The *Unofficial* Revit 2012 Certification Exam Guide

Elise Moss

ISBN: 978-1-58503-679-0

Schroff Development Corporation

www.SDCpublications.com

Schroff Development Corporation
P.O. Box 1334
Mission, KS 66222
(913) 262-2664
www.SDCpublications.com

Publisher: Stephen Schroff

Trademarks
The following are registered trademarks of Autodesk, Inc.: AutoCAD, AutoCAD Architectural Desktop, Revit, Autodesk, AutoCAD Design Center, Autodesk Device Interface, VizRender, and HEIDI
Microsoft, Windows, Word, and Excel are either registered trademarks or trademarks of Microsoft Corporation.
All other trademarks are trademarks of their respective holders.

Copyright 2011 by Elise Moss
All rights reserved. No part of this book may be reproduced, stored in a retrieval system, or transcribed in any form or by any means – electronic, mechanical, photocopying, recording, or otherwise – without the prior written permission of Schroff Development Corporation.

IT IS A VIOLATION OF UNITED STATES COPYRIGHT LAWS TO MAKE COPIES IN ANY FORM OR MEDIA OF THE CONTENTS OF THIS BOOK FOR EITHER COMMERCIAL OR EDUCATIONAL PURPOSES WITHOUT EXPRESS WRITTEN PERMISSION.

Moss, Elise
    The Unofficial Revit 2012 Certification Exam Guide
    Elise Moss
ISBN: 978-1-58503-679-0

Examination Copies:
Books received as examination copies are for review purposes only and may not be made available for student use. Resale of examination copies is prohibited.

Electronic Files:
Any electronic files associated with this book are licensed to the original user only. These files may not be transferred to any other party.

The authors and publisher of this book have used their best efforts in preparing this book. These efforts include the development, research, and testing of material presented. The author and publisher shall not be held liable in any event for incidental or consequential damages with, or arising out of, the furnishing, performance, or use of the material herein.

Printed and bound in the United States of America.

Preface

This book is geared towards users who have been using Revit for at least six months and are ready to pursue their official Autodesk certification. Autodesk offers two certification exams for Revit: an Associate certificate and a Professional certificate. It is advisable to take both exams. You can locate the closest testing center on Autodesk's website.

I wrote this book because I teach a certification preparation class at SFSU. I also teach an introductory Revit class using my Revit Basics text. I heard many complaints from students who had taken my Revit Basics class when they had to switch to the Autodesk AOTC courseware for the exam preparation class. Students preferred the step by step easily accessible instruction I use in my texts. When my support staff advised me that Autodesk had informed them that there would not be an exam guide available for Revit 2010, I decided to tackle my own guide. Because of the interface changes between Revit 2008 (the last year an AOTC guide is available) and 2010, I did not feel comfortable using a 2008 textbook to prepare students for a 2010 certification test. I have since updated the text for 2011, and now for 2012.

This textbook includes exercises which simulate the knowledge users should have in order to pass the certification exam. I advise my students to do each exercise two or three times to ensure that they understand the user interface and can perform the task with ease.

I have endeavored to make this text as easy to understand and as error-free as possible…however, errors may be present. Please feel free to email me if you have any problems with any of the exercises or questions about Revit in general.

Acknowledgements

A special thanks to Rick Rundell, Gary Hercules, James Cowan, Christie Landry, and Steve Burri, two Autodesk employees who are tasked with supporting and promoting Revit.

Additional thanks to Will Harris, Scott Davis, James Balding, Rob Starz, and all the other Revit users out there who provided me with valuable insights into the way they use Revit.

Thanks to Stephen Schroff and Mary Schmidt, who work tirelessly to bring these manuscripts to you, the user, and provide the important moral support authors need.

My eternal gratitude to my life partner, Ari, my biggest cheerleader throughout our years together.

An additional thank you to my son, Daniel Stassart, who provided the photograph used in the Revit rendering on the cover of this text. The photograph is of a fun house clown he designed for Saratoga High School's Grad Night 2010.

Elise Moss
Elise_moss@mossdesigns.com

TABLE OF CONTENTS

Preface — i

Acknowledgements — ii

Table of Contents — iii

Introduction - FAQs

Lesson One
Building Information Modeling and Revit Basics
  Exercise 1-1
  Quick Access Toolbar — 1-3
  Exercise 1-2
  Exploring the User Interface — 1-7
  Exercise 1-3
  Recover and Use Backup Files — 1-8
  Exercise 1-4
  Design Options — 1-11

  Practice Associate Exam — 1-24

Lesson Two
The Basics of Building a Model
  Exercise 2-1
  Wall Options — 2-2
  Exercise 2-2
  Placing a Wall Sweep — 2-5
  Exercise 2-3
  Create a Wall Sweep Style — 2-10
  Exercise 2-4
  Create a Custom Profile — 2-12
  Exercise 2-5
  Create a Compound Wall — 2-15
  Exercise 2-6
  Stacked Walls — 2-23
  Exercise 2-7
  Chained Walls — 2-33
  Exercise 2-8
  Dividing a Wall into Parts — 2-35
  Exercise 2-9
  Creating an In-Place Mass — 2-43
  Exercise 2-10
  Editing an In-Place Mass — 2-60
  Exercise 2-11
  Mass Properties — 2-68

  Practice Associate Exam — 2-72

Lesson Three
Component Families
    Exercise 3-1
    Level-Based Component   3-2
    Exercise 3-2
    Creating a Family   3-4
    Exercise 3-3
    Identifying a Family   3-16

    Practice Associate Exam   3-17

Lesson Four
View Properties
    Exercise 4-1
    Creating a Level   4-2
    Exercise 4-2
    Story vs. Non-Story Levels   4-4
    Exercise 4-3
    Creating Column Grids   4-8
    Exercise 4-4
    Setting View Depth   4-15
    Exercise 4-5
    Create a Cropped View   4-16
    Exercise 4-6
    Change View Display   4-18
    Exercise 4-7
    Reveal Hidden Elements   4-21
    Exercise 4-8
    Create a View Template   4-22
    Exercise 4-9
    Create a Scope Box   4-28

    Practice Associate Exam   4-33

Lesson Five
Dimensions and Constraints
    Exercise 5-1
    Placing Permanent Dimensions   5-2
    Exercise 5-2
    Modifying Dimension Text   5-7
    Exercise 5-3
    Converting Temporary Dimensions to Permanent Dimensions   5-10
    Exercise 5-4
    Applying Constraints   5-12

    Practice Associate Exam   5-16

Lesson Six
Developing the Building Model

Exercise 6-1	Modifying a Floor Perimeter	6-2
Exercise 6-2	Modifying a Ceiling	6-5
Exercise 6-3	Creating Stairs	6-9
Exercise 6-4	Creating a Roof by Footprint	6-14
Exercise 6-5	Creating a Roof by Extrusion	6-16
Exercise 6-6	Creating a Sloped Ceiling	6-21

Practice Associate Exam   6-27

Lesson Seven
Detailing and Drafting

Exercise 7-1	Creating Drafting Views	7-2
Exercise 7-2	Save and Re-Use a Drafting View	7-7
Exercise 7-3	Adding Tags	7-9
Exercise 7-4	Creating a Detail View	7-12
Exercise 7-5	Creating a Detail Group	7-19
Exercise 7-6	Import and Edit DWG Details	7-23
Exercise 7-7	Creating a Drafting View	7-28
Exercise 7-8	Revision Control	7-37
Exercise 7-9	Modify a Revision Schedule	7-41
Exercise 7-10	Add Revision Clouds	7-44
Exercise 7-11	Aligning Views Between Sheets	7-49

Practice Associate Exam   7-53

Lesson Eight
Construction Documentation

Exercise 8-1	Creating a Door Schedule	8-2
Exercise 8-2	Creating a Legend	8-5
Exercise 8-3	Adding Rooms to a Floor Plan	8-12

Exercise 8-4
Creating an Area Scheme . . . 8-15
Exercise 8-5
Creating an Area Plan . . . 8-18
Exercise 8-6
Creating a Room Schedule . . . 8-23
Exercise 8-7
Creating a Drawing List . . . 8-26
Exercise 8-8
Create a Note Symbol . . . 8-29
Exercise 8-9
Add Notes . . . 8-34
Exercise 8-10
Create a Material TakeOff Schedule . . . 8-36
Exercise 8-11
Creating a Mass Floor Schedule . . . 8-39

Practice Associate Exam . . . 8-41

Lesson Nine
Presenting the Building Model
Exercise 9-1
Creating a Toposurface . . . 9-2
Exercise 9-2
Defining Camera Views . . . 9-11
Exercise 9-3
Graphic Display Options . . . 9-14
Exercise 9-4
Assigning Settings . . . 9-17
Exercise 9-5
Place a Decal . . . 9-19
Exercise 9-6
Custom Render Settings . . . 9-25

Practice Associate Exam . . . 9-27

Lesson Ten
Collaboration
Exercise 10-1
Monitoring a Linked File . . . 10-3
Exercise 10-2
Interference Checking . . . 10-8
Exercise 10-3
Using Shared Coordinates . . . 10-12
Exercise 10-4
Point Clouds . . . 10-18
Exercise 10-5
Worksets . . . 10-22

Practice Associate Exam . . . 10-29

About the Author

Introduction

FAQs

The first day of class students are understandably nervous and they have a lot of questions about getting certification. Throughout the class, I am peppered with the same or similar questions.

Why is this textbook the "Unofficial" Guide?

Autodesk reserves the right to publish any official training courseware. I have used and continue to use Autodesk courseware when I teach, but I have found that it is easier for me to teach from my own books. I did contact Autodesk and check if there would be any objection to the publication of an unofficial guide and was told that as long as I did not violate any copyrights this book could be published.

What is the difference between the Associate Level and Professional Exam?

The associate level exam is closed book, closed notes, closed software, closed neighbor. The student must rely on their memory of Revit's user interface, including dialog boxes and tools. Both exams use a "secure" browser, which means that you cannot cut and paste or copy from the browser. For the Professional Exam, you have the Revit software open and use the Alt-TAB shortcut key to flip from the secure browser to the software application to do each problem.

It is helpful during both exams to have a piece of paper and a pencil so you can make notes.

You do not need a calculator for either exam and calculators are against the rules anyway.

What are the exams like?

The first time you take the exam, you will create an account with a login. Be sure to write down your login name and password. You will need this regardless of whether you pass or fail.

If you fail and decide to retake the exam, you want to be able to log in to your account.

If you pass, you want to be able to log in to download your certificate and other data.

Both exams are timed. This means you only have one to two minutes for each question. You have the ability to "mark" a question to go back if you are unsure. This is a good idea because a question that comes later on in the exam may give you a clue or an idea on how to answer a question you weren't sure about.

Both exams pull from a question "bank" and no two exams are exactly alike. Two students sitting next to each other taking the same exam will have entirely different experiences and an entirely different set of questions. However, each exam covers specific topics. For example, you will get at least one question about BIM or Revit projects. You will probably not get the same question as your neighbor.

At the end of the exam, the browser will display a screen listing the question numbers, the answers you chose, and indicate any marked or incomplete questions. The questions themselves are not displayed on this page. Any questions where you forgot to select an answer will be marked incomplete with a capitol I. Questions that you marked will display the letter M. You can click on those answers and the browser will link you back directly to those questions so you can review them and modify your answers.

I advise my students to mark any questions where they are struggling and move forward, then use any remaining time to review those questions. A student could easily spend ten to fifteen minutes pondering a single question and lose valuable time on the exam.

Once you have completed your review, you will receive a prompt to END the exam. Some students find this confusing as they think they are quitting the exam and not receiving a score. Once you end the exam, you may not change any of your answers. There will be a brief pause and then you will see a screen where you will be notified whether you passed or failed. You will also see which questions you missed, listed by the question number. Again, you will not see any of the actual questions. However, you will see the topic, so you might see that you missed Question 4 and that question is on view properties.

You will have to rely on your memory to recall what question was about view properties. Some students might find this confusing because they didn't even know that particular question fit into the view properties category.

If you failed the test, you do want to note which categories you missed. For example, you might have missed a question on BIM, a question on view properties, and a question on constraints. Write these down. Then review those topics both in this guide and in the software to help prepare you to retake the exam.

How many times can I take the test?

You can take the test as many times as you like until you pass. There is no waiting period between re-takes, so if you fail the exam on Tuesday, you can come back on Wednesday and try again. Of course, this depends on the testing center where you take the exam.

Do a lot of students have to re-take the test or do they pass on the first try?

About half of my students pass the exam on the first try, but it definitely depends on the student. Some people are better at tests than others. My youngest son excels at "multiple guess" style exams, which is what the associate certification exam is. He can pretty much ace any multiple guess exam you give him regardless of the topic. Most students are not so fortunate. Some students find a timed test extremely stressful. For this reason, I have created a simulated version of both the associate and the professional level exams for my students simply so they can practice taking an on-line timed exam. This has the effect of "conditioning" their responses so they are less stressed taking the actual exam.

Some students find the multiple choice style extremely confusing, especially if they are non-native English speakers. There are exams available in many languages, so if you are not a native English speaker, check with the testing center about the availability of an exam in your native language.

Why take a certification exam?

The competition for jobs is steep and employers can afford to be picky. Being certified provides employers with a sense of security knowing that you passed a difficult exam that requires a basic skill set. It is important to note that the certification exam does not test your ability as a designer or drafter. The certification exam tests your knowledge of the Revit software. This is a fine distinction, but it is an important one.

If you pass the exam, you have the option of having your name published on Autodesk's website as a Certified Associate or Certified Professional. Some employers and headhunters use that list to find a potential new hire. You do not have to have your name published if you don't want to be bothered.

How long is the certification good for?

Your certification is good for a particular year of software. It does not expire. If you pass and are certified for Revit 2012, you are always certified for Revit 2012. That said, you are not certified for Revit 2015 or Revit 2020. Most employers want you to be certified within a couple of years of the most current release, so if you wish to maintain your "competitive edge" in the employment pool, expect that you will have to take the certification exam every two to three years. I recommend students take an "update" class from an Autodesk Authorized Training Center before they take the exam to improve their chances of passing. Autodesk recently changed their requirements and if you have a prior certification, then you only need to re-take the Professional exam to be re-certified. However, this may change, so check with your testing center about the current requirements for certification.

How much does it cost?

The cost for the exam is posted on Autodesk's website. Autodesk charges students less than professionals, so if you are a student or unemployed, check to see if you qualify for a discount or a free exam. Members of AUGI, Autodesk User Group International, also qualify for a discount or a free exam. Membership in AUGI is free. It is worth it to check with the testing center to find out what criteria is necessary to qualify for a discount or free exam.

Can I take the exam at home?

No. Autodesk requires users to take the exam in a proctored setting. When I proctor an exam, I ask my students to show valid ID, such as a driver's license. This is to ensure that the certification process maintains a certain level of integrity and meaningfulness. Otherwise, a user could pay someone to take the exam for him.

Do I need to be able to use the software to pass the exam?

This sounds like a worse question than intended. Some of my students have taken the Revit classes, but have not actually gotten a job using Revit yet. They are in that Catch-22 situation where an employer requires experience or certification to hire them but they can't pass the exam because they aren't using the software every day. For those students, I advise some self-discipline where they schedule at least six hours a week for a month where they use the software – even if it is on a "dummy" project – before they take the exam. That will boost the odds in their favor.

Is the professional exam a lot harder than the associate exam?

Most of my students tell me that they find the associate exam considerably harder than the professional exam. The associate exam is a set of thirty multiple choice questions about the Revit software. Because students do not have the software open, they must rely on their memory and their ability to recall tasks. The professional exam is a set of twenty exercises. For each exercise, the user must open a Revit file, perform a specific task, and then answer a question. If they performed the task properly, the answer will be correct. It is a good idea if you have time to do each task twice just to verify your answer. You can take the professional exam first and then the associate exam, if you prefer. You must pass **both** exams to be certified in Revit.

What happens if I pass?

Because you are taking the test in a testing center, you want to be sure you wrote down your login information. That way when you get back to your home or office, you can login to Autodesk's certification center and download your certificate. You also can download a logo which shows you are a Certified Associate or Certified Professional that you can post on your website or print on your business card.

How many times can I log into Autodesk's testing center?

You can log in as often as you like. The tests you have taken will be listed as well as whether you passed or failed.

Can everybody see that I failed the test?

Autodesk is kind enough to keep it a secret if you failed the exam. Nobody knows unless you tell them. If you passed the test, people only see that information if you selected the option to post that result. Regardless, only you and Autodesk will know whether you passed or failed unless *you* choose to share that information.

Can I change my mind? I said I didn't want it posted if I passed and now I am looking for a job.

Yes, you are allowed to change your mind. Log on to the Autodesk testing site and email them using the Contact Link. Provide them with your user name, email address, and the test results you want posted. They will verify that you passed and update their database listing. This may take a week or longer. So, if you change your mind, let them know right away. Do not go on a job interview and say you are certified without bringing along your certificate as proof. Many employers will check your claim against Autodesk's database.

What if I need to go to the bathroom during the exam or take a break?

You are allowed to "pause" the test. This will stop the clock. You then alert the proctor that you need to leave the room for a break. When you return, you will need the proctor to approve you to re-enter the test and start the clock again.

How many questions can I miss?

The Associate exam has 30 questions. The required passing score is 80%. This means you can miss as many as six questions and still pass.

The Professional exam has 20 questions. The required passing score is 80%. This means you can miss as many as four questions and still pass.

Do I have to take both tests? Can't I just take the Professional Exam?

In order to receive the Professional certificate, you must pass both the Associate and Professional exams. However, you can take the Professional exam before the Associate exam, if you prefer.

How much time do I have for each exam?

The associate exam has a one hour time limit. That is roughly two minutes per question.

The professional exam has a ninety minute time limit. That is roughly three minutes per question.

Can I ask for more time?

You can make arrangements for more time if you are a non-English speaker or have problems with tests. Be sure to speak with the proctor about your concerns. Most proctors will provide more time if you truly need it. However, my experience has been that most students are able to complete the exam with time to spare. I have only had one or two students that felt they "ran out of time".

What happens if the computer crashes during the test?

Don't worry. Your answers will be saved and the clock will be stopped. Simply reboot your system. Get Revit launched again (if you are taking the professional exam) and let the proctor know when you are ready to start the exam again, so you can re-enter the testing area in your browser.

Do I have to take both exams if I want to be re-certified?

The short answer is 'Yes'. If you passed the associate and professional level exams for a previous release, you need to take both exams again to be certified for the current release.

Is there a practice test I can take?

Yes, Autodesk has set up an on-line assessment test to help you prepare to take the real exam.

Does it cost anything to take the practice test?

Yes, depending on the test it costs between $18 and $30.

Can I take the practice test more than one time?

No, you can only take the practice exam once per payment. That is why I set up a practice exam for my students, so they could practice multiple times without having to pay any money.

Can I have access to the practice exams you set up for your students?

If you are a registered student at SFSU, I can grant you access. Otherwise, no. I have had students come out of state to take my Revit class because they feel it gives them an advantage.

What sort of questions do you get in the Associate exam?

Many students complain that the questions are all about Revit software and not about building design or the uniform building code. Keep in mind that this test is to determine your knowledge about Revit software. This is not an exam to see if you are a good architect or designer.

The associate level exam has several question types:

One best answer – this is a multiple choice style question. You can usually arrive at the best answer by figuring out which answers do NOT apply.

Select all that apply – this can be a confusing question for some users because unless they know how *many* possible correct answers there are, they aren't sure. In some cases, you may be provided with the hint of selecting two or three out of five possible choices.

Point and click – this has a java-style interface. You will be presented with a picture, and then asked to pick a location on the picture to simulate a user selection. When you pick, a mark will be left on the image to indicate your selection. Each time you pick in a different area, the mark will shift to the new location. You do not have to pick an exact point…a general target area is all that is required.

Matching format – you probably are familiar with this style of question from elementary school. You will be presented with two columns. One column may have assorted terms and the second column the definitions. You then are expected to drag the terms to the correct definition to match the items.

What sort of questions do you get in the Professional exam?

Each question follows the same process. You will be asked to open a file. You may be asked to open a specific view or a sheet. This tests your ability to navigate around Revit, so be familiar with the Project Browser and how it works. You may be asked to orient the model to a specific orientation or level. You will then be required to perform a specific task, either adding or modifying an element or determining an element's properties. You will then be asked to fill an answer into an input box. The answer will be either text or numeric. The answer must match exactly with what is presented on screen, so it is best to Copy and Paste between Revit and the secure browser. If you miss a punctuation mark, use the wrong case, or spell something wrong, your answer will be marked wrong.

If you are unsure about a question in the Professional exam and want to mark it for review, perform a SaveAs Copy of the file, so you don't lose any work you did.

Any tips?

I suggest you read every question at least twice. Some of the wording on the questions is tricky.

Be well rested and be sure to eat before the exam. Most testing centers do not allow food, but they may allow water. Keep in mind that you can take a break if you need one.

Relax. Maintain perspective. This is a test. It is not fatal. If you fail, you will not be the first person to have failed this exam. Failing does not mean you are a bad designer or architect or even a bad person. It just means you need to study the software more.

If you are taking the Professional exam, have Revit open and ready to go before you start the test. Verify that you know where the drawing files are located so you don't have to search for them every time you need to open a file. Write down the file path on your scratch paper just in case you panic. Don't close the file. Occasionally, different questions will use the same file, so if you already have the file open that saves time. You will not open and use every file in the data set, so do not open every file in anticipation of using it. Practice switching windows before the exam. Open Internet

Explorer and open a session of Revit. Then use the Alt-Tab to switch between the windows. Practice this until you are comfortable.

Remember to write down your login name and password for your account. The proctor will not be able to help you if you forget.

Lesson One

Building Information Modeling and Revit Basics

This lesson addresses the following Associate level exam questions:

- Building Information Modeling
- User Interface
- Building Elements
- Revit Projects

There will be at least one question on the Associate exam regarding Building Information Modeling. You will be expected to understand what BIM means and how it works. Autodesk is extremely proud that Revit is BIM software.

BIM means that Revit uses intelligent objects to create and manage a building model. In AutoCAD, you draw a set of lines to symbolize a door. In Revit, you place a door object which has parameters embedded in the object. These parameters contain data concerning the door: everything from the material, cost, and size to function and manufacturer information. This information can be leveraged to be used in schedules and in Excel spreadsheets. You can create an unlimited number of views for your building model and they all reside in a single file.

Revit boasts "bidirectional associativity," which means that if you make a change in one view, all related views also update.

Revit has parametric relationships within the model. For example, floors are constrained to walls, so if a wall is shifted in any direction, the floor will automatically update.

When you first launch Revit, a startup window named Recent Files is displayed.

The Unofficial Revit 2012 Certification Exam Guide

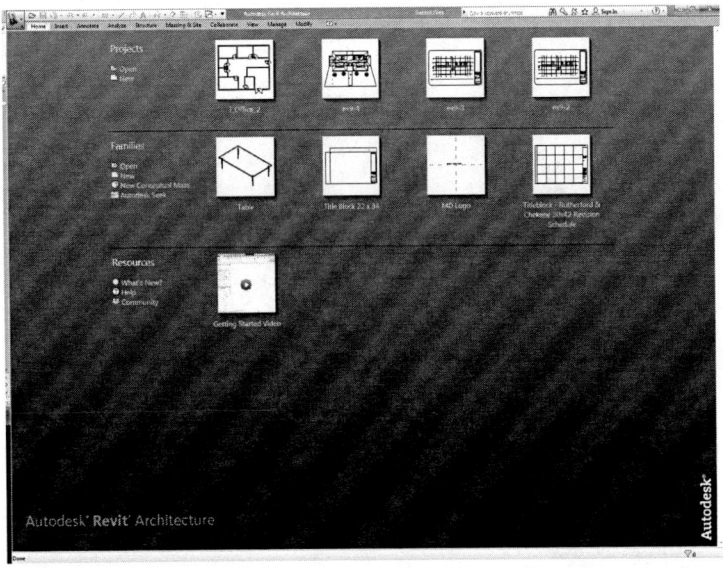

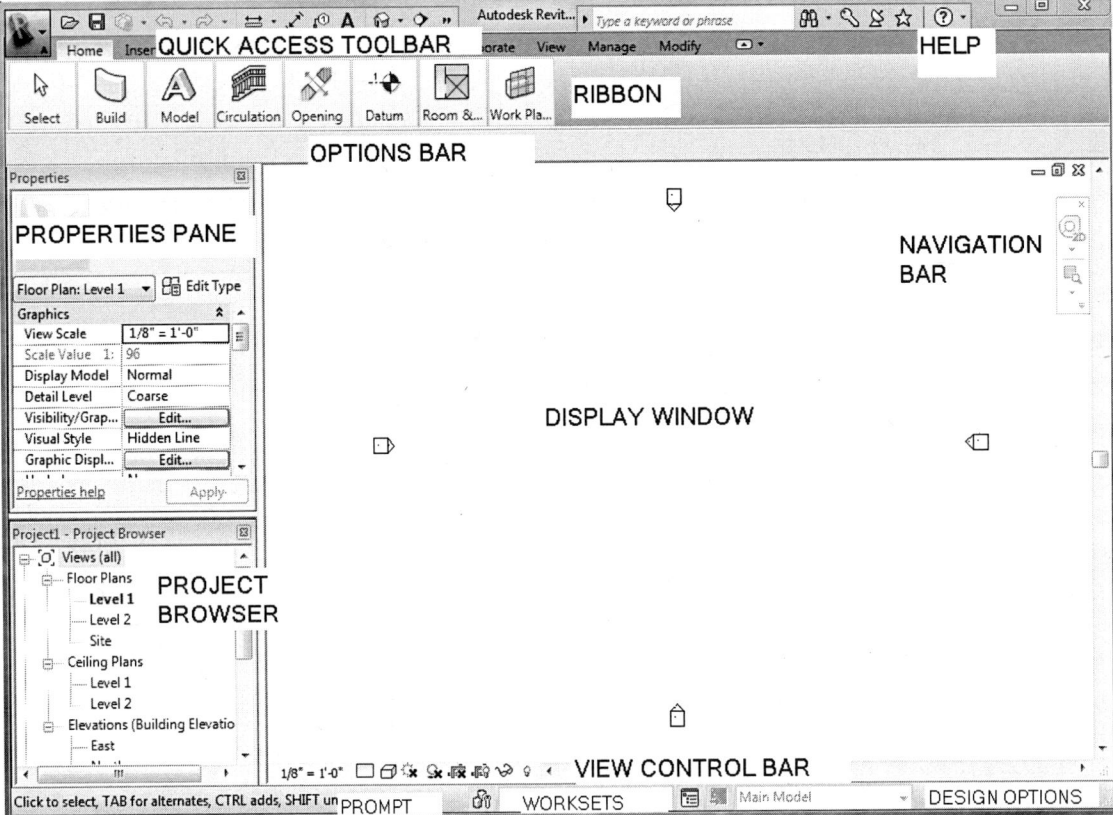

In the Associate exam, you will be expected to identify any or all of the labeled items shown.

Building Information Modeling and Revit Basics

Command Exercise
Exercise 1-1 – Quick Access Toolbar

Drawing Name: **(none, start from scratch)**
Estimated Time to Completion: 10 Minutes

Scope

Learn how to add and remove tools from the Quick Access Toolbar.

Solution

1. 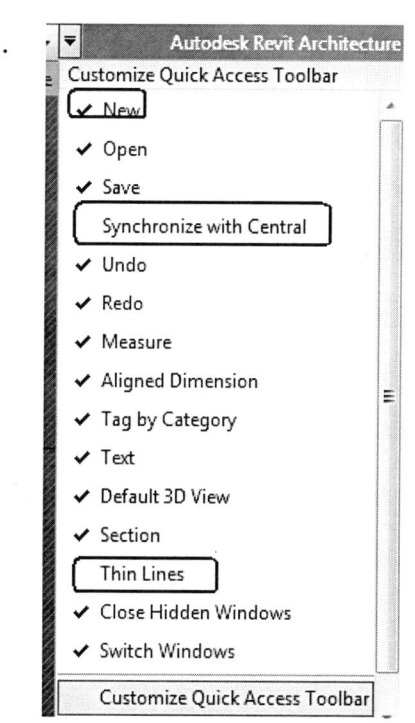 Select the drop-down arrow on the Quick Access Toolbar.

   Enable **New**.
   Disable **Synchronize with Central**.
   Disable **Thin Lines**.

2. The Quick Access Toolbar updates with the new settings.

   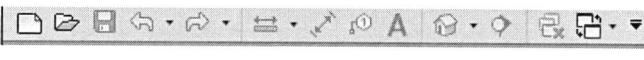

3. 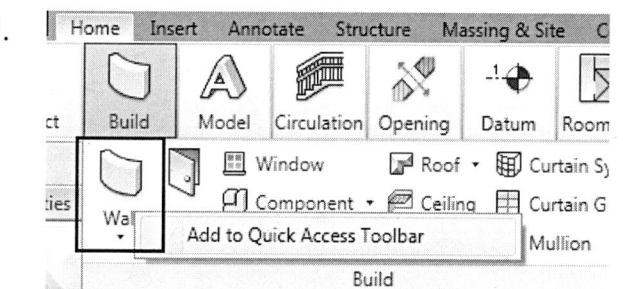 Place your mouse over the Wall tool on the Home ribbon.

   Right click and select **Add to Quick Access Toolbar**.

4. The Wall tool is added to the Quick Access Toolbar.

1-3

The Unofficial Revit 2012 Certification Exam Guide

5. Select the **Wall** tool and place a wall in the drawing area.
   Select the Wall and note that the ribbon changes to Modify mode.

6. 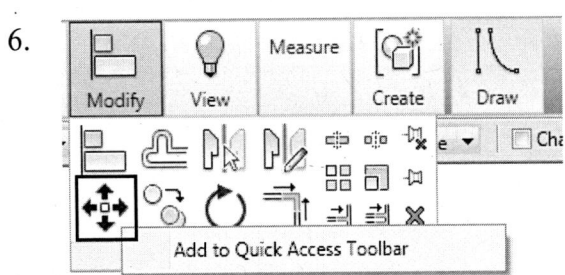 Right click on the **Move** tool.
   Select **Add to Quick Access Toolbar**.

7.

   The Quick Access Toolbar now displays the Move tool.

8. Left click anywhere in the drawing area.

9. Right click on the **Wall** tool and select **Remove from Quick Access Ribbon**.

   10. The Wall tool is removed.

 The Quick Access Toolbar acts like the ribbon as some tools may become disabled depending on the mode you are in.

1-4

Building Elements are used to create a building design. There are five classes of building elements: host, component, datum, annotation, and view. Building elements fall into three categories: Model, View, and Annotation. To pass the Associate exam, users need to identify which category a building element falls in.

Each element falls into a category, such as wall, column, door, window, furniture, etc. Each category contains different families. Each family can have more than one type. The type is usually determined by the size or parameters assigned to that family.

These are very difficult concepts for many students, especially if they have been used to dealing with lines, circles, and arcs.

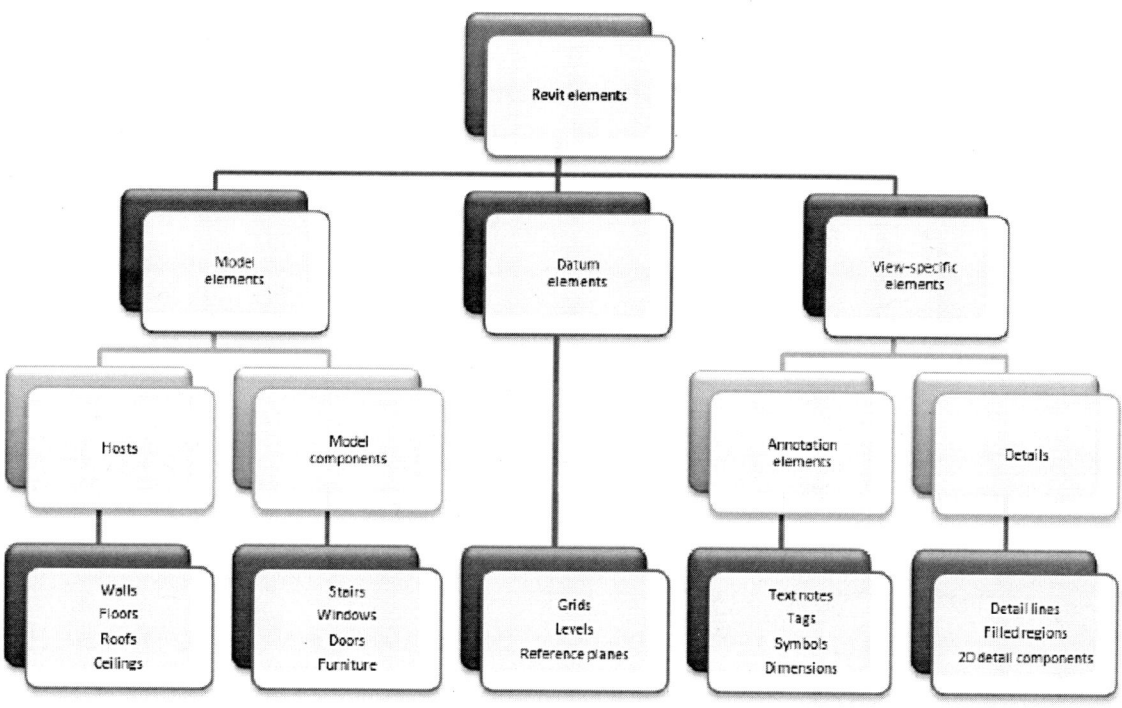

Revit elements are separated into three different types of elements: Model, Datum and View-specific. Users are expected to know if an element is model, datum or view-specific.

Model elements are broken down into categories. A category might be a wall, window, door, or floor. If you look in the Project Browser, you will see a category called Families. If you expand the category, you will see the families for each category in the current project. Each family may contain multiple types.

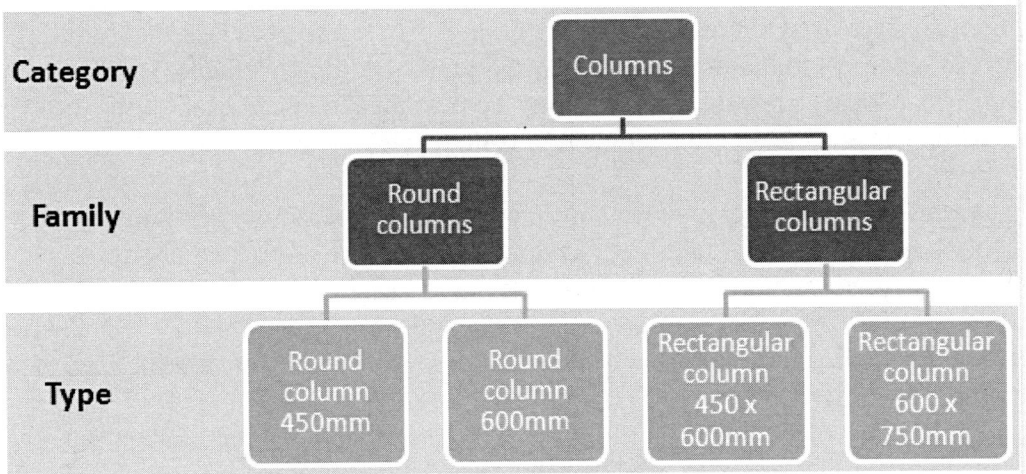

Every Revit file is considered a Project. A Revit project consists of the Project Environment, components, and views. The Project Environment is managed in the Project Browser.

Building Information Modeling and Revit Basics

Command Exercise

Exercise 1-2 – Exploring the User Interface

Drawing Name: **c_user interface.rvt**
Estimated Time to Completion: 5 Minutes

Scope

Review the user interface to prepare for the exam.

Solution

1. The file will open in a 3D view. Note that there is a ViewCube in the upper left corner.

2. Open the Level 1 Floor Plan view.

3. Note that the ViewCube is no longer visible and has been replaced with the Navigation Bar.

   The ViewCube is only visible in 3D views.

Command Exercise

Exercise 1-3 – Recover and Use Backup Files

Drawing Name: **new**
Estimated Time to Completion: 5 Minutes

Scope

Recover and Use Backup Files

Solution

1. Close any open projects.
   Press **New** under Projects.

2. Go to **File→Save As→Project**.

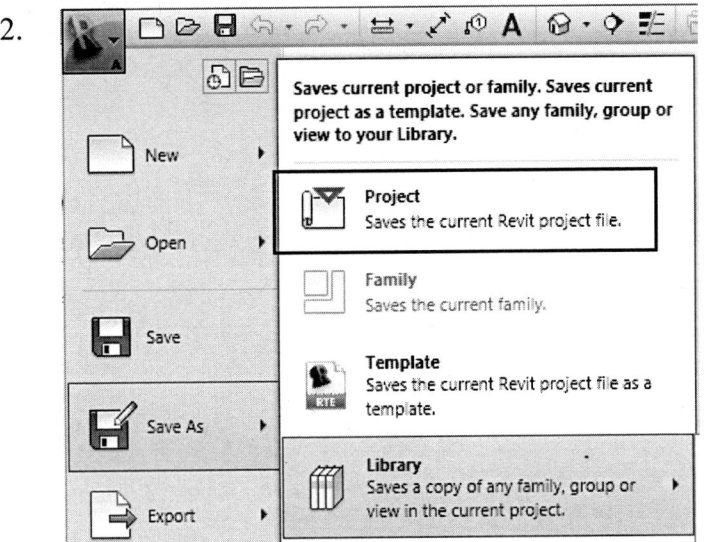

3. Select the Options button next to the file name.

Building Information Modeling and Revit Basics

4. 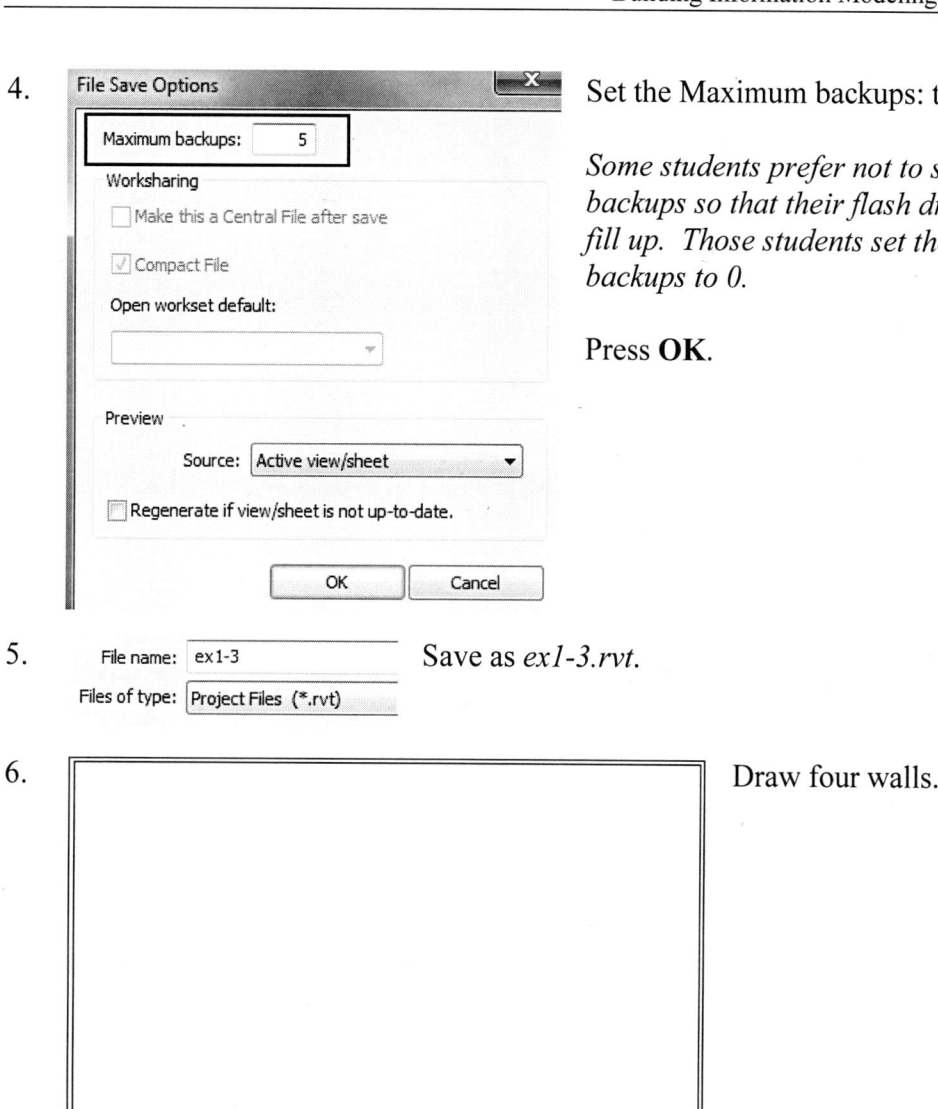 Set the Maximum backups: to **5**.

   Some students prefer not to save any backups so that their flash drive doesn't fill up. Those students set the number of backups to 0.

   Press **OK**.

5. File name: ex1-3
   Files of type: Project Files (*.rvt)

   Save as *ex1-3.rvt*.

6. [blank rectangle] Draw four walls.

7. 💾 Press **Save**.

8.  Add two more walls. Add a door.

9. 💾 Press **Save**.

1-9

The Unofficial Revit 2012 Certification Exam Guide

10. 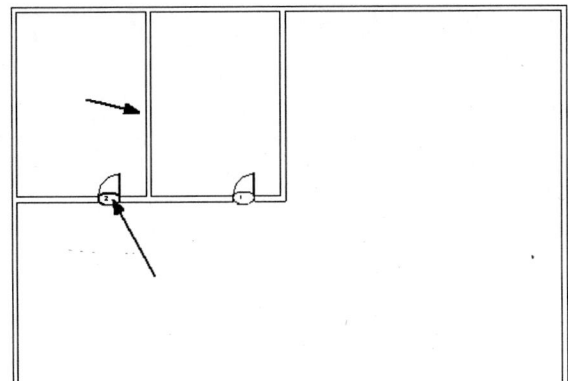 Add one wall.
    Add one door.

11.  🖫 Press **Save**.

12. 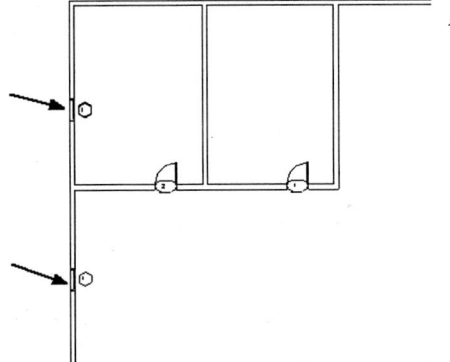 Add two windows.

13.  🖫 Press **Save**.

14.  📂 Select **Open**.

15. ex1-3.0001   8/12/2010 10:05 AM   Note that you have several versions of ex1-3.
    ex1-3.0002   8/12/2010 10:05 AM
    ex1-3.0003   8/12/2010 10:08 AM   The .0000x indicates the backup number.
    ex1-3   8/12/2010 10:09 AM

16. 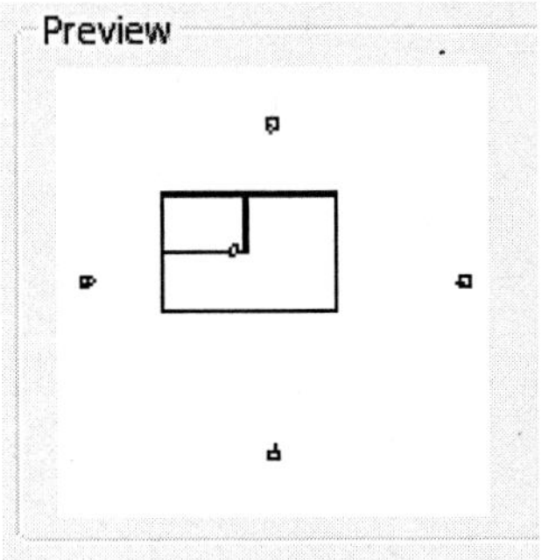 Note that you can highlight a version and check in the preview window which backup you want to select.

17. Open *ex1-3.0001.rvt*.
    This is the first save you did.

18. [ex1-3.0001 - Floor Plan: Level 1]   Note the file name at the top of the screen.

19. Close all files without saving.

1-10

Building Information Modeling and Revit Basics

Command Exercise

Exercise 1-4 – Design Options

Drawing Name: **i_Design_Options**
Estimated Time to Completion: 5 Minutes

Scope

Use of Design Options

Solution

1. 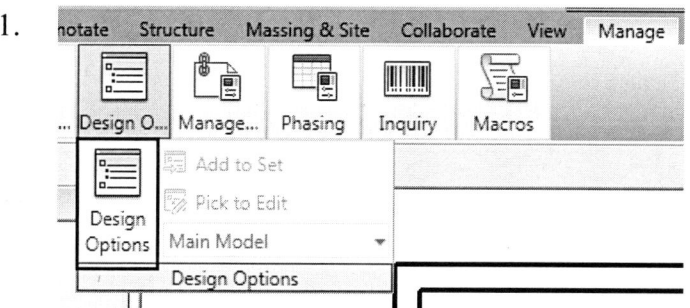 Activate the **Manage** ribbon.

   Select **Design Options** under the Design Options panel.

2. 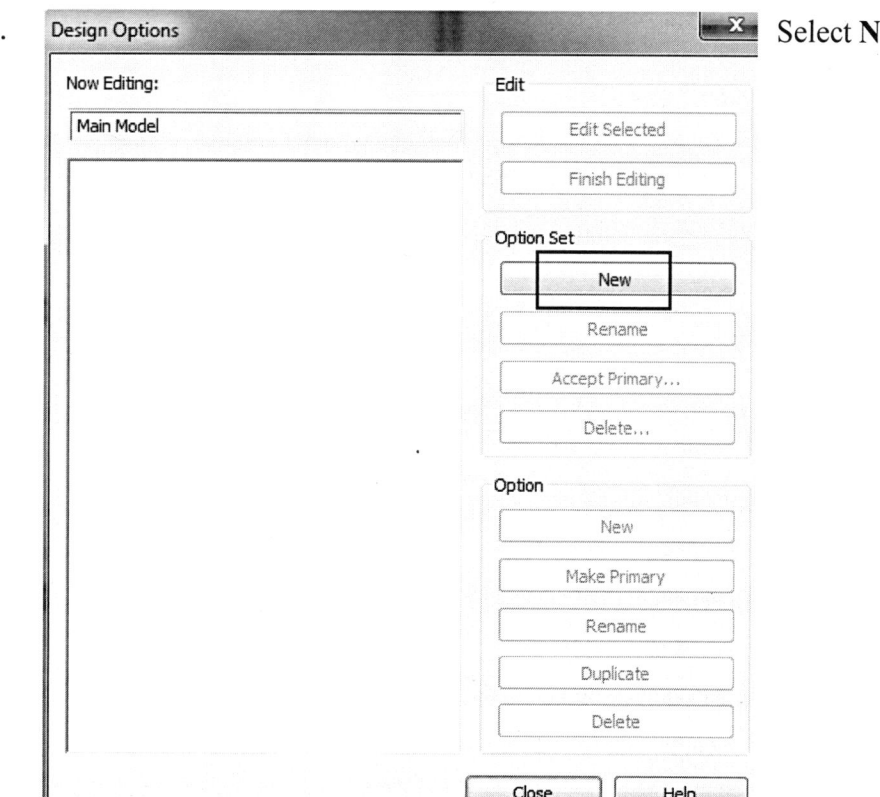 Select **New**.

1-11

The Unofficial Revit 2012 Certification Exam Guide

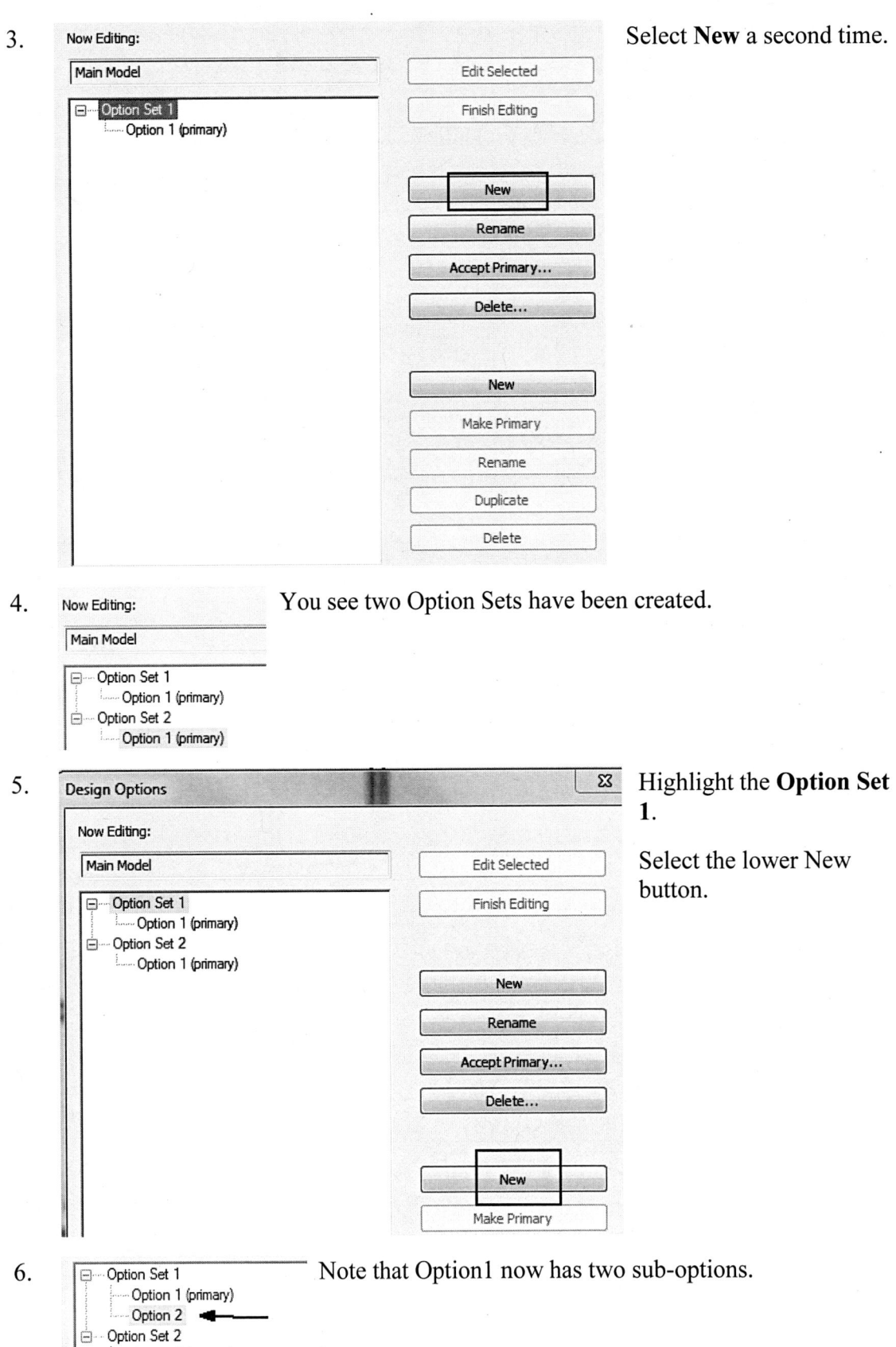

3. Select **New** a second time.

4. You see two Option Sets have been created.

5. Highlight the **Option Set 1**.

   Select the lower New button.

6. Note that Option1 now has two sub-options.

1-12

Building Information Modeling and Revit Basics

7. Highlight the **Option Set 2**.

Select the lower New button.

8. Note that Option 2 now has two sub-options.

9. Highlight **Option Set 1**.

Select **Rename**.

10. Rename Option Set 1 **South Entry Door Options**.

Press **OK**.

11. Highlight **Option 1 (primary)** under the South Entry Door Options.

12. Select **Rename**.

13. Rename to **Dbl Glass Door - No Trim**.

Press **OK**.

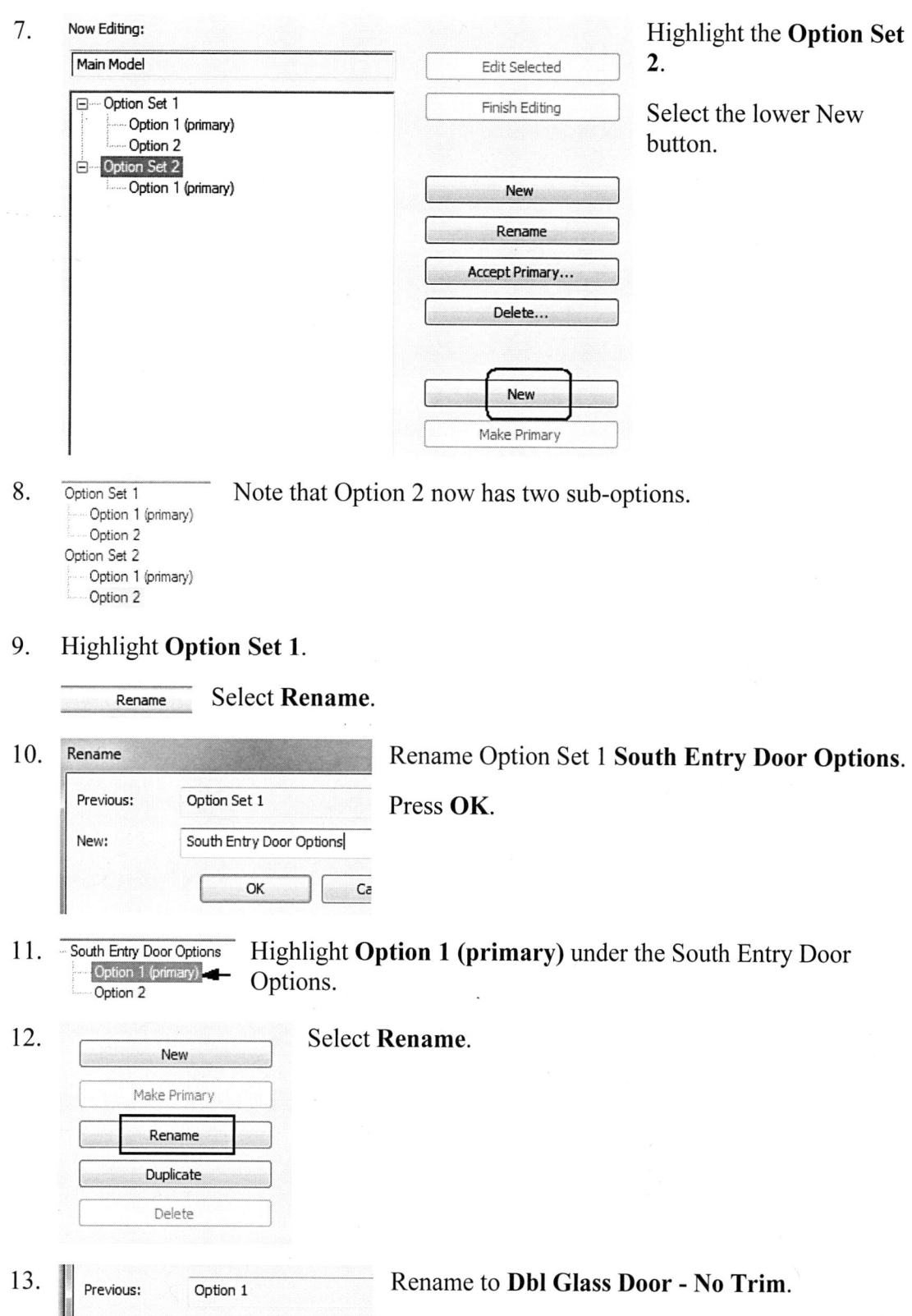

1-13

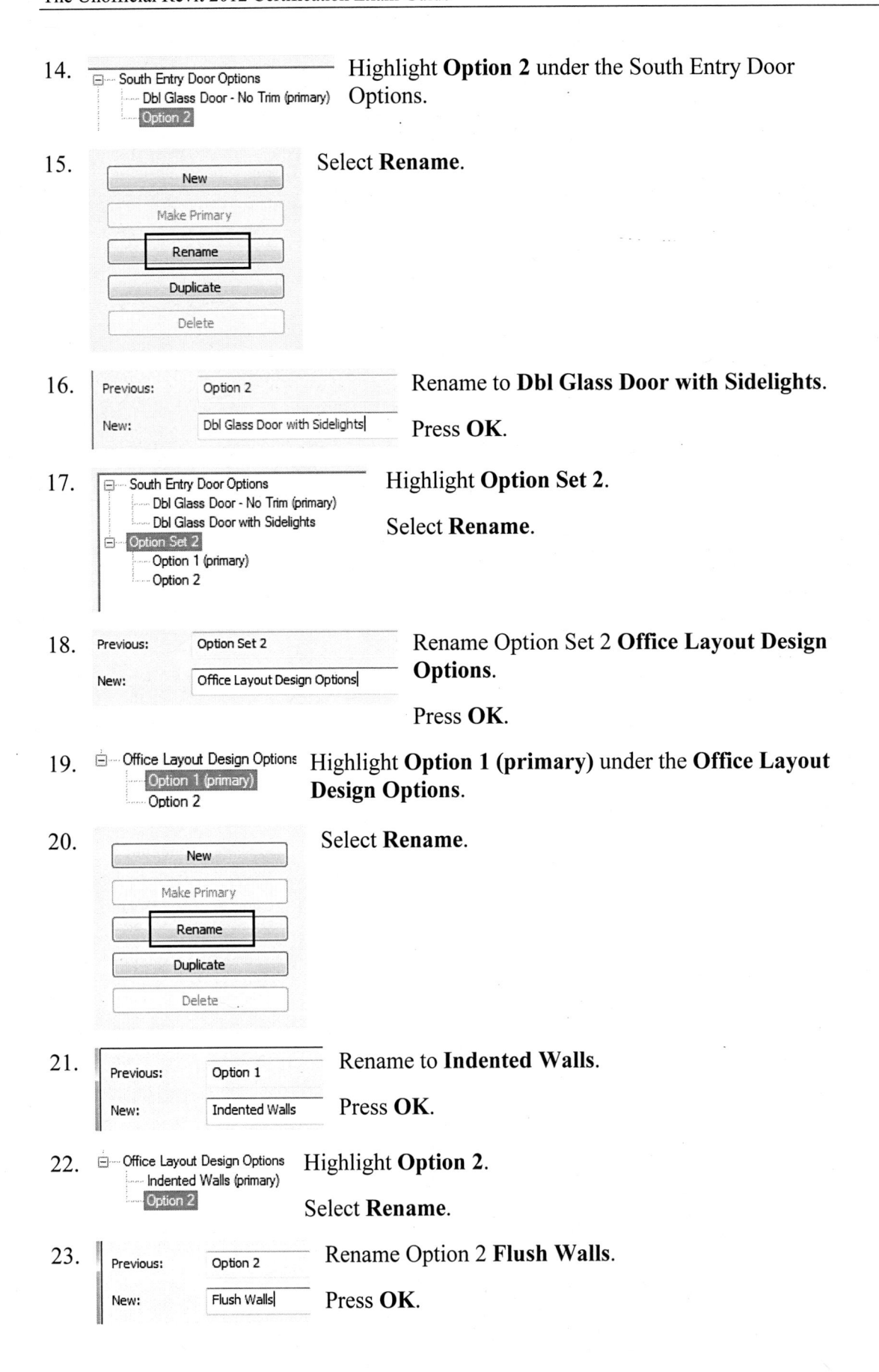

The Unofficial Revit 2012 Certification Exam Guide

14. Highlight **Option 2** under the South Entry Door Options.

15. Select **Rename**.

16. Rename to **Dbl Glass Door with Sidelights**.
    Press **OK**.

17. Highlight **Option Set 2**.
    Select **Rename**.

18. Rename Option Set 2 **Office Layout Design Options**.
    Press **OK**.

19. Highlight **Option 1 (primary)** under the **Office Layout Design Options**.

20. Select **Rename**.

21. Rename to **Indented Walls**.
    Press **OK**.

22. Highlight **Option 2**.
    Select **Rename**.

23. Rename Option 2 **Flush Walls**.
    Press **OK**.

1-14

Building Information Modeling and Revit Basics

24. Close the Design Options dialog.

25. 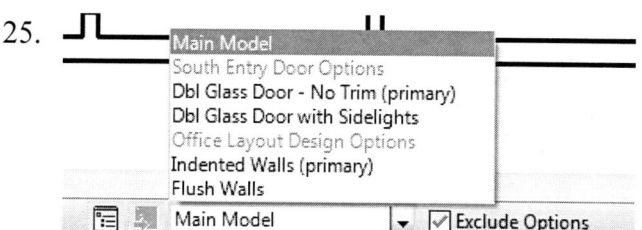 Note in the bottom of the window, you can select which Option set you want active.

26. Using **Duplicate View→Duplicate**, create four copies of the Level 1 view.

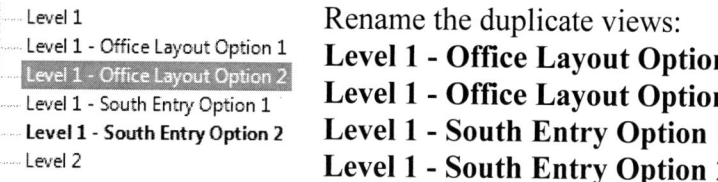

Rename the duplicate views:
Level 1 - Office Layout Option 1
Level 1 - Office Layout Option 2
Level 1 - South Entry Option 1
Level 1 - South Entry Option 2

27. 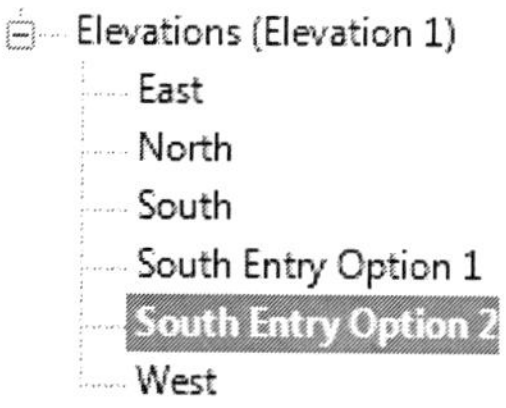 Using **Duplicate View→Duplicate**, create two copies of the South Elevation view.

Rename the duplicate views:
South Entry Option 1
South Entry Option 2

28. Activate **Level 1 - South Entry Option 1**.

29. 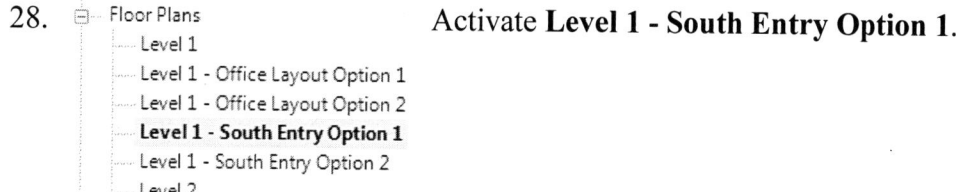 In the Properties pane:
Select Edit for **Visibility/Graphics Overrrides**.

30. 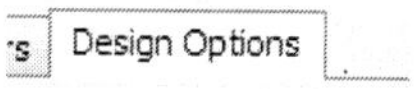 Select the **Design Options** tab.

31. 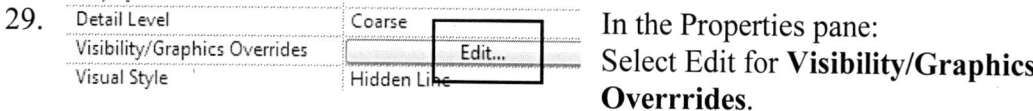 Set Option Set 1 to **Dbl Glass Door - No Trim (primary)**.

Press **OK**.

32. 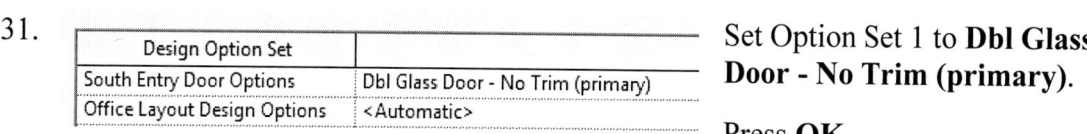 Set the Design Option to **Dbl Glass Door - No Trim (primary)**.

33. 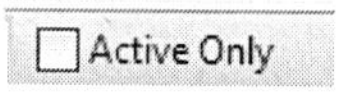 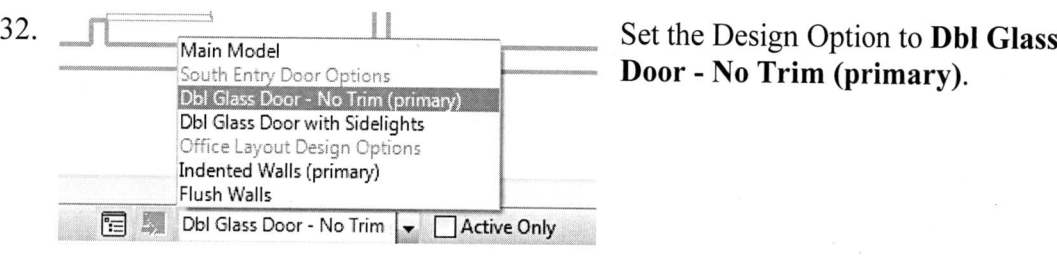 Uncheck **Active Only**.

1-15

34. 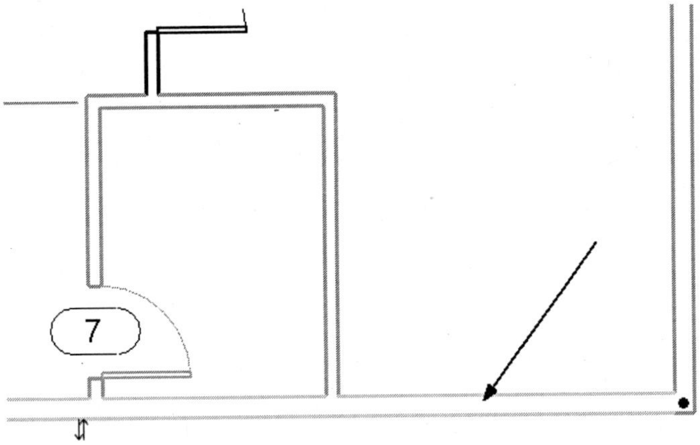 Select the south horizontal wall.

35. 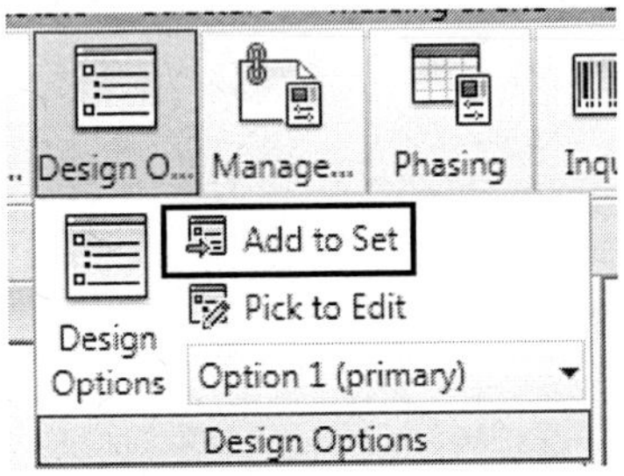 Activate the **Manage** ribbon.

    Under Design Options, select **Add to Set**.

    The selected wall is added to the **Dbl Glass Door - No Trim (primary)** *set.*

36. Activate the **Home** ribbon.

    Select the **Door** tool from the Build panel.

37. 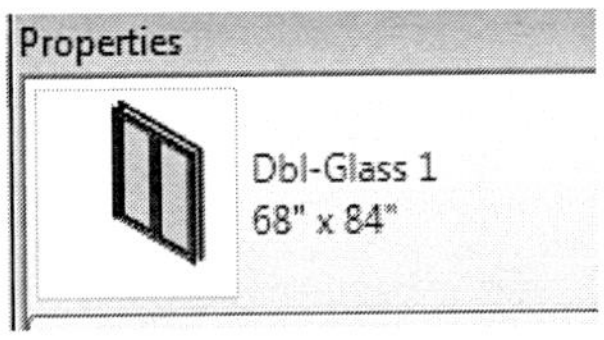 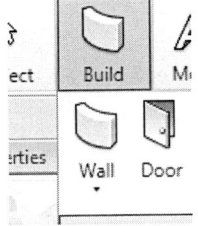 Set the Door type to **Dbl-Glass 1: 68" x 84"**.

38. 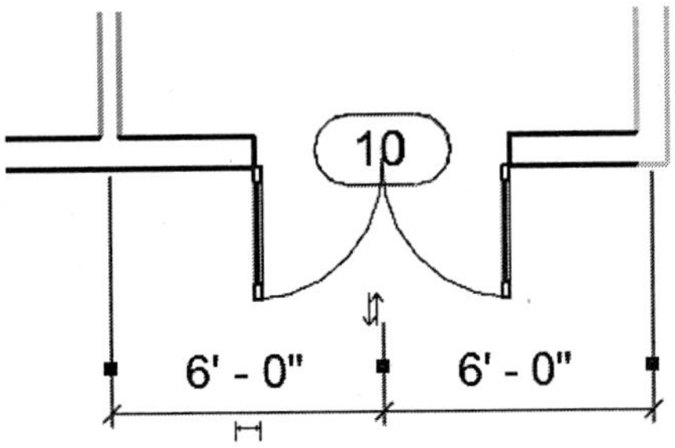 Place the door as shown.

39. 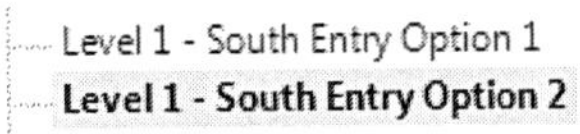 Activate **Level 1 - South Entry Option 2**.

40. 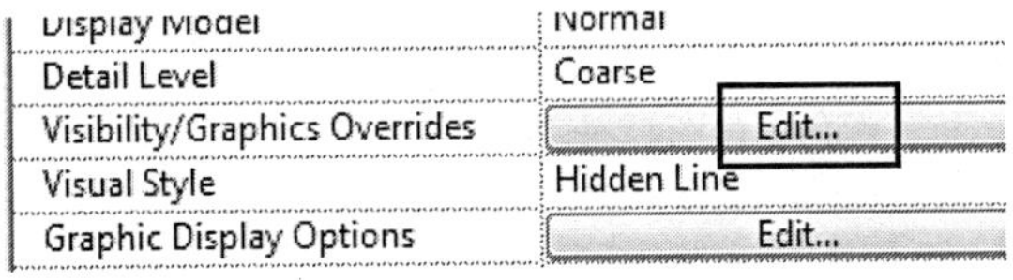 In the Properties pane: Select **Edit** Visibilities/Graphics Overrides.

Building Information Modeling and Revit Basics

41. Activate the **Design Options** tab.

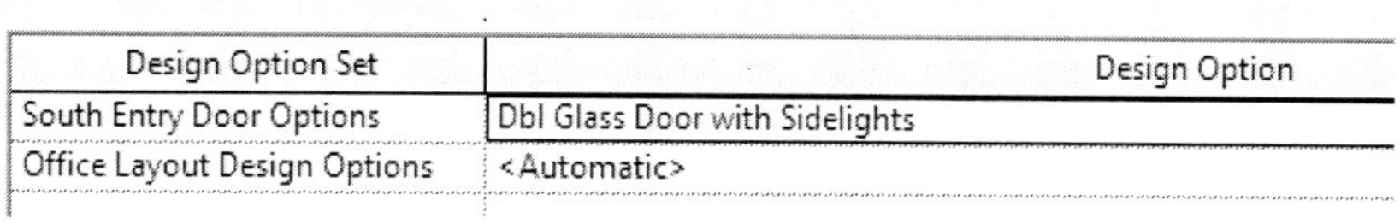

Design Option Set	Design Option
South Entry Door Options	Dbl Glass Door with Sidelights
Office Layout Design Options	<Automatic>

Set **Dbl Glass Door with Sidelights** on South Entry Door Options.

Press **OK**.

42. 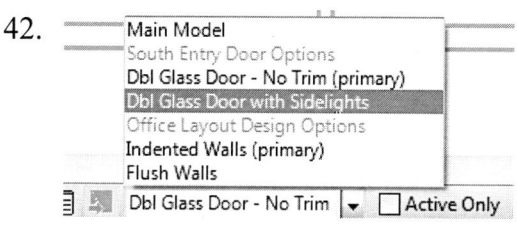 Set the Design Option to **Dbl Glass Door with Sidelights**.

43.  Uncheck **Active Only**.

44. 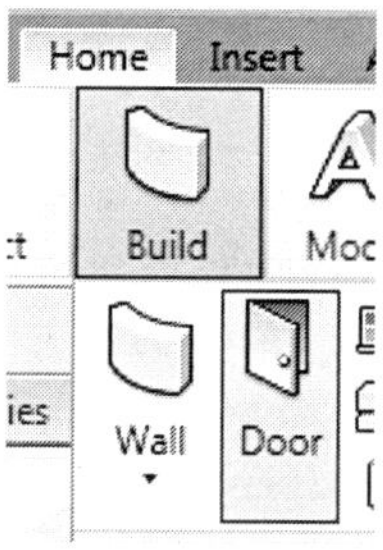 Activate the **Home** ribbon.

Select the **Door** tool from the Build panel.

45. 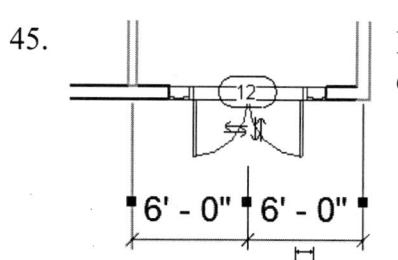 Place a **Double-Raised Panel with Sidelights: 68″ x 80″** door as shown.

46. Activate the **South Entry Option 1** elevation.

47. 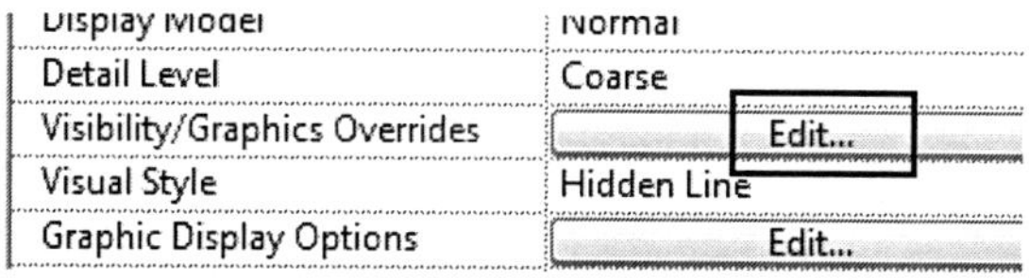 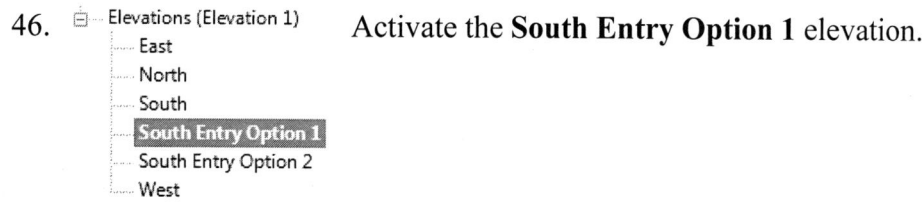 In the Properties pane:
Select **Edit** Visibilities/Graphics Overrides.

1-17

48. Activate the **Design Options** tab.

Design Option Set	
South Entry Door Options	Dbl Glass Door - No Trim (primary)
Office Layout Design Options	<Automatic>

    Set **Dbl Glass Door - No Trim** on South Entry Door Options.

    Press **OK**.

49. Activate the **South Entry Option 2** elevation.

50.
Display Model	Normal
Detail Level	Coarse
Visibility/Graphics Overrides	Edit...
Visual Style	Hidden Line
Graphic Display Options	Edit...

    In the Properties pane:
    Select **Edit** Visibilities/Graphics Overrides.

51. Activate the **Design Options** tab.

Design Option Set	
South Entry Door Options	Dbl Glass Door with Sidelights
Office Layout Design Options	<Automatic>

    Set **Dbl Glass Door with Sidelights** on South Entry Door Options.

    Press **OK**.

52. Sheets (all)
    - A101 - South Entry Door Option
    - A102 - Office Layout Options

    Activate the Sheet named **South Entry Door Options**.

53.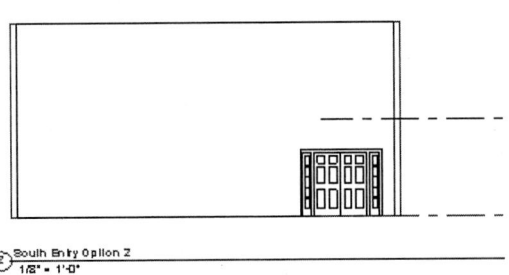

    Drag and drop the two South Entry Option elevation views on the sheet.

54. Switch to 3D view.

55. Use **Duplicate View→Duplicate** to create two new 3D views.

    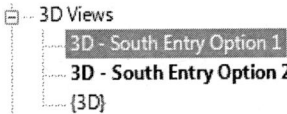

    Rename the views:
    3D - South Entry Option 1
    3D - South Entry Option 2

Building Information Modeling and Revit Basics

56. Activate **3D - South Entry Option 1**.

57. In the Properties pane: Select **Edit** Visibilities/Graphics Overrides.

58. Activate the **Design Options** tab.

    Set **Dbl Glass Door - No Trim** on South Entry Door Options.

    Press **OK**.

59. Activate **3D - South Entry Option 2**.

60. In the Properties pane: Select **Edit** Visibilities/Graphics Overrides.

61. Activate the **Design Options** tab.

    Set **Dbl Glass Door with Sidelights** on South Entry Door Options.

    Press **OK**.

62. Activate the Sheet named **South Entry Door Options**.

63. Drag and drop the 3D views onto the sheet.

1-19

64. Activate **Level 1 - Office Layout Option 1**.

65. In the Properties pane:
    Select Edit for **Visibility/Graphics Overrrides**.

66. Select the **Design Options** tab.

67. Set Option Set 1 to **Indented Walls (primary)**.
    Press **OK**.

68. Set the Design Option to **Indented Walls (primary)**.

69. Uncheck **Active Only**.

70. Select the Wall tool from the Home ribbon.
    Select the Basic Wall: INterior - 5" Partition (2-hr).

71. Place the two walls indicated.

    The vertical wall is placed at the midpoint of the small horizontal wall.

    The horizontal wall is aligned with the wall indicated by the red line.

72. Activate the **Home** ribbon.
    Select the **Door** tool from the Build panel.

1-20

Building Information Modeling and Revit Basics

73. Place a **Sgl Flush 36″ x 80″** door as shown.

74. Activate **Level 1 - Office Layout Option 2**.

75. In the Properties pane:
Select Edit for **Visibility/Graphics Overrrides**.

76. Select the **Design Options** tab.

77. Set Office Layout Design Options to **Flush Walls**.

Press **OK**.

78. Set the Design Option to **Flush Walls**.

79. Uncheck **Active Only**.

80. Activate the **Home** ribbon.

Select the **Wall** tool from the Build panel.

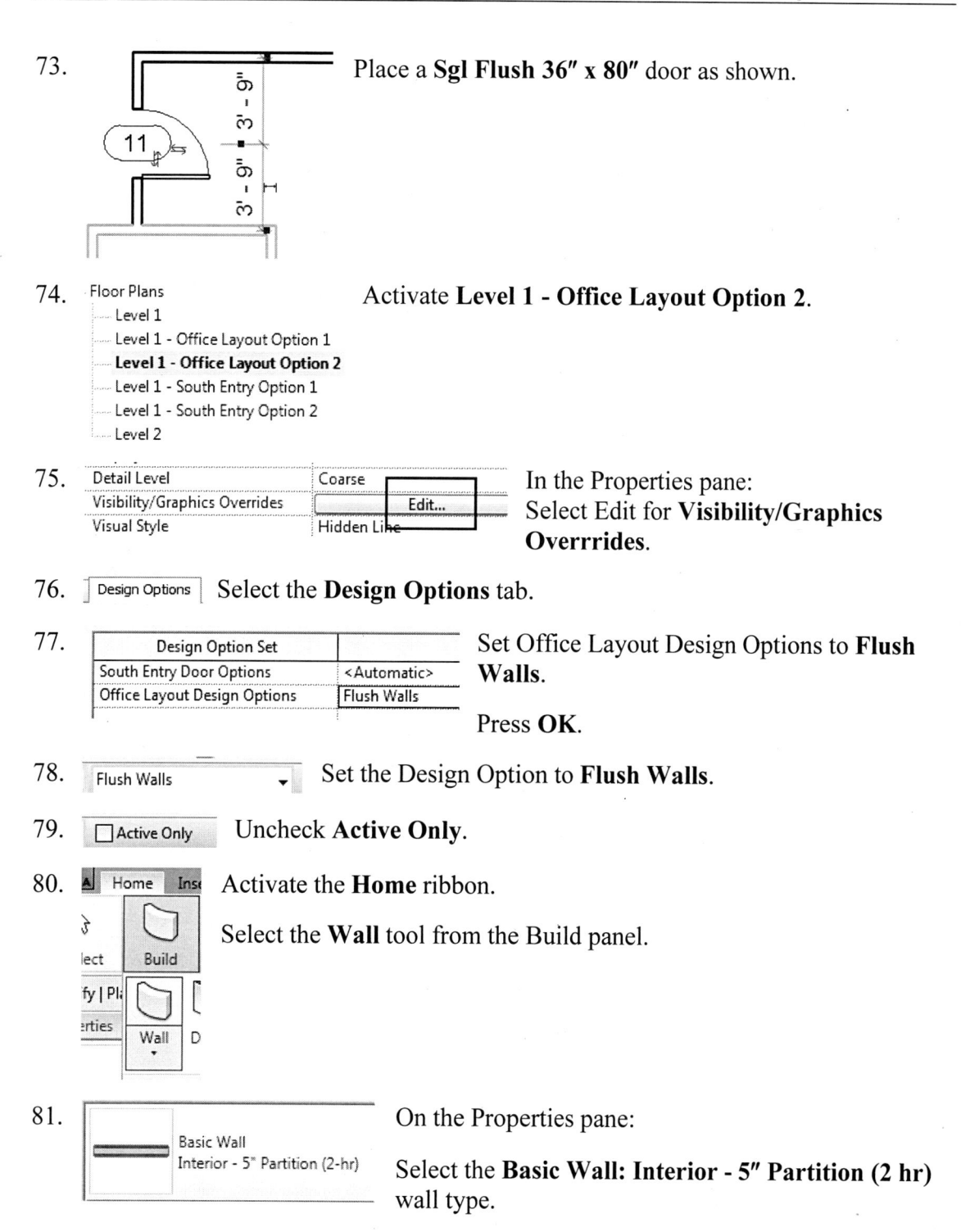

81. On the Properties pane:

Select the **Basic Wall: Interior - 5″ Partition (2 hr)** wall type.

1-21

82. 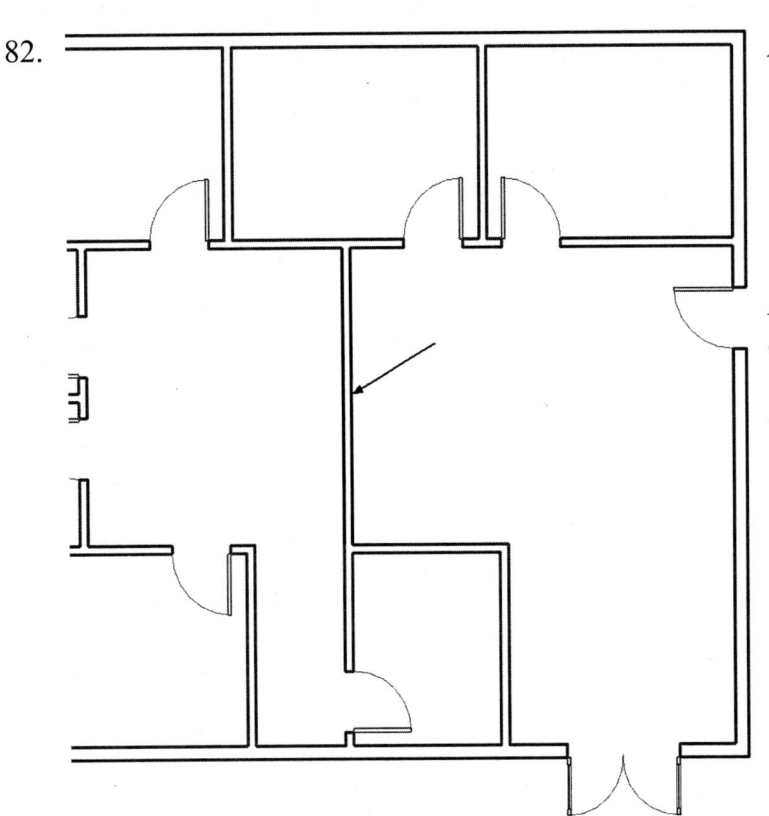 Add the wall shown.

Note that the walls and door added for the Indented Walls option are not displayed.

83. 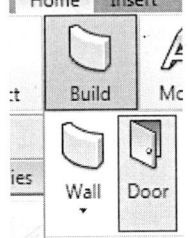 Activate the **Home** ribbon.

Select the **Door** tool from the Build panel.

84. 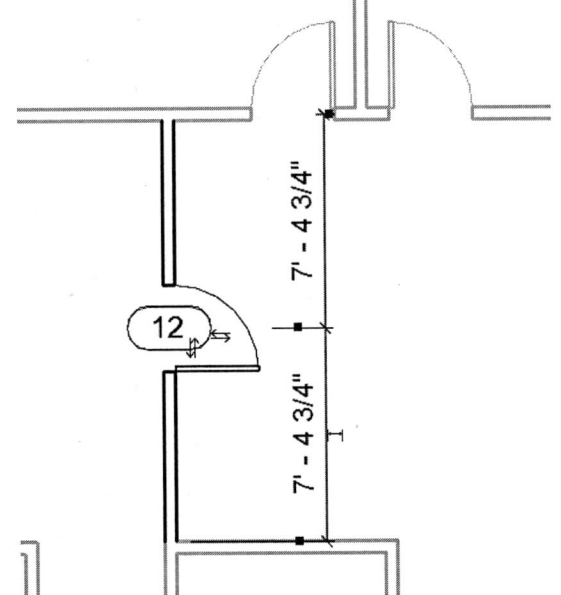 Place a **Sgl Flush 36″ x 80″** door as shown.

85. Activate the **Manage** ribbon.

    Select **Design Options** on the Design Options panel.

86. Select **Finish Editing**.

    Close the dialog.

87. Change the Design Option to **Main Model**.

88. Note that if you hover your mouse over the element, it will display which Option set it belongs to.

    This only works if Active Only or Exclude Options is disabled.

89. Activate the Sheet named **Office Layout Options**.

90. Drag and drop the two Office Layout options onto the sheet.

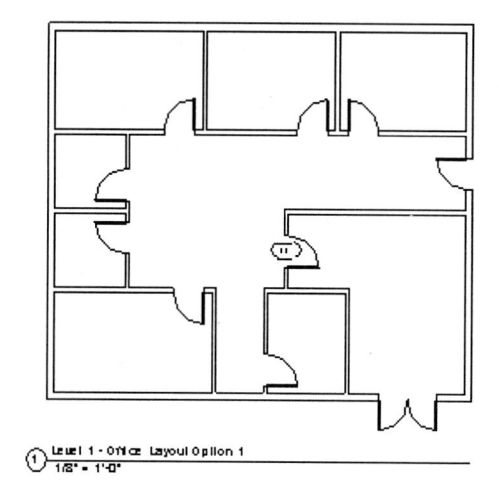

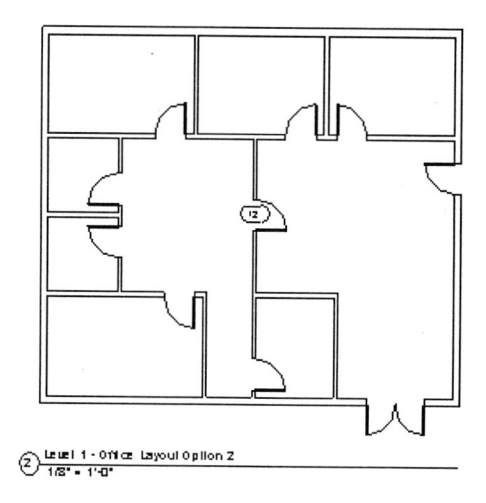

91. Close without saving.

Practice Associate Exam

1. Select the answer which is NOT an example of bidirectional associativity:
   A. Flip a section line and all views update
   B. Draw a wall in plan view and it appears in all other views
   C. Change an element type in a schedule and the change is displayed in the floor plan view as well
   D. Flip a door orientation so the door swing is on the exterior of the building.

2. Select the answer which is NOT an example of a parametric relationship:
   A. A floor is attached to enclosing walls. When a wall moves, the floor updates so it remains connected to the walls.
   B. A series of windows are placed along a wall using an EQ dimension. The length of the wall is modified and the windows remain equally spaced.
   C. A door is placed in a wall. The wall is moved and the door remains constrained in the wall.
   D. A shared parameter file is loaded to the server

3. Which tab does NOT appear on Revit's ribbon?
   A. Home
   B. Basics
   C. Insert
   D. View

4. Which item does NOT appear in the Project Browser?
   A. Families
   B. Groups
   C. Callouts
   D. Notes

5. Which is the most recently saved backup file?
   A. office.0001
   B. office.0002
   C. office.0003
   D. office.0004

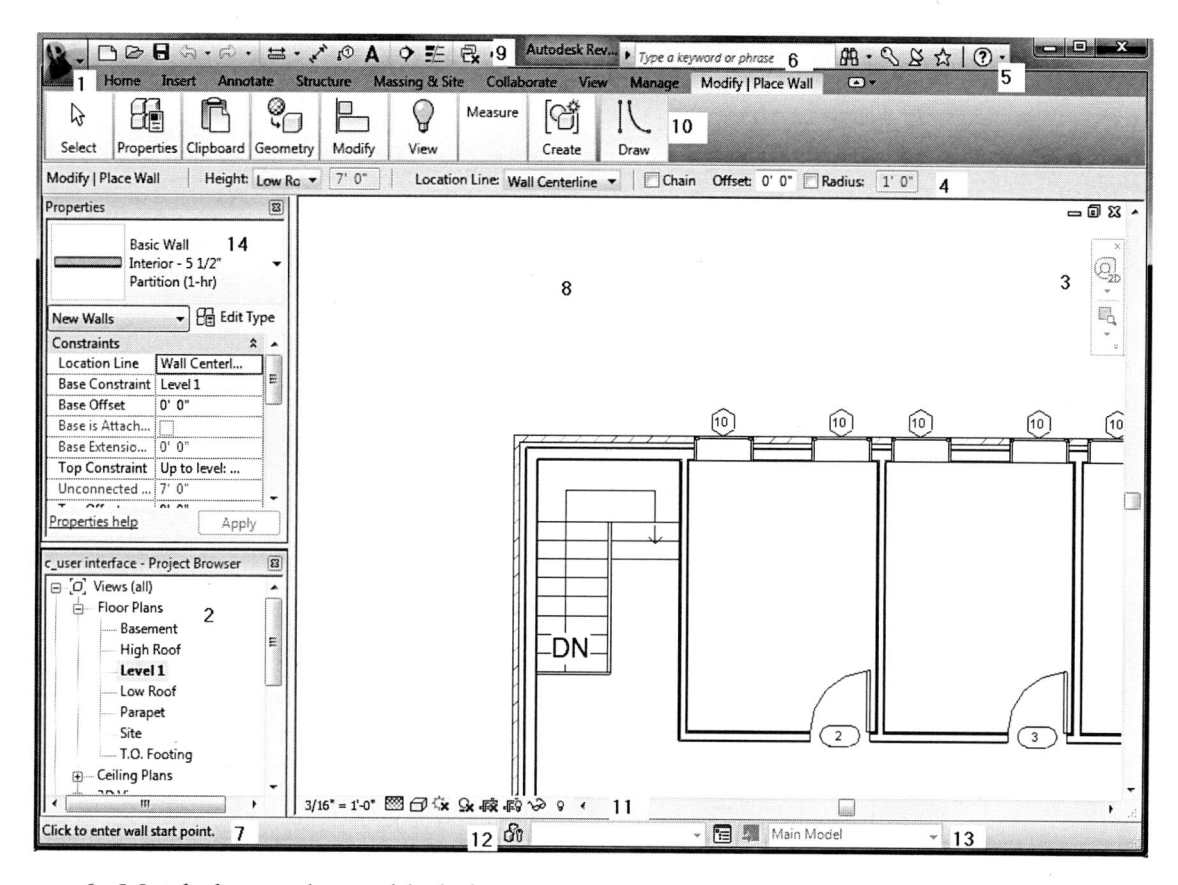

6. Match the numbers with their names.

View Control Bar	InfoCenter
Project Browser	Status Bar
Navigation Bar	Properties Pane
Options Bar	Application Menu
Design Options	Drawing Area
Help	Quick Access Toolbar
Ribbon	Worksets

7. When using design options, the active option is the _____
   - A. preferred design option in the design option set
   - B. part of the building that is not defined using design options
   - C. design options currently being edited
   - D. collection of all design options

Answers:

1) D; 2) D; 3) B; 4) D; 5) D; 6) 1- Application Menu, 2- Project Browser, 3- Navigation Bar, 4- Options Bar, 5- Help, 6- InfoCenter, 7- Status Bar, 8- Drawing Area, 9- Quick Access Toolbar, 10- Ribbon, 11- View Control Bar, 12- Worksets, 13- Design Options; 7) D

Notes:

Lesson Two

The Basics of Building a Model

This lesson addresses the following Associate and Professional level exam questions:

- Wall Properties
- Compound Walls
- Stacked Walls
- Doors and Windows
- In-Place Mass

In the Professional exam, most of the wall problems follow these steps:

- Place a wall of a specific element type. (Be able to select wall type.)
- Place a wall by setting the location line. (Understand how to use the location line setting.)
- Place a wall using different Option Settings. (Understand how to use the Options Settings when placing a wall.)
- After placing the wall, place a dimension to determine if the wall was placed correctly.
- After placing the wall, inspect the element properties to determine if the wall was placed correctly.

In the Associate exam, the user will need to be familiar with the different parameters in walls and compound walls. The user should also know which options are applied to walls and when those options are available.

Command Exercise

Exercise 2-1 – Wall Options

Drawing Name: **i_firestation_basic_plan.rvt**
Estimated Time to Completion: 10 Minutes

Scope

Exploring the different wall options

Solution

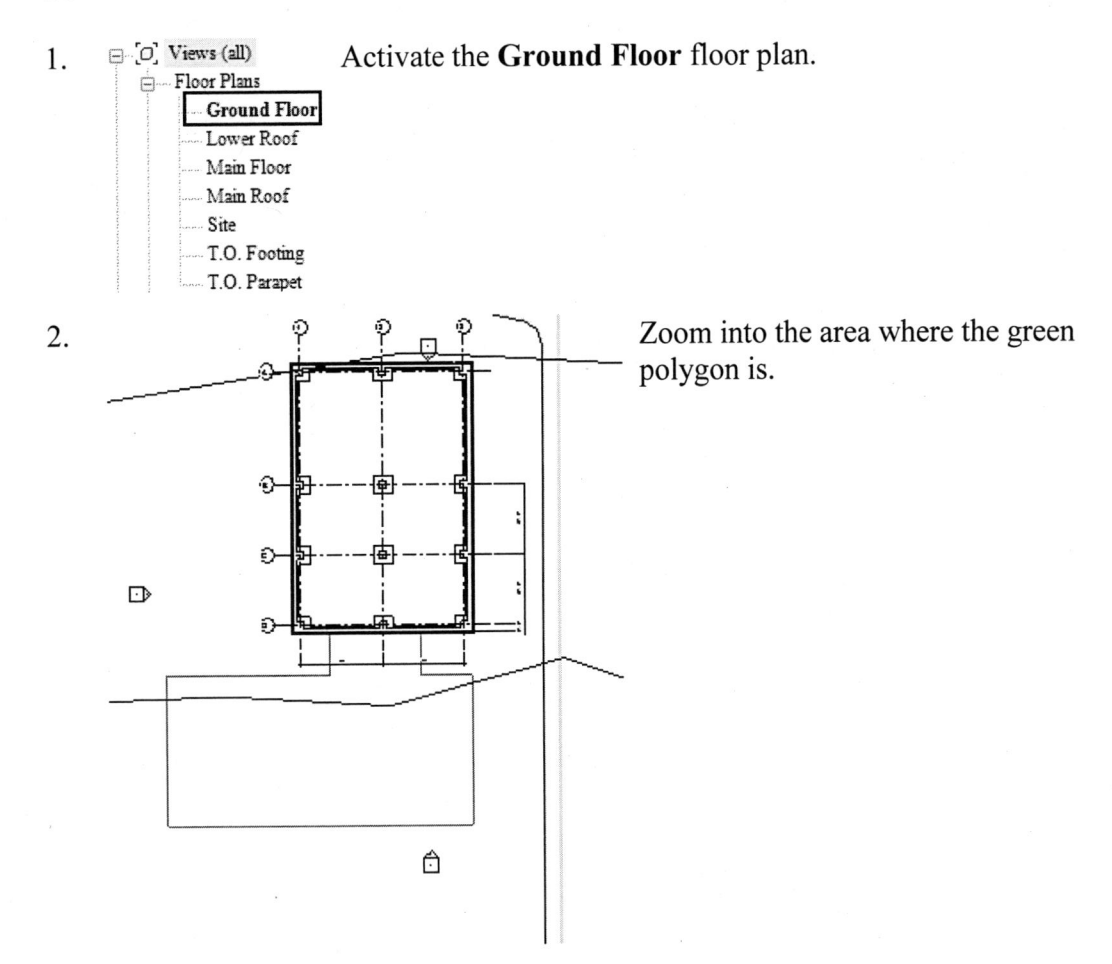

1. Activate the **Ground Floor** floor plan.

2. Zoom into the area where the green polygon is.

3. Select **Wall** from the Home ribbon.

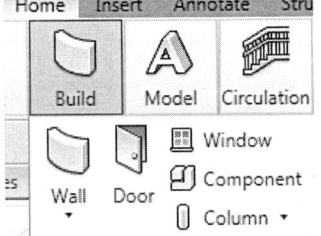

2-2

The Basics of Building a Model

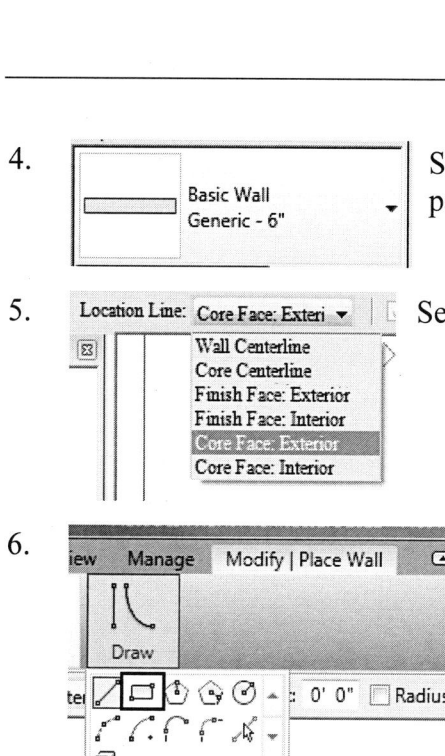

4. Set the Wall Type to **Generic – 6″** in the Properties pane.

5. Set the Location Line to **Core Face:Exterior**.

6. Select the **Rectangle** tool on the Draw panel.

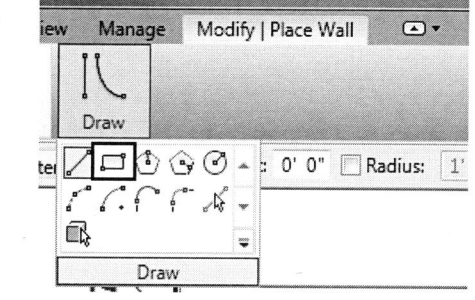

7. Select the two points indicated to place the rectangle.

8. Select the **Line** tool from the Draw panel.

9. Start the line at the midpoint of the lower horizontal wall.

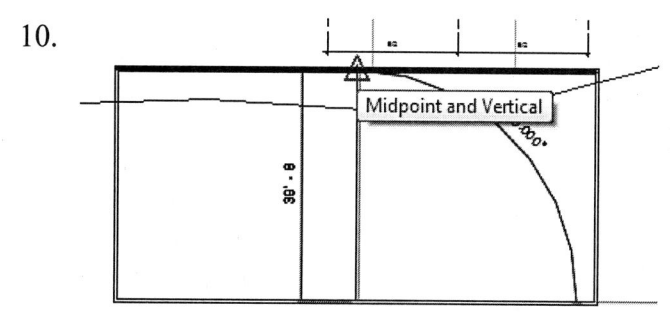

10. Bring the line end up to the midpoint of the upper horizontal wall.

    Left click to finish placing the wall.

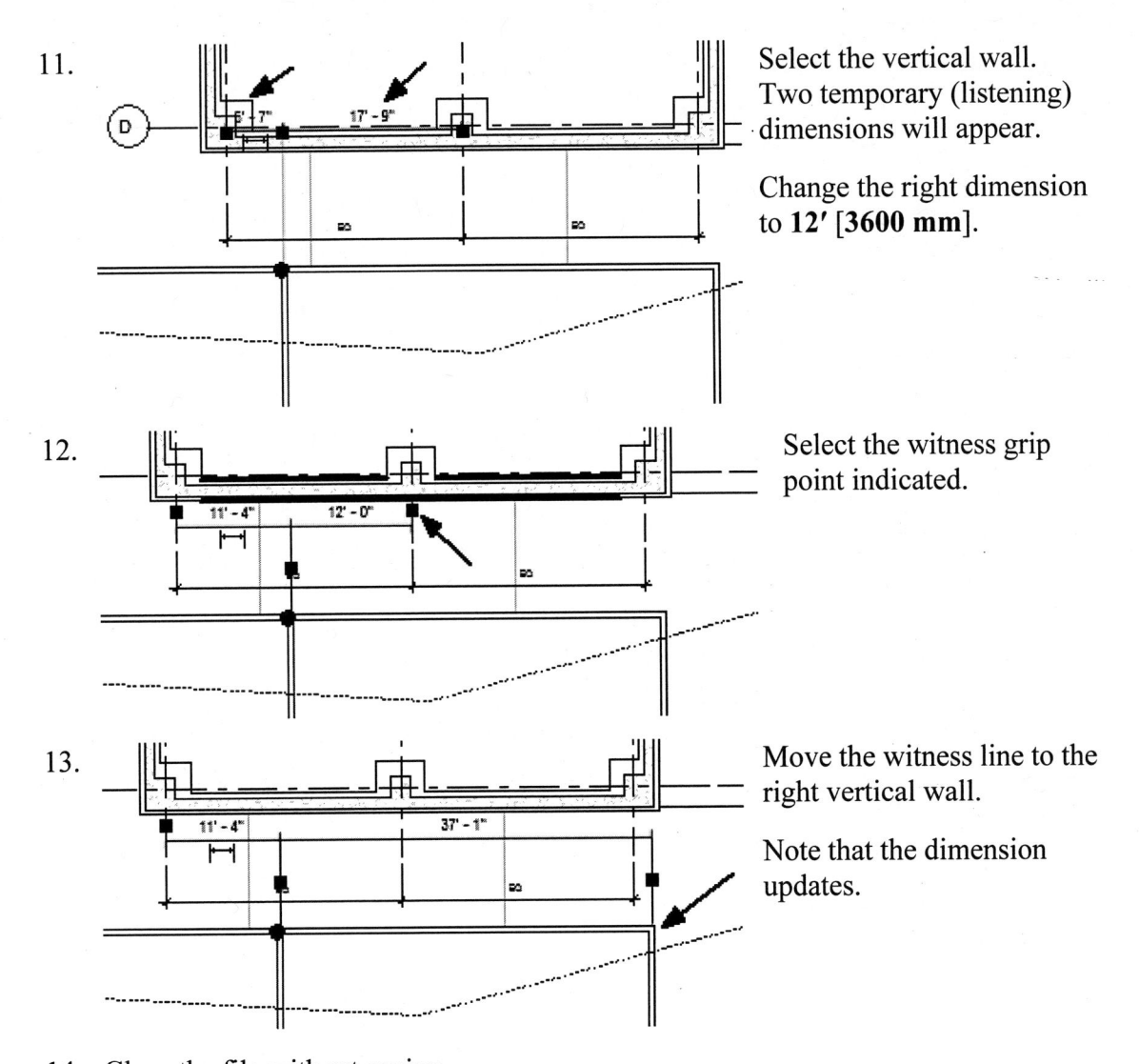

11. Select the vertical wall. Two temporary (listening) dimensions will appear.

    Change the right dimension to **12′ [3600 mm]**.

12. Select the witness grip point indicated.

13. Move the witness line to the right vertical wall.

    Note that the dimension updates.

14. Close the file without saving.

Command Exercise

Exercise 2-2 – Placing a Wall Sweep

Drawing Name: **i_walls.rvt**
Estimated Time to Completion: 20 Minutes

Scope

Placing a wall sweep.

Solution

1. Activate **Level 1** Floor Plan.

2. Select the **Wall** tool from the Home ribbon on the Build panel.

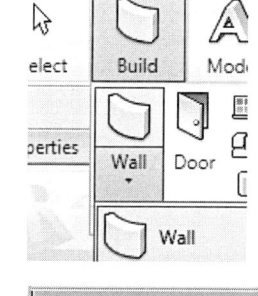

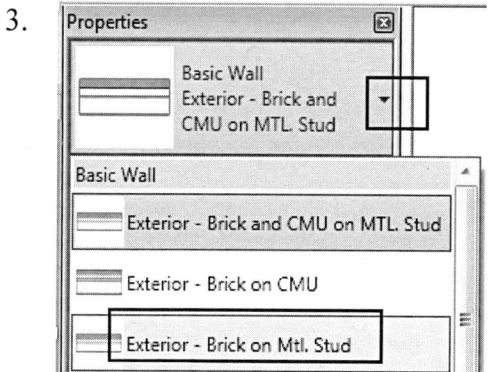

3. Set the wall type to **Exterior - Brick on Mtl. Stud** using the Type Selector on the Properties pane.

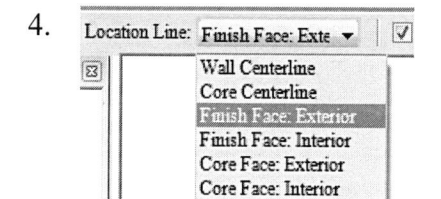

4. Set the Location Line to **Finish Face: Exterior**.

5. Select the **Pick Line** mode from the Draw panel.
   Select the four green lines.

   Note that when you pick the lines, the side of the line you use determines which side of the line is used for the exterior side of the wall.

6. The lines should be aligned to the exterior side of the walls.

   Set the Detail Level to **Medium**.

7. Type **VV** to bring up the Visibility/Graphics dialog.

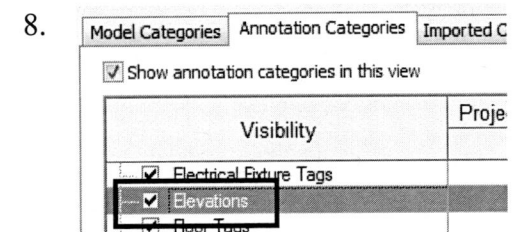

8. Enable the visibility of Elevations.

   Press **OK**.

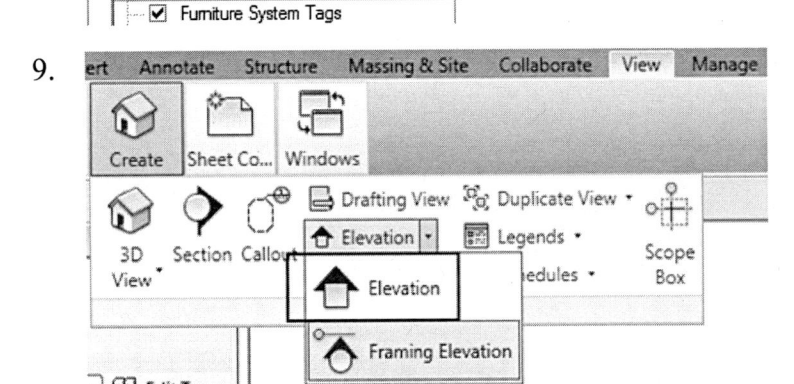

9. Activate the **View** ribbon.

   Select the **Elevation** tool on the Create panel.

10. Place an elevation in the center of the room.

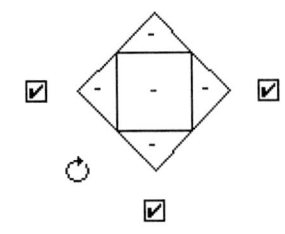

    Place a check mark on each box to create an elevation for each interior wall.

The Basics of Building a Model

11. In the Project Browser, you will see that four elevation views have been created.

12. If you hover your mouse over a triangle, a tooltip will appear with the name of the linked view.

13. Rename the elevation views to East Interior, North Interior, South Interior and West Interior.

14. If you pick on the triangle part of the elevation, you will see the view depth (Far Clip Offset) of that elevation view.

15. Activate the **South Interior** View.

16. Use the grips to extend the elevation view beyond the walls.

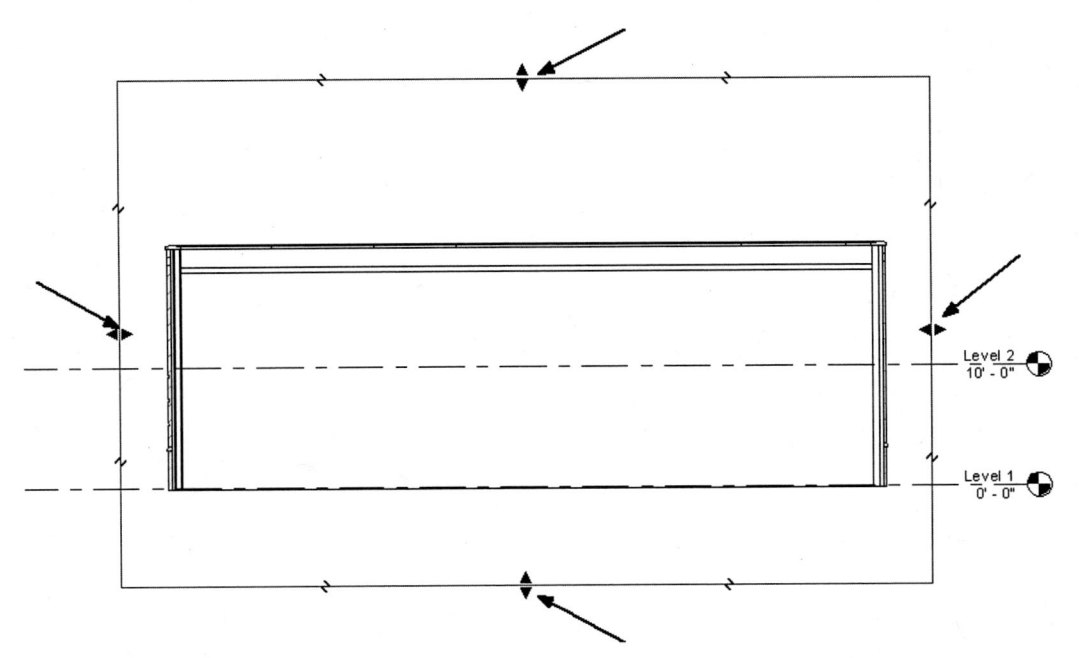

17. Activate the **Home** ribbon.

    Select the **Wall Sweep** tool.

    The Wall Sweep tool is only available in elevation, 3D or section views.

18. Place the sweep so it is toward the top of the wall.

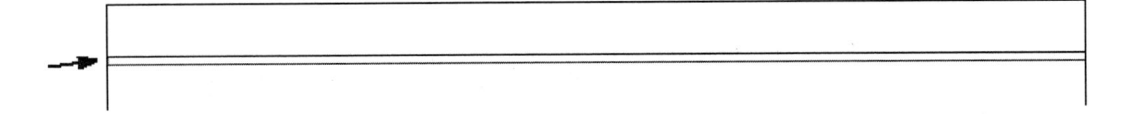

The Basics of Building a Model

19. In the Properties pane, adjust the Offset from Level to **18′ 0″**.

20. Switch to a 3D view.

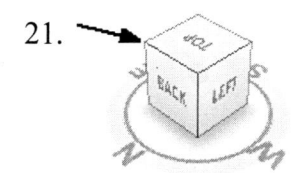

21. Select the top corners of the view cube to orient the view so you can see the wall sweep.

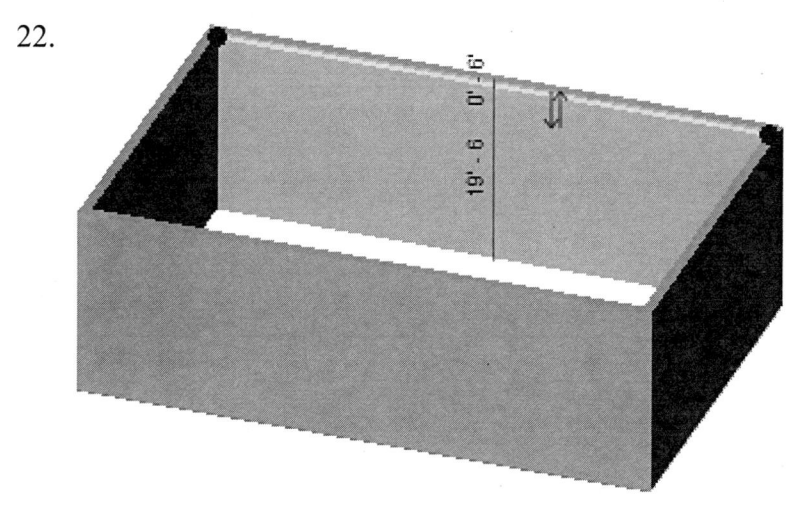

22. Select the wall sweep that was placed.

    It will highlight when selected.

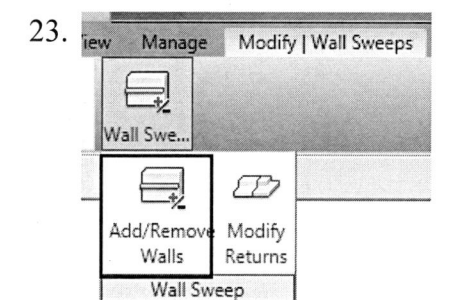

23. Select **Add/Remove Walls** from the ribbon.

    Select the other walls.
    Orbit around to inspect.

24. Save as *ex2-2.rvt*.

2-9

Command Exercise

Exercise 2-3 – Create a Wall Sweep Style

Drawing Name: **ex2-2.rvt**
Estimated Time to Completion: 15 Minutes

Scope

Creating a wall sweep style.
Loading a Profile.

Solution:

1. Activate the **South Interior** View.

2. Activate the **Insert** ribbon.

   Select **Load Family**.

3. Browse to the **Profiles** folder.

4. Load the following profiles:

   Base-3.rfa
   Crown 1.rfa

   You can load more than one file at a time by holding down the CTRL key.

5. Press **Open**.

The Basics of Building a Model

6. Activate the **Home** ribbon.

   Select the **Wall Sweep** tool.

   The Wall Sweep tool is only available in elevation, 3D or section views.

7. Select **Edit Type** from the Properties pane.

8. Select **Duplicate**.

9. Enter **Base Moulding** in the Name field.

   Press **OK**.

10. Set the Profile to **Base 3 : 3 1/2" x 9/16"**.
    Set the Material to **Plastic - Vinyl Cove Base**.

    Press **OK** to exit the dialog.

11. Place the baseboard on the bottom of the wall.

12. Save as *ex2-3.rvt*.

Command Exercise

Exercise 2-4 – Create a Custom Profile

Drawing Name: **ex2-3.rvt**
Estimated Time to Completion: 20 Minutes

Scope

Creating a custom profile.
Using the custom profile in a wall sweep.

Solution

1. Select **Open**.

2. Scroll on the left pane to the **Imperial Library**.

3. Browse to the **Profiles** folder.

4. Open *Base 3.rfa*.

5. Save the file as *Base 4.rfa*.

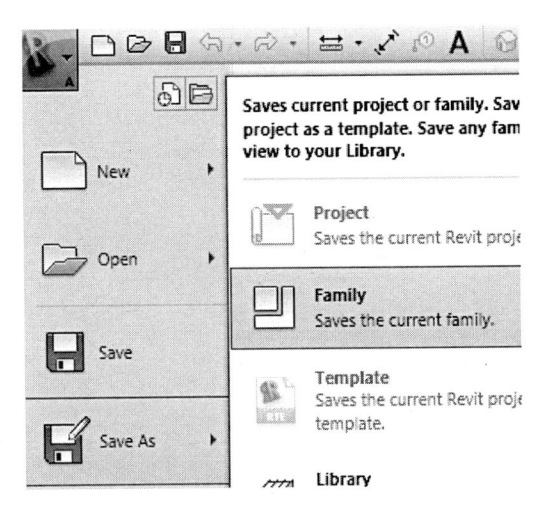

6. Activate the Home ribbon.

   Select the **Types** tool on the Properties pane.

The Basics of Building a Model

7. Note that several sizes are available for this profile.

   Use the Apply button to see how the profile changes depending on the size selected.

   Press **OK** to close the Types dialog.

8. Modify the profile.

   I eliminated the offset on the left and simplified the top.

   Verify that the profile still flexes properly using the different types.

9. Save the new profile.

10. Activate the Modify ribbon.

    Select **Load into Project**.

11. Close the family file.

12. Activate the **South Interior** View.

13. Select the base wall sweep.

2-13

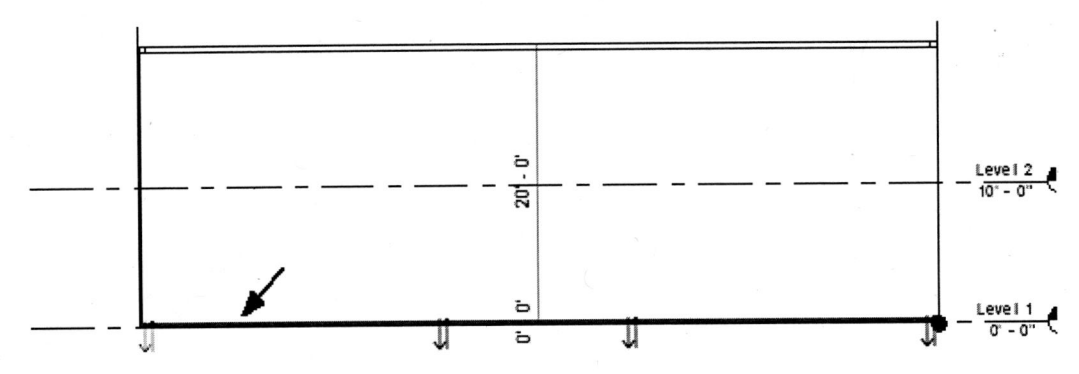

14. 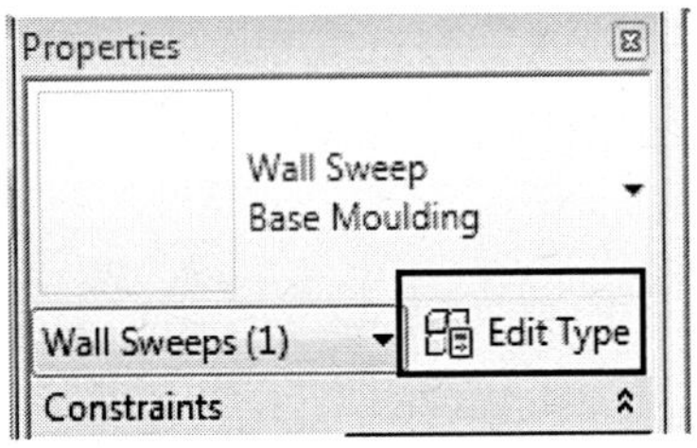 Select **Edit Type** from the Properties pane.

15. 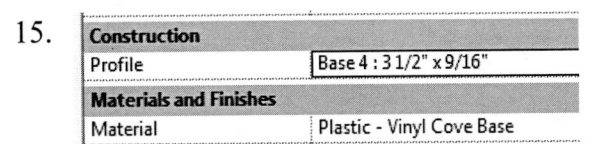 Select **Base 4: 3 1/2" x 9/16"** for the Profile.

    This is the new profile you just created and loaded into the project.

    Press **OK**.

16. Save as *ex2-4.rvt*.

Command Exercise

Exercise 2-5 – Create a Compound Wall

Drawing Name: **ex2-4.rvt**
Estimated Time to Completion: 40 Minutes

Scope

Creating a custom profile.
Using the custom profile in a Compound Wall.

Revit defines a compound wall as a wall that consists of multiple vertical layers.

Solution

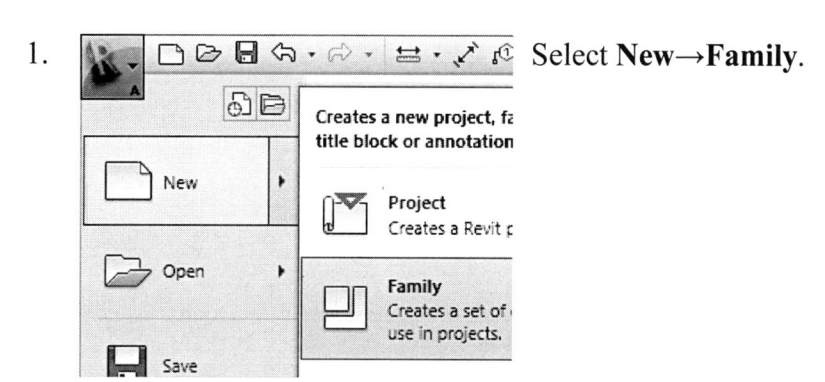

1. Select **New→Family**.

2. Locate the *Profile.rft* file.
   Select **Open**.

3. Select the **Line** tool on the Detail panel.

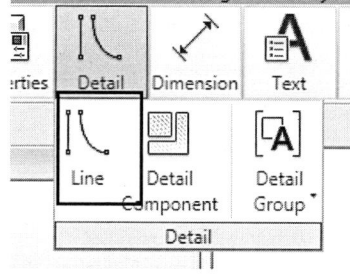

4. Select the **Rectangle** tool on the Draw panel.

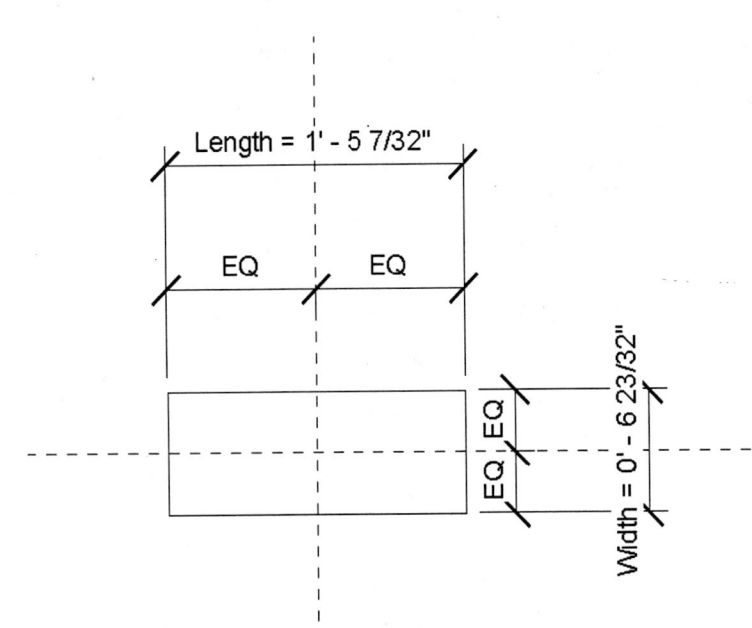

5. Create a rectangle centered on the reference planes.

   The orientation of the rectangle is important for the stud to appear properly in the wall.

   Add a length label and a width label to the dimensions.

6. The dimension tool is located on the Home ribbon.
   To add a label, select the dimension, right click and select Edit Label.

7. Activate the Home ribbon.

   Select the **Types** tool from the Properties panel.

8. Select **New** under Family Types.

9. Enter **Stud - 2″ x 4″** in the Name field.

   Press **OK**.

10. Set the Width to **1 1/2″**.
    Set the Length to **3 1/2″**.

    Press **Apply** to see the profile update.

11. Press **OK** to close the dialog.

12. Select **Save**.

The Basics of Building a Model

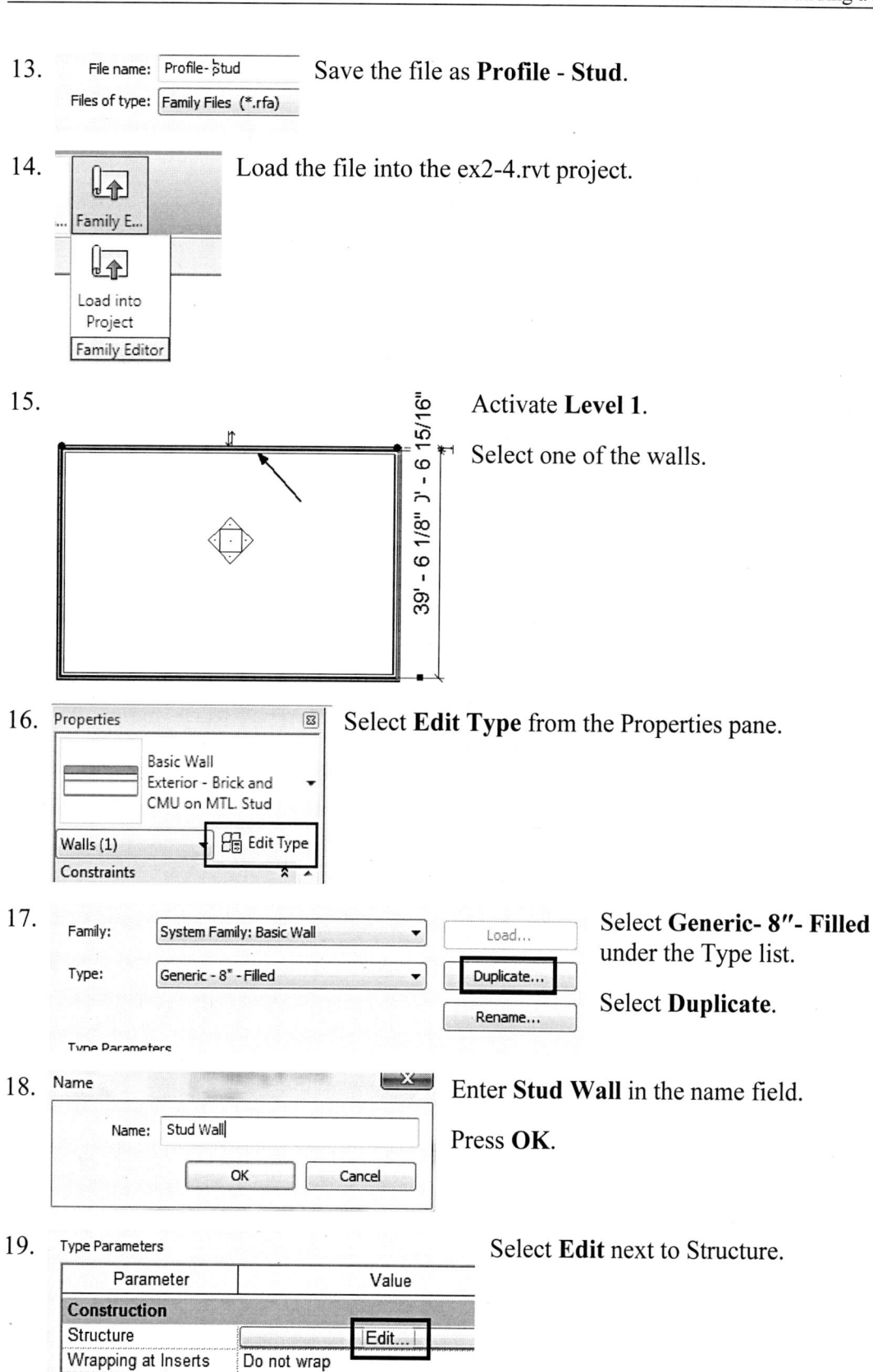

13. Save the file as **Profile - Stud**.

14. Load the file into the ex2-4.rvt project.

15. Activate **Level 1**.

    Select one of the walls.

16. Select **Edit Type** from the Properties pane.

17. Select **Generic- 8″- Filled** under the Type list.

    Select **Duplicate**.

18. Enter **Stud Wall** in the name field.

    Press **OK**.

19. Select **Edit** next to Structure.

2-17

20. Create the following layer structure:
   Layer 1: Finish 1 [4] Siding Clapboard ½"
   Layer 2: Core Boundary
   Layer 3: Substrate [2] Wood – Sheathing – Plywood ½"
   Layer 4: Thermal/Air Layer Air Barrier- Air Infiltration 3 ½"
   Layer 5: Core Boundary
   Layer 6: Finish [2] (5) Gypsum Wall Board ½"

21. Switch the Preview window to display a section view.

22. Select the **Sweeps** button.

23. Select **Load Profile**.

24. Locate the *Profile-Stud.rfa* profile you created. Press Open.

25. Select **Add**.

26. Locate the Stud profile that was loaded.

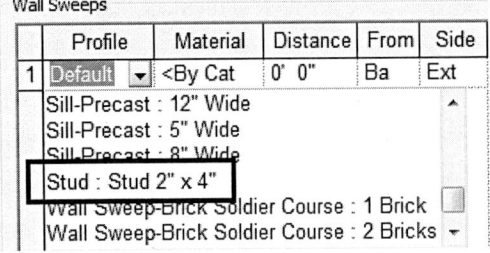

27. Set the material to **Wood-Stud Layer**.

28. We want to locate the stud profile so it is between the gypsum board and the plywood sheath.

29.

	Material	Distance	From	Side	Offset	Flip	Setback
1	Wood - Stud Layer	-0' 0 3/4"	Top	Interior	-0' 2 1/4"	☐	0' 0"
2	Wood - Stud Layer	0' 0 3/4"	Base	Interior	-0' 2 1/4"	☐	0' 0"

To have the profile place properly:

Set the first Wall Sweep at a distance of -3/4" from the Top.
Offset it -2 ¼" from the interior side.

Select **Add** to add the second wall sweep.
Set the second Wall Sweep at a distance of ¾" from the Base.
Offset it -2 ¼" from the interior side.
Press **OK**.

30. Zoom into the top and bottom of the wall to verify the placement of the stud.

31. Press **OK** to close the dialog.

32. Switch to a 3D view.

33. Determine which wall is the stud wall.
    If you select the wall, you will see the wall type displayed in the ribbon.

    Basic Wall
    Stud Wall

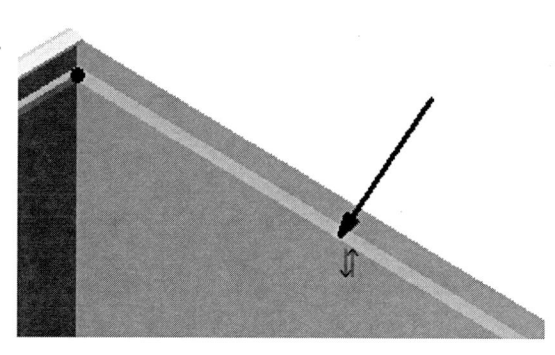

34. Select the wall sweep that has been placed on the wall.

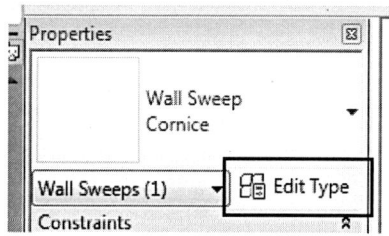

35. Select **Edit Type** from the Properties Pane.

2-19

36. Select **Duplicate**.

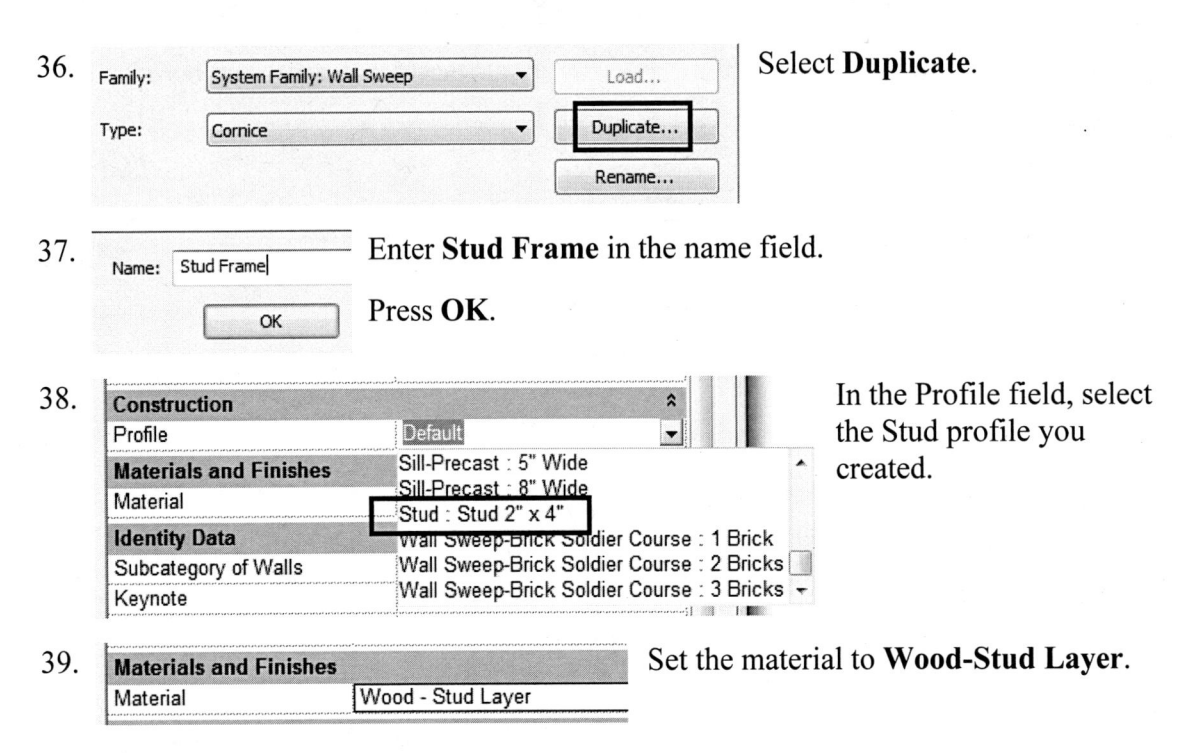

37. Enter **Stud Frame** in the name field.

    Press **OK**.

38. In the Profile field, select the Stud profile you created.

39. Set the material to **Wood-Stud Layer**.

40. Press **OK**.

41. Release the wall sweep you have selected by left clicking anywhere in the drawing window.

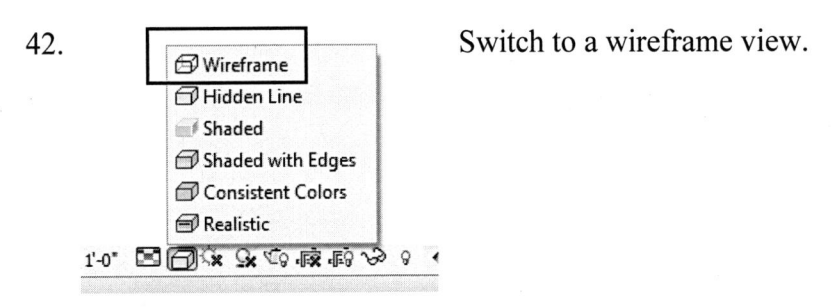

42. Switch to a wireframe view.

43. 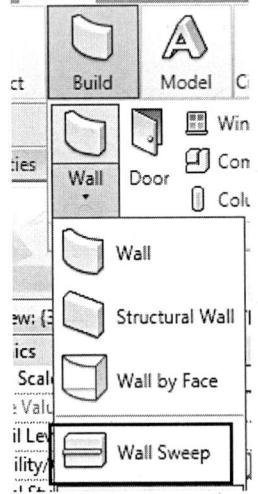 Select **Wall Sweep** from the Home ribbon.

2-20

The Basics of Building a Model

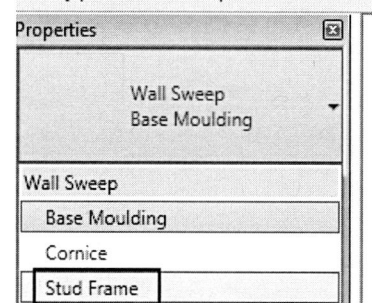

44. Select **Stud Frame** from the element type drop-down list in the Properties pane.

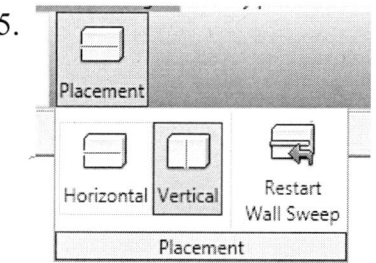

45. Select **Vertical** orientation on the Placement panel.

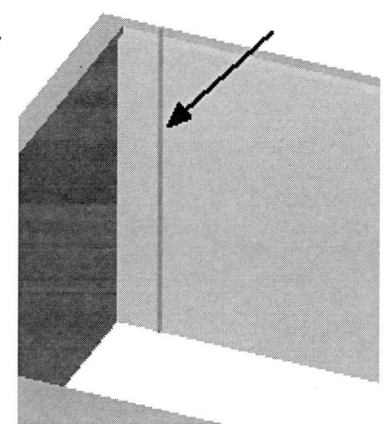

46. Place the stud on the wall.

    Cancel out of the command.

47. Switch to **Level 1** floor plan for a plan view.

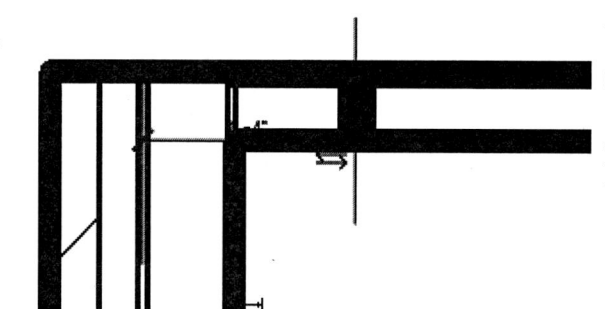

48. Use the **Move** tool to position the stud inside the wall.

    Adjust the distance so the stud is located 16″ from the wall end.

2-21

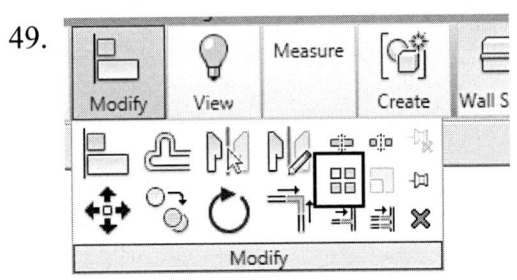

49. Select the wall stud.
Select the **Array** tool on the Modify panel.

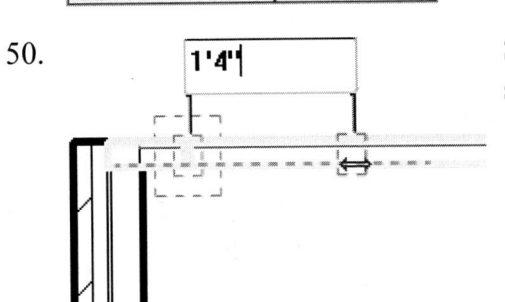

50. Set the center to center distance between the studs to **1′ 4″**.

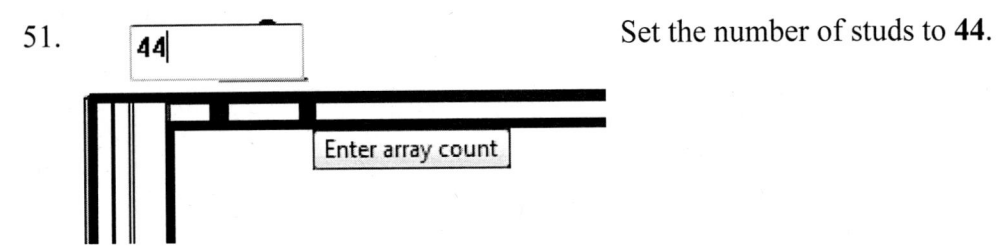

51. Set the number of studs to **44**.

Depending on your system, it may take a few minutes to generate the array.

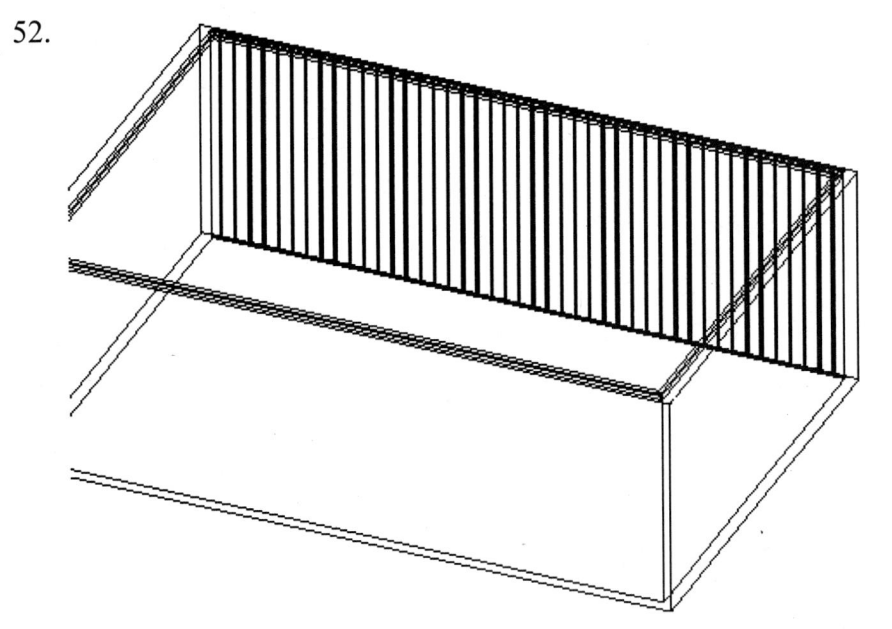

52. Switch to a 3D view.

    Set it to wireframe.

    You see a stud-framed wall.

53. Save as *ex2-5.rvt*.

Command Exercise

Exercise 2-6 – Stacked Walls

Drawing Name: **i_stacked_walls.rvt**
Estimated Time to Completion: 60 Minutes

Scope

Defining a stacked wall structure

Revit defines a stacked wall as a wall that has 2 or more horizontal layers, each consisting of different materials and surfaces.

Solution

1. Open *i_stacked_walls.rvt*.

2. Activate **Level 1**.

3. Select the left vertical wall.

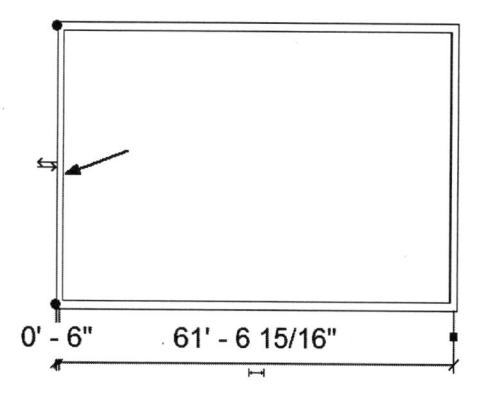

4. Select **Edit Type** on the Properties pane.

5. Select **Duplicate**.

6. Type **Exterior - Concrete Foundation**. Press **OK**.

7. Select Edit Structure.

8. Switch the view to **Section: Modify Type**.

9.

	Function	Material	Thickness
1	Finish 1 [4]	Masonry - Brick	0' 6"
2	Structure [1]	Concrete	0' 6"
3	**Core Boundary**	**Layers Above Wrap**	**0' 0"**
4	Substrate [2]	Wood - Sheathing - plywood	0' 2"
5	Thermal/Air Lay	Misc. Air Layers - Air Space	0' 1"
6	Structure [1]	Wood - Stud Layer	0' 6"
7	Substrate [2]	Wood - Sheathing - plywood	0' 2"
8	**Core Boundary**	**Layers Below Wrap**	**0' 0"**
9	Finish 2 [5]	Gypsum Wall Board	0' 0 3/4"

Add Layers as follows:
Layer 1: Finish 1 [4] Masonry - Brick 6″
Layer 2: Structure [1] Concrete 6″
Layer 3: Core Boundary
Layer 4: Substrate [2] Wood - Sheathing 2″
Layer 5: Thermal Air Lay - Misc Air Layers - Air Space 1″
Layer 6: Structure [1] Wood - Stud Layer 6″
Layer 7: Substrate [2] Wood - Sheathing 2″
Layer 8: Core Boundary
Layer 9: Finish 2 [5] Gypsum Wall Board 3/4″

10. Select **Split Region**.

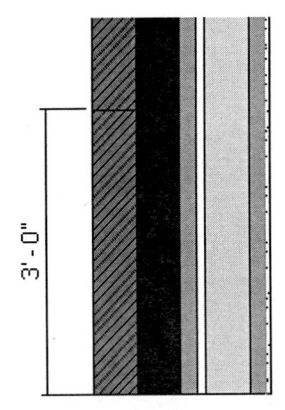

11. Cut the Layer 1: brick layer 3′-0″ from the base.

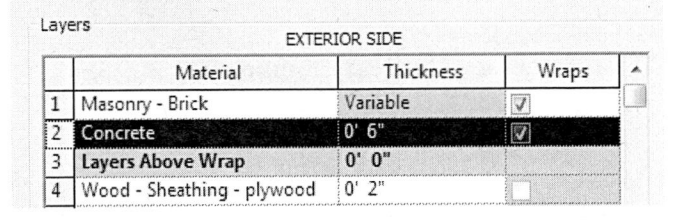

12. Highlight the **Layer 2: Concrete** Layer.

	Material	Thickness	Wraps
1	Masonry - Brick	Variable	✓
2	Concrete	0' 6"	✓
3	**Layers Above Wrap**	**0' 0"**	
4	Wood - Sheathing - plywood	0' 2"	

13. Pick on the **Assign Layers** button.

The Basics of Building a Model

14. 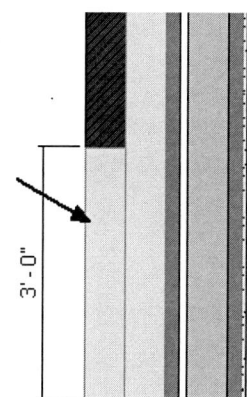 Select the lower region of the brick layer that was just split.

    The upper region will now be brick and the lower region will be concrete.

    It may take some practice before you are able to do this.

15. 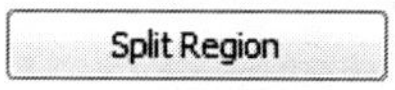 [Split Region] Select **Split Region**.

16. 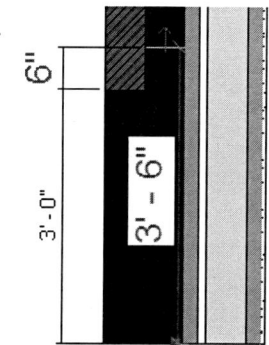 Cut the Layer 2: concrete 3'-6" from the base.

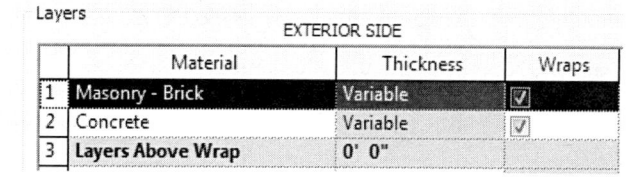

17. Highlight the **Layer 1: Masonry Brick** Layer.

	Material	Thickness	Wraps
1	Masonry - Brick	Variable	☑
2	Concrete	Variable	☑
3	Layers Above Wrap	0' 0"	

18.  [Assign Layers] Pick on the **Assign Layers** button.

19. 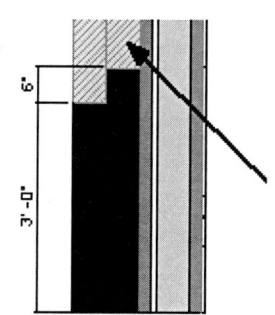 Highlight the Masonry brick layer.

    Select the upper region of layer 2.

    The upper region will now be brick and the lower region will be concrete.

    It may take some practice before you are able to do this.

20. 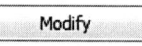 [Modify] Select **Modify**.

21. Select the base of the concrete Layer 1 component.

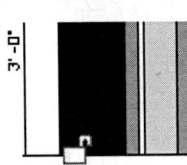

22. A small lock will appear.

    Click on the lock to unlock it.

23. Select **Modify**.

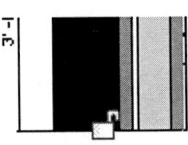

24. Select the base of Layer 2: Concrete.

    Click on the lock to unlock it.

25. Press **OK** to close the dialogs.

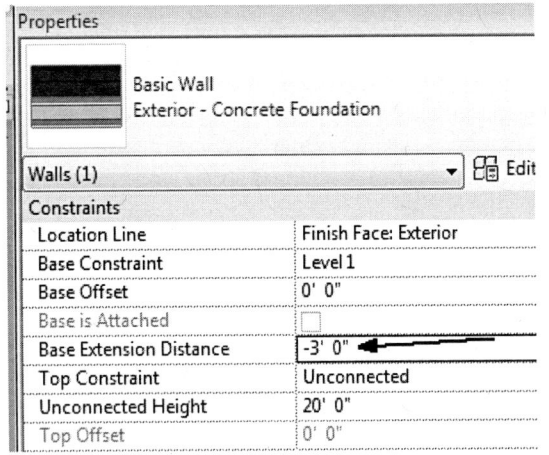

26. Select the wall with the Exterior - Concrete Foundation wall type.

    In the Properties pane:

    Set the Base Extension Distance to **-3' 0"**.

    Left click in the display window to release the selection.

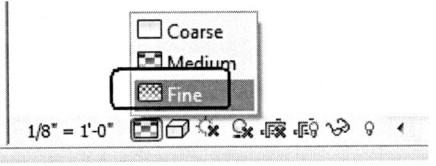

27. Set the display to Medium or Fine to see the wall layers.

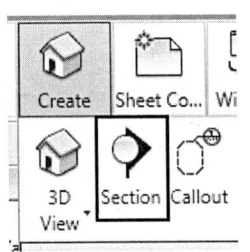

28. Activate the View ribbon.

    Select the Section tool from the Create panel.

The Basics of Building a Model

29. Place a small section on the wall you just defined.

Activate the section view.

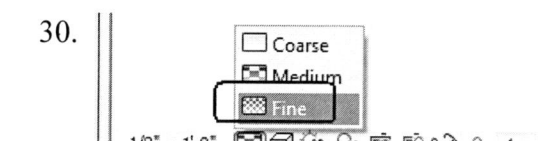

30. Set the display to Medium or Fine to see the wall layers.

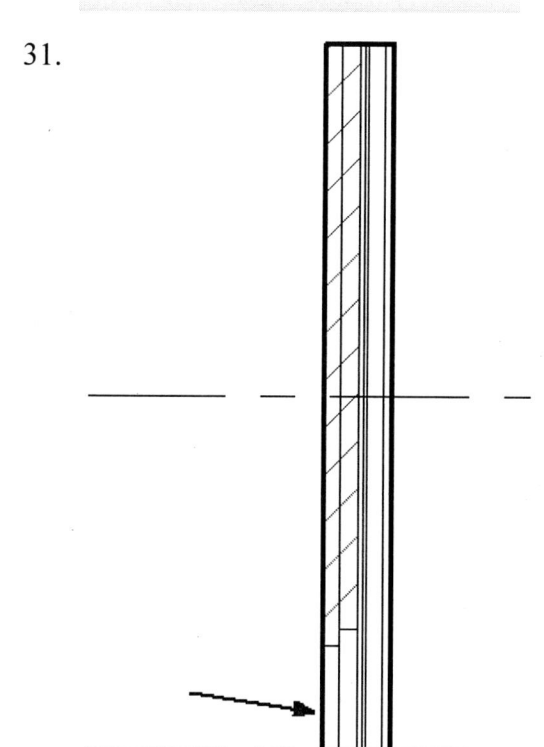

31. Note the concrete section is below the base level.

Select the wall.

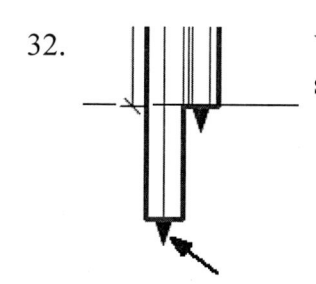

32. You can use the grips to adjust the base depth of the concrete section.

2-27

33. Activate **Level 1**.

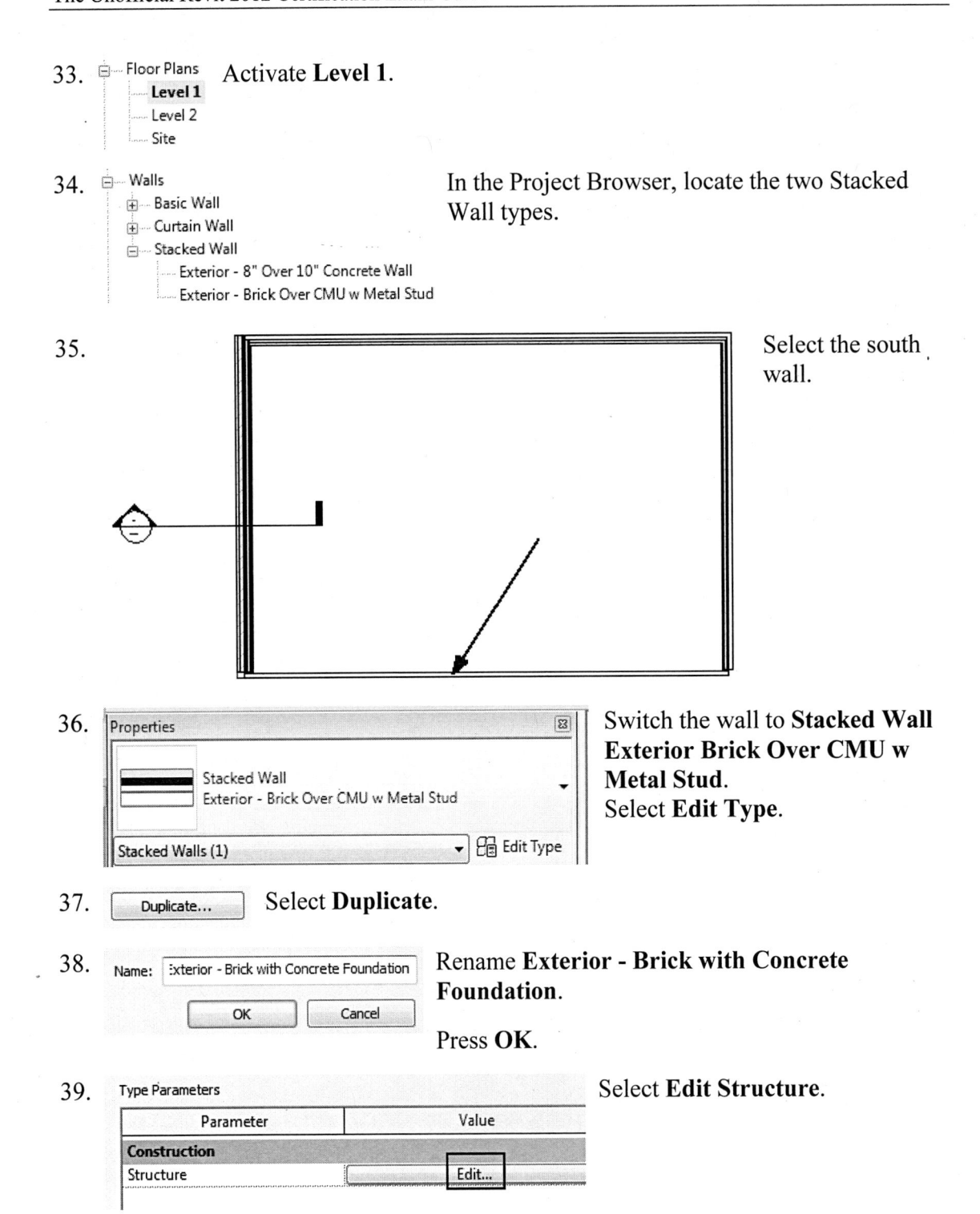

34. In the Project Browser, locate the two Stacked Wall types.

35. Select the south wall.

36. Switch the wall to **Stacked Wall Exterior Brick Over CMU w Metal Stud**.
    Select **Edit Type**.

37. Select **Duplicate**.

38. Rename **Exterior - Brick with Concrete Foundation**.
    Press **OK**.

39. Select **Edit Structure**.

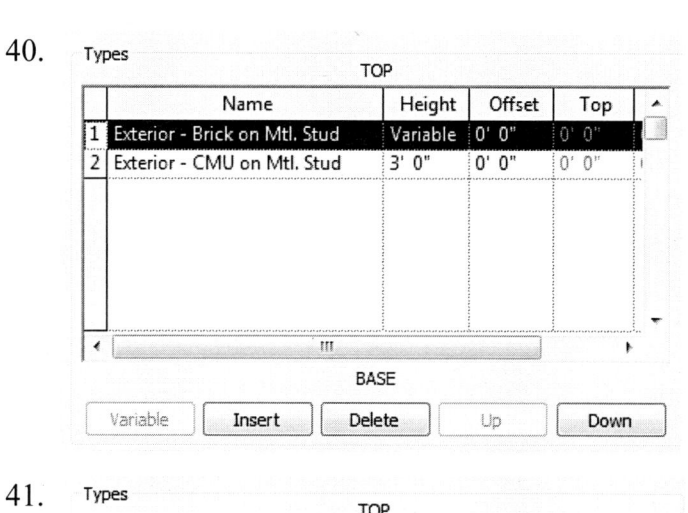

40. Note the stacked wall uses different layers going from Top to Base instead of Exterior to Interior.

Each layer is a wall type instead of a component material.

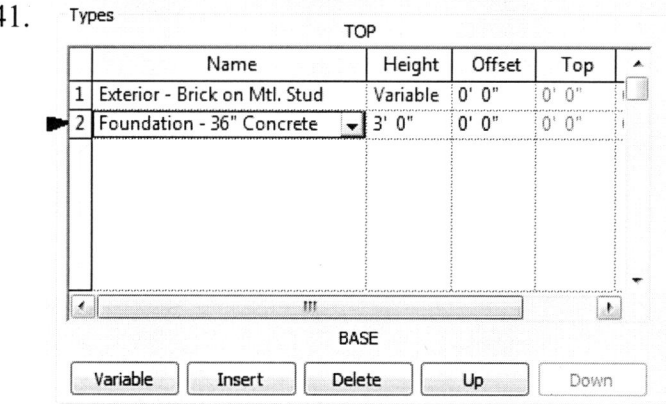

41. Change Layer 2 to **Foundation - 36″ Concrete**.

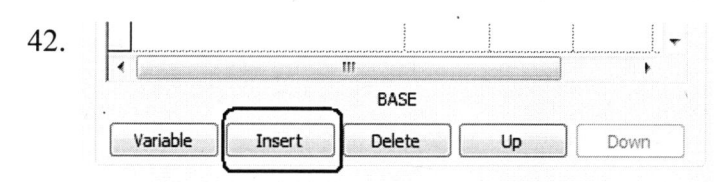

42. Select **Insert**.

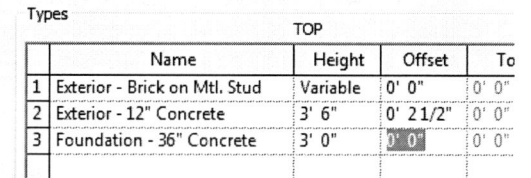

43. Set the new layer to:

    Exterior - **12″ Concrete**.
    Set the Height to **3′ 6″**.
    Set the Offset to **2 1/2″**.

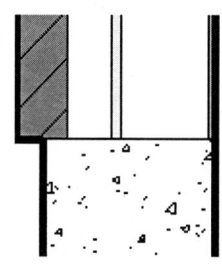

44. You can zoom into the preview window to check the offset value.

2-29

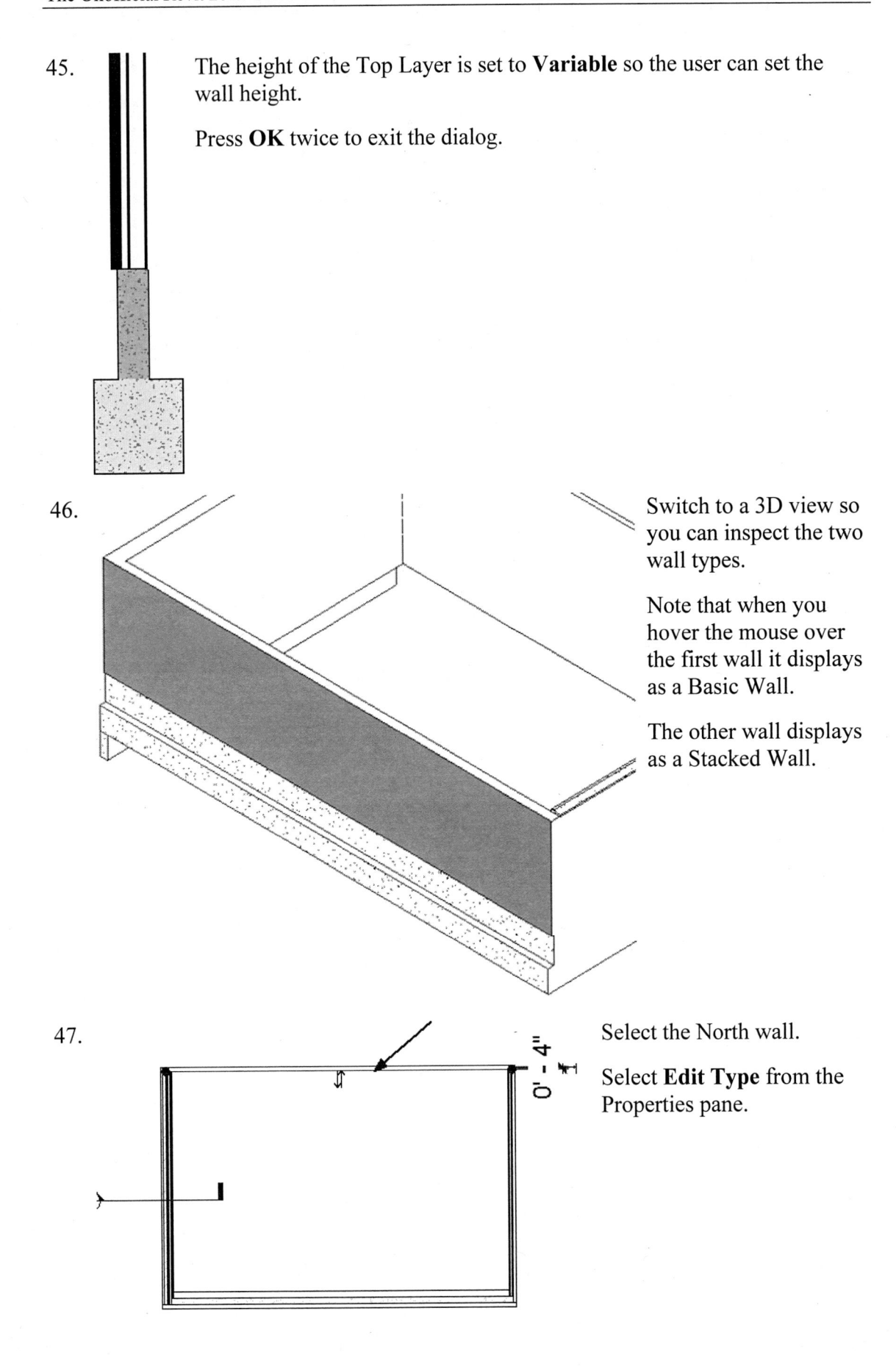

45. The height of the Top Layer is set to **Variable** so the user can set the wall height.

    Press **OK** twice to exit the dialog.

46. Switch to a 3D view so you can inspect the two wall types.

    Note that when you hover the mouse over the first wall it displays as a Basic Wall.

    The other wall displays as a Stacked Wall.

47. Select the North wall.

    Select **Edit Type** from the Properties pane.

2-30

The Basics of Building a Model

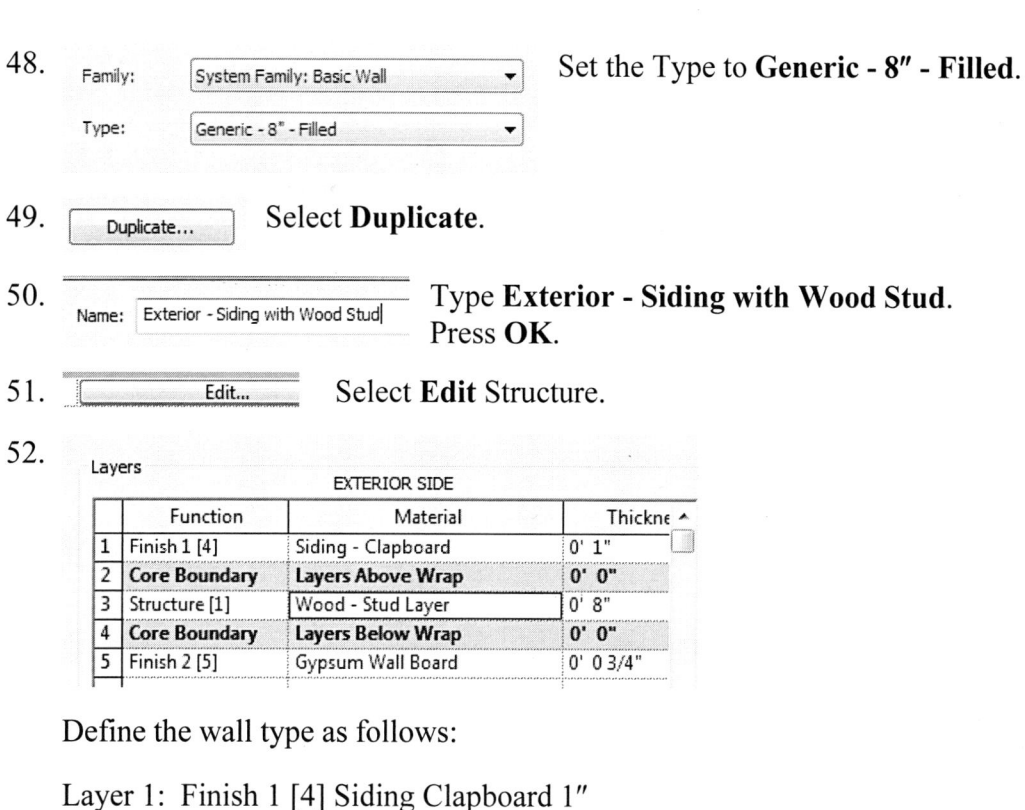

48. Set the Type to **Generic - 8" - Filled**.

49. Select **Duplicate**.

50. Type **Exterior - Siding with Wood Stud**. Press **OK**.

51. Select **Edit** Structure.

52.

	Function	Material	Thickness
1	Finish 1 [4]	Siding - Clapboard	0' 1"
2	Core Boundary	Layers Above Wrap	0' 0"
3	Structure [1]	Wood - Stud Layer	0' 8"
4	Core Boundary	Layers Below Wrap	0' 0"
5	Finish 2 [5]	Gypsum Wall Board	0' 0 3/4"

Define the wall type as follows:

Layer 1: Finish 1 [4] Siding Clapboard 1"
Layer 2: Core Boundary
Layer 3: Structure [1] Wood Stud Layer 8"
Layer 4: Core Boundary
Layer 5: Finish 2 [5] Gypsum Wall Board 3/4"

53. Press **OK** to close all dialogs.

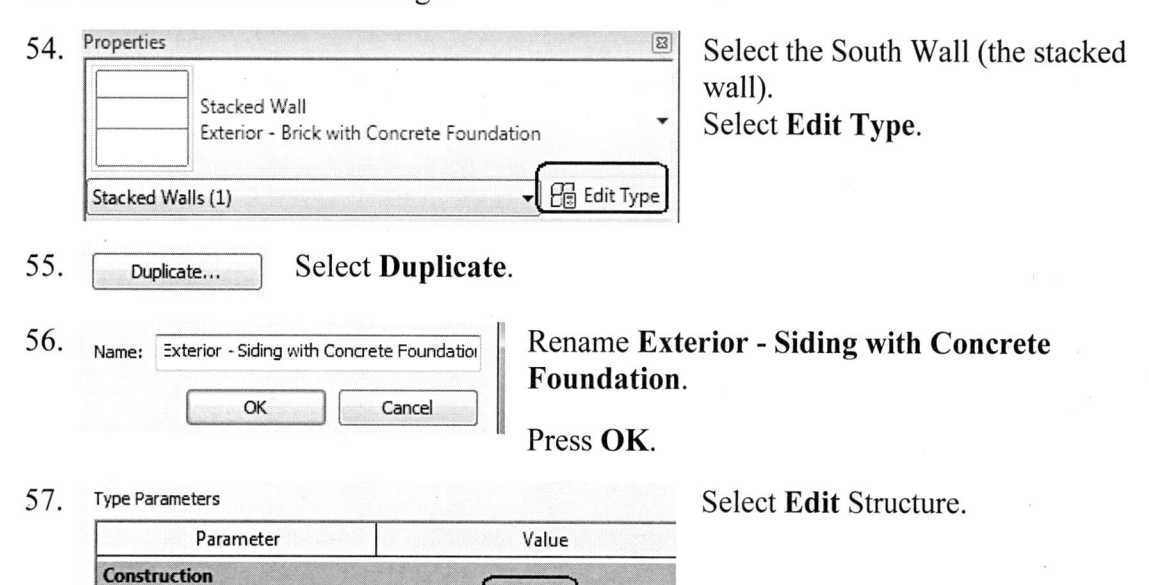

54. Select the South Wall (the stacked wall).
Select **Edit Type**.

55. Select **Duplicate**.

56. Rename **Exterior - Siding with Concrete Foundation**.
Press **OK**.

57. Select **Edit** Structure.

2-31

58.

	Name	Height	Offset	
1	Exterior - Siding with Wood Stu	Variable	0' 0"	0' 0'
2	Exterior - 12" Concrete	3' 6"	0' 1 1/4"	0' 0'
3	Foundation - 36" Concrete	3' 0"	0' 0"	0' 0'

Set Layer 1 to the new wall type: **Exterior - Siding with Wood Stud**.

Adjust the Offset for Layer 2: Exterior - 12" Concrete to **1 1/4"**. Press **OK** to close all dialogs.

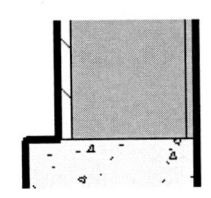

59. You can zoom into the preview window to check the offset.

Press **OK** twice to close the dialogs.

60. Switch to a 3D view.

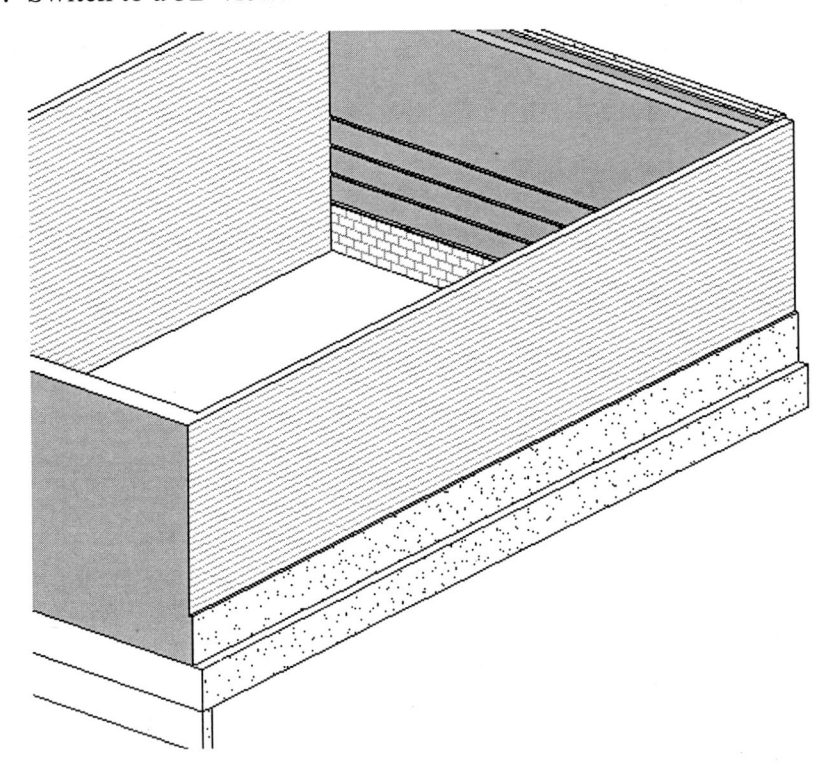

61. Close without saving.

Command Exercise

Exercise 2-7 – Chained Walls

Drawing Name: **i-walls.rvt**
Estimated Time to Completion: 10 Minutes

Scope

Using TAB to select walls.
Using CTRL to copy selected items.
Using SHIFT to move selected items.

Solution

1. Open *i-walls.rvt*.

2. Select the **Wall** tool from the Home ribbon.

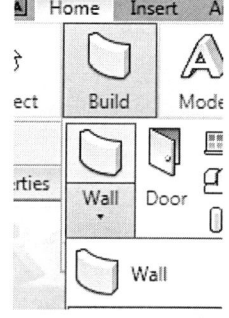

3. Select the **Brick and CMU on MTL. Stud** wall style on the Properties pane.

4. Enable **Chain**.

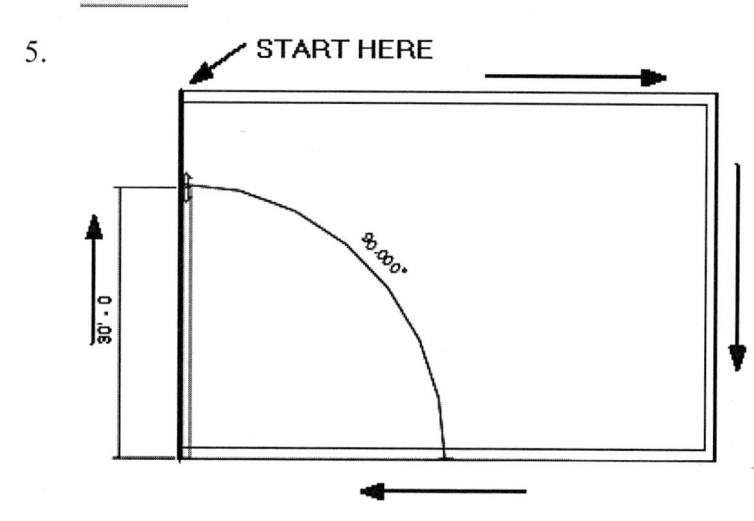

5. Select the upper left vertex of the rectangle and draw the walls to place following the direction of the arrows.

   Right click to cancel or press ESC to finish placing walls.

2-33

6. 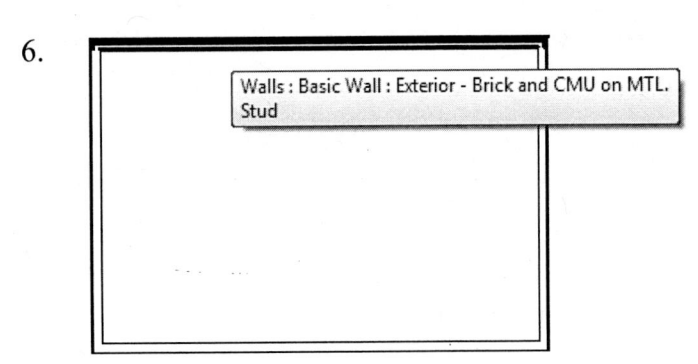 Place the mouse over one of the walls so it highlights. DO NOT SELECT.

   Press the TAB key.
   All the walls highlight.
   Left pick to select all four walls.

7. Press the CONTROL key and hold down the left mouse to drag the walls to the right.

The CONTROL key is used to create copies of selected elements.

8. 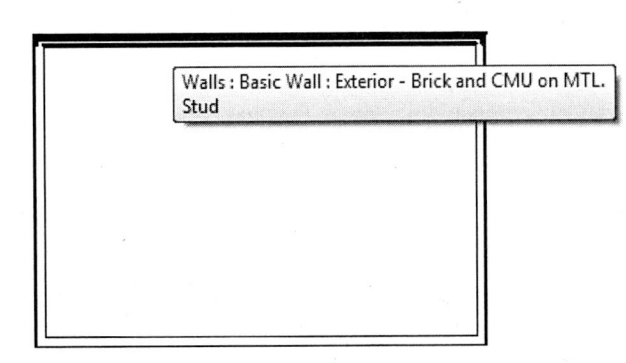 Place the mouse over one of the walls so it highlights. DO NOT SELECT.

   Press the TAB key.
   All the walls highlight.
   Left pick to select all four walls.

9. Press the SHIFT key to move the selected walls.

10. Close the file without saving.

The Basics of Building a Model

Command Exercise

Exercise 2-8 – Dividing a Wall into Parts

Drawing Name: **wall_parts.rvt**
Estimated Time to Completion: 45 Minutes

Scope

Use of parts to apply materials to a wall

Solution

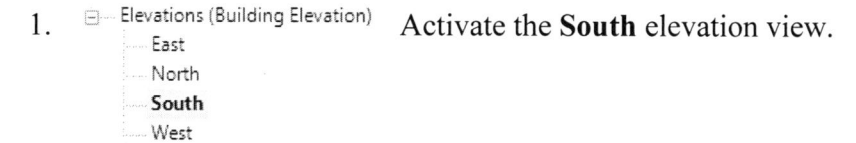

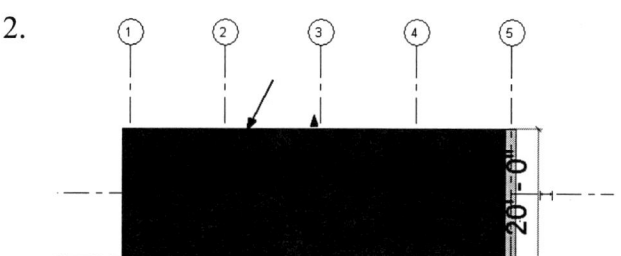

1. Activate the **South** elevation view.

2. Select the wall so it highlights.

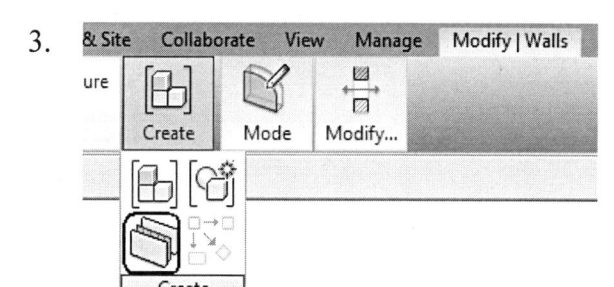

3. Select the **Create Parts** tool on the Create panel.

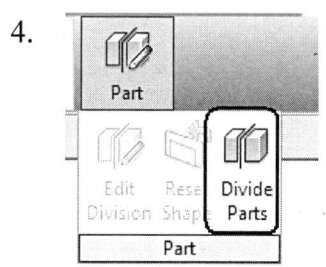

4. Select **Divide Parts** on the Part panel.

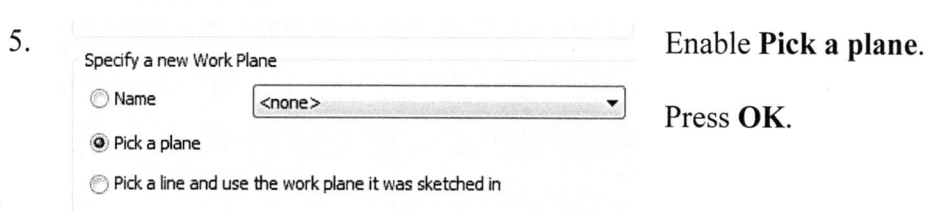

5. Enable **Pick a plane**.

   Press **OK**.

2-35

6. Pick the front of the wall for the workplane.

7. Select the **Add** tool from the Divided Parts panel.

8. Select **Intersecting References** from the References panel.

9. Set Filter to **All**.

   This allows you to see Grids and Levels.

10. Place a check next to the **Grids**.

    Press **OK**.

The Basics of Building a Model

11. 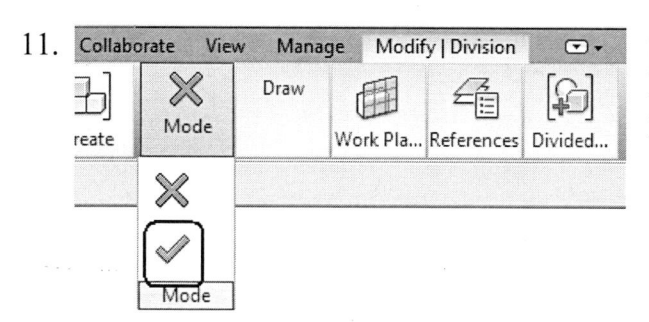 Select the **green check** on the Mode panel to finish dividing the parts.

12. 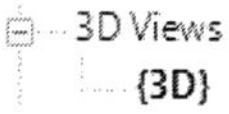 Switch to a 3D view.

13. 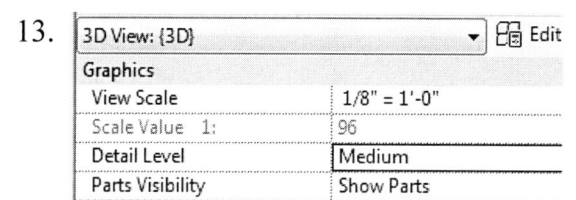 In the Properties pane:

    Set the Detail Level to **Medium**.
    Set the Parts Visibility to **Show Parts**.

14. 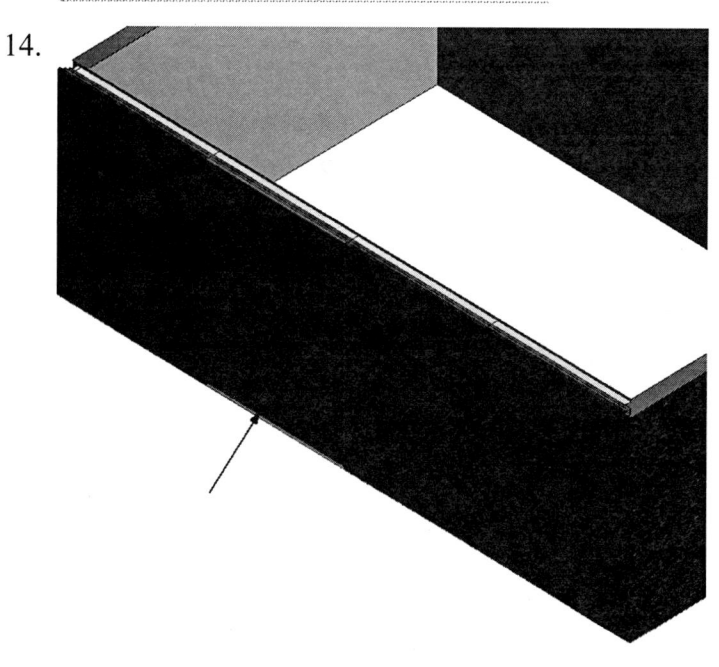 Select the second panel/part.

15. In the Properties panel:

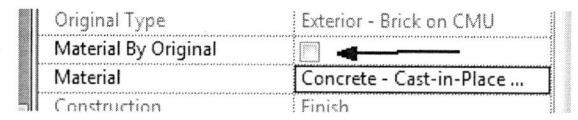

    Uncheck **Material by Original**.
    Left click in the Material column to assign a material.

16. 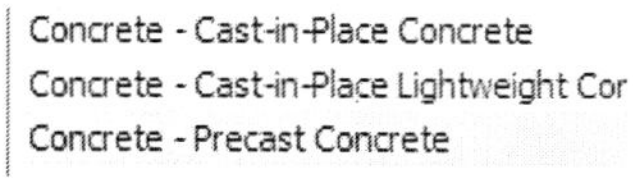 Select the **Concrete - Precast Concrete** material.

17.  Enable **Use Render Appearance for Shading**.

    Press **OK**.

2-37

18.

The wall changes to show the new material.

19.

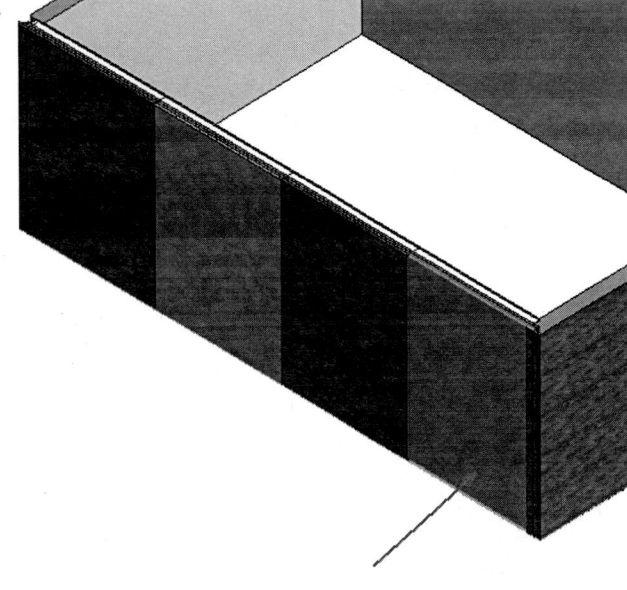

Select the fourth panel/part.

20. In the Properties panel:

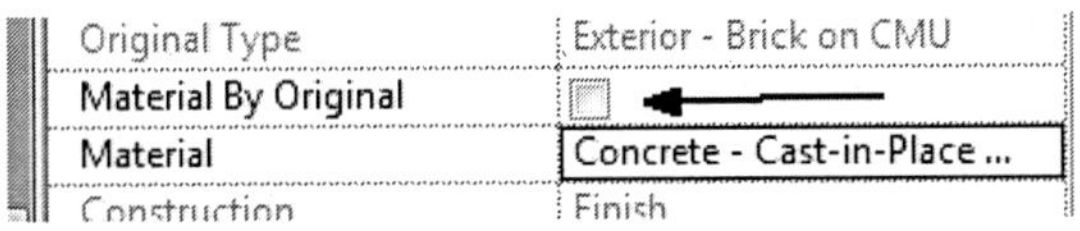

Uncheck **Material by Original**. Left click in the Material column to assign a material.

21. 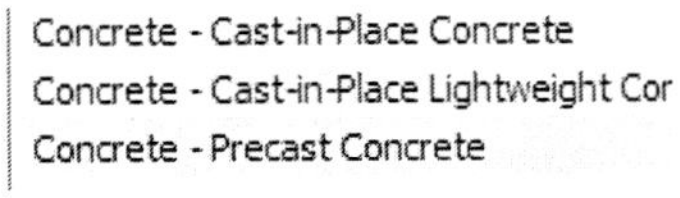 Concrete - Cast-in-Place Concrete
Concrete - Cast-in-Place Lightweight Cor
Concrete - Precast Concrete

Select the **Concrete - Precast Concrete** material.

22.  Shading
☑ Use Render Appearance for Shading

RGB 087-088-086

Enable **Use Render Appearance for Shading**.

Press **OK**.

The Basics of Building a Model

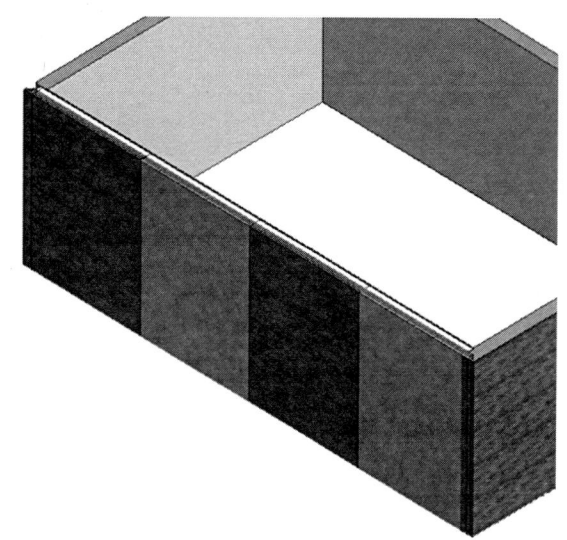

23. The wall changes to show the new material.

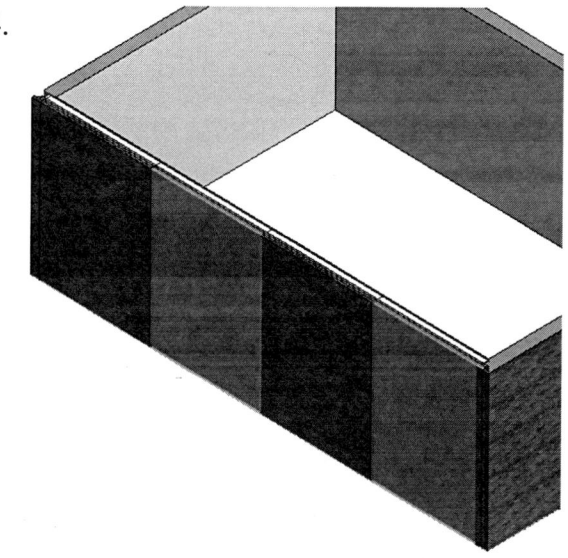

24. Hold down the CTRL key and select the two concrete panels.

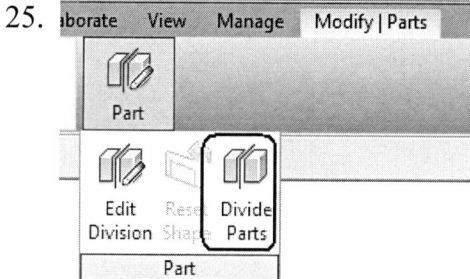

25. Select the **Divide Parts** tool from the Part panel.

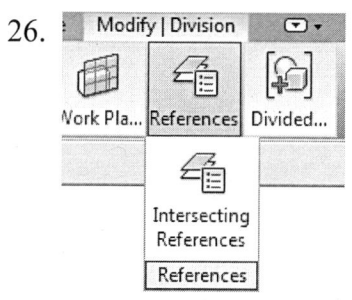

26. Select **Intersecting References** from the References panel.

2-39

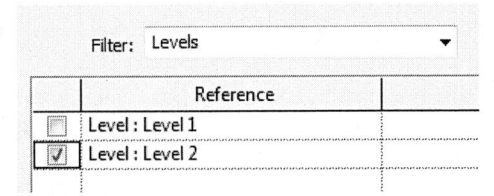

27. Place a check next to the **Level 2**.

Press **OK**.

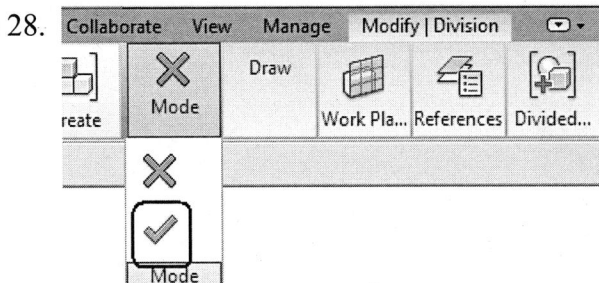

28. Select the **green check** on the Mode panel to finish dividing the parts.

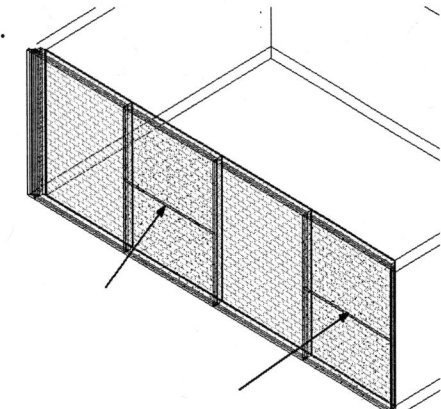

29. The concrete panels are now divided into two sections.

Shown in wireframe so you can see the divisions easily.

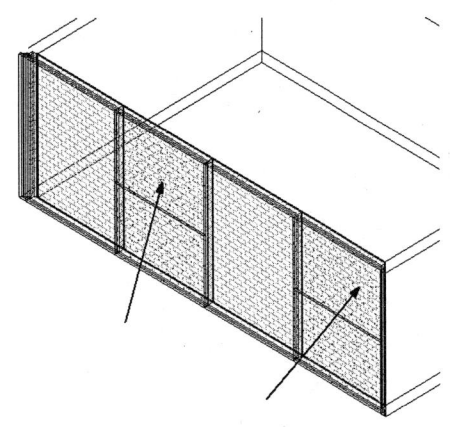

30. Hold down the CTRL key and select the two top sections of the concrete panels.

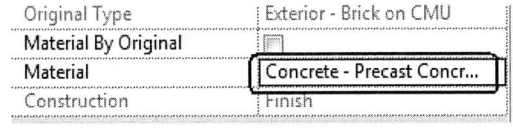

31. In the Properties panel:

Left click in the Material column to assign a material.

32. Select the **Masonry-Stone** material.

The Basics of Building a Model

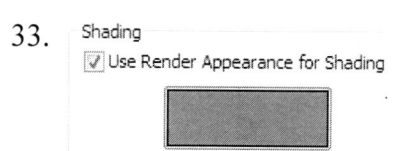

33. Enable **Use Render Appearance for Shading**.

Press **OK**.

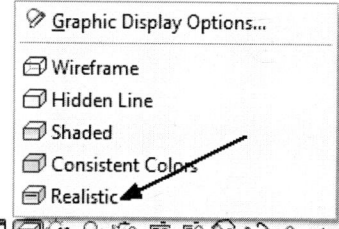

34. Set the display to **Realistic**.

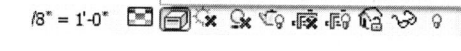

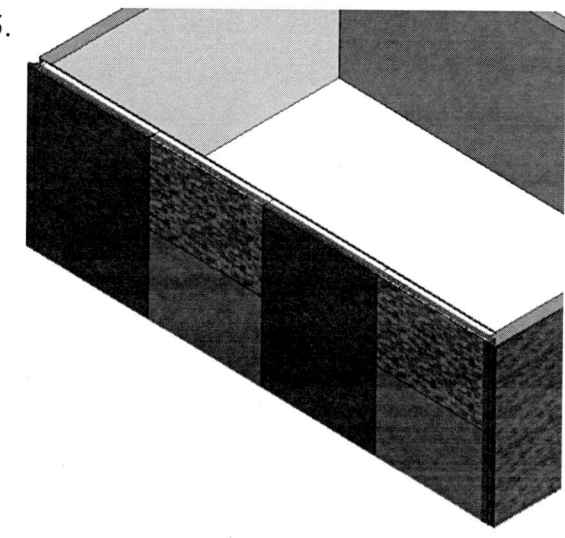

35. The new materials are assigned.

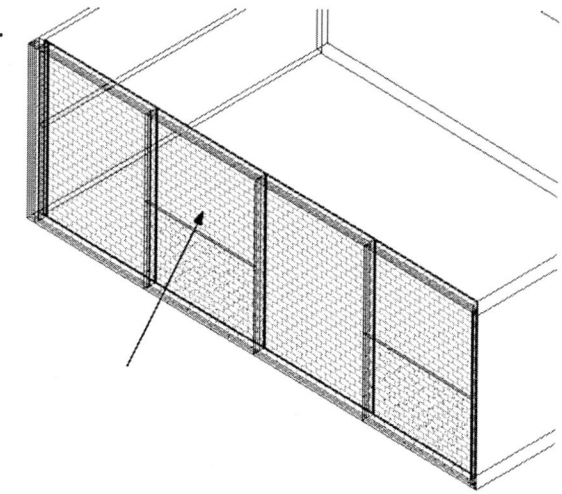

36. Select the top part indicated.

Note that no grips are available when a part is selected.

Shown in wireframe so you can see the divisions easily.

37. Enable **Show Shape Handles** on the Properties pane.

2-41

The Unofficial Revit 2012 Certification Exam Guide

38.  Use the top shape handle to lower the material 3'-10" from the top of the wall.

39. 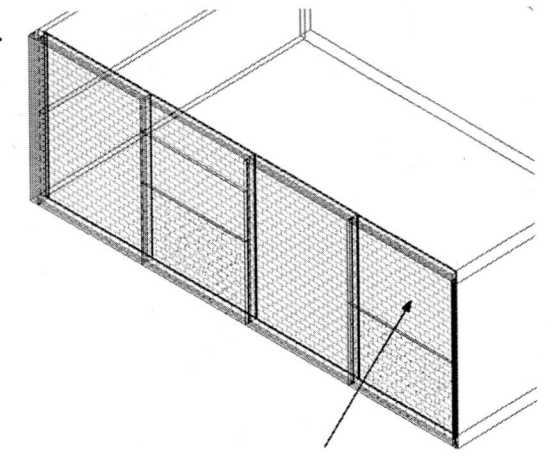 Select the top part indicated.

   Note that no grips are available when a part is selected.

   Shown in wireframe so you can see the divisions easily.

40. 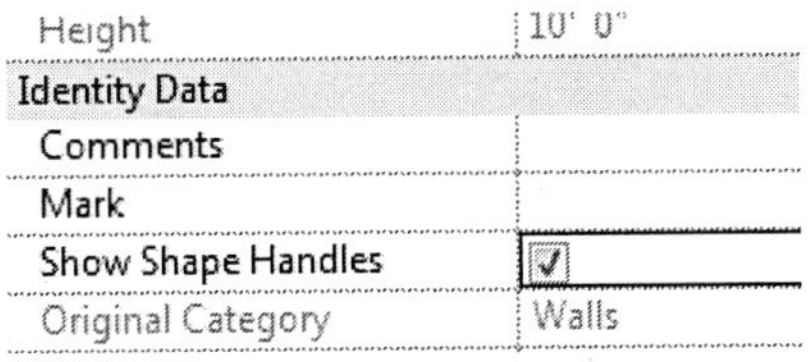 Enable **Show Shape Handles** on the Properties pane.

41. 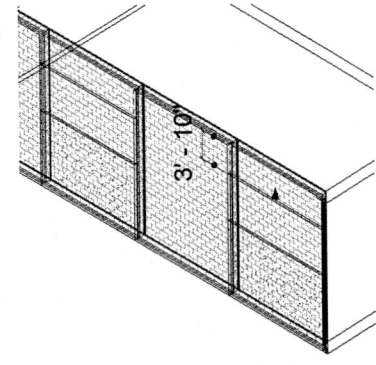 Use the top shape handle to lower the material 3'-10" from the top of the wall.

42. 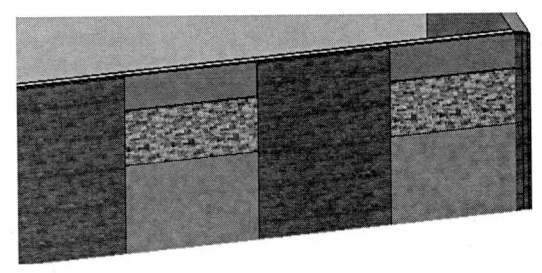 Switch to a **Realistic** display.

   Orbit the model to inspect your new wall.

   Save as *ex2-8.rvt*.

2-42

The Basics of Building a Model

Command Exercise

Exercise 2-9 – Creating an In-Place Mass

Drawing Name: **in_place_mass.rvt**
Estimated Time to Completion: 60 Minutes

Scope

Use of in-place masses to create a conceptual model

Solution

1. Activate the **Site** plan view.

2. Activate the **Massing & Site** ribbon.

3. Select the **In-Place Mass** tool from the Conceptual Mass panel.

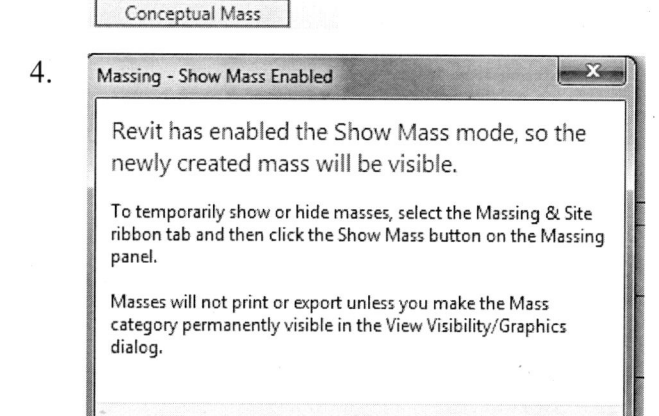

4. Revit displays a message indicating that visibility of masses has been turned on.

    Press **Close**.

2-43

5. Name your first mass **Building 1**.

   Press **OK**.

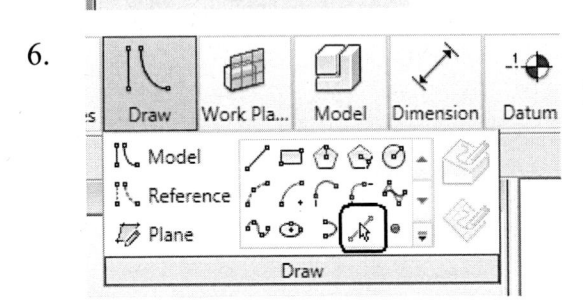

6. Select the **Pick Line** tool from the Draw panel.

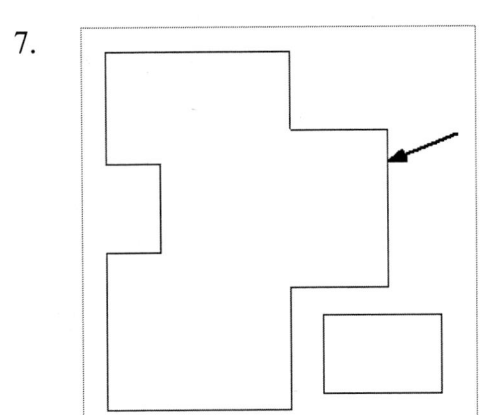

7. Pick the lines for the building in the upper right quadrant.

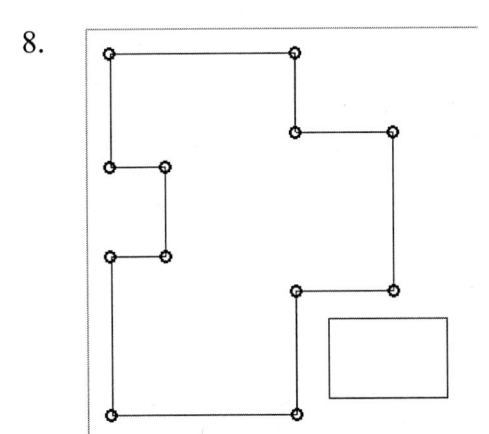

8. When you select the sketch, it should form a closed boundary.

   Make sure there are no overlapping lines.

9. Switch to a **3D** view.

10. Select the sketch.

    Select **Form→Create Form→Solid Form**.

2-44

The Basics of Building a Model

11. Click on the dimension.
Change it to **70′ 0″**.

Press **ENTER**.
Left click in the display window to release the selection.

12. Select **Finish Mass** from the In-Place Editor panel.

13. Activate the **Site** plan view.

14. Activate the **Massing & Site** ribbon.

15. Select the **In-Place Mass** tool from the Conceptual Mass panel.

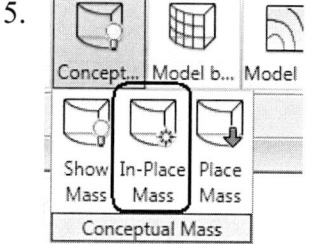

16. Name your mass **Building 2**.
Press **OK**.

17. Select the **Pick Line** tool from the Draw panel.

2-45

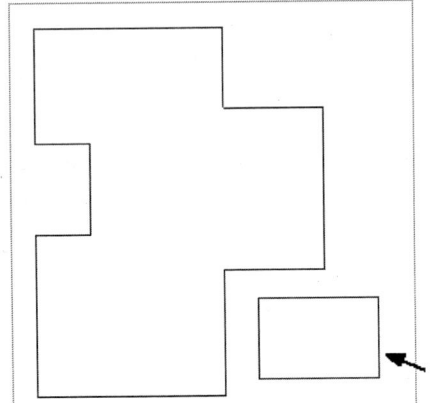

18. Pick the lines for the small building in the upper right quadrant.

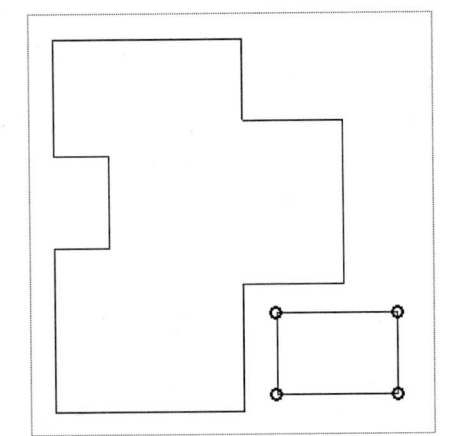

19. When you select the sketch, it should form a closed boundary.

    Make sure there are no overlapping lines.

20. Switch to a **3D** view.

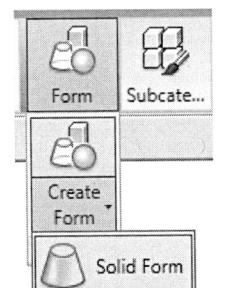

21. Select the sketch.

    Select **Form→Create Form→Solid Form**.

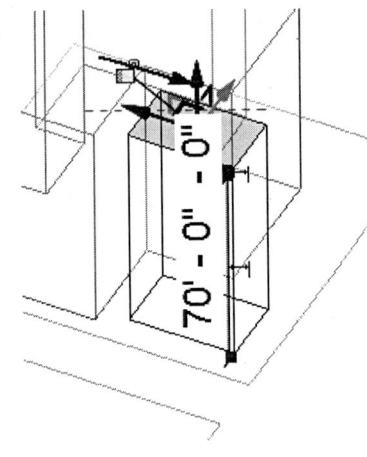

22. Select the blue Z-axis.

    Drag the building up until the dimension displays **70'-0"**.

    Left click in the display window to release the selection.

The Basics of Building a Model

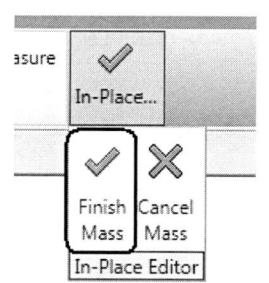

23. Select **Finish Mass** from the In-Place Editor panel.

24. Activate the **Site** plan view.

25. Activate the **Massing & Site** ribbon.

26. Select the **In-Place Mass** tool from the Conceptual Mass panel.

27. Name your mass **Building 3**.

    Press **OK**.

28. Select the **Pick Line** tool from the Draw panel.

2-47

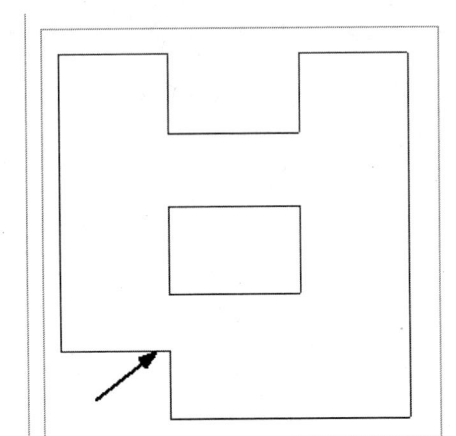

29. Pick the lines for the building in the upper left quadrant.

    Select both the inner and outer boundaries.

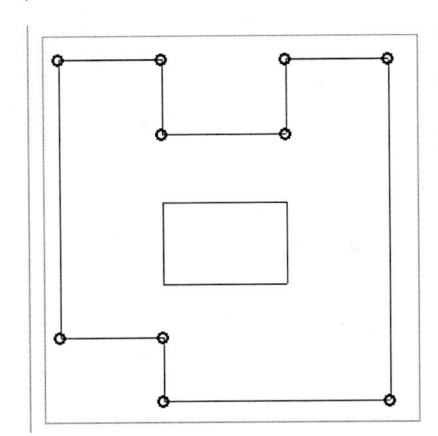

30. When you select the sketch, it should form a closed boundary.

    Make sure there are no overlapping lines.

31. Switch to a **3D** view.

32. Select the outer sketch.

    Select **Form→Create Form→Solid Form**.

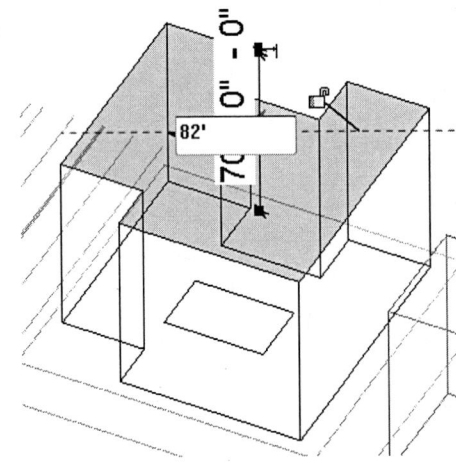

33. Select the Blue Z-axis.

    Drag the building up until the dimension displays **82'-0"**.

    Left click in the display window to release the selection.

2-48

The Basics of Building a Model

34. 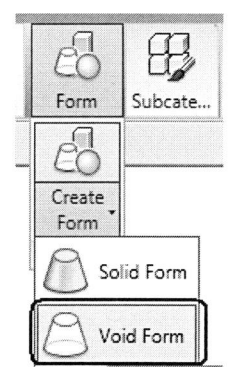 Select the inner sketch.

    Select **Form→Create Form→Void Form**.

35. 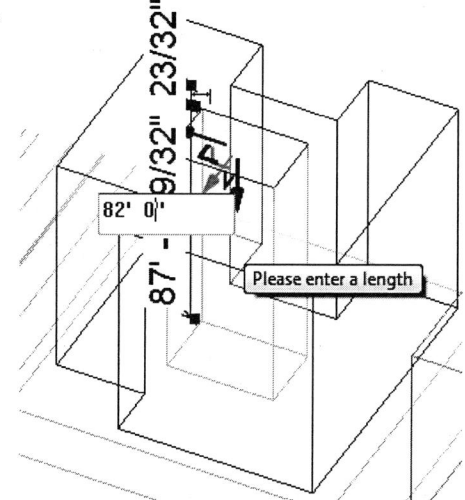 Select the blue Z-axis.

    Drag the void down until the dimension displays **82′-0″**.

    Left click in the display window to release the selection.

36. 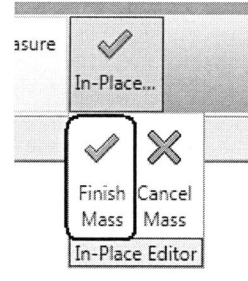 Select **Finish Mass** from the In-Place Editor panel.

37. 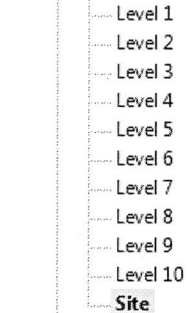 Activate the **Site** plan view.

38. 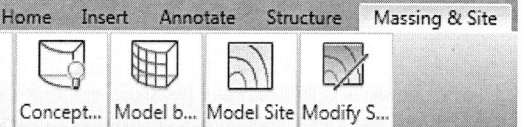 Activate the **Massing & Site** ribbon.

2-49

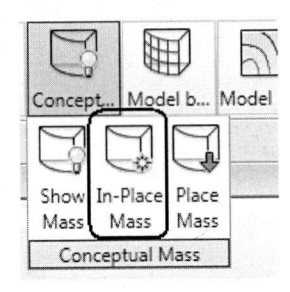

39. Select the **In-Place Mass** tool from the Conceptual Mass panel.

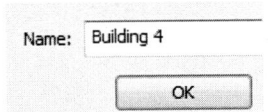

40. Name your mass **Building 4**.

    Press **OK**.

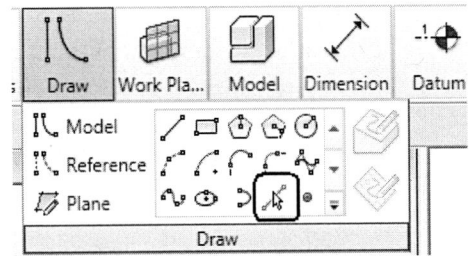

41. Select the **Pick Line** tool from the Draw panel.

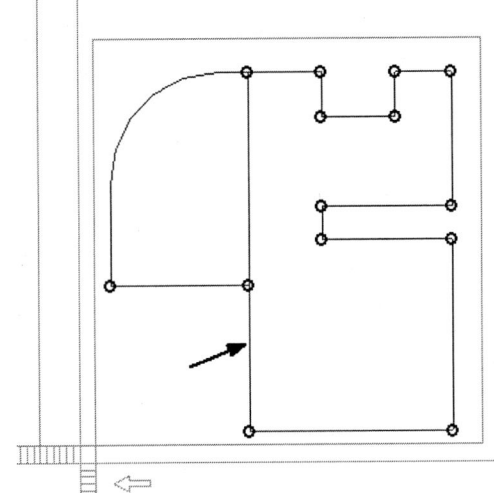

42. Pick the lines for the building in the lower left quadrant.

    You will need to use the TRIM tool from the Modify panel to trim the lower left side of the sketch.

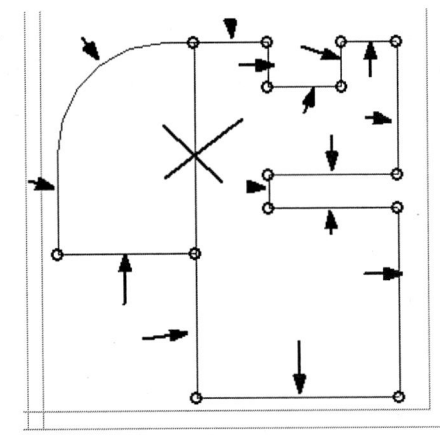

43. When you select the sketch, it should form a closed boundary.

    Make sure there are no overlapping lines. Arrows indicate the sketch components. I have x'd out the line which needs to be trimmed out.

44. Switch to a **3D** view.

The Basics of Building a Model

45. 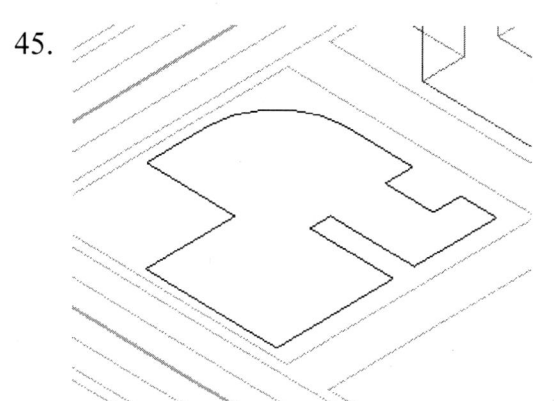 Select the sketch.

46. 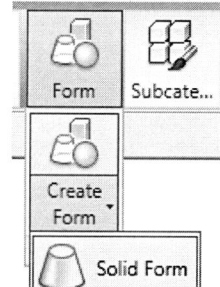 Select **Form→Create Form→Solid Form**.

47. 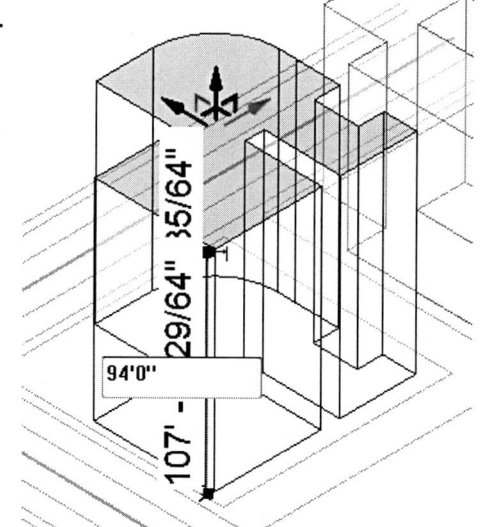 Select the Blue Z-axis.

    Drag the building up until the dimension displays **94'-0"**.

    Left click in the display window to release the selection.

48. 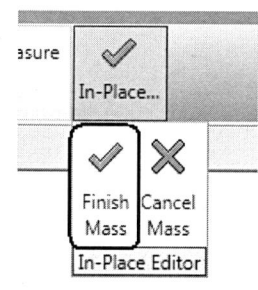 Select **Finish Mass** from the In-Place Editor panel.

2-51

49. Activate the **Site** plan view.

50. Activate the **Massing & Site** ribbon.

51. Select the **In-Place Mass** tool from the Conceptual Mass panel.

52. Name the mass **Towers**.

    Press **OK**.

53. Select the **Rectangle** tool from the Draw panel.

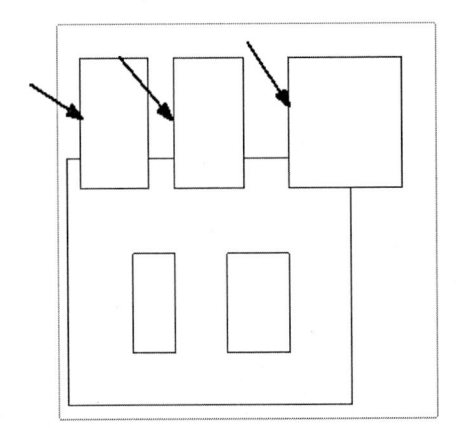

54. Trace over the top three rectangles in the fourth quadrant.

55. Switch to a **3D** view.

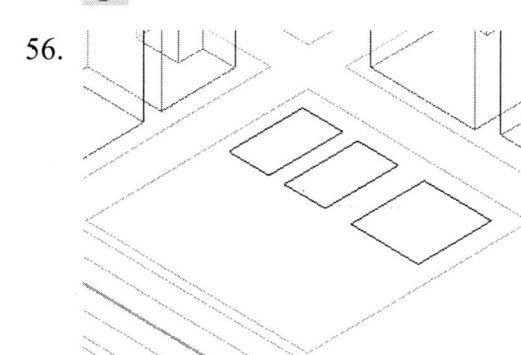

56. Select the left rectangle.

    You can only use one closed polygon at a time for a solid form.

57. Select **Form→Create Form→Solid Form**.

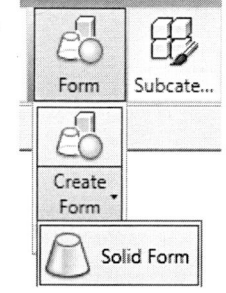

58. Select the Blue Z-axis.

    Drag the building up until the dimension displays **106'-0"**.

    Left click in the display window to release the selection.

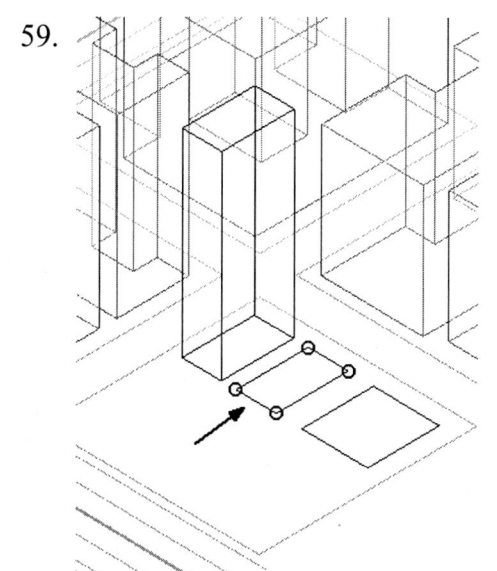

59. Select the middle rectangle.

2-53

60. 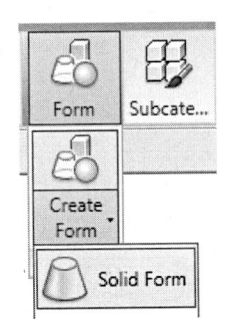 Select **Form→Create Form→Solid Form**.

61. 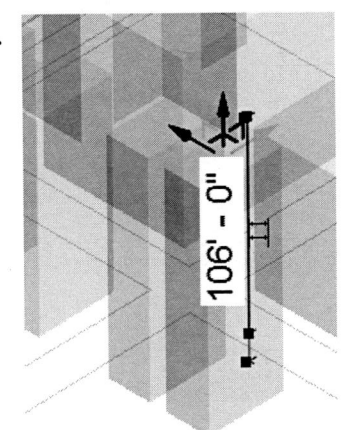 Select the Blue Z-axis.

    Drag the building up until the dimension displays **106'-0"**.

    Left click in the display window to release the selection.

62. 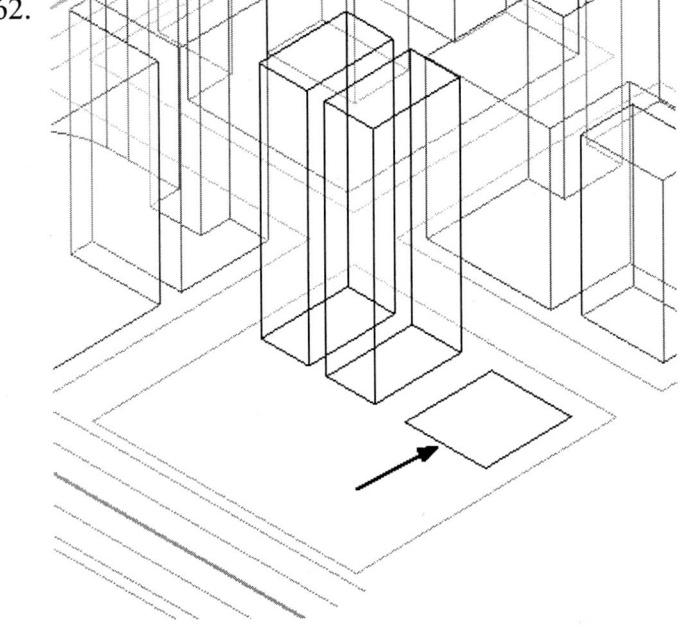 Select the right rectangle.

63. 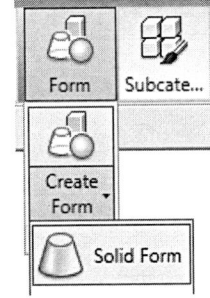 Select **Form→Create Form→Solid Form**.

2-54

The Basics of Building a Model

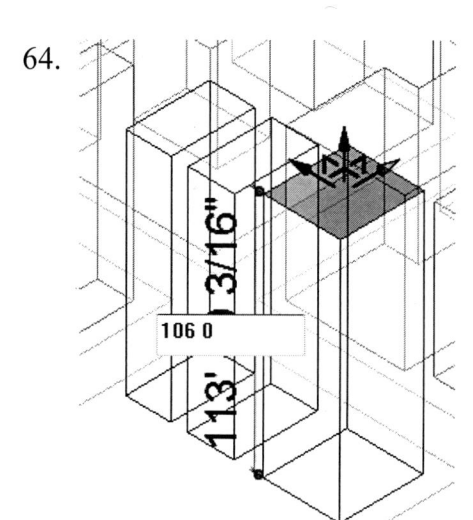

64. Select the blue Z-axis.

Drag the building up until the dimension displays **106'-0"**.

Left click in the display window to release the selection.

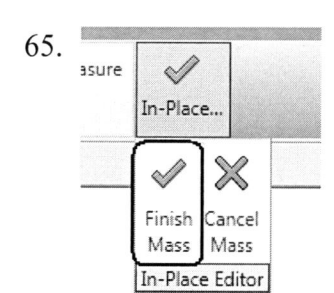

65. Select **Finish Mass** from the In-Place Editor panel.

66. Activate the **Site** plan view.

67. Activate the **Massing & Site** ribbon.

68. Select the **In-Place Mass** tool from the Conceptual Mass panel.

2-55

The Unofficial Revit 2012 Certification Exam Guide

69. Name the mass **Building 5**.

    Press **OK**.

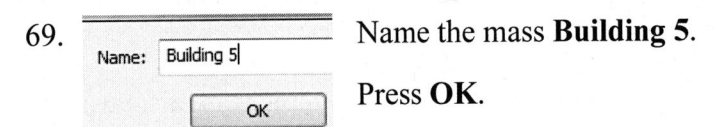

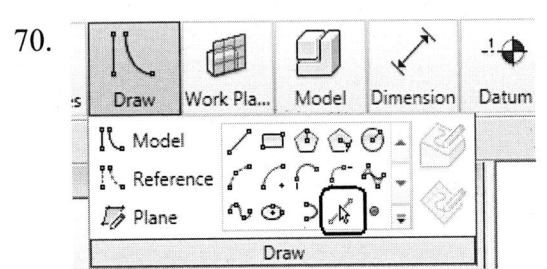

70. Select the **Pick Line** tool from the Draw panel.

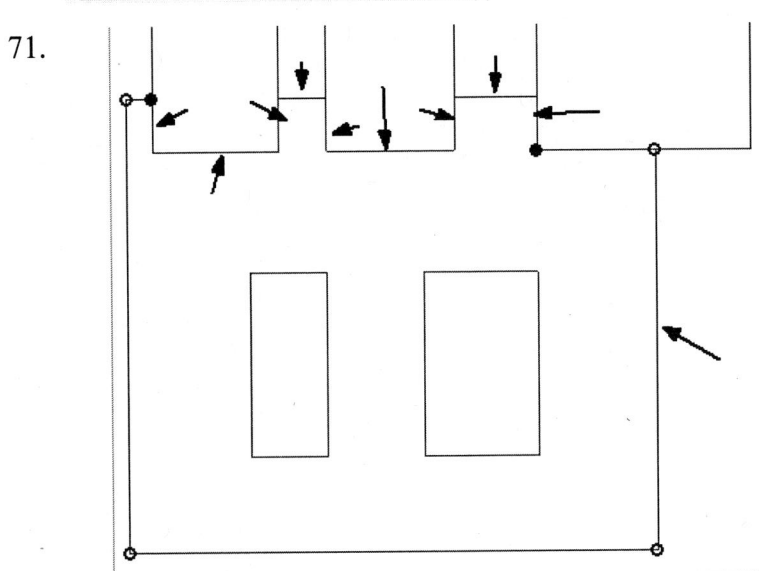

71. Pick the lines for the sketch in the lower right quadrant.

    Use **Draw Line** to complete the sketch.

    Use the **Rectangle** tool to create two sketches for the internal rectangles.

    These will be voids.

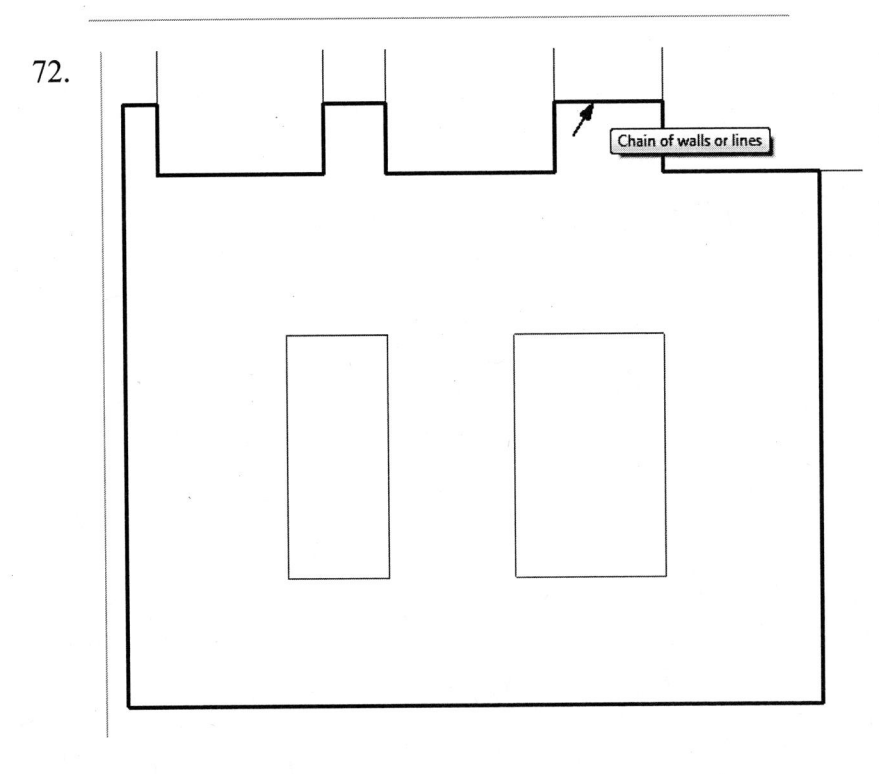

72. When you select one of the lines of the sketch, you should see the entire sketch highlight.

    If you don't see a continuous loop, there are either missing lines or overlapping/ duplicate lines.

    Check the sketch for overlapping lines by deleting a line, then click UNDO if it is not a duplicate.

The Basics of Building a Model

73. Switch to a **3D** view.

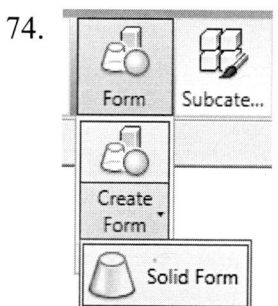

74. Select the outside boundary sketch.

   Select **Form→Create Form→Solid Form**.

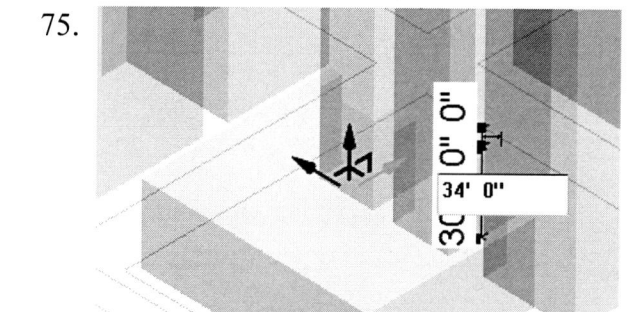

75. Select the Blue Z-axis.

   Drag the building up until the dimension displays **34'-0"**.

   Left click in the display window to release the selection.

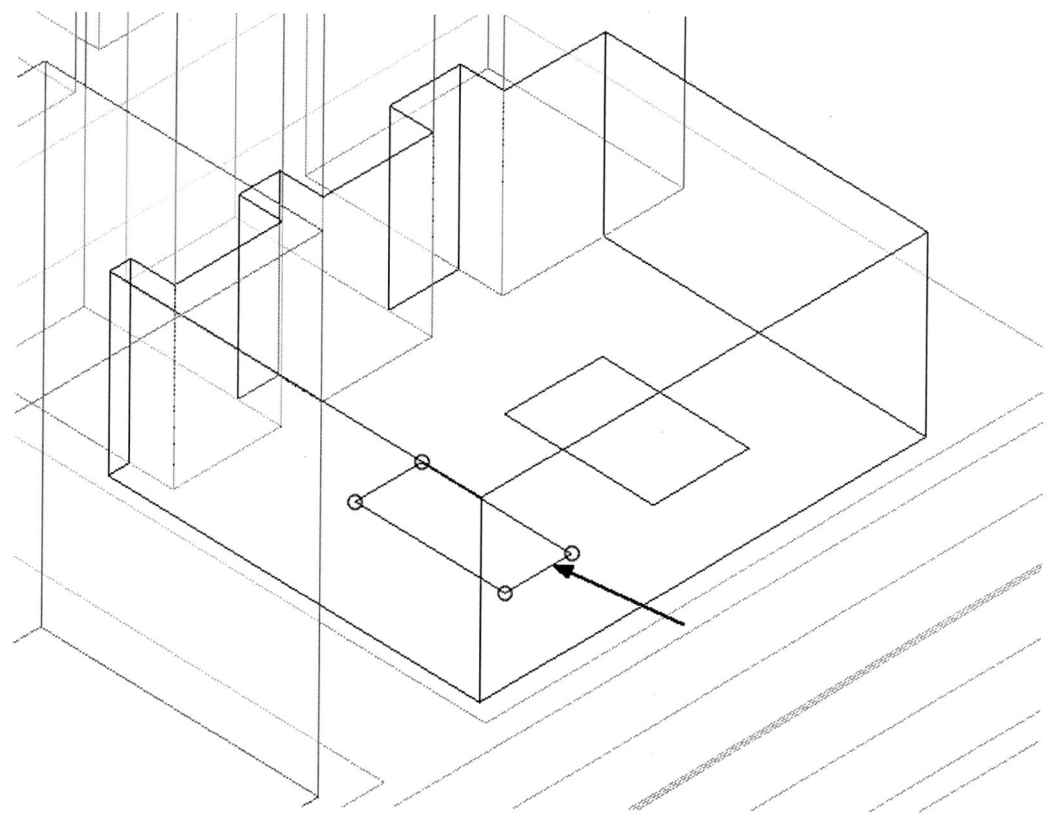

76. Select the left rectangle.

2-57

77. Select **Form→Create Form→Void Form**.

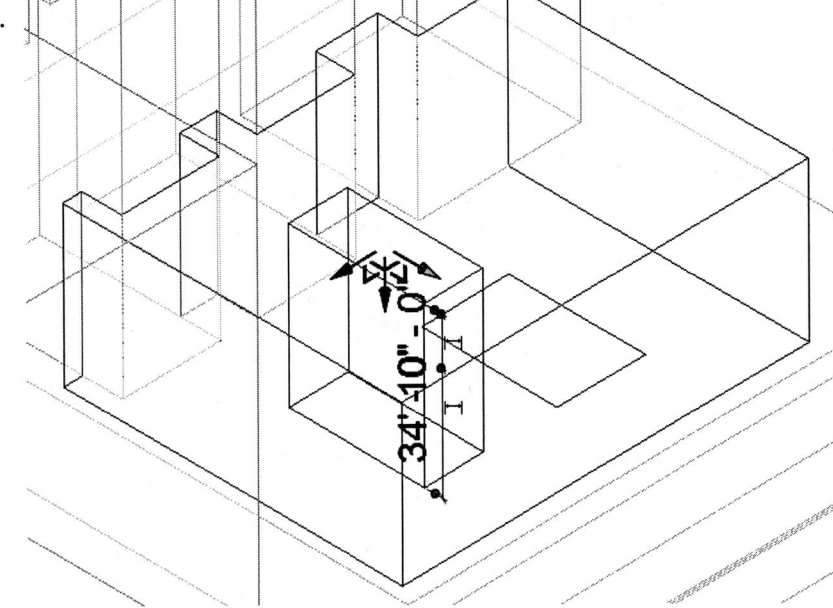

78. Select the blue Z-axis.

    Drag the building up until the dimension displays **34'-0"**.

    Left click in the display window to release the selection.

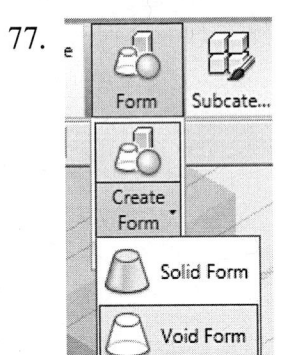

79. Select the right rectangle.

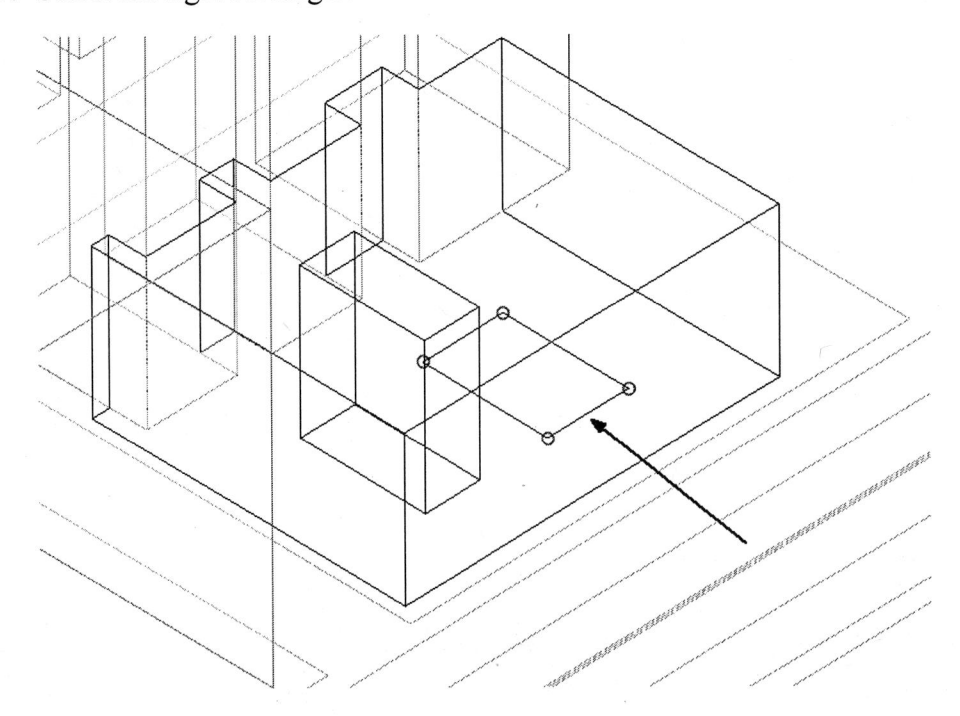

2-58

The Basics of Building a Model

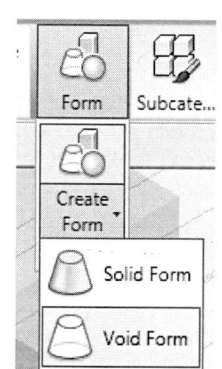

80. Select the sketch.

    Select **Form**→**Create Form**→**Void Form**.

81. Select the Blue Z-axis.

    Drag the building up until the dimension displays **34′-0″**.

    Left click in the display window to release the selection.

82. Select **Finish Mass** from the In-Place Editor panel.

83. Close without saving.

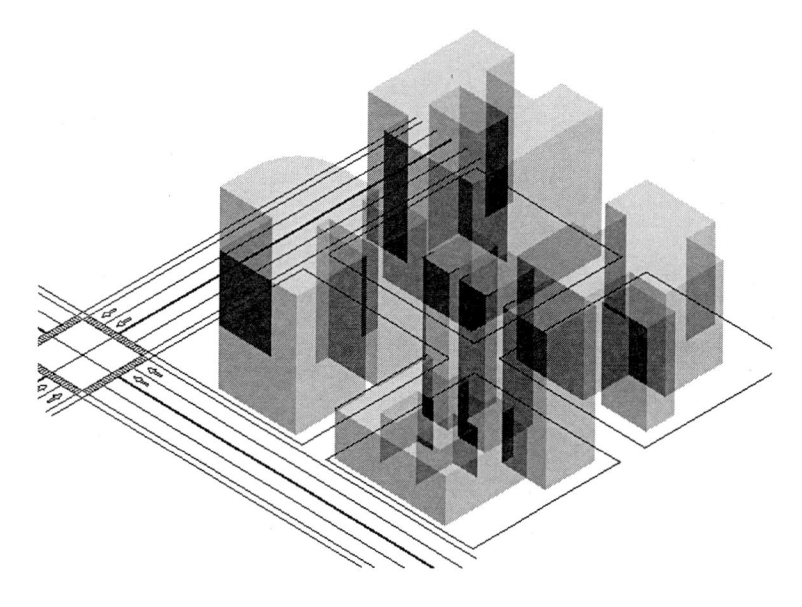

2-59

Command Exercise

Exercise 2-10 – Editing an In-Place Mass

Drawing Name: **editing_masses.rvt**
Estimated Time to Completion: 30 Minutes

Scope

Editing in-place masses to develop a conceptual model

Solution

1. Select **Building 3** in the NW quadrant.

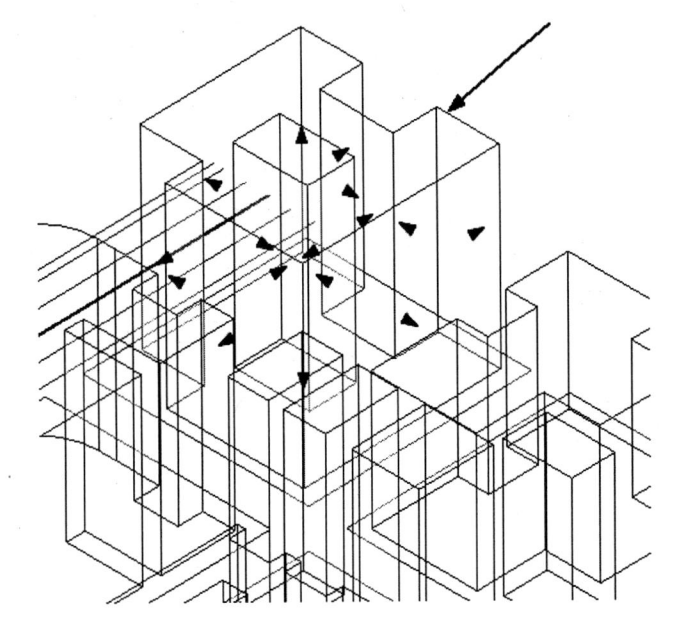

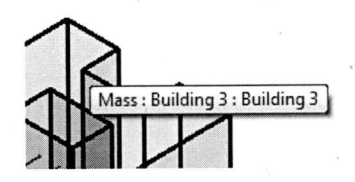

   If you hover your mouse over a mass, it will display the mass name assigned.

2. Select **Edit In-Place** from the Model panel.

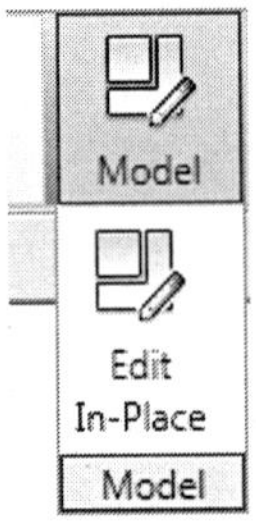

3. Use the **TAB** key to cycle through the selections until you have selected the top face.

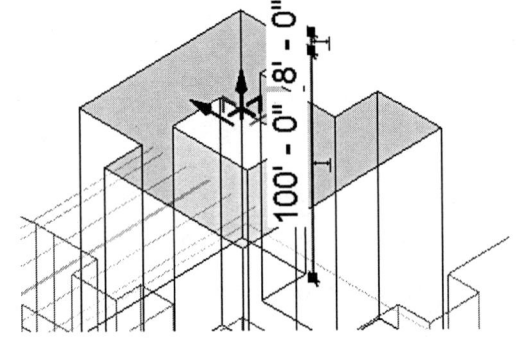

   Change the height of the mass to **100'-0"**.

The Basics of Building a Model

4. 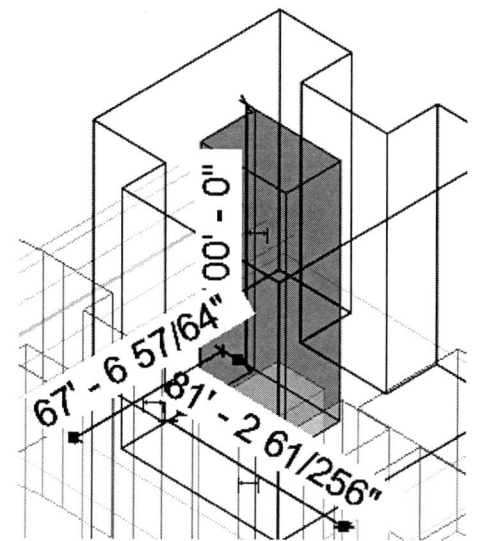 Use the **TAB** key to cycle through the selections until you have selected the void.

   Change the height of the mass to **100'-0"**.

5. 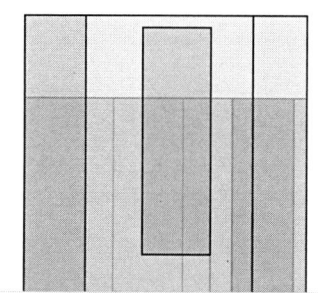 If you switch to a Left view, you can check the void to see if it really is aligned on the top and bottom.

6. 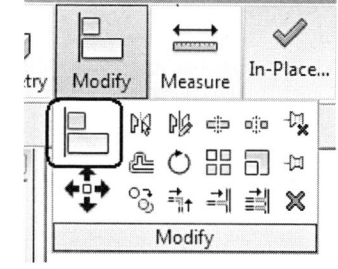 You can also use the ALIGN tool on the Modify panel to align the top of the void with the top of the solid form.

   Select ALIGN. Use the TAB key to select the top of the solid form. Then, use the TAB key to select the top of the void.

   Repeat for the bottom.

7. 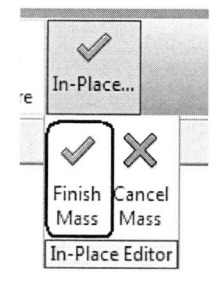 Select **Finish Mass** on the In-Place Editor panel when you are done editing the mass.

2-61

8. Select Building 4.

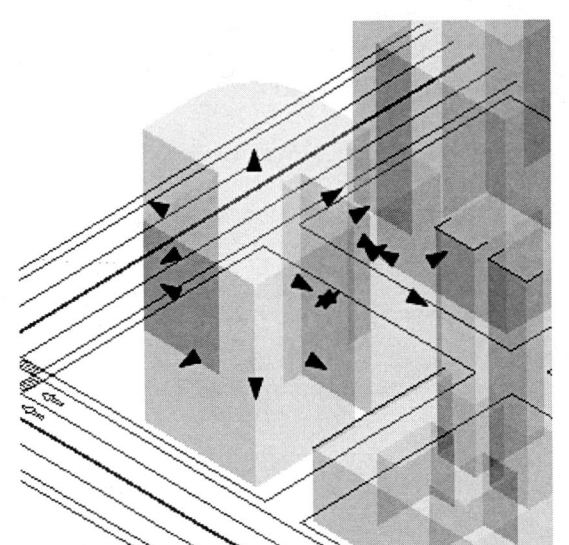

9. Select **Edit In-Place** from the Model panel.

10. Rotate the view using the ViewCube.

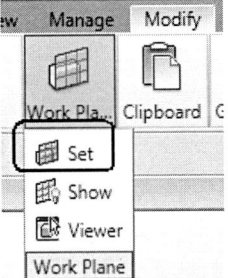

11. Select **Set Work Plane** from the Work Plane panel.

The Basics of Building a Model

12. Select the face indicated.

13. Select **Show Work Plane** from the Work Plane panel.

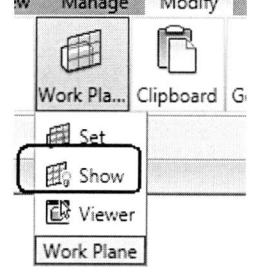

    The color of the selected face will change.

14. Select **Viewer** from the Work Plane panel.

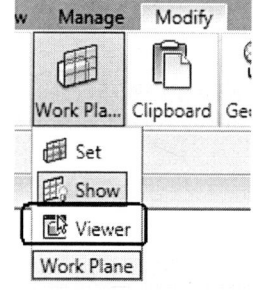

15. A window will open with a normal (perpendicular) view to the active work plane.

2-63

16. Select the **Rectangle** tool from the Draw panel.

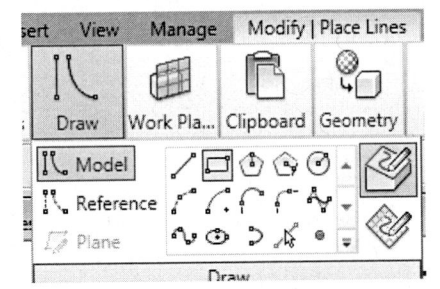

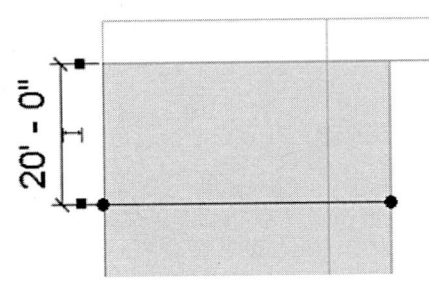

17. Draw a rectangle that is 20′ high using the Viewer window.

To adjust the dimension, select the bottom line and the temporary dimension will appear.

You can also use the ALIGN tool to set the sides of the rectangle collinear to the mass.

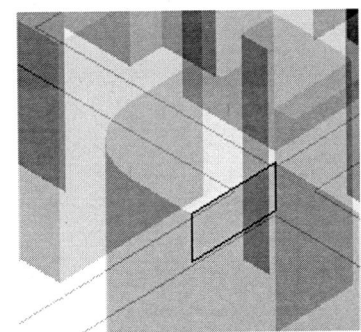

18. Check the placement of the rectangle in the 3D view.

    Close the Viewer window.

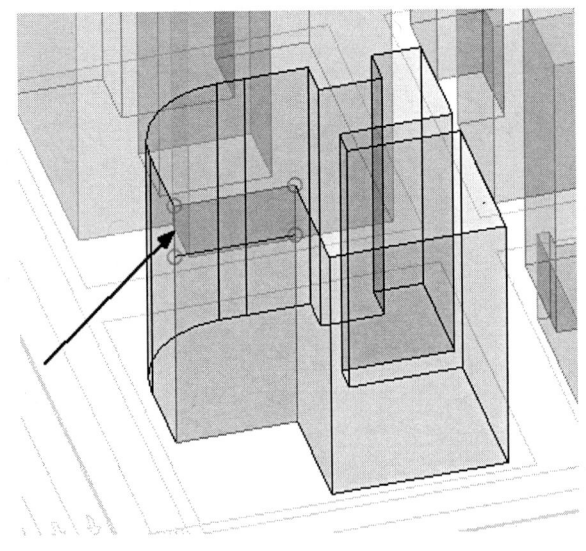

19. Select the sketch.

The Basics of Building a Model

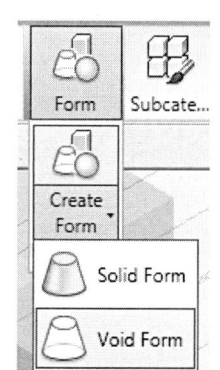

20. Select **Form→Create Form→Void Form**.

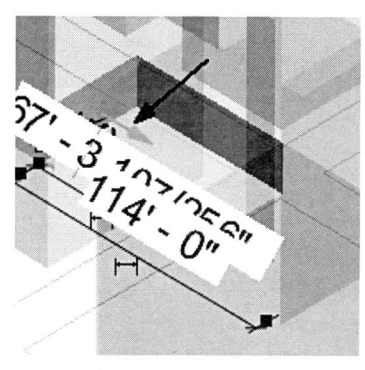

21. Use the green Axis to drag the void form through the existing mass.

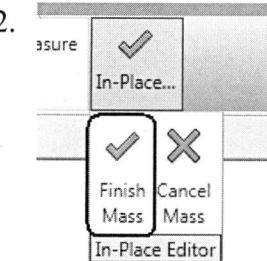

22. Select **Finish Mass** from the In-Place Editor panel.

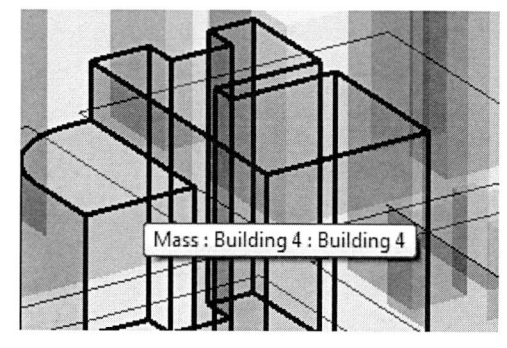

23. Select **Building 4**. (This is the building you just modified.)

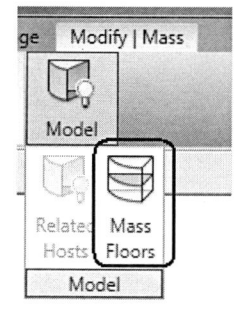

24. Select **Mass Floors** from the Model panel.

2-65

25. 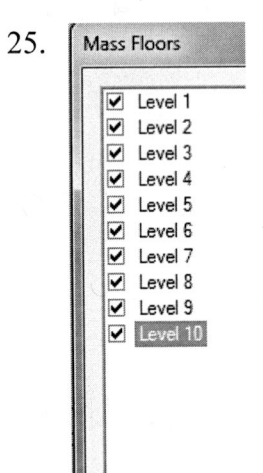 Enable all the Levels.

    Press **OK**.

26. 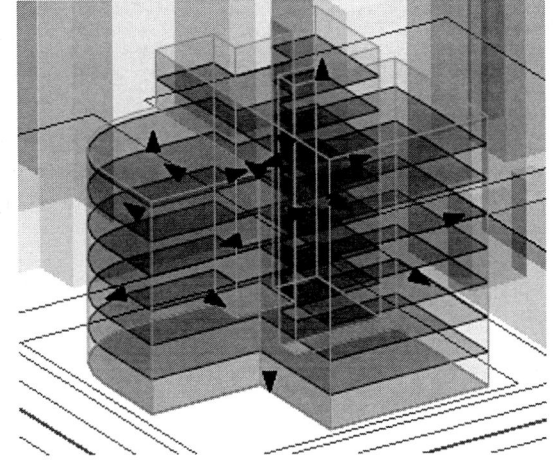 Floors are placed at each level.

27. 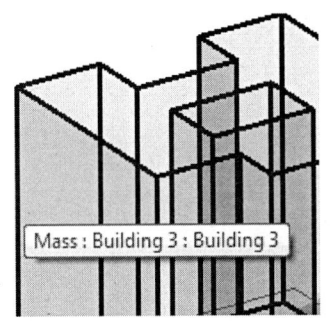 Select Building 3.

28. 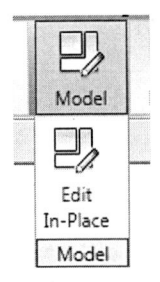 Select **Edit In-Place** from the Model panel.

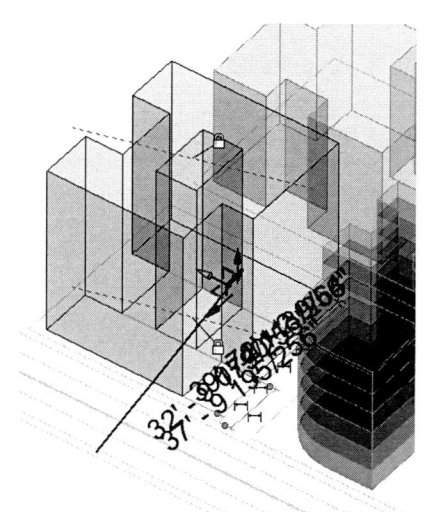

29. Select the face indicated.

    You should see the shape handle axis tool.

    You can use the TAB key to cycle through the selection until the face is highlighted then left click.

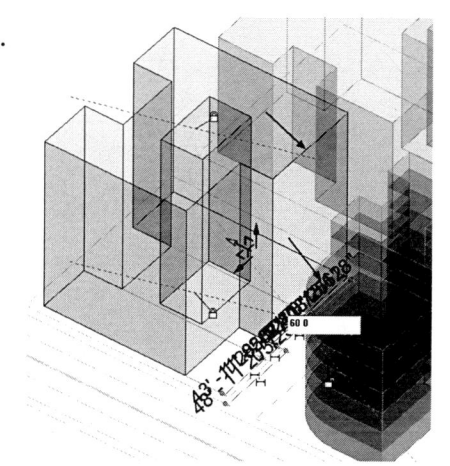

30. Adjust the dimension using the red axis.

    It may be difficult to see the distance. You can also select the temporary dimension and set it to 60' 0". The arrows indicate the edge which is being adjusted.

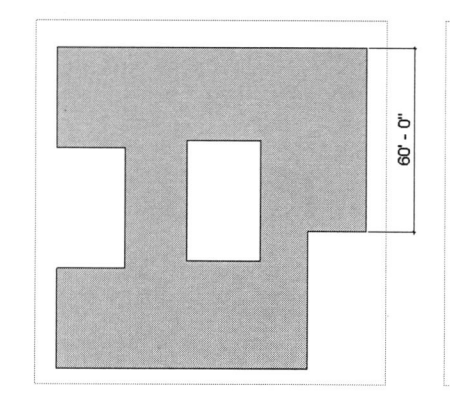

31. To verify that the face was moved properly, switch to a Top view using the view cube.

    Then use the MEASURE tool to verify the dimension.

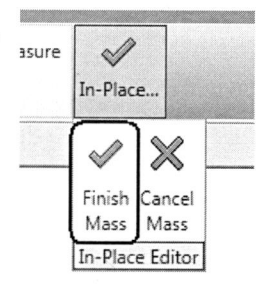

32. Select **Finish Mass** from the In-Place Editor panel.

33. Save the file as *ex2-10.rvt*.

The Unofficial Revit 2012 Certification Exam Guide

Command Exercise

Exercise 2-11 – Mass Properties

Drawing Name: **new**
Estimated Time to Completion: 15 Minutes

Scope

Modifying a conceptual mass

Solution

1. Start a new project using the Default template.

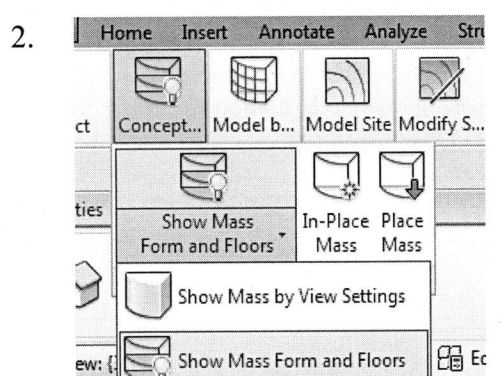

2. Activate the Massing & Site ribbon.

   Enable **Show Mass Form and Floors** from the Conceptual Mass panel.

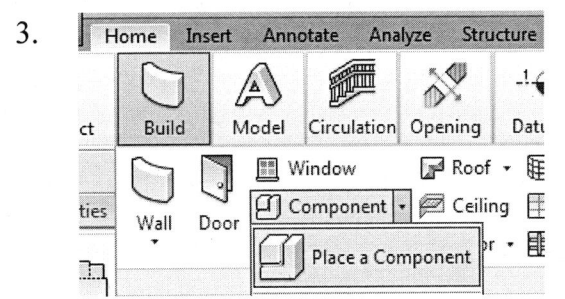

3. Activate the Home ribbon.

   Select the **Component→Place a Component** tool on the Build panel.

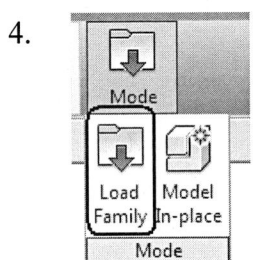

4. Select **Load Family** from the Mode panel.

5. Browse to the *Mass* folder.

2-68

The Basics of Building a Model

6. Select the *Rectangle-Blended* mass.

   Press **Open**.

7. On the ribbon:

   Select **Place on Work Plane** on the Placement panel.

8. Place in the window.

   Right click and select Cancel twice to exit the command.

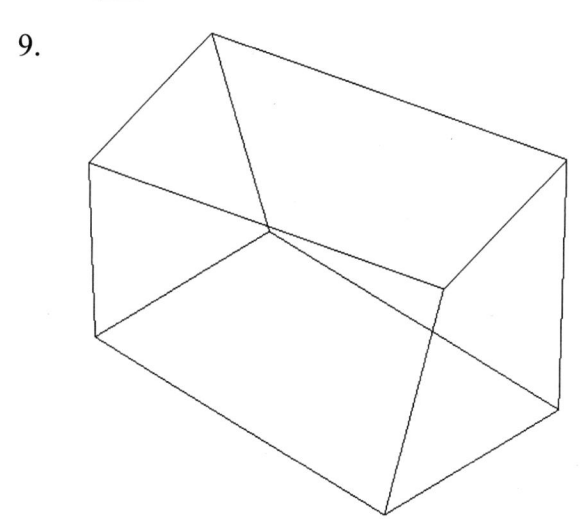

9. Switch to a 3D view.

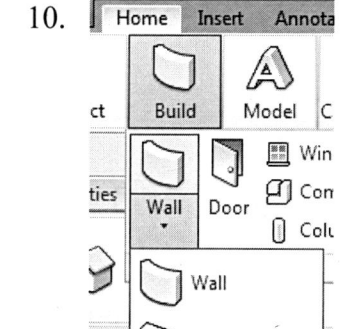

10. Activate the Home ribbon.

    Select the **Wall→Wall by Face** tool on the Build panel.

2-69

11. Set the wall type to **Generic - 12″** using the Type Selector.

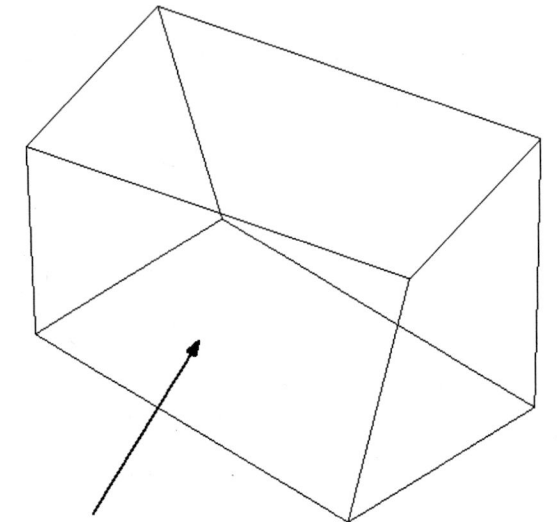

12. Select the face indicated.

    Left click in the window to exit the command.

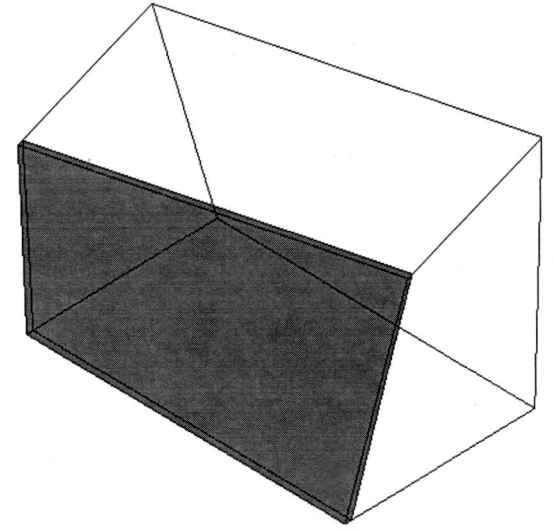

13. Select the wall you just placed.

    What is the area of the wall?

14. You should see the Volume and Area in the Properties pane.

    Volume 1494.54 CF
    Area   1503.14 SF

15. Close without saving.

The Basics of Building a Model

- The default material for a mass is 5 percent transparent.

- Masses will not print unless the category is enabled in Visibility/Graphics Overrides.

- Masses are created from a single closed profile.

- Masses are a nested entity. In order to modify the profile, you have to open the mass up for editing and then open the desired form component up for editing.

- Masses can be comprised of multiple forms, a combination of voids and solids.

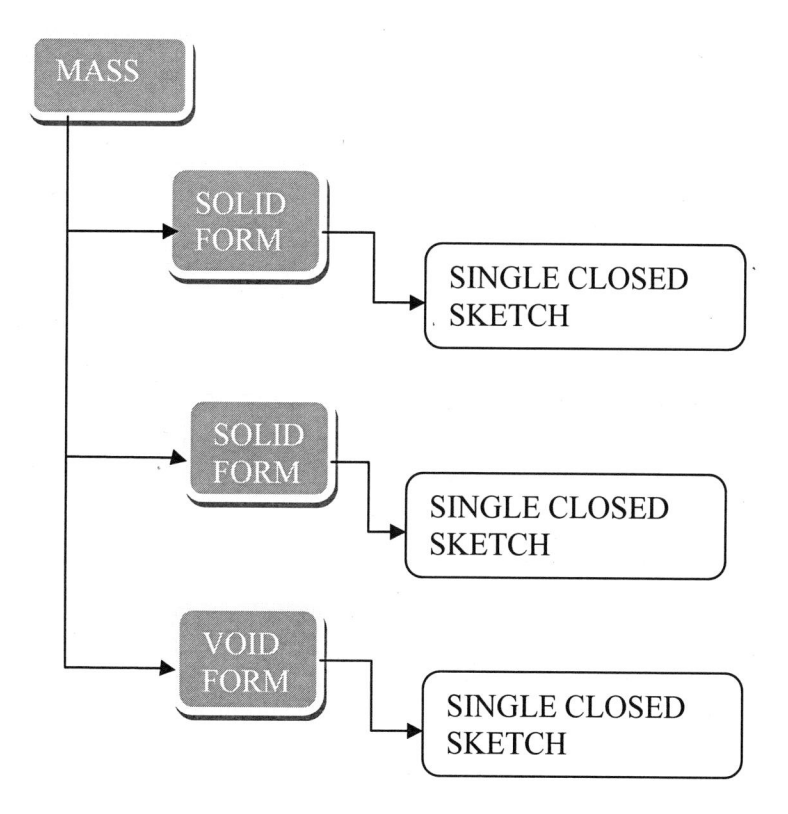

```
MASS ──┬── SOLID FORM ──── SINGLE CLOSED SKETCH
       ├── SOLID FORM ──── SINGLE CLOSED SKETCH
       └── VOID FORM ───── SINGLE CLOSED SKETCH
```

Practice Associate Exam

1. Which of the following can NOT be defined prior to placing a wall?

   A. Unconnected Height
   B. Base Constraint
   C. Location Line
   D. Profile
   E. Top Offset

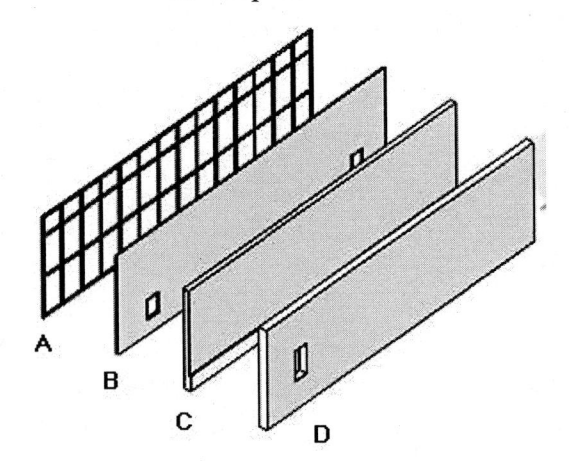

2. Identify the stacked wall.

3. Walls are system families. Which name is NOT a wall family?

   A. BASIC
   B. COMPOUND
   C. CURTAIN
   D. COMPLICATED

4. Select the TWO which are wall type properties:

   A. COARSE FILL PATTERN
   B. LOCATION LINE
   C. TOP CONSTRAINT
   D. FUNCTION
   E. BASE CONSTRAINT

5. Select ONE item that is used when defining a compound wall:

   A. MATERIAL
   B. SWEEPS
   C. GRIDS
   D. LAYERS
   E. FILL PATTERN

6. Enabling the Chain command when placing walls does the following:

   A. Creates a daisy chain of walls.
   B. Constrains the walls together so they can be moved and copied as a set.
   C. Reduces the number of clicks required when placing walls.
   D. Places a compound wall.

7. Use this key to cycle through selections:
    A. TAB
    B. CTL
    C. SHIFT
    D. ALT

8. When working with a mass, you can use levels to define mass _____
    A. Roofs
    B. Floors
    C. Ceilings
    D. Walls

9. To create a mass that is unique in a project, use the _____ Mass tool.
    A. In-Place
    B. Component
    C. System
    D. By Face

10. Selecting a work plane:
    A. Automatically changes the relative coordinate system
    B. Changes the project location
    C. Changes the level
    D. Determines the depth of an extrusion

11. The construction of a stacked wall is defined by different wall _____.
    A. Types
    B. Layers
    C. Regions
    D. Instances

12. To change the structure of a basic wall you must modify it's:
    A. Type Parameters
    B. Instance Parameters
    C. Structural Usage
    D. Function

13. Select THREE element types than can be created using mass faces:
    A. Doors
    B. Walls
    C. Levels
    D. Floors
    E. Roofs

14. Select TWO methods used to create a conceptual design using mass families;
    A. Go to the Applications Menu and select New→Conceptual Mass.
    B. Go to the Massing & Site ribbon and select Place Mass.
    C. Go to the Applications Menu and select New→Family
    D. Go to the Massing & Site ribbon and select In-Place Mass
    E. Go to the Applications Menu and select New→Project

15. In order to place a wall or floor on a mass face, the face must be:
    A. Horizontal
    B. Vertical
    C. Either Horizontal or Vertical
    D. Curved or spherical
    E. None of the above

16. To divide a floor or wall into parts, you can use the following (select all that apply):
    A. Lines
    B. Levels
    C. Grids
    D. Circles
    E. Arcs

17. To display parts in a view:
    A. Go to the Massing & Site ribbon and select Show Mass.
    B. On the View Properties pane: set Parts Visibility to Show Parts
    C. Go to the Visibility/Graphics dialog and enable Parts.
    D. Go to Temporary Hide/Isolate and Reset

18. To assign a different material to a part, select the part and:
    A. On the Properties pane: Enable Material by Original
    B. Right click and select Assign Material
    C. On the Modify ribbon, select Paint from the Geometry Panel.
    D. On the Properties pane: Uncheck Material by Original, then assign a material in the material field.

Answers:
1) D; 2) C; 3) D; 4) A & D; 5) D; 6) C; 7) A; 8) B; 9) A; 10) A; 11) A; 12) A; 13) B, D, & E; 14) A & D; 15) E; 16) A, B, C, & D; 17) B; 18) D

Lesson Three

Component Families

This lesson addresses the following Associate and Professional exam questions:

- Load Component Families
- Adding Components to a Project
- Creating families

Users should be able to understand the difference between a hosted and non-hosted component. A hosted component is a component that must be placed or constrained to another element. For example, a door or window is hosted by a wall. You should be able to identify what components can be hosted by which elements. Walls are non-hosted. Whether or not a component is hosted is defined by the template used for creating the component. A wall, floor, ceiling or face can be a host.

Some components are level-based, such as furniture, site components, plumbing fixtures, casework, roofs and walls. When you insert a level-based component, it is constrained to that level and can only be moved within that infinite plane.

Components must be loaded into a project before they can be placed. Users can pre-load components into a template, so that they are available in every project.

Users should be familiar with how to use Element and Type Properties of components in order to locate and modify information.

There are 3 kinds of families in Revit Architecture:

- system families
- loadable families
- in-place families

System families are walls, ceilings, stairs, floors, etc. These are families which can only be created by using an existing family, duplicating, and redefining. These families are loaded into a project using a project template.

Loadable families are external files. These include doors, windows, furniture, and plants.

In-place families are components which are created inside of a project and are unique to that project.

Command Exercise

Exercise 3-1 – Level-Based Component

Drawing Name: **i_components.rvt**
Estimated Time to Completion: 10 Minutes

Scope

Moving a component from one level to the next.

Solution

1. Activate the **Main Floor** floor plan.

2. Select the table element indicated.

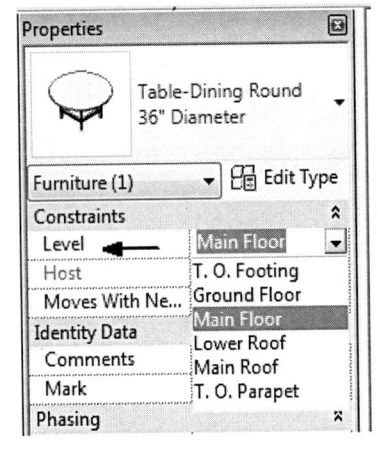

3. On the Properties pane:

   Change the Level parameter to **Ground Floor**.

Component Families

4. Activate **Ground Floor**.

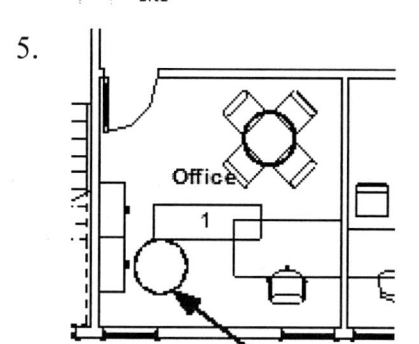

   - Floor Plans
     - **Ground Floor**
     - Lower Roof
     - Main Floor
     - Main Roof
     - Site

5. The table is in the same location on the Ground Floor.

6. Close the file without saving.

The Unofficial Revit 2012 Certification Exam Guide

Command Exercise

Exercise 3-2 – Creating a Family

Drawing Name: **park bench.dwg**
Estimated Time to Completion: 80 Minutes

Scope

Create a Revit family from an AutoCAD symbol.

Solution

1. Close any open files.

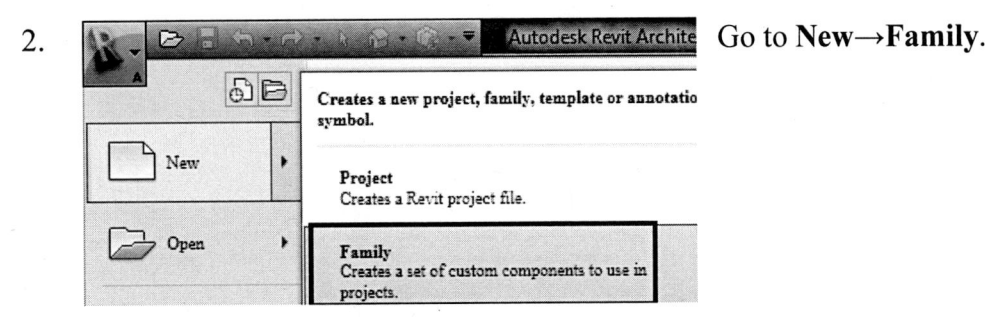

2. Go to **New→Family**.

3. Select the *Furniture.rft* from the Imperial templates.

4. Activate the **View** ribbon.

   Select **Tile** under the Window panel.

5. Double click the title for the **Elevation:Right** window to enlarge it.

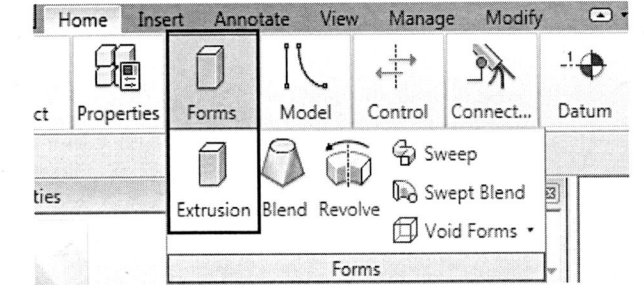

6. Activate the **Home** ribbon.

   Select **Forms→Extrusion**.

3-4

Component Families

7. Activate the **Insert** ribbon.

   Select the **Import CAD** tool from the Import panel.

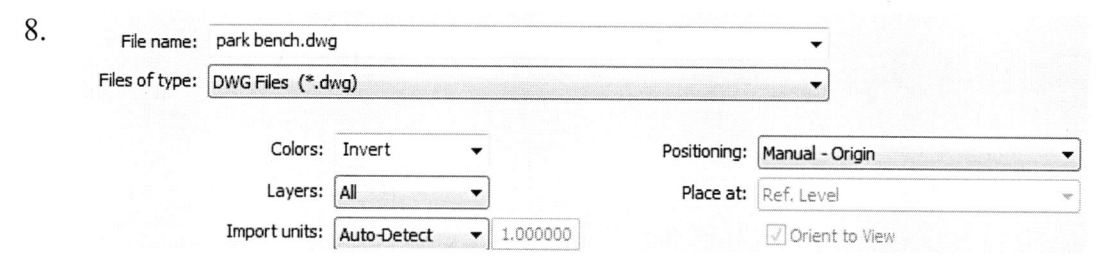

8. Locate the *park bench.dwg* file.
   Set the positioning to Manual-Origin.
   Press Open.

9. The park bench will appear as shown.

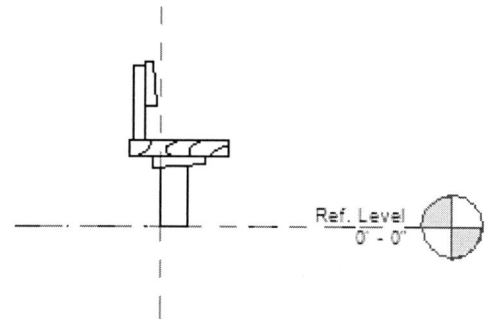

10. On the Properties pane:

    Set the Extrusion End to **4'-0"**.

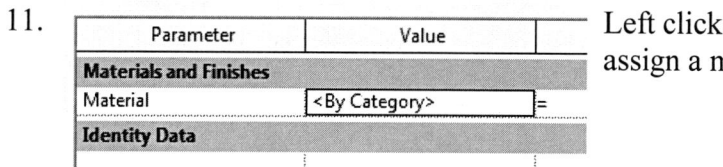

11. Left click in the **Material** column to assign a material.

12. Highlight the **Default** Material.
    Select the **Copy Material** tool located in the lower left of the dialog.

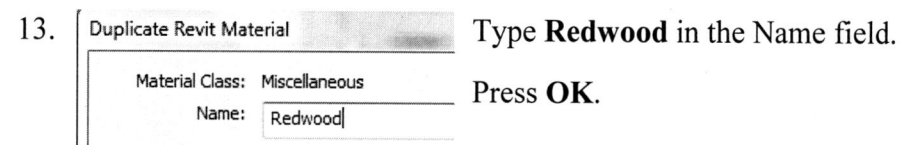

13. Type **Redwood** in the Name field.

    Press **OK**.

3-5

14. Enable **Use Render Appearance for Shading** on the Graphics tab.

15. Do a search for **redwood**.

16. Select the redwood material.

    Press **OK**.

17. Redwood is listed in the Properties pane.

18. Clean up the sketch so that there are no self-intersecting lines.

    Use the TRIM and SPLIT tools.

19. Select the **Green Check** under Mode to **Finish Extrusion**.

20. Select extrusion.

    In the Properties pane:

    Set the Material to **Redwood**.

Component Families

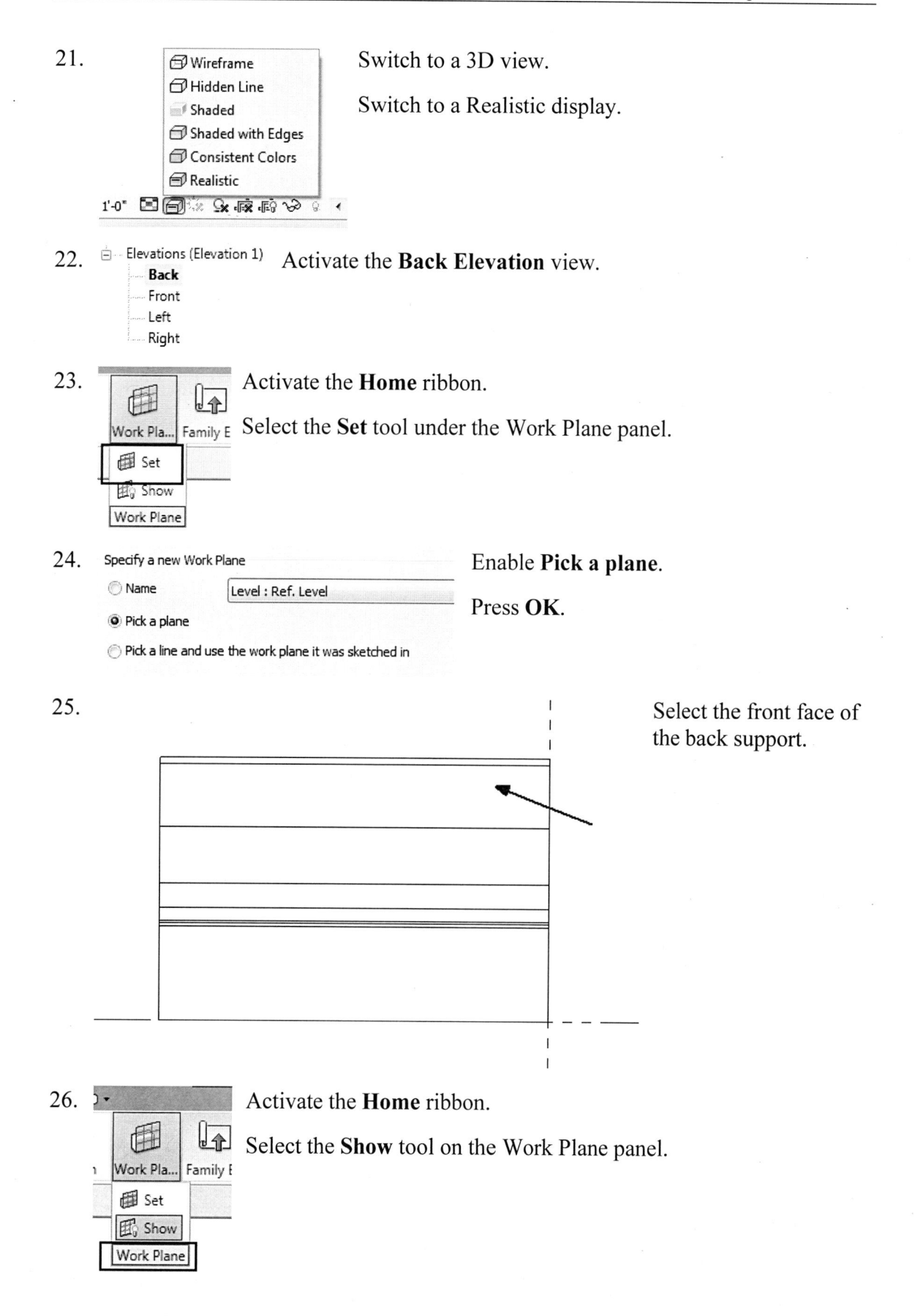

21. Switch to a 3D view.

    Switch to a Realistic display.

22. Activate the **Back Elevation** view.

23. Activate the **Home** ribbon.

    Select the **Set** tool under the Work Plane panel.

24. Enable **Pick a plane**.

    Press **OK**.

25. Select the front face of the back support.

26. Activate the **Home** ribbon.

    Select the **Show** tool on the Work Plane panel.

3-7

27. The active work plane will display as a light blue rectangle.

    Verify that the active work plane is the front face of the back support.

28. Select **Forms→Extrusion**.

29. Select **Material** from the Properties Pane.

30. Activate the **Materials** tab.

31. Highlight the **Default** Material.
    Select the **Copy Material** tool located in the lower left of the dialog.

32. Type **Nameplate** in the Name field.
    Press **OK**.

33. Enable **Use Render Appearance for Shading** on the Graphics tab.

34. Select the **Appearance** tab.
    Type **aluminum** in the search field to search for the aluminum materials.

35. Select the **Anodized - Blue-Gray** material.

    Press **OK**.

36. Set the Extrusion End to **1/4"**.

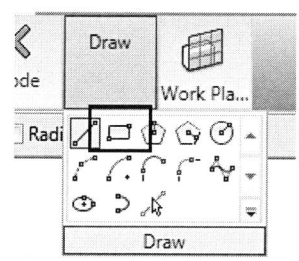

37. Select the **Rectangle** tool from the Draw panel.

38. Draw a rectangle on the seat face.

    Use dimensions to center it on the surface.

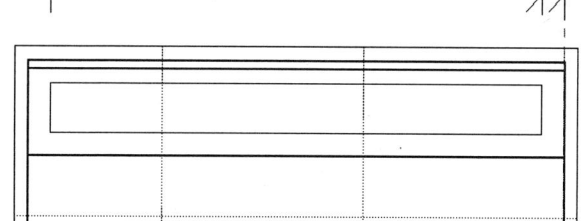

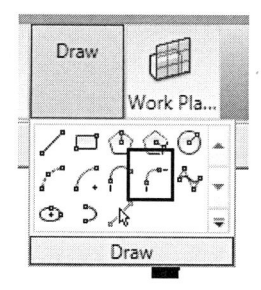

39. Use the Fillet Arc tool to fillet the corners of the rectangle.

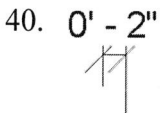

40. Set the corners to 1" radius.

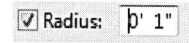

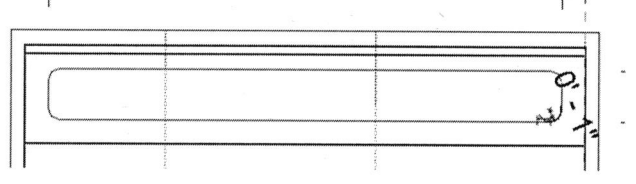

3-9

41. Select the **green check** under Mode to **Finish Extrusion**.

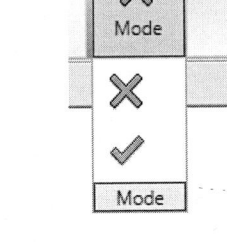

42. Switch to a 3D view to inspect your model.

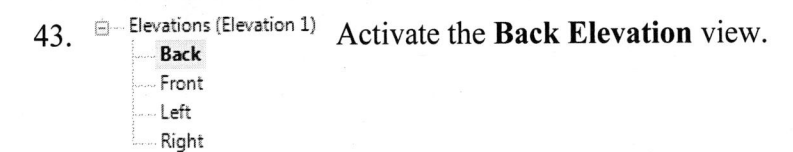

43. Activate the **Back Elevation** view.

44. Activate the **Home** ribbon.

    Select the **Set** tool under the Work Plane panel.

45. Enable **Pick a plane**.

    Press **OK**.

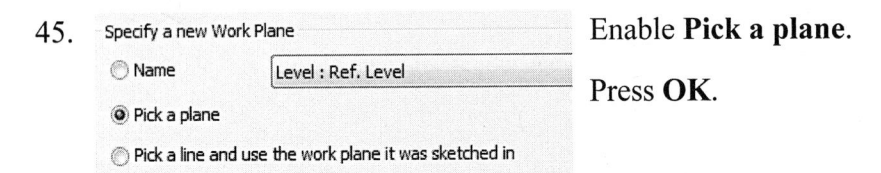

46. Select the front surface of the nameplate.

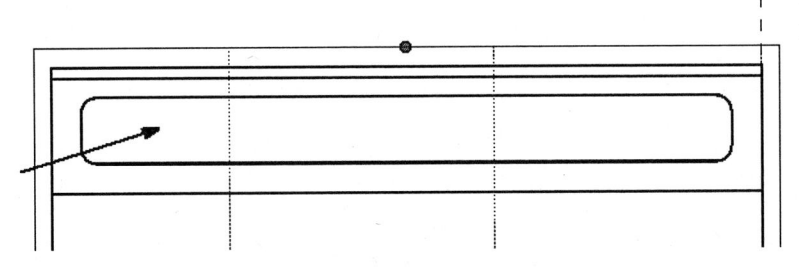

    The active work plane will shift to the new location.

Component Families

47. Select **Model Text** from the Model panel on the Home ribbon.

48. Type **In Memory of Our Fallen Soldiers** in the Edit Text dialog.

    Press **OK**.

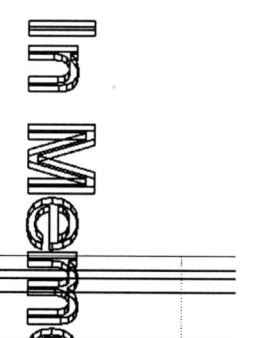

49. Click to place in the view.

    Right click and select **Cancel** to exit the command.

The space bar is not available to rotate the text in the Model Text command.

50. Select the Model text.

    Select **Edit Type** in the Properties Pane.

51. Select **Duplicate**.

52. Name the new type **Model Text 2**.

    Press **OK**.

53. Change the Text Size to **2"**.

    Press **OK**.

54. Use the Rotate and Move tools from the Modify panel to position the text.

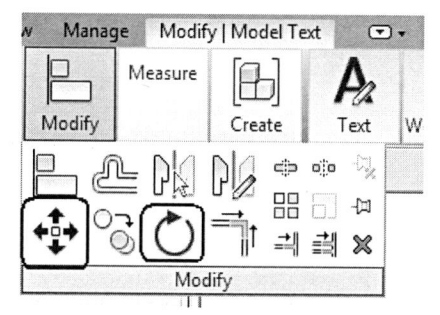

3-11

55. Set the Depth to **1/8"**.

56. Select **Material** from the Properties Pane.

57. Activate the Materials tab.

Highlight the **Default** Material.
Select the **Copy Material** tool located in the lower left of the dialog.

58. Type **Nameplate Text** in the Name field.

Press **OK**.

59. Select the **Appearance Property Sets** tab.

Highlight **Metallic Paint**.

60. Select the Satin - Gold color.

61. Select the **Graphics** tab.

Place a check on the Use Render Appearance for Shading.

Press **OK**.

62. Activate the Home ribbon.

Disable visibility of the work plane by selecting **Show** on the Work Plane panel.

3-12

Component Families

63. Switch to a 3D View.

64. Turn off the visibility of the work plane.

65. Set the Display to **Realistic**.

66. The model so far.

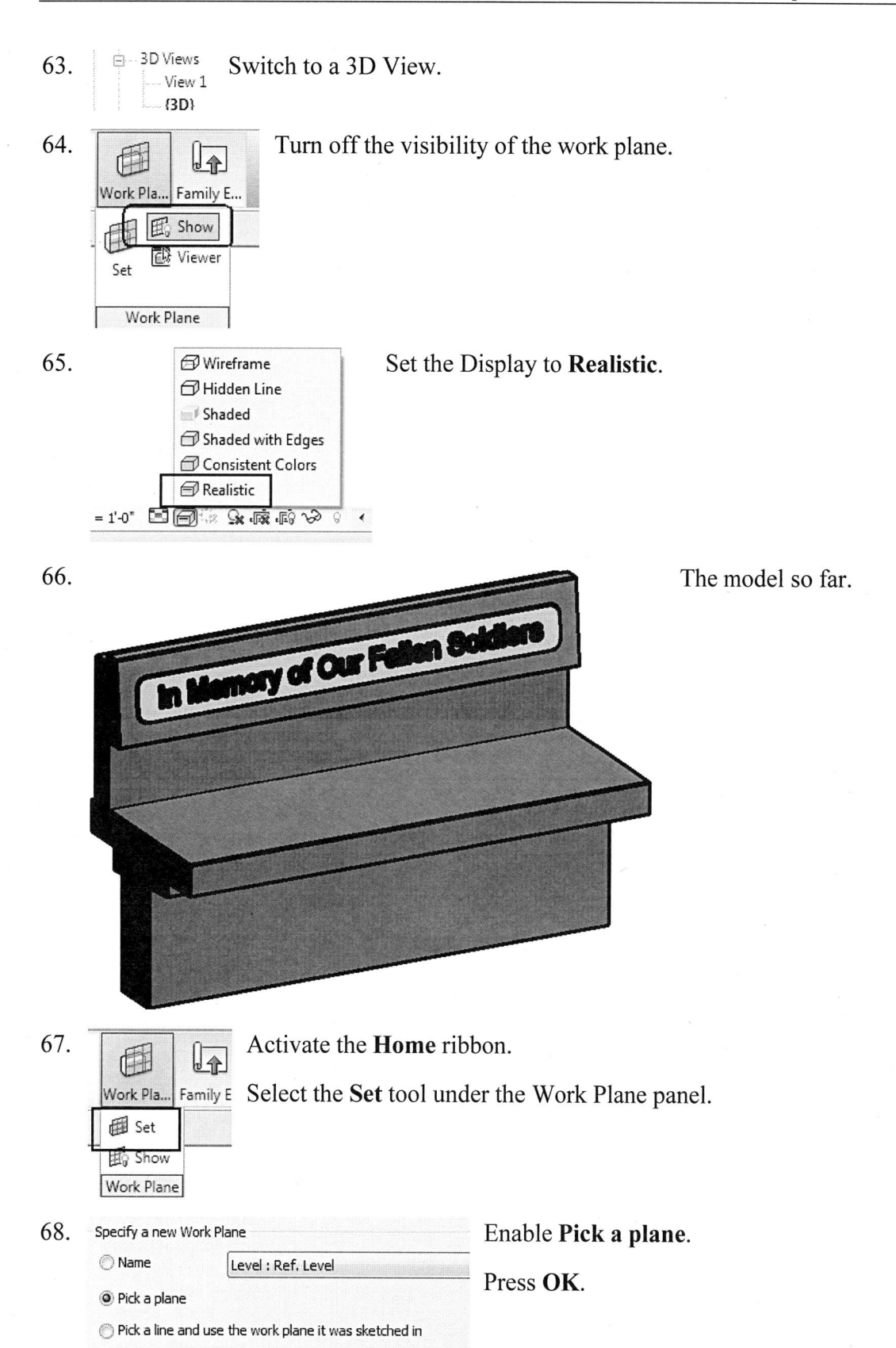

67. Activate the **Home** ribbon.

Select the **Set** tool under the Work Plane panel.

68. Enable **Pick a plane**.

Press **OK**.

3-13

69. Select the front surface of the bench leg area.

The active work plane will shift to the new location.

70. Activate the **Back Elevation** view.

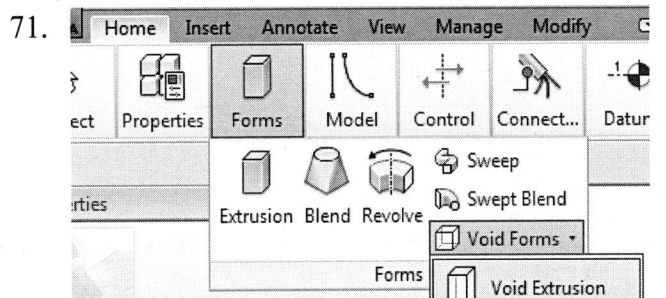

71. Select **Forms→Void Extrusion** from the Home ribbon.

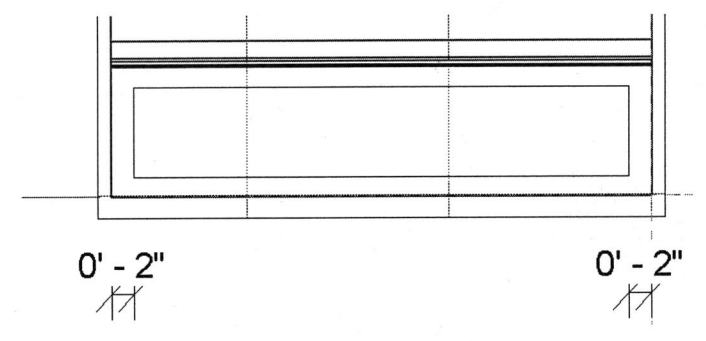

72. Use the Rectangle tool from the Draw panel to place a rectangle centered on the face.

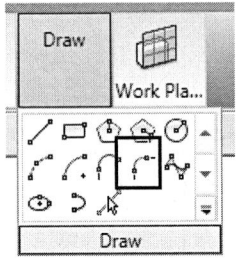

73. Use the Fillet Arc tool to fillet the corners of the rectangle.

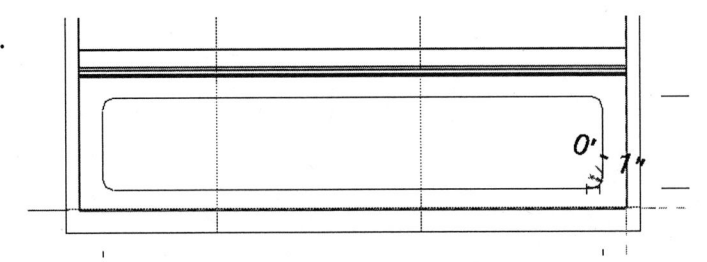

74. Set the corners to 1" radius.

3-14

Component Families

75. Set the depth of the void extrusion **8"**.

Press **Apply**.

76. Select the **green check** under Mode to finish the void.

77. Switch to a wire frame view to see the void.

Use the grips to adjust the void position so it goes entirely through the park bench.

78. Save as *park bench.rfa*.

This is a loadable family which can be loaded and used in any project.

3-15

Command Exercise
Exercise 3-3 – Indentifying a Family

Drawing Name: **i_firestation_elem.rvt**
Estimated Time to Completion: 5 Minutes

Scope

Identify different elements and their families.

Solution

1. Open *i_firestation_elem.rvt*.

2. Activate the **South** elevation.

3. Select the second window from the left.

4. Select the **30" W** from the window type list in the Properties pane.

5. Use the Measure tool from the Quick Access toolbar to check the distance between the outside edges of the two left windows.

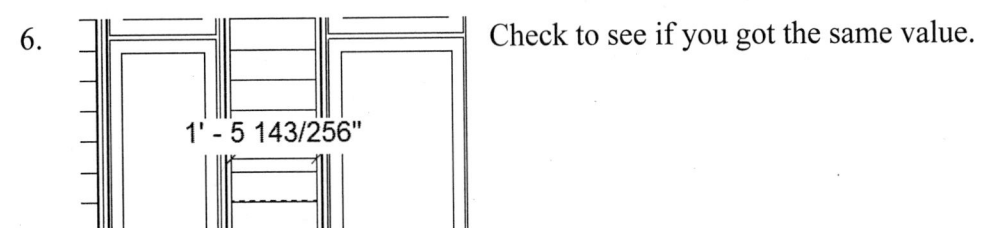

6. Check to see if you got the same value.

   1' - 5 143/256"

7. Close without saving.

Practice Associate Exam

1. If a level-based component is moved from Level 1 to Level 2 by changing the Element Properties, the new location is:
   A. At the origin.
   B. Corresponds to the location on the previous level.
   C. Where the user selects it to be.
   D. None of the above.

2. Families in the Project Browser are organized by:
   A. Instance, then Category, then Family
   B. Family, then Instance
   C. Category, then Family, then Type
   D. Family, then Type

3. A _____ is a group of elements with a common set of properties - called parameters - and a related graphical representation.
   A. view
   B. family
   C. project
   D. model
   E. mass

4. Select TWO characteristics you can specify for a family type:
   A. Category
   B. Materials
   C. Levels
   D. Views
   E. Dimensions

5. Select the THREE types of families:
   A. Datum
   B. View
   C. System
   D. Model
   E. Mass

6. The surface pattern for a material is set in the _____ tab of the Materials dialog.
   A. Physical
   B. Identity
   C. Render Appearance
   D. Graphics

7. To create a new system family you:
   A. Use a Revit family template
   B. Modify the instance parameters of an existing similar family
   C. Duplicate a similar system family and modify the type parameters
   D. Modify the type parameters of a similar system family.

8. In the Generic Model family template, you are provided with:
   A. Levels
   B. Reference Planes
   C. Grids
   D. Grid Guides

9. To create an opening in an extrusion when defining a model family, you need to place a:
   A. Opening
   B. Void
   C. Hole
   D. Cut

10. A(n) _____ family exists only in the project and can not be loaded into other projects.
    A. massing
    B. system
    C. loadable
    D. in-place
    E. model

Answers:
1) B; 2) C; 3) B; 4) B & E; 5) C, D, & E; 6) D; 7) C; 8) B; 9) B; 10) B

Lesson Four

View Properties

This lesson addresses the following Associate and Professional exam questions:

- View Properties
- Object Visibility Settings
- Section Views
- Elevation Views
- View Templates
- Scope Boxes

The Project Browser lists all the views available in the project. Any view can be dragged and dropped onto a sheet. Once a view is used or consumed on a sheet, it cannot be placed a second time on a sheet – even on a different sheet. Instead, you must create a duplicate view. You can create as many duplicate views as you like. Each duplicate view may have different annotations, line weight settings, detail levels, etc. Annotations are associated to a view. If a view is deleted, any annotations are also deleted.

Revit has bidirectional associativity. This means that changes in one view are automatically reflected in all associated views. For example, if you modify the dimensions or locations of a window in one view, the change is reflected in all the associated views, including the 3D view.

You can control the appearance of Revit elements using Object Visibility Settings. These settings control line color, line type, and line weight. You can create templates which have different Object Visibility Settings for different project types.

Command Exercise
Exercise 4-1 – Creating a Level

Drawing Name: **i_levels.rvt**
Estimated Time to Completion: 5 Minutes

Scope

Placing a level.

Solution

1. Activate the **South Elevation**.

   The level names have been turned off.

2. Select each level and place a check in the square that appears. This will turn on visibility of the level name.

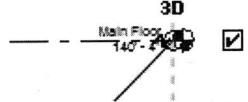

3. You should be able to identify the names for each level.

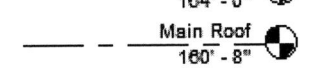

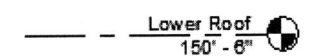

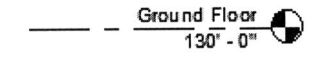

   T.O. Parapet 164' - 0"
   Main Roof 160' - 8"
   Lower Roof 150' - 6"
   Main Floor 140' - 4"
   Ground Floor 130' - 0"
   T.O. Footing 126' - 0"

4. Select the **Level** tool from the Home ribbon.

View Properties

5. Place a level **5'-0"** above the Main Floor.

6. Note the elevation value for the new level.

7. Close without saving.

Command Exercise

Exercise 4-2 – Story vs. Non-Story Levels

Drawing Name: **story_levels.rvt**
Estimated Time to Completion: 15 Minutes

Scope

Understanding the difference between story and non-story levels
Converting a non-story level to a story level.

Solution

1. Activate the **South Elevation**.

2. Select each level and place a check in the square that appears. This will turn on visibility of the level name.

3. Study the Main Floor level.

   Notice that it is the color black while all the other levels are blue.

   The Main Floor level is a non-story or reference level. It does not have a view associated with it.

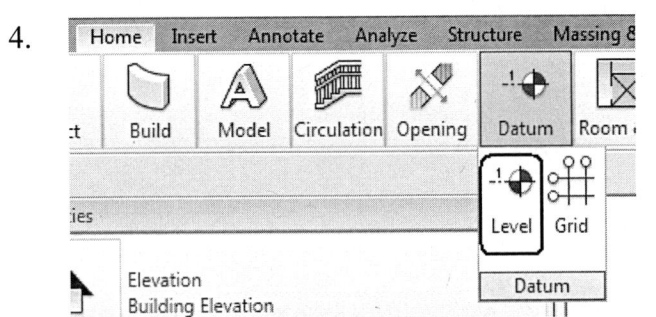

4. Activate the Home ribbon.

   Select the **Level** tool on the Datum panel.

5. On the Options bar:

   Uncheck **Make Plan View**.

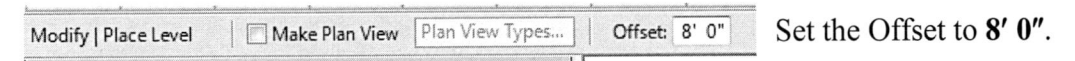

   Set the Offset to **8' 0"**.

View Properties

6. Select the **Pick** tool on the Draw panel.

7. Select the Main Floor level.

   Verify that the preview shows the level will be placed 8' 0" ABOVE the Main Floor level.

8. The level is placed above the Main Floor.

   Right click and select Cancel twice to exit the Level command.

9. Select the Elbow control on the new level to add a jog.

10. Note that the new level is also a non-story or reference level.

    Check in the Project Browser and you will see that no associated views were created with the new level.

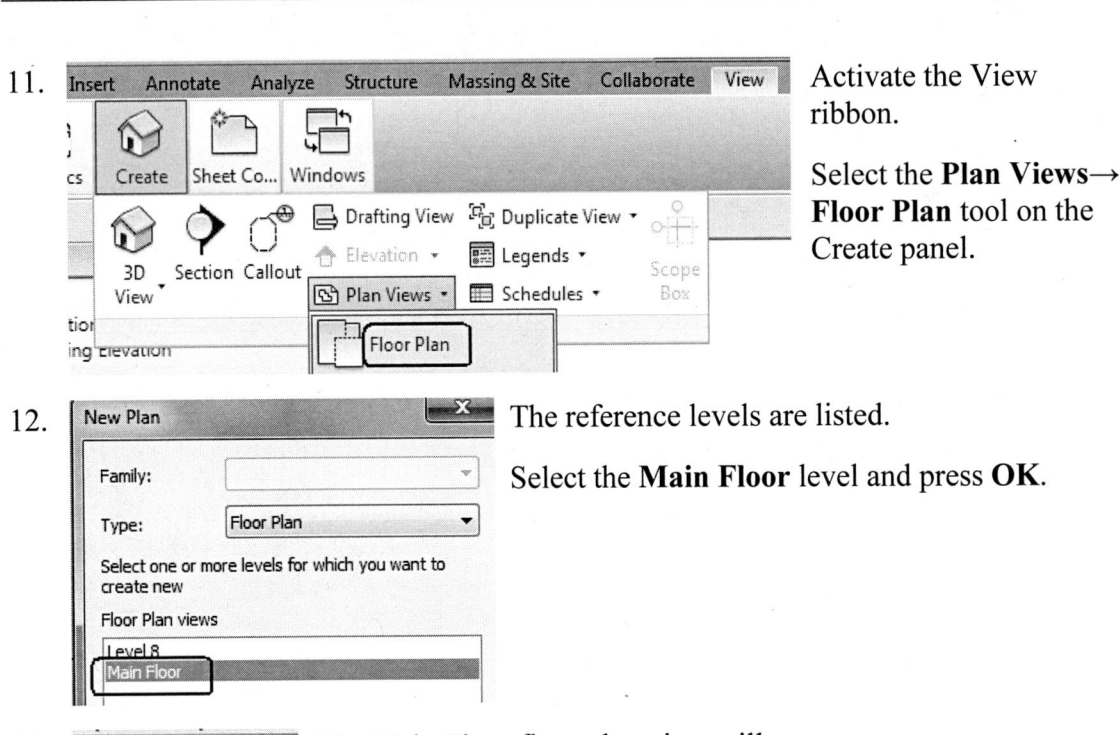

11. Activate the View ribbon.

   Select the **Plan Views→ Floor Plan** tool on the Create panel.

12. The reference levels are listed.

   Select the **Main Floor** level and press **OK**.

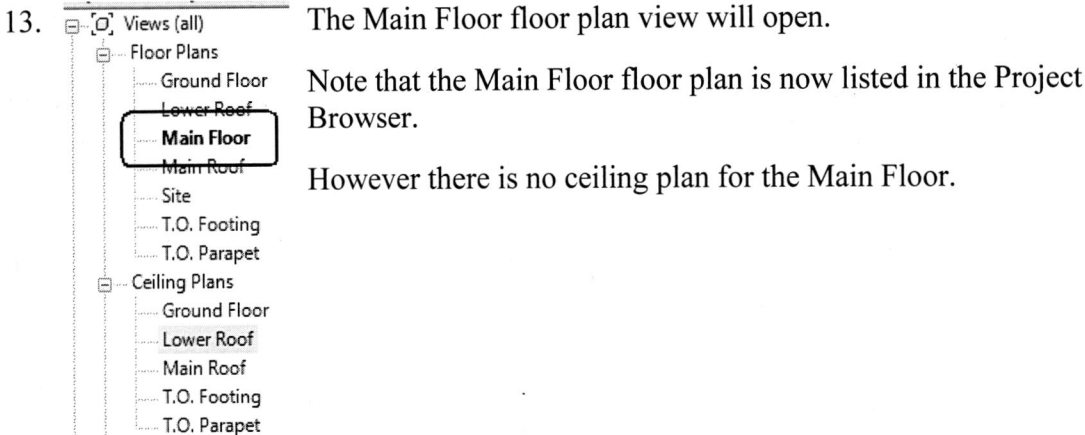

13. The Main Floor floor plan view will open.

   Note that the Main Floor floor plan is now listed in the Project Browser.

   However there is no ceiling plan for the Main Floor.

14. 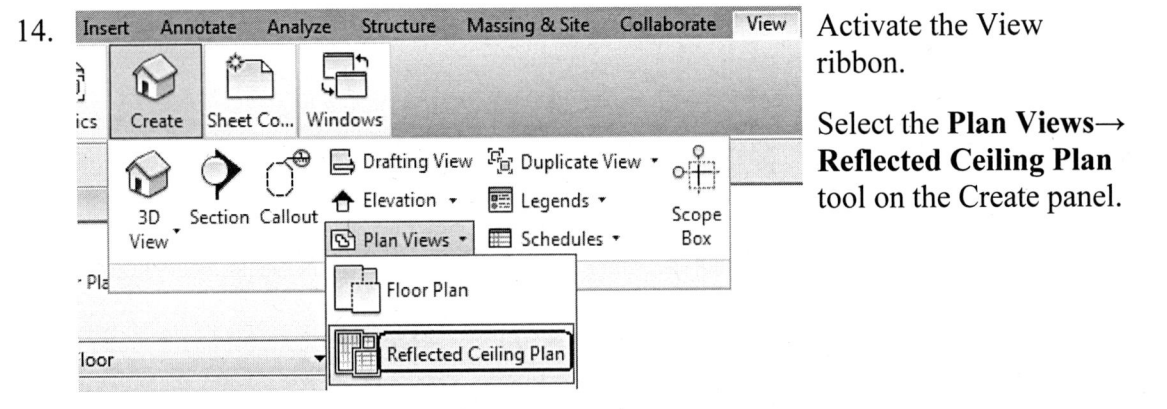 Activate the View ribbon.

   Select the **Plan Views→ Reflected Ceiling Plan** tool on the Create panel.

View Properties

15. The reference levels are listed.

Select the **Main Floor** level and press **OK**.

16. The Main Floor floor ceiling plan view will open.

17. Activate the **South Elevation**.

18. The Main Floor level is now the color Blue to indicate it has associated views.

19. Close the file without saving.

4-7

The Unofficial Revit 2012 Certification Exam Guide

Command Exercise
Exercise 4-3 – Creating Column Grids

Drawing Name: **i_grids.rvt**
Estimated Time to Completion: 10 Minutes

Scope

Placing column grids.

Solution

1. Activate the **Ground Floor** view.

2. Zoom into the building area displayed.

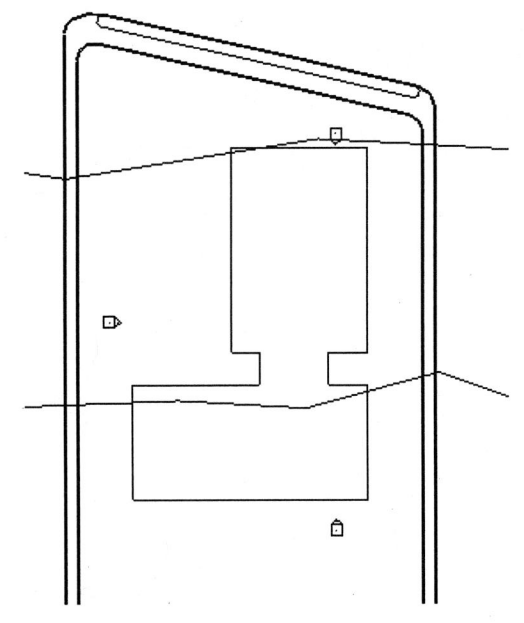

3. Select the **Grid** tool on the Datum panel from the Home ribbon.

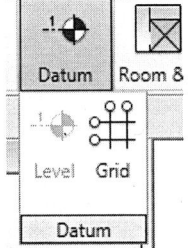

4-8

View Properties

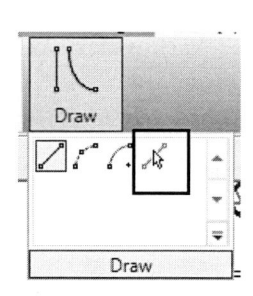

4. Select the **Pick Lines** mode from the Draw panel.

5. Set the Offset to **2'-0"** [**600 mm**] on the Options bar.

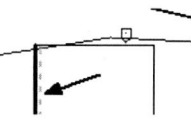

6. Click to place a vertical grid line as shown.

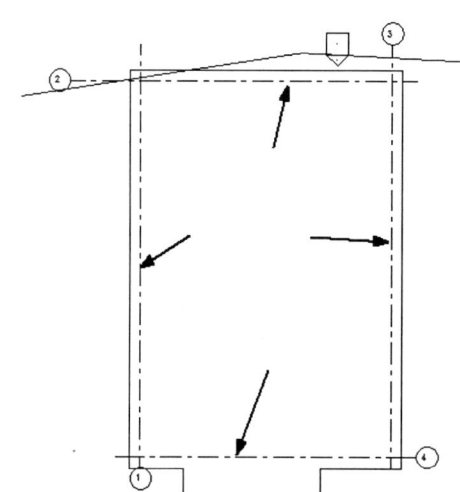

7. Place gridlines as shown.

Use the grips by the heads to drag the grid bubbles into position.

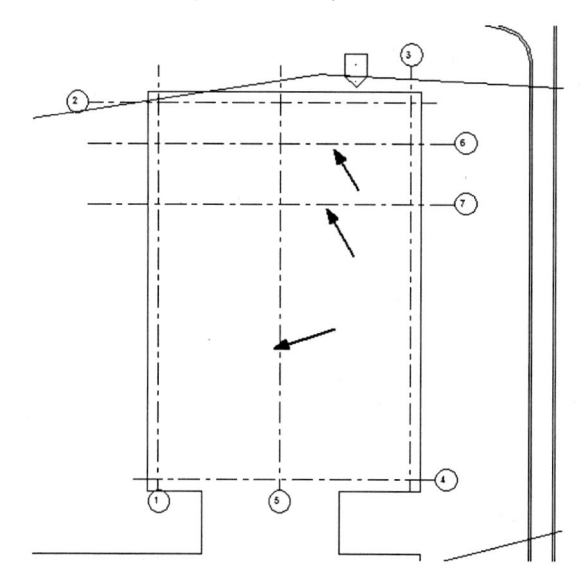

8. Add a vertical grid line as shown.

Add two horizontal grid lines as shown.

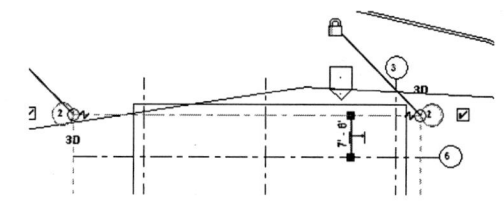

9. Place a check on both rectangles to make bubbles visible on both sides of the grid line.

4-9

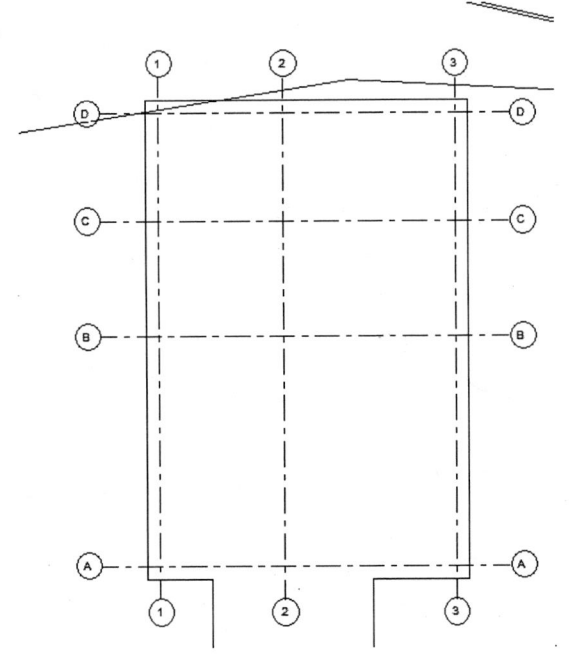

10. Label the horizontal grid lines A-D. The alpha labeled grids are incremented from bottom to top.

    Label the vertical grid lines 1-3. The number labeled grids are incremented from left to right.

    Enable the grid bubbles on both ends.

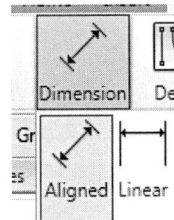

11. Activate the **Annotate** ribbon.

    Select the **ALIGNED** dimension tool from the Dimension panel.

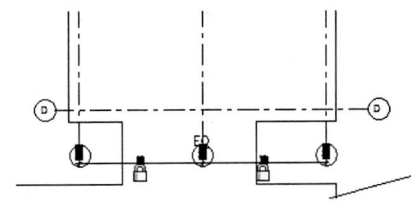

12. Place a continuous dimension between the three vertical grid lines.

    Enable the EQ toggle.

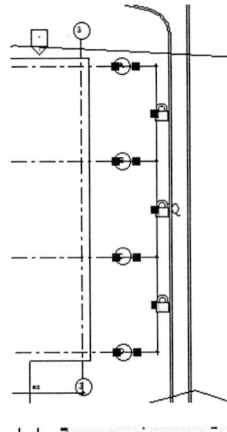

13. Place a continuous dimension between the horizontal grid lines.

    Enable the EQ toggle.

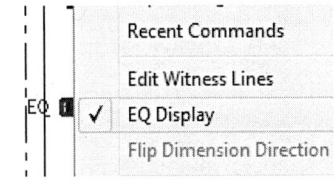

14. Select the vertical dimensions.
    Right click and toggle **EQ Display** off.

15. 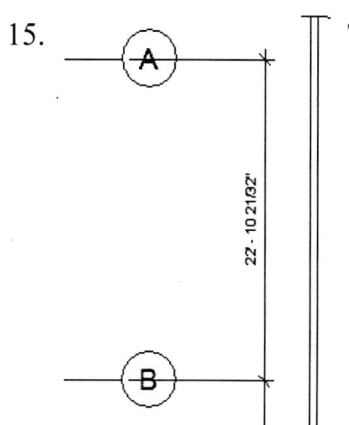 The dimension is now visible.

16. 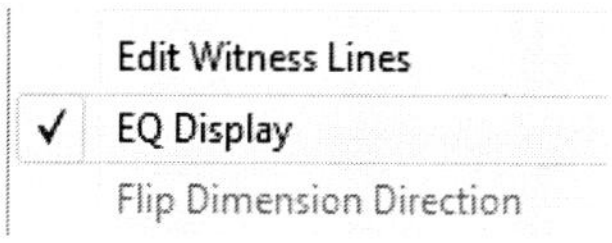 Select the horizontal dimensions.
    Right click and toggle **EQ Display** off.

17. 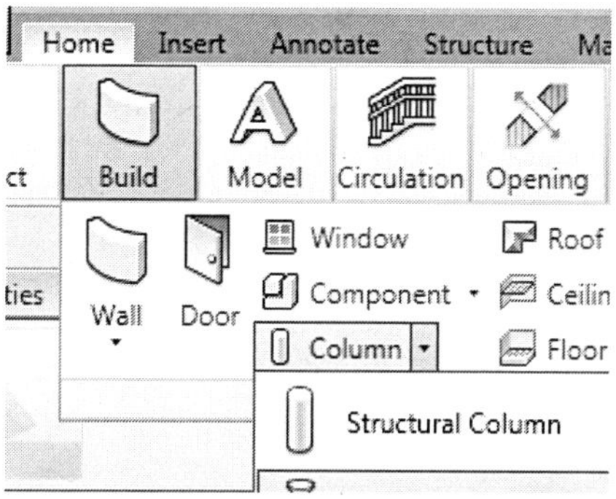 Select the **Structural Column** tool from the Build panel on Home ribbon.

18. 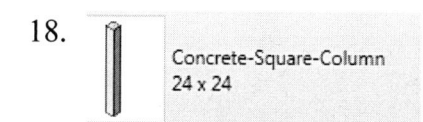 Select the **24 x 24 Concrete Square Column [600 x 600 mm]** from the Type Selector list on the Properties pane.

19. 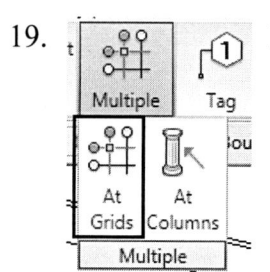 Enable the **At Grids** option to place columns at grid intersections.

4-11

20. Select each grid line.

    A column will be placed at each grid intersection.

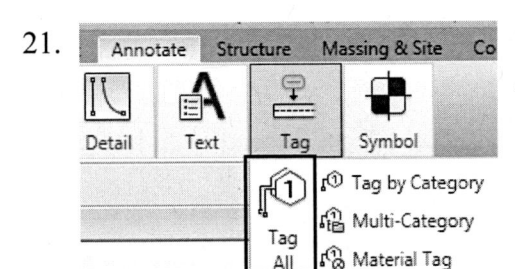

21. Select **Tag All** from the Tag panel on the Annotate ribbon.

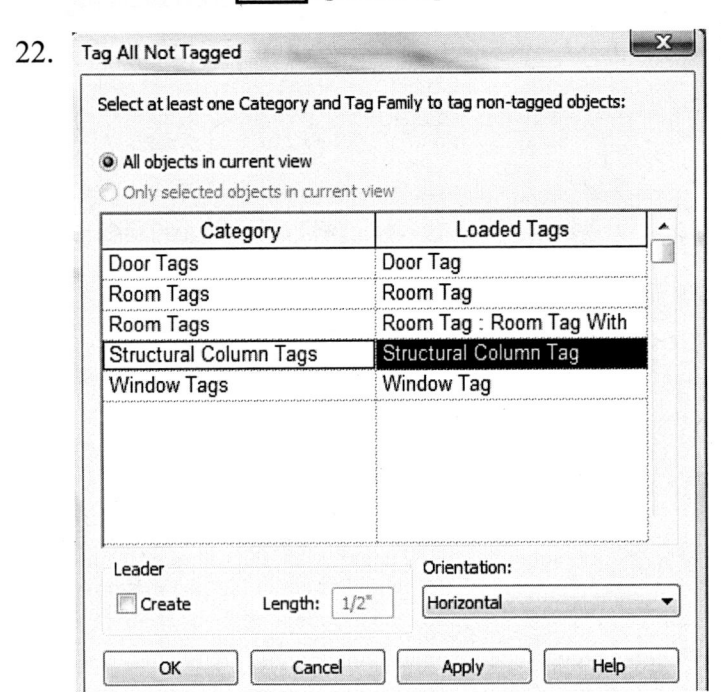

22. Highlight the **Structural Column Tag**.

    Press **OK**.

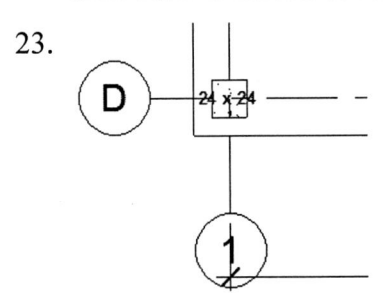

23. The column is labeled with the Column Type.

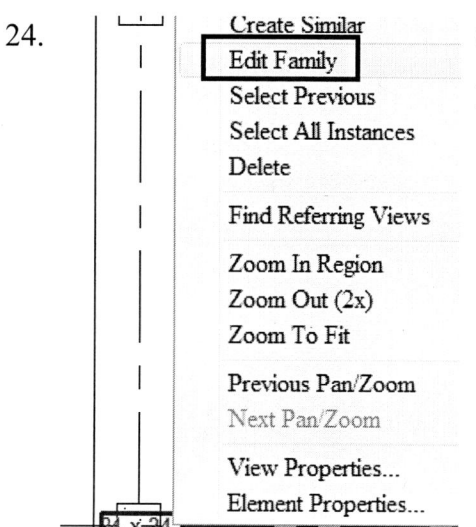

24. Select one of the structural column tags.

Right click and select **Edit Family**.

25. Go to **File→Save As→Family**.

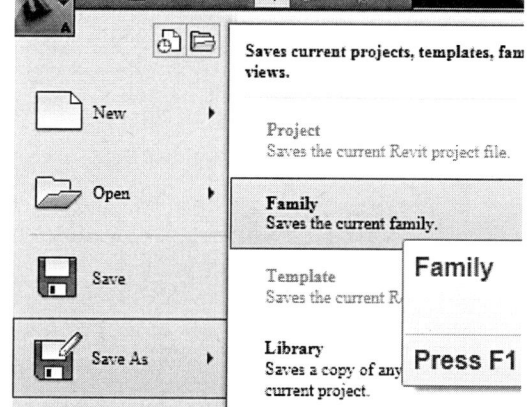

26. Rename the tag *Structural Column Location Tag.rfa*.

27. Select the text.

Select the **Edit** button in the Label field on the Properties pane.

28. Use the Add and Remove tools to remove the Column ID and add the Column Location Mark.

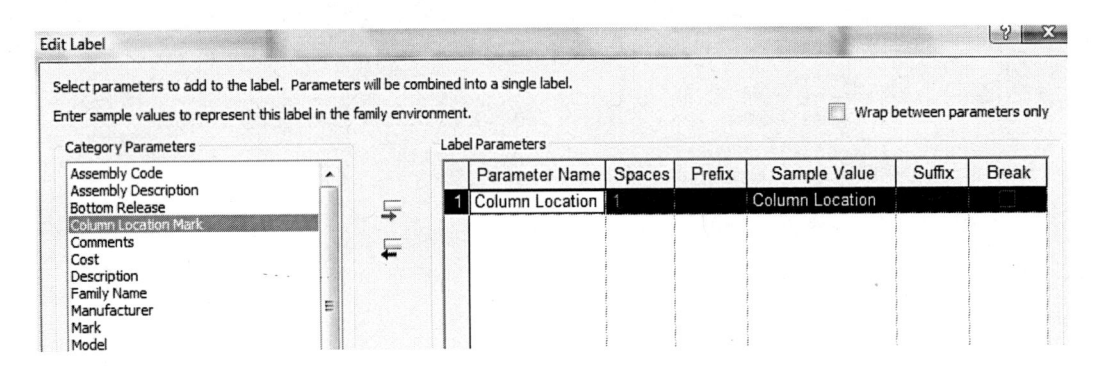

29. Press **OK**.

30. Save the file.

31. Select the **Load into Project** tool.

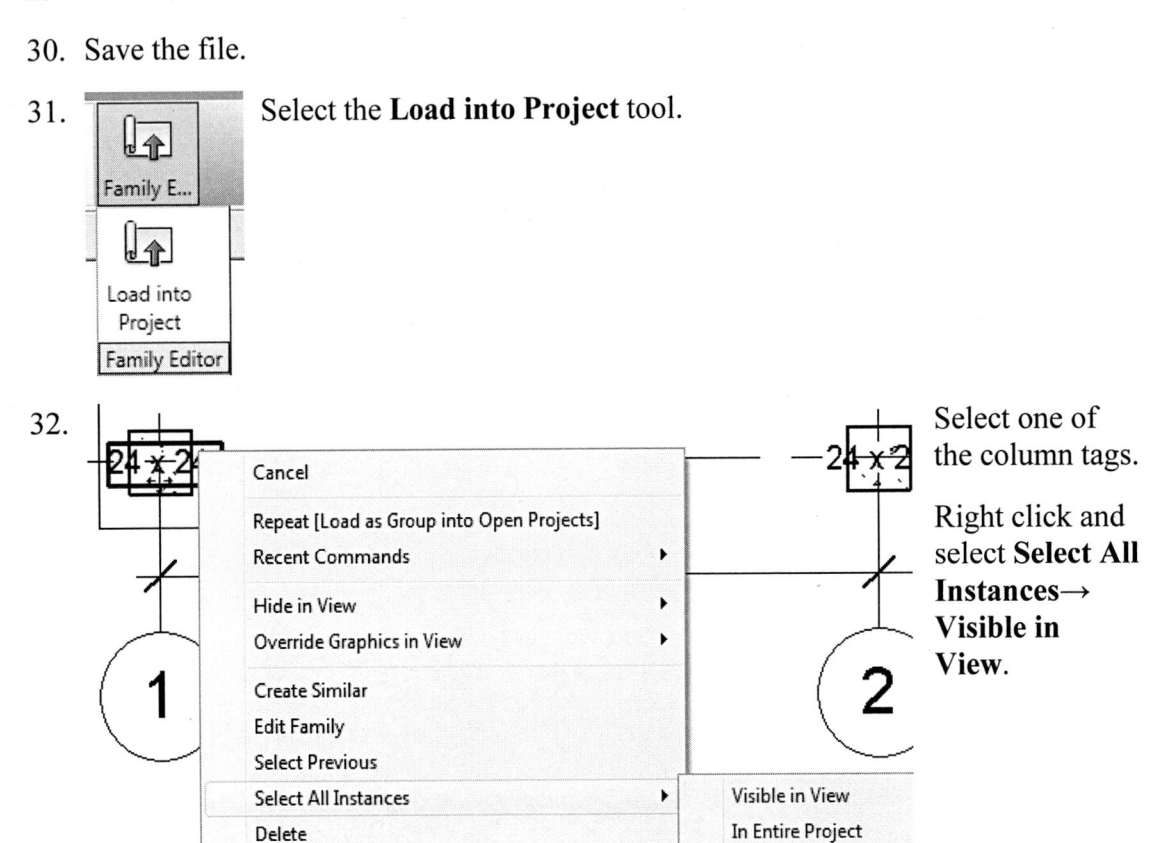

32. Select one of the column tags.

    Right click and select **Select All Instances→ Visible in View**.

33.  Select the **Structural Column Location Tag** from the Type Selector on the Properties pane.

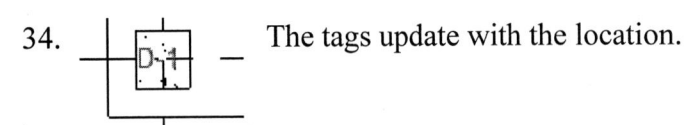

34. The tags update with the location.

35. Close without saving.

Command Exercise

Exercise 4-4 – Setting View Depth

Drawing Name: **i_firestation_basic_plan.rvt**
Estimated Time to Completion: 5 Minutes

Scope

Determine the view depth of a view

Solution

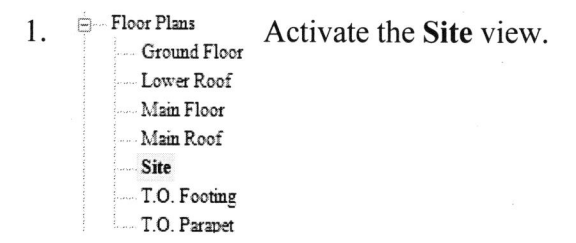

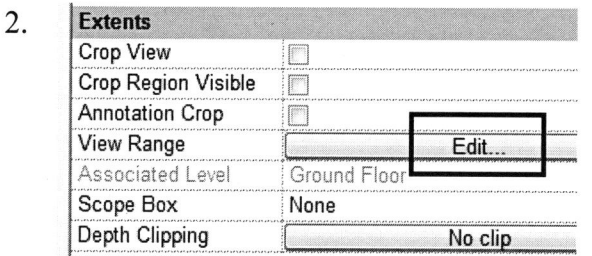

1. Activate the **Site** view.

2. In the Properties pane:

   Scroll down to **View Range**.
   Select the **Edit** button.

3. Determine the **View Depth**.

4. Press **OK**.

5. Close without saving.

The Unofficial Revit 2012 Certification Exam Guide

Command Exercise

Exercise 4-5 – Create a Cropped View

Drawing Name: **i_firestation_managing_views.rvt**
Estimated Time to Completion: 10 Minutes

Scope

Create a cropped view

Solution

1. Activate the **Main Floor – Furniture Plan** view.

2. In the Properties Pane:

    Scroll down the window and:

    Enable **Crop View**.
    Enable **Crop Region Visible**.

4. Zoom out.

    Select the viewport rectangle.

4-16

View Properties

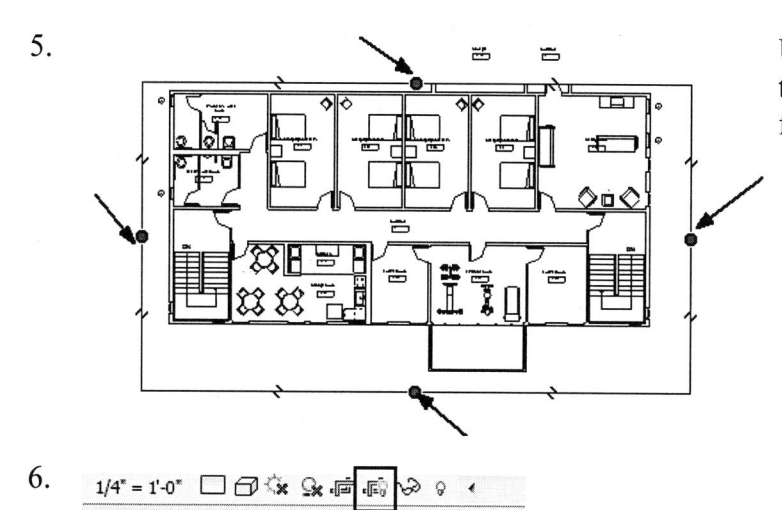

5. Use the bubbles to position the viewport so that only the furniture floor plan is visible.

6. Select **Hide Crop Region** using the tool in the View Control bar.
Press **OK**.

7. Close without saving.

The Unofficial Revit 2012 Certification Exam Guide

Command Exercise

Exercise 4-6 – Change View Display

Drawing Name: **i_firestation_managing_views.rvt**
Estimated Time to Completion: 15 Minutes

Scope

Use Temporary Hide/Isolate to control visibility of elements.
Change Line Width Display
Change Object Display Settings

Solution

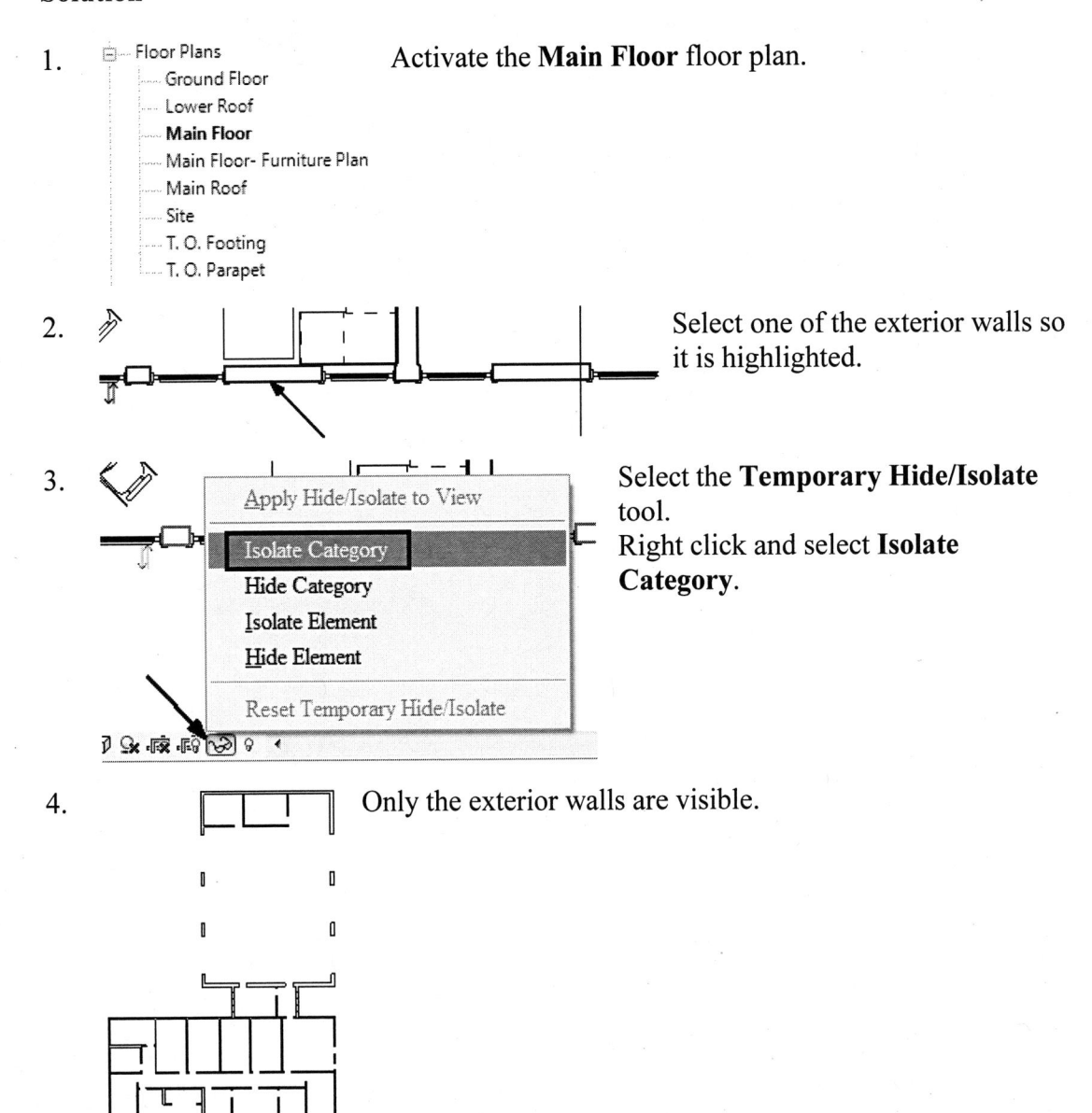

1. Activate the **Main Floor** floor plan.

2. Select one of the exterior walls so it is highlighted.

3. Select the **Temporary Hide/Isolate** tool.
   Right click and select **Isolate Category**.

4. Only the exterior walls are visible.

4-18

View Properties

5. Select the **Temporary Hide/Isolate** tool. Right click and select **Reset Temporary Hide/Isolate**.

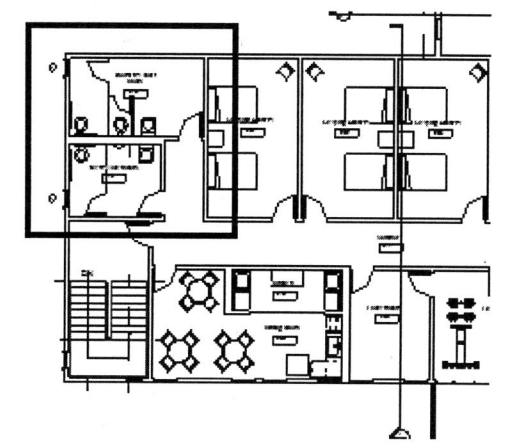

6. Zoom into the region where the lavatories are located.

7. Change the view scale to **1/8″ = 1′-0″**.

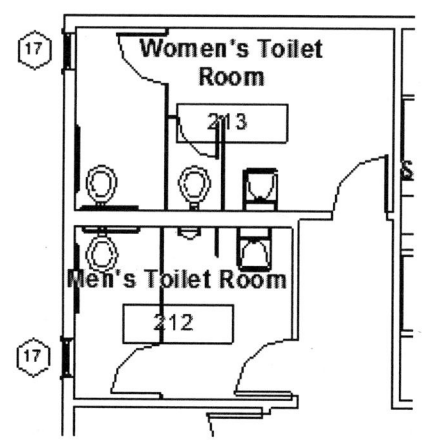

8. Note that the room tags scale to the view.

9. Activate the **Modify** ribbon.

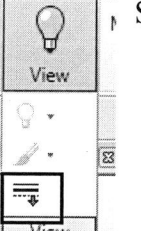

10. Select the **Linework** tool on the View panel.

11. Set the Line Style to **Overhead**.

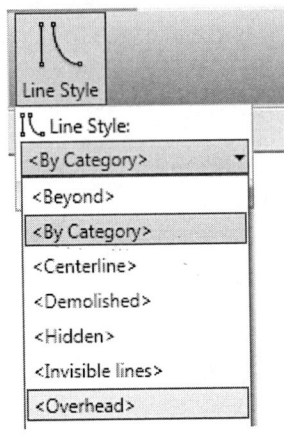

12. Select the door swing on the toilet cubicle.

13. Note that the door swing's appearance changes.

14. Activate **Section 1**.

15. Activate the Manage ribbon.

    Select **Settings→Object Styles**.

16. Expand the **Doors** category on the Model Objects tab.
    Change the Line Weight, Line Color, and Line Pattern for the Panel and Frame.
    Press **Apply** to see the changes.
    You can move the dialog over so you can see how the display is changed.

17. Close without saving.

View Properties

Command Exercise

Exercise 4-7 – Reveal Hidden Elements

Drawing Name: **i_visibility.rvt**
Estimated Time to Completion: 5 Minutes

Scope

Turn on the display of hidden elements

Solution

1. Activate **the Ground Floor Admin Wing** floor plan.

   Floor Plans
   - Ground Floor
   - **Ground Floor Admin Wing**
   - Lower Roof
   - Main Floor
   - Main Roof

2. Select the **Reveal Hidden Elements** tool.

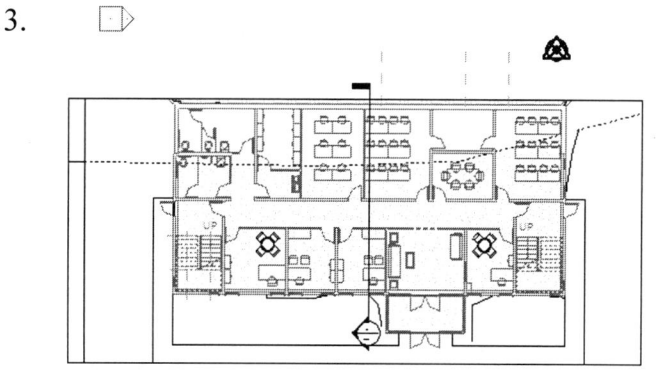

3. Items highlighted in magenta are hidden.

   Window around the two tables while holding down the CONTROL key to select them.

4. Select **Unhide element** from the ribbon.

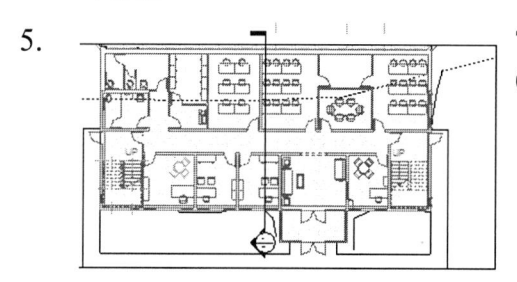

5. The tables will no longer be displayed as magenta (hidden elements).

6. Select the **Close Hidden Elements** tool.

7. The view will be restored.

8. Close without saving.

4-21

Command Exercise

Exercise 4-8 – Create a View Template

Drawing Name: **i_view_templates.rvt**
Estimated Time to Completion: 30 Minutes

Scope

Create a view template
Apply view settings to a view

Solution

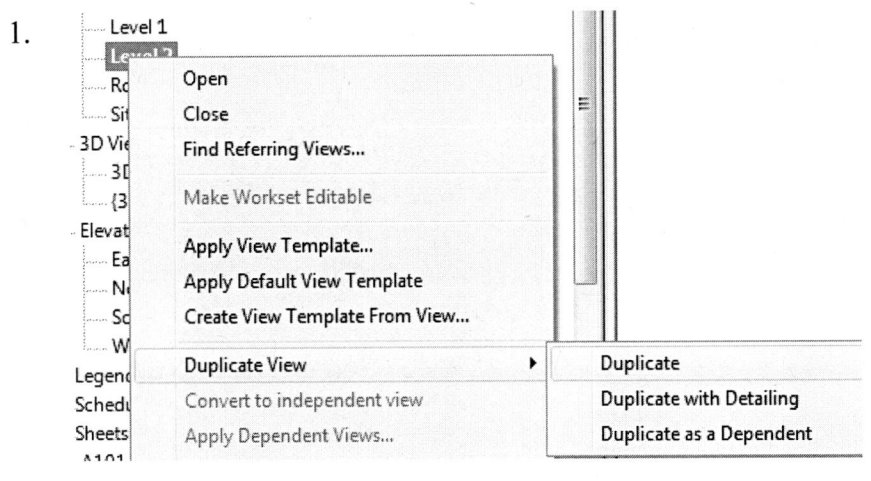

1. Highlight **Level 2** in the Project browser. Right click and select **Duplicate View→Duplicate**.

2. Rename the Copy of Level 2 to **Level 2 Furniture**.

3. Activate the **Level 2 Furniture**.

   In the Properties pane:

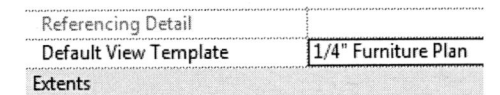

   Set the Default View Template to **1/4" Furniture Plan**.

   Compare the Copy of Level 2 view with the Level 2 view.

4. Use the Tile tool on the View window to display a window with the Level 2 view and a window with the Level 2 Furniture view.

This way you can compare the two views side by side.

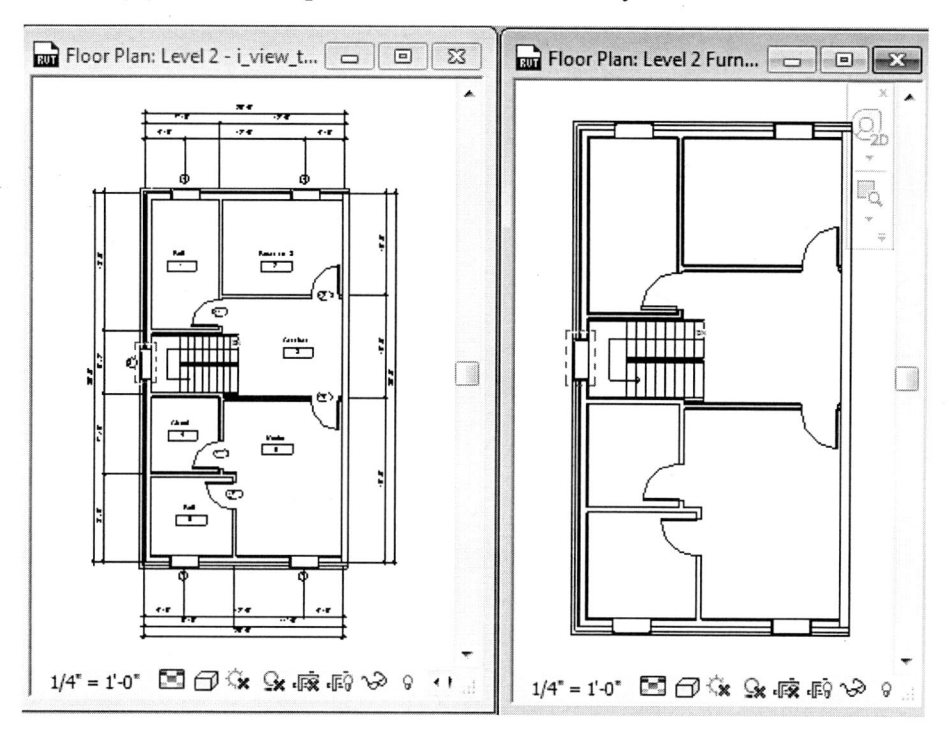

5. Click in the window with the Level 2 view.
   In the Properties pane:

   | Referencing Detail | 3 |
   | Default View Template | 1/4" Architectural Plan |

   Scroll down and you will see that the Default View template is set to 1/4" Architectural Plan.

6. 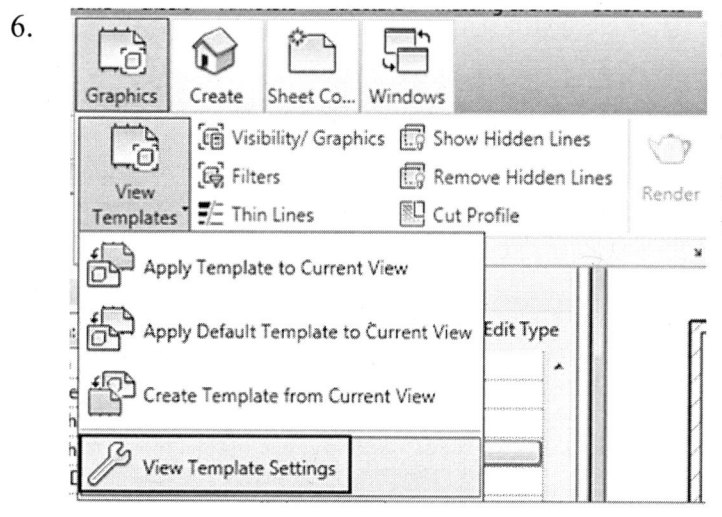 Click in the window with the Level 2 Furniture view.

   Activate the View ribbon.

   Select **View Template Settings** under the Graphics panel.

7. 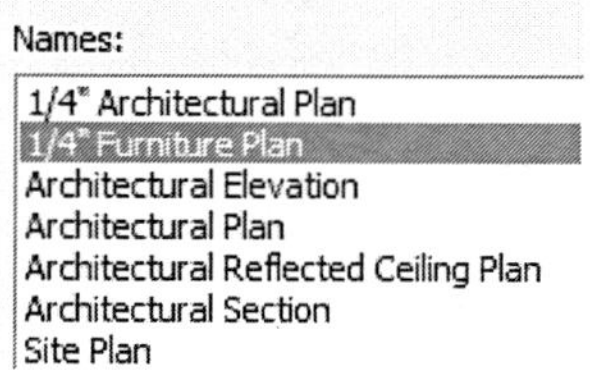 Highlight the **1/4" Furniture Plan** view template.

4-23

8. Select **Edit** in the V/G Overrides Annotation field.

9. Disable Plan Region.

   Press **OK**.

   Press **Apply**.

   Press **OK** to close the dialog.

10. Click on **Reveal Hidden Elements**.

11. Select the corner sink.

12. Right click and select **Unhide in View → Category**.

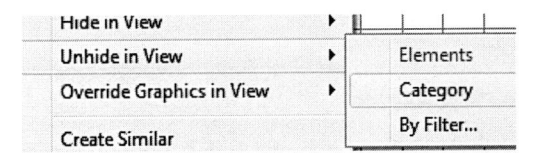

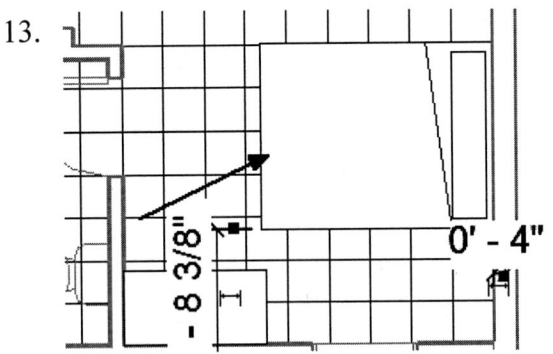

13. Select the bed.

14. Right click and select **Unhide in View → Category**.

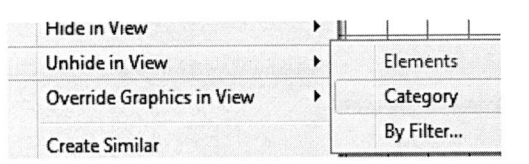

15. Close **Reveal Hidden Elements**

View Properties

16. Compare the two views.

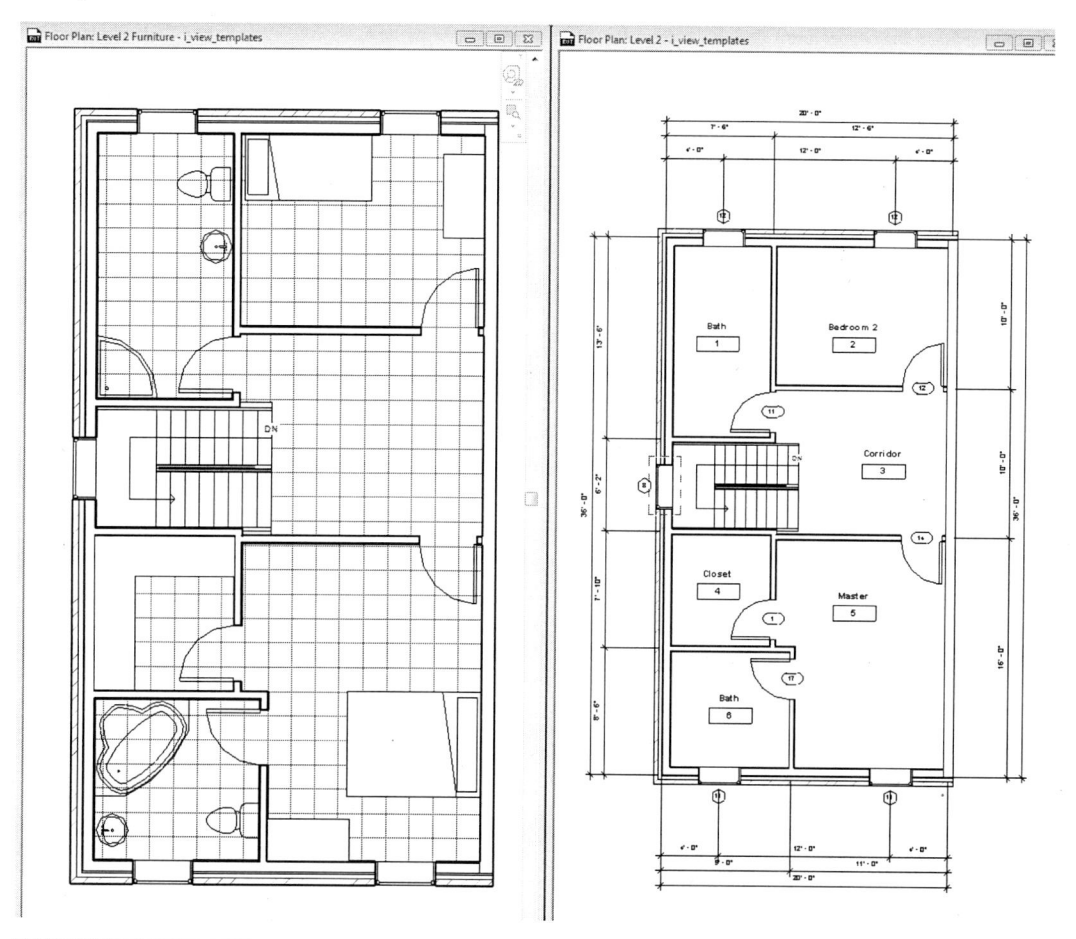

17. Click in the window with the Level 2 Furniture view.

   Activate the View ribbon.

   Select **View Template Settings** under the Graphics panel.

18. Highlight the **1/4″ Furniture Plan** view template.

4-25

19. Select **Edit** in the V/G Overrides Model field.

20. Select **Object Styles**.

21. Expand the **Furniture** category.

22. Select **New** under Modify Subcategories.

23. Type **Bedroom**.

    Assign it as a subcategory of Furniture.

    Press **OK**.

24. You see Bedroom listed under Furniture.

25. Expand the **Plumbing Fixtures** category.

26. Select **New** under Modify Subcategories.

27. Type **Toilet**.

    Assign it as a subcategory of **Plumbing Fixtures**.

    Press **OK**.

28. Select **New** under Modify Subcategories.

29. Type **Sink**.

    Assign it as a subcategory of **Plumbing Fixtures**.

    Press **OK**.

4-26

View Properties

30. The new subcategories are displayed in the object settings dialog.

31. Press **OK** to close all dialogs.

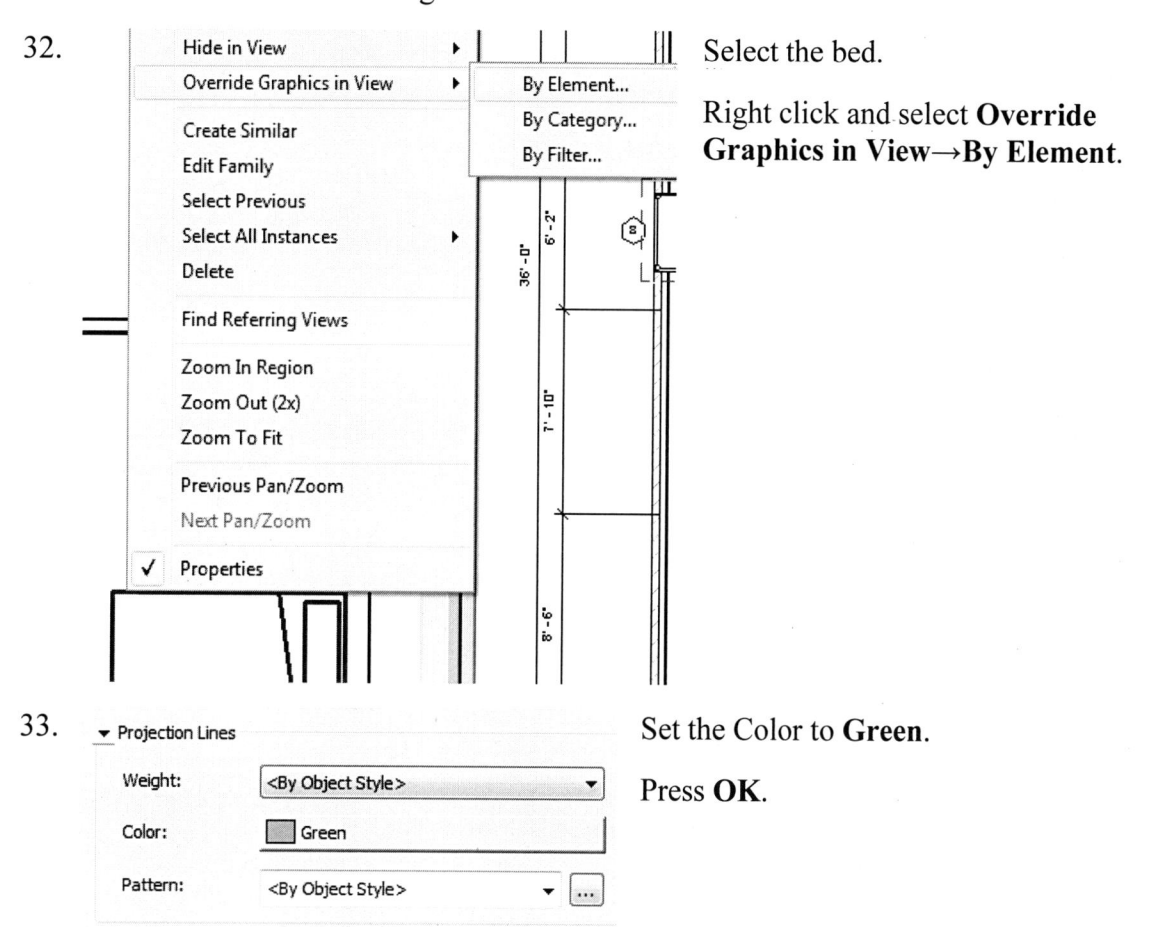

32. Select the bed.

    Right click and select **Override Graphics in View→By Element**.

33. Set the Color to **Green**.

    Press **OK**.

34. Close the file without saving.

4-27

The Unofficial Revit 2012 Certification Exam Guide

Command Exercise

Exercise 4-9 – Create a Scope Box

Drawing Name: **i_scope_box.rvt**
Estimated Time to Completion: 5 Minutes

Scope

Create and apply a scope box.
Scope boxes are used to control the visibility of grid lines and levels in views.

Solution

1. Activate the **Level 1** floor plan.

2. Activate the **Home** ribbon.

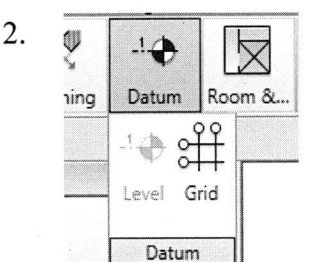

   Select the **Grid** tool from the Datum panel.

3. Set the Offset to **2′ 0″** on the Options bar.

4. Select the **Pick Lines** tool from the Draw panel.

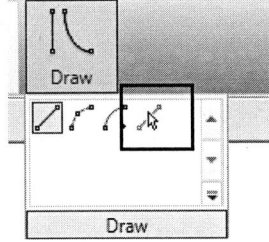

4-28

View Properties

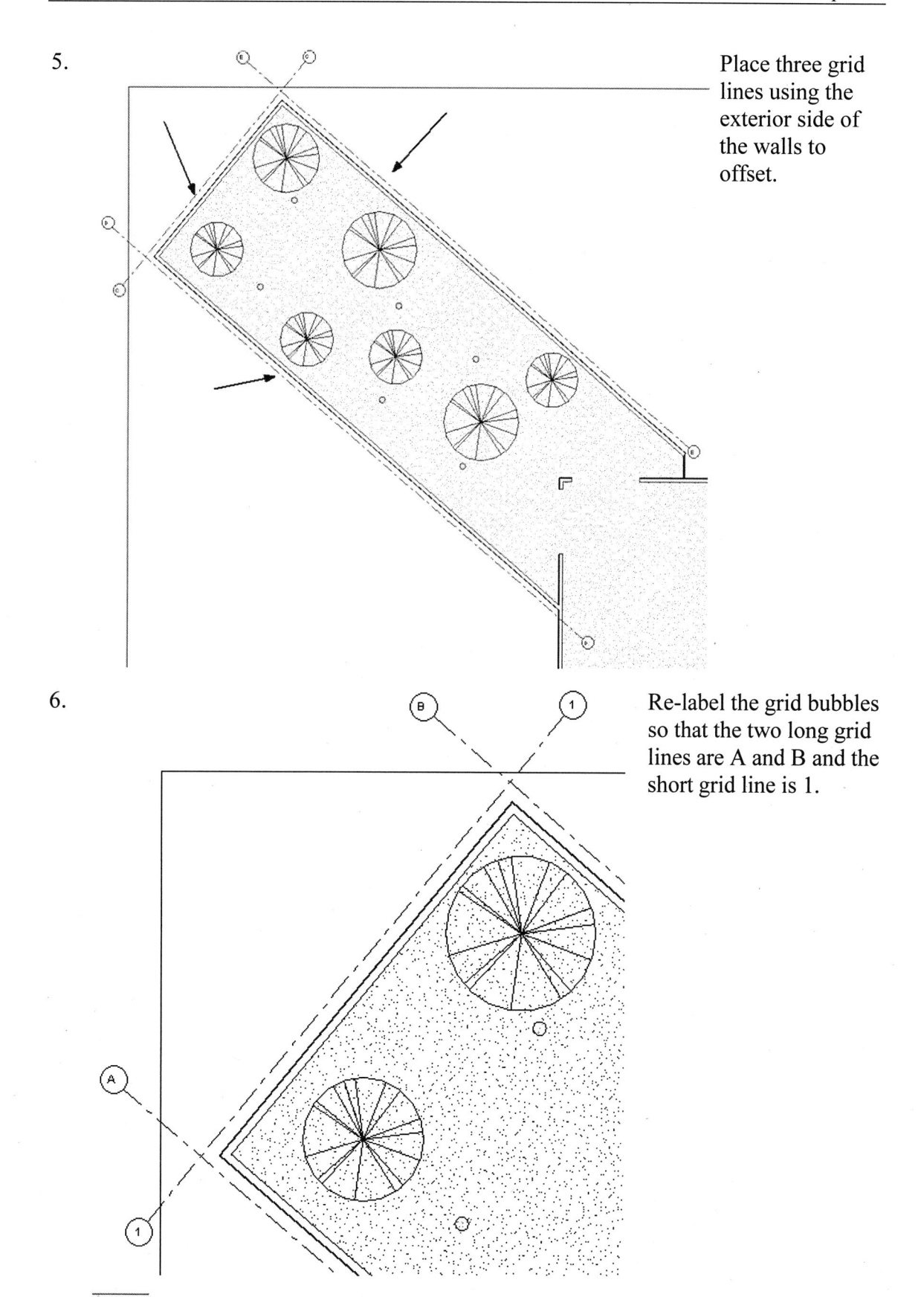

5. Place three grid lines using the exterior side of the walls to offset.

6. Re-label the grid bubbles so that the two long grid lines are A and B and the short grid line is 1.

7. Select the **Measure** tool from the Quick Access toolbar.

4-29

8. Measure one side of the yard area.

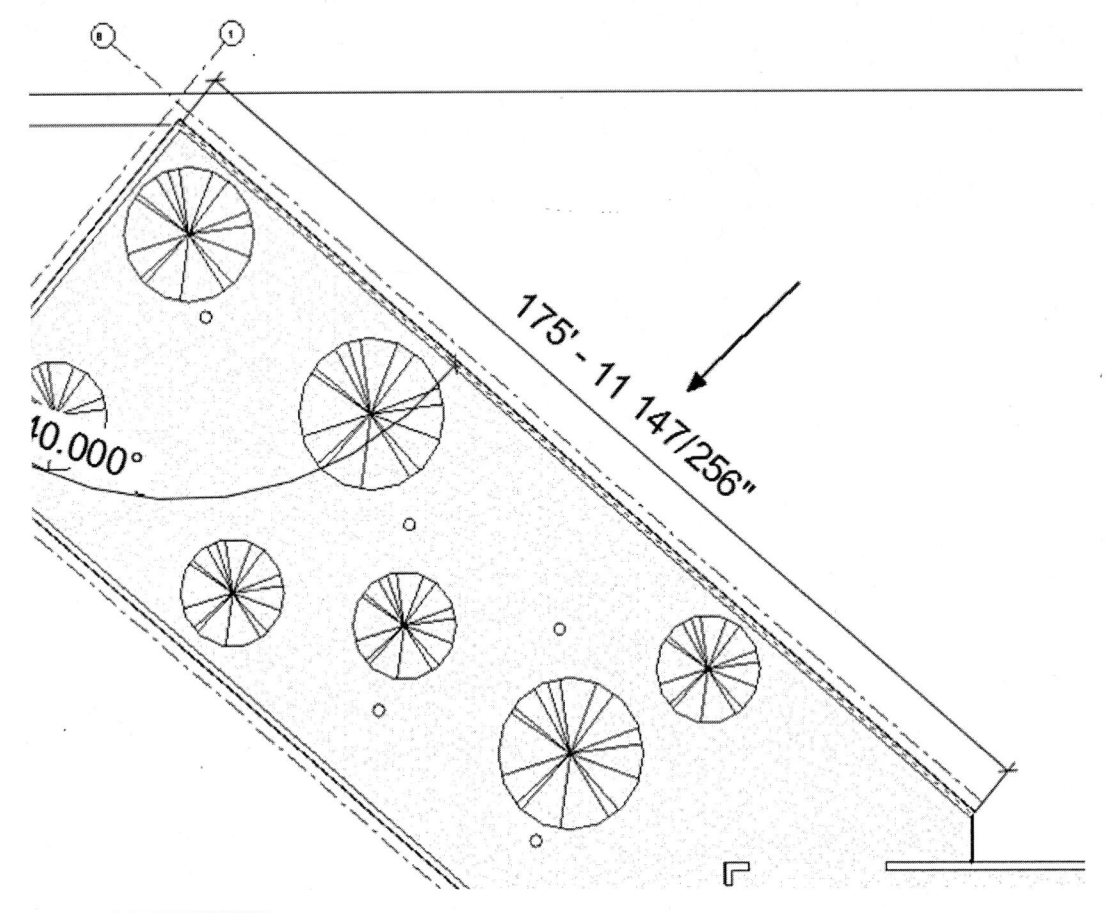

9. Activate the **Home** ribbon.

   Select the **Grid** tool from the Datum panel.

10. Set the Offset to **180′ 0″** on the Options bar.

11. Select the **Pick Lines** tool from the Draw panel.

View Properties

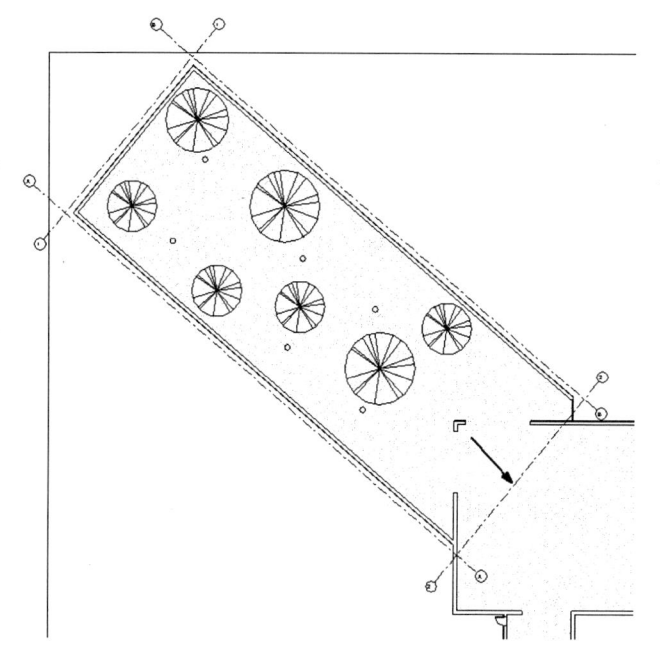

12. Place the lower grid line by selecting the upper wall and offsetting 180′.

Re-label the grid line **2**.

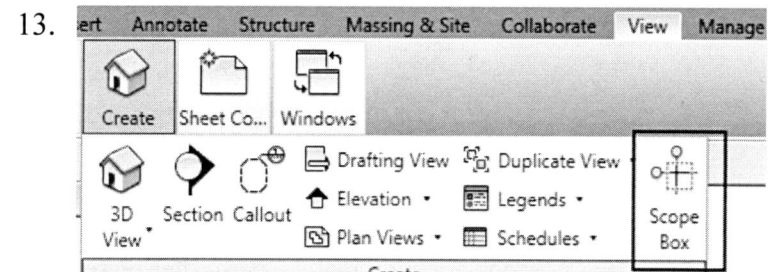

13. Activate the **View** ribbon.

Select the **Scope Box** tool from the Create panel.

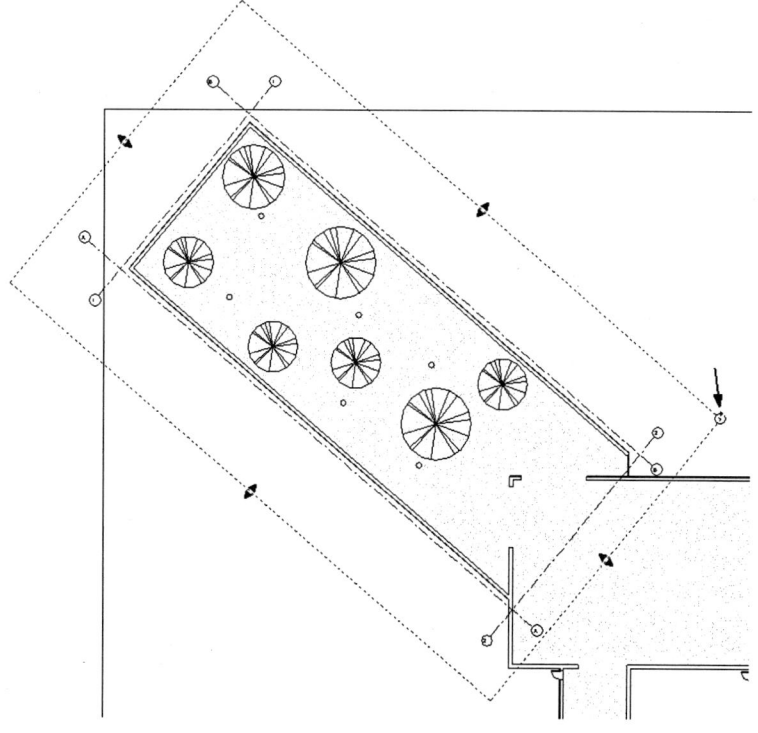

14. Place the scope box.

Use the Rotate icon on the corner to rotate the scope box into position.

Use the blue grips to control the size of the scope box.

4-31

15. Select the grid line labeled **B**.

16. In the Properties pane:

    Set the Scope Box to Scope Box 1, the scope box which was just placed.

17. Repeat for the other three grid lines.

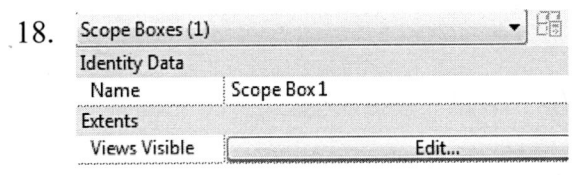

18. Select the Scope Box.

    Select **Edit** next to Views Visible in the Properties pane.

19.
Elevation	Elevation 1 - a	Invisible	None
Floor Plan	Level 1	Visible	None
Floor Plan	Level 2	Visible	Invisible
Floor Plan	Site	Visible	None
Floor Plan	Level 3	Visible	None

    Set the Level 2 Floor Plan Override Invisible.

    Press **OK**.

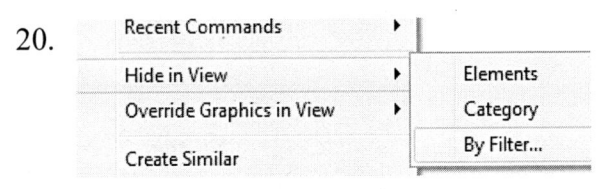

20. Select the scope box.

    Right click and select **Hide in View → Elements**.

    The scope box is no longer visible in the view.

21. Activate Level 2.

    The grid lines and scope box are not visible.

22. Close the file without saving.

4-32

Practice Associate Exam

1. Straight grid lines are visible in the following view types:
   A. ELEVATION
   B. PLAN
   C. 3D
   D. SECTION
   E. DETAIL

2. Which two shortcut keys launch the Visibility/Graphics dialog?
   A. VG
   B. VV
   C. VE
   D. VW
   E. F5

3. True or False: Objects hidden using the Temporary Hide/Isolate tool are not visible, but they are still printed.

4. Select the THREE options for Detail Level for a view:
   A. COARSE
   B. SHADED
   C. FINE
   D. HIDDEN
   E. WIREFRAME
   F. MEDIUM

5. True or False: If you delete a view, the annotations placed in the view are also deleted.

6. True or False: A camera can not be placed in an elevation view.

7. Scope boxes control the visibility of:
   A. Elements
   B. Plumbing Fixtures
   C. Object Styles
   D. Grid lines and levels

8. To change the graphic appearance of your model from Hidden Line to Realistic, you:
   A. Modify the Rendering Settings in the View Control Bar
   B. Edit Visibility/Graphics Overrides
   C. Change graphic display options in View Properties
   D. Click Visual Styles on the View Control Bar

9. A story level is the color:
    A. Yellow
    B. Blue
    C. Black
    D. Green

10. If you create a level using the COPY or ARRAY tool, what type of level is created?
    A. Story
    B. Non-Story or Reference
    C. Elevation
    D. Plan

11. This type of level does not have a PLAN view associated to it:
    A. Story
    B. Non-Story or Reference
    C. Elevation
    D. Plan

12. In which view type can you place a level?
    A. PLAN
    B. LEGEND
    C. 3D
    D. CONSTRUCTION
    E. ELEVATION

Answers:
1) A, B & D; 2) A & B; 3) True; 4) A, C & F; 5) True; 6) False; 7) D; 8) D; 9) C; 10) B; 11) A; 12) E

Lesson Five

Dimensions and Constraints

This lesson addresses the following Associate and Professional exam questions:

- Constraints
- Temporary and Permanent Dimensions

Dimensions are system families. They are in the Annotation category. They have type and instance properties.

Revit has two types of dimensions: temporary and permanent.

A temporary dimension is displayed when an element is placed or selected. In order to modify a temporary dimension, you must select the element. Listening dimensions are temporary dimensions that appear when elements are being added and positioned.

A permanent dimension is placed using the Dimension tool. In order to modify a permanent dimension, you must move the element to a new position. The permanent dimension will automatically update. To reposition an element, you can modify the temporary dimension or move the element using listening dimensions.

When you enter dimension values using feet and inches, you do not have to enter the units. You can separate the feet and inches values with a space and Revit will fill in the units. If a single unit is entered, for example '10', Revit assumes that value is 10 feet, not 10 inches.

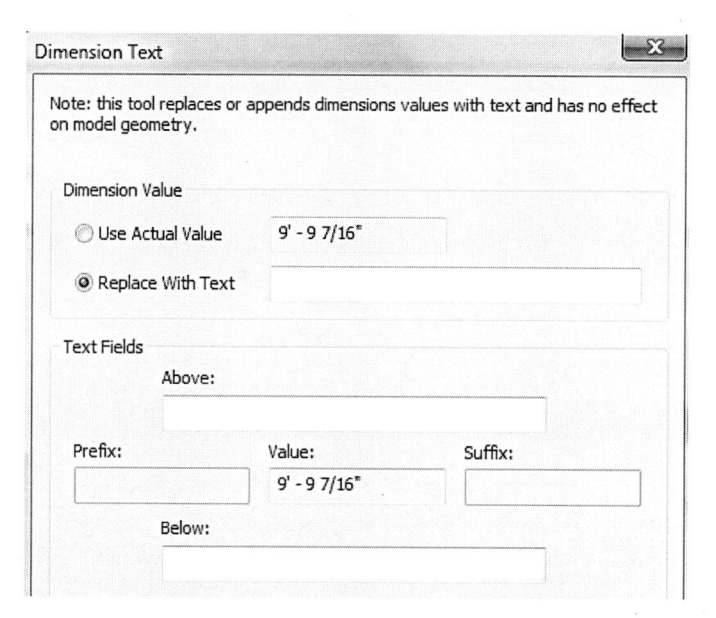

To override a dimension value, select the permanent dimension and enable Replace with Text and put in the desired text.

You can also add additional notes using the Text Fields for Above, Prefix, Suffix, or Below.

The Unofficial Revit 2012 Certification Exam Guide

Command Exercise

Exercise 5-1 – Placing Permanent Dimensions

Drawing Name: **i_dimensions.rvt**
Estimated Time to Completion: 20 Minutes

Scope

Placing dimensions

Solution

1. Activate the **Ground Floor Admin Wing** floor plan.

   Floor Plans
   — Ground Floor
   — **Ground Floor Admin Wing**
   — Lower Roof
   — Main Floor
   — Main Floor Admin Wing
   — Main Roof

2. Activate the Modify ribbon.

   Select the **Match Properties** tool from the Clipboard panel.

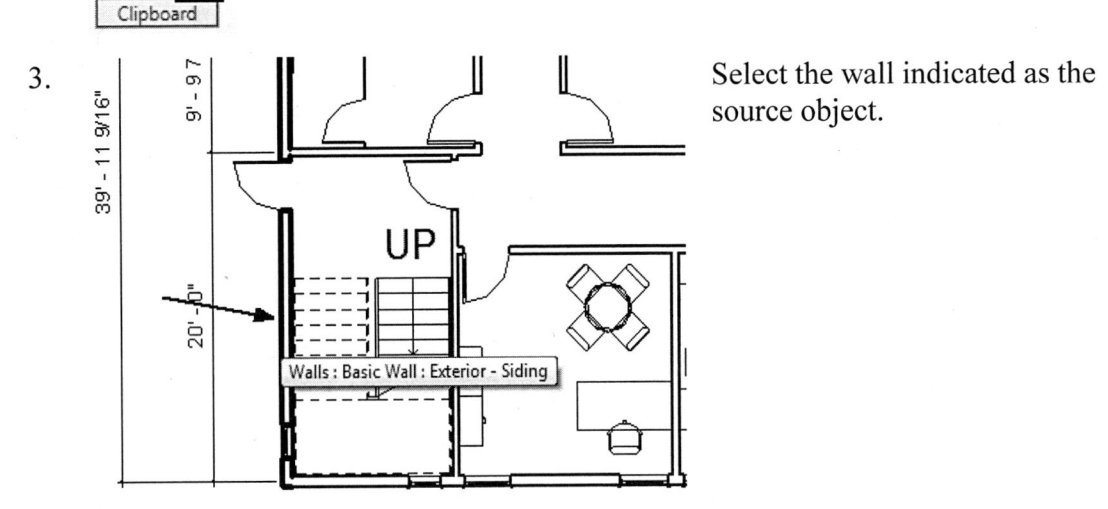

3. Select the wall indicated as the source object.

4. Select the wall indicated as the target object.

Dimensions and Constraints

5. 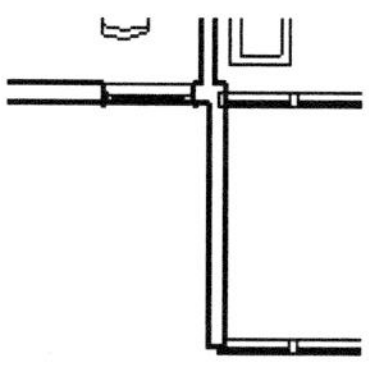 Note that the curtain wall changed to an Exterior-Siding wall.

6. 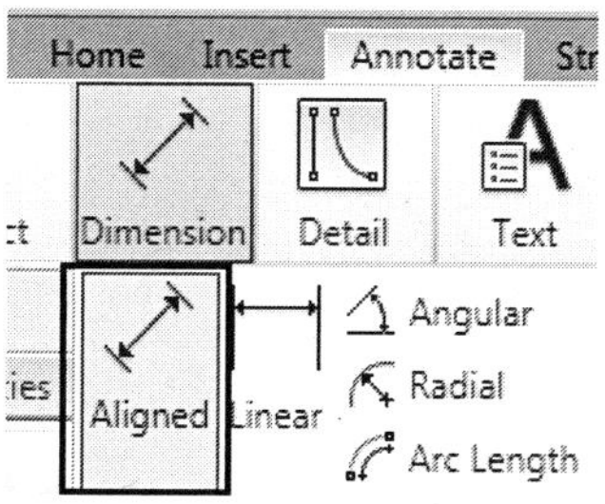 Activate the Annotate ribbon.

   Select the **Aligned Dimension** tool.

7. 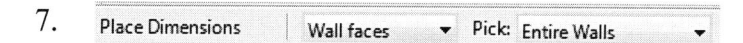 On the Options bar, set the dimensions to select the **Wall faces**.

8. On the Options bar, set the dimensions to **Pick Entire Walls**.

9. Pick the wall indicated.

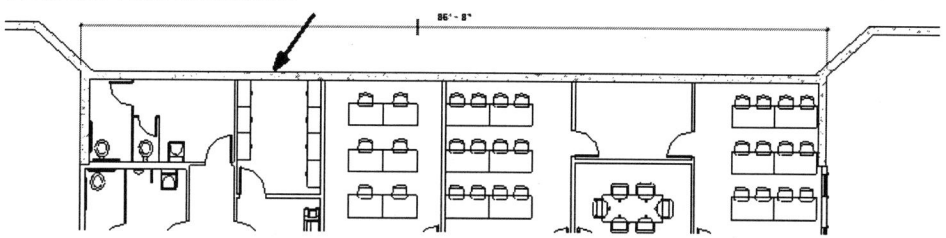

   Move the mouse above the selected wall to place the dimension.

10. Note the entire wall is selected and the dimensions are located at the faces of the walls.
    Cancel or escape to end the Dimension command.

11. Select the dimension.

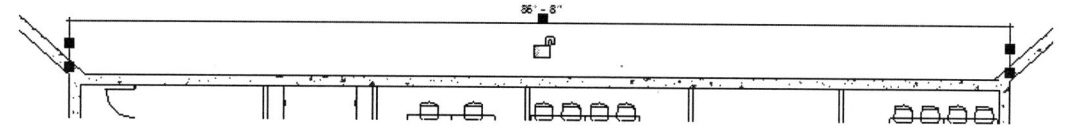

    Note that there are several grips available.

12. Select the second grip indicated on the left.

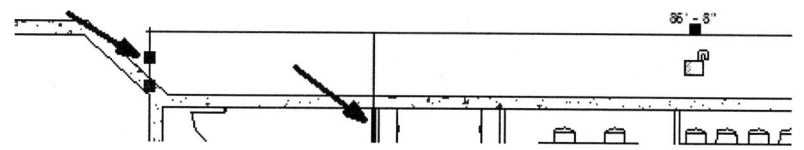

    Move the witness line to the wall face indicated by the arrow in the center of the image.

13. Note that the witness line automatically snaps to the wall face.

5-3

14. On the Options bar, change the Prefer to **Wall centerlines**.

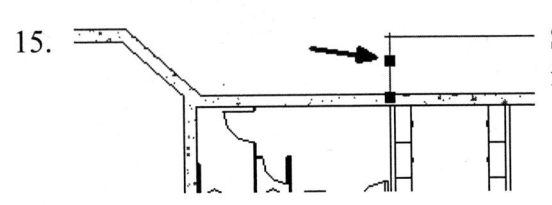

15. Select the dimension and activate the grip indicated.

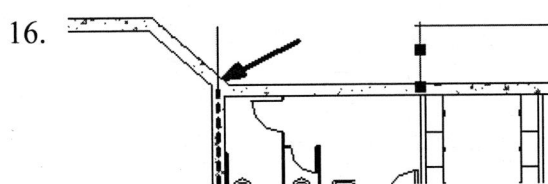

16. Drag the witness line to the center of the left wall.

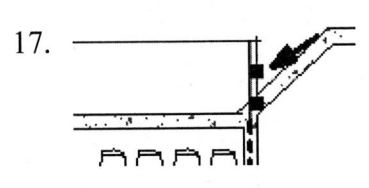

17. Use the grip on the right side of the dimension to shift the witness line to the wall centerline.

18. 85'-8" Note how the dimension value updates.

19. Select the **Aligned** tool.

20. Set Pick to Individual References on the options bar.

21. Select the centerlines of the walls indicated.

Dimensions and Constraints

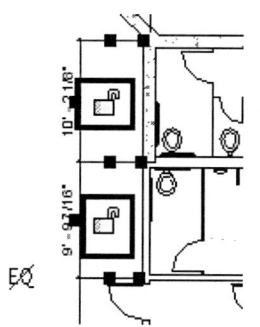

22. Select the two locks to switch the permanent dimensions to *locked* dimensions. This means these distances will not be changed.

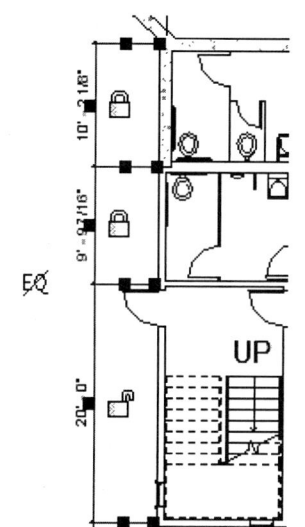

23. You should see two of the padlocks as closed and one as open.

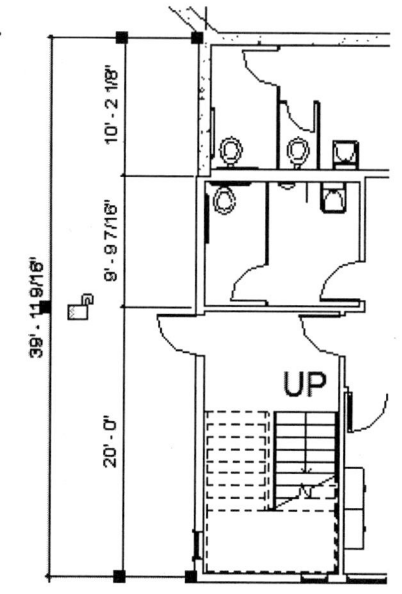

24. Place an overall dimension using the wall centerlines.

5-5

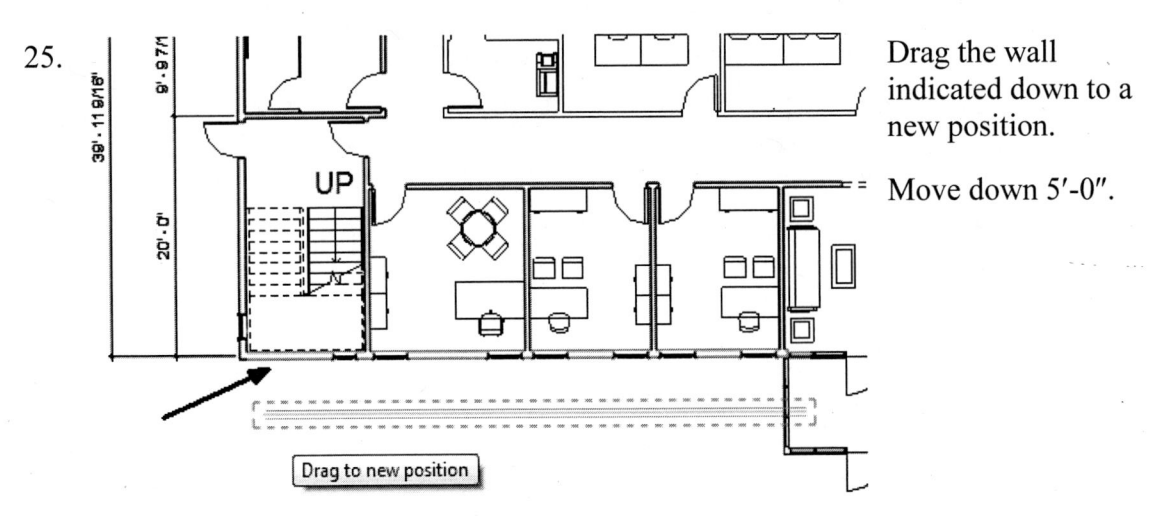

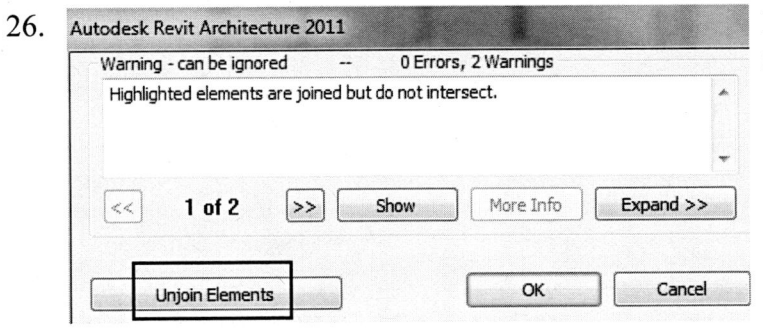

25. Drag the wall indicated down to a new position.

Move down 5'-0".

26. If you get an error message, select **Unjoin Elements**.

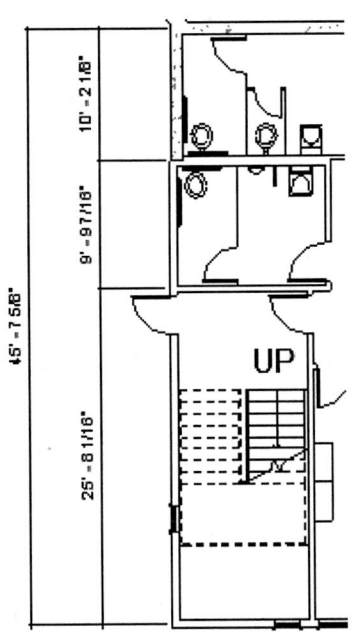

Note that the two locked dimensions did not change. Only the unlocked dimension updated.

27. Close without saving.

Command Exercise

Exercise 5-2 – Modifying Dimension Text

Drawing Name: **dimtext.rvt**
Estimated Time to Completion: 15 Minutes

Scope

Replace Dimension Text
Restore DimensionText
Modify DimensionText

Solution

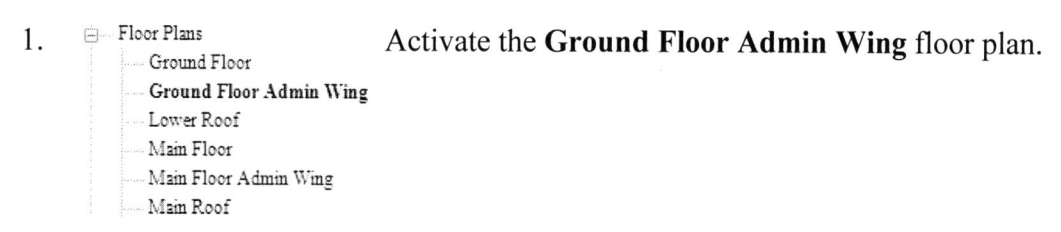

1. Activate the **Ground Floor Admin Wing** floor plan.

2. 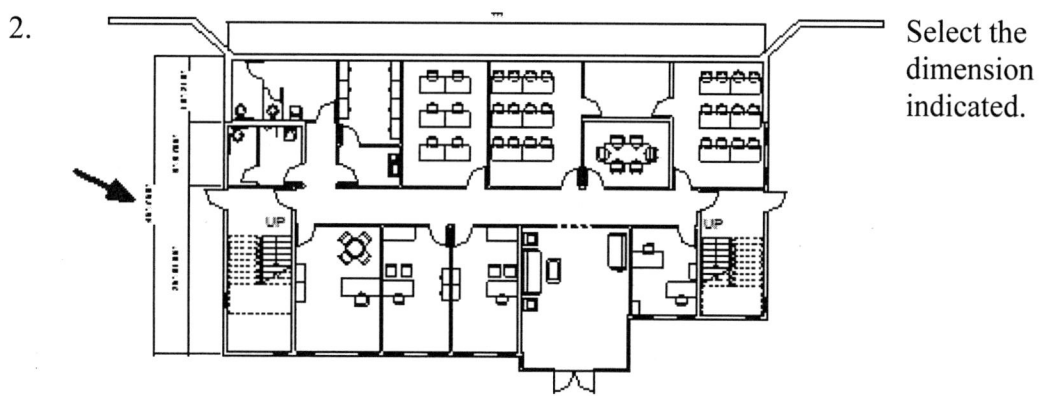 Select the dimension indicated.

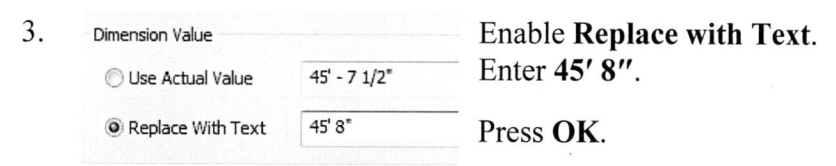

3. Enable **Replace with Text**.
   Enter **45' 8"**.
   Press **OK**.

4. 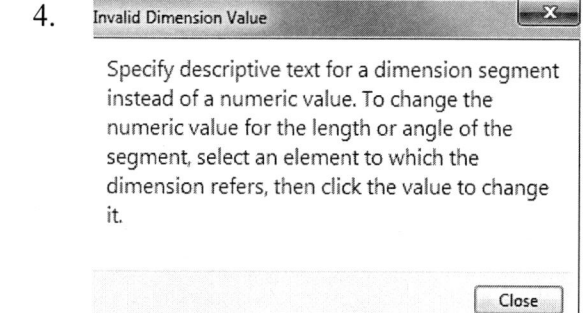 You will get an error message stating that you cannot change the numeric value without moving the element to correspond with that value.

   Press **Close**

5-7

5. Enable **Replace with Text**.
Enter **OVERALL**.

Press **OK**.

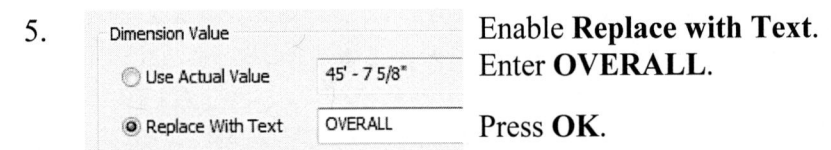

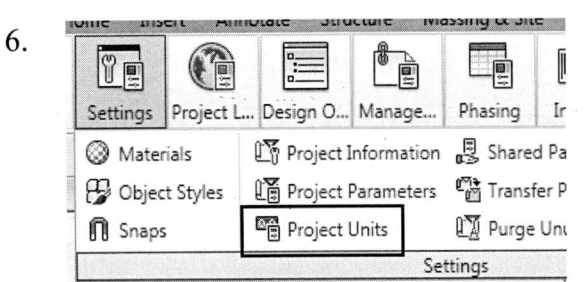

6. Activate the **Manage** ribbon.

Select **Project Units** on the Settings panel.

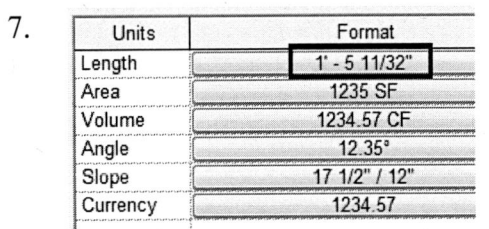

7. Select the **Length** button under the Format column.

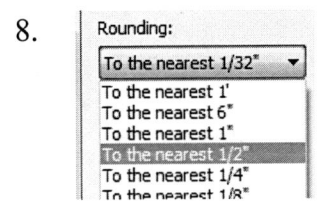

8. Set the Rounding **To the nearest ½″**.

Press **OK** until all dialogs are closed.

9. Note that the dimensions update to the new rounding.

Dimensions and Constraints

10. Select the 10' 2" dimension to be edited.

11. In the Below field, type: **WOMEN'S LAVATORY**.

    Press **OK**.

12. Note how the dimension updates.

13. Select the dimension with **???**.

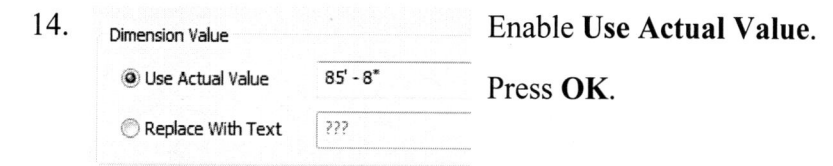

14. Enable **Use Actual Value**.

    Press **OK**.

15. Close without saving.

Command Exercise

Exercise 5-3 – Converting Temporary Dimensions to Permanent Dimensions

Drawing Name: **i_dimensions.rvt**
Estimated Time to Completion: 10 Minutes

Scope

Place dimensions using different options.
Convert temporary dimension to permanent

Solution

1. 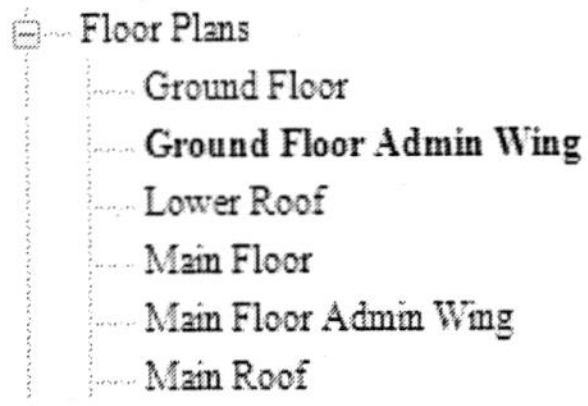 Activate the **Ground Floor Admin Wing** floor plan.

2. 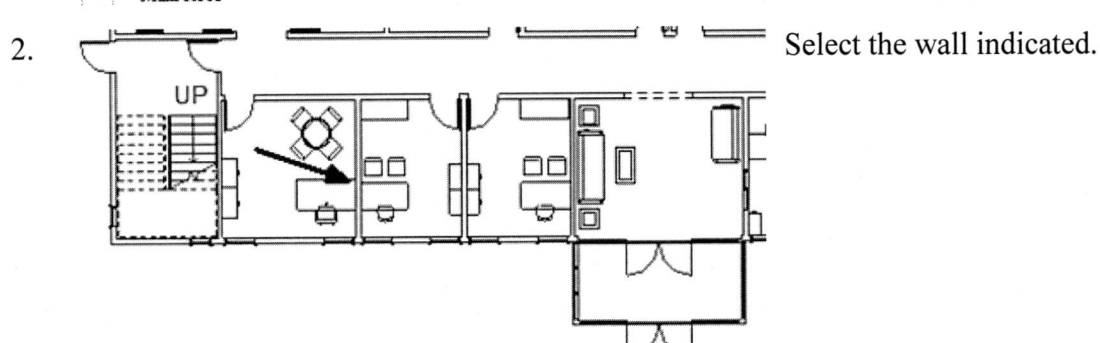 Select the wall indicated.

3. 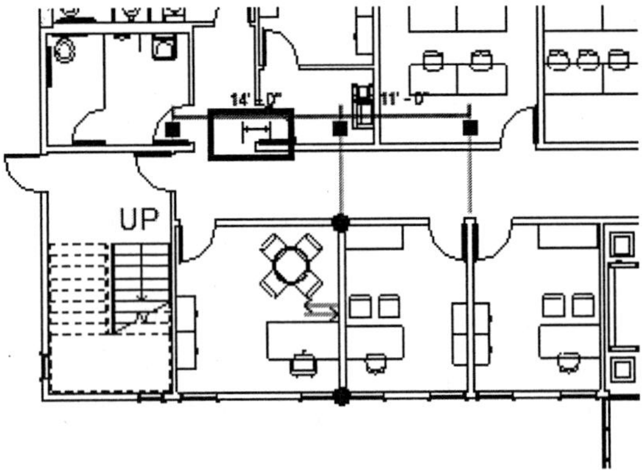 Two dimensions will appear.

   There is a small dimension icon visible.

   This icon converts a temporary dimension to a permanent dimension.

   Left click on this icon.

Dimensions and Constraints

4. The dimensions are now converted to permanent dimensions.

   Drag the dimensions below the view.

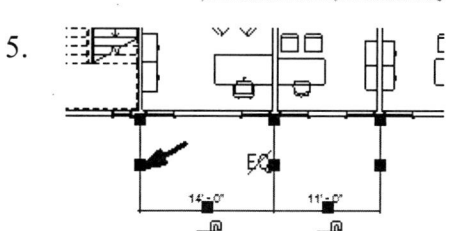

5. Click on the dimensions so they highlight.

   Click on the witness line grip indicated.

6. Notice how each time the grip is clicked on, the witness line shifts from the wall centerline to the face of the wall.

7. Select the grip at the endpoint of the witness line. Drag the endpoint to increase the gap between the wall and the witness line.

   Release the grip.

8. Select the witness line grip indicated.

   Drag the witness line to the outer wall. Note that if the witness line is set to the outer wall face it maintains that orientation.

   Release.

   The dimension updates.

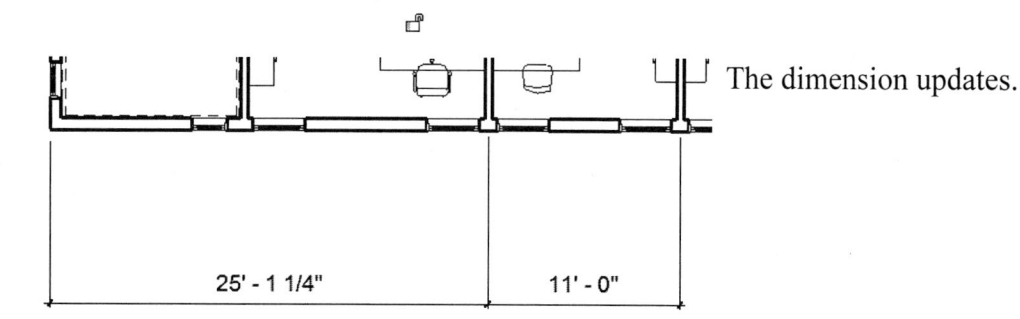

9. Close without saving.

5-11

Command Exercise

Exercise 5-4 – Applying Constraints

Drawing Name: **i_constraints.rvt**
Estimated Time to Completion: 20 Minutes

Scope

Using the Align tool to constrain elements

Solution

1. Activate the **Main Floor** floor plan.

2. Select the interior wall indicated.

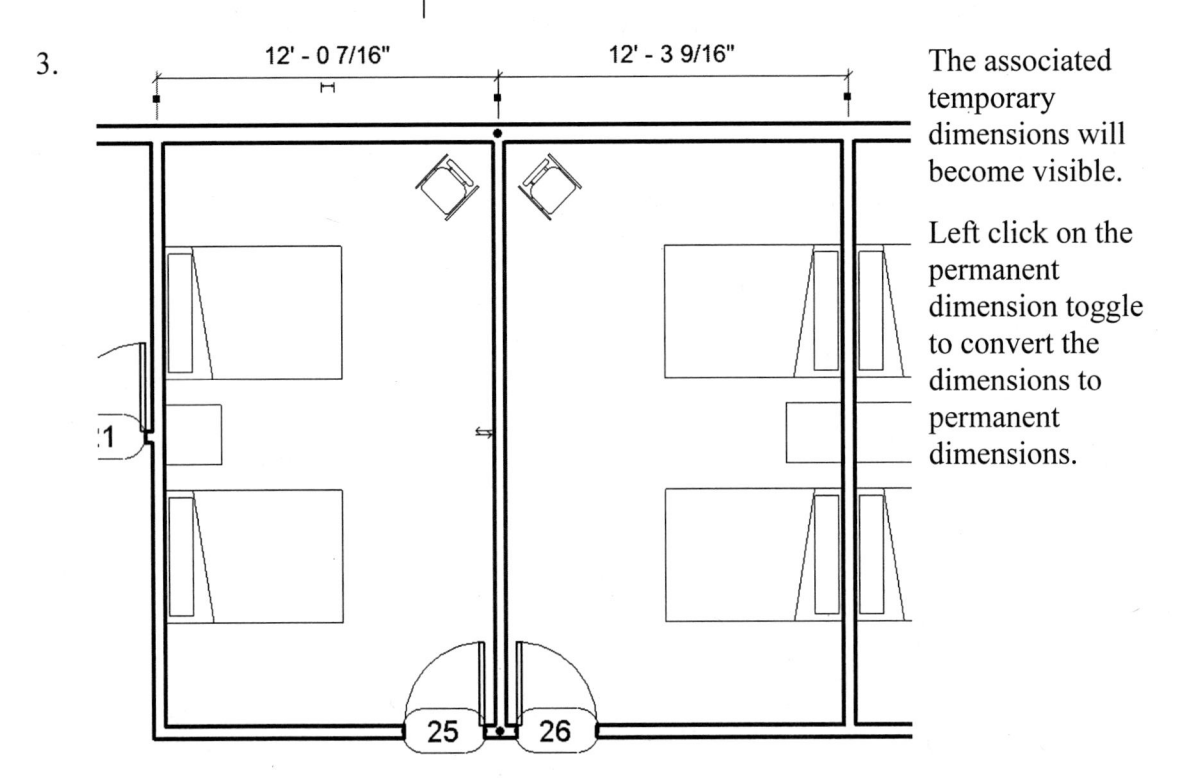

3. The associated temporary dimensions will become visible.

   Left click on the permanent dimension toggle to convert the dimensions to permanent dimensions.

Dimensions and Constraints

4. Left click anywhere in the display window.

   In the Properties pane:

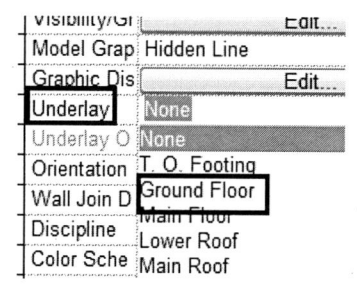

   Scroll down to the **Underlay** parameter.

   Set the Underlay to **Ground Floor**.

   This will make the ground floor visible in the graphics window. Elements on the ground floor will be displayed in a lighter shade.

   Press **OK** to close the dialog.

5. Note in the upper left corner the interior walls are not aligned.

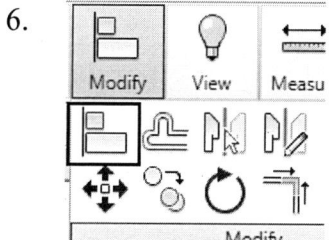

6. Activate the **Modify** ribbon.

   Select the **Align** tool from the Modify panel.

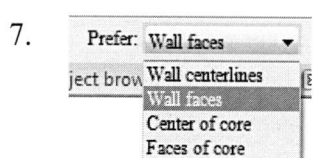

7. Set the preference to **Wall faces** on the Options bar.

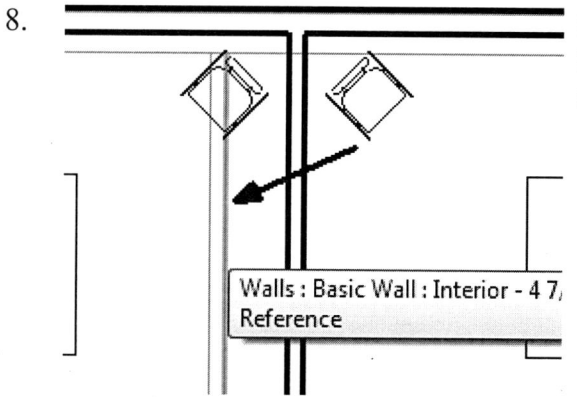

8. Select the right side of the ground floor interior wall as the source for the alignment.

5-13

The Unofficial Revit 2012 Certification Exam Guide

9. Select the right side of the main floor interior wall as the target for the alignment (this is the wall that will be shifted).

10. A warning dialog will appear due to the door location. Ignore the warning. ***Don't move the door or wall.***

11. Lock the alignment in place so that the walls remain constrained together.

12. Right click and select Cancel to exit the Align mode.

13. Activate the **Ground Floor** floor plan.

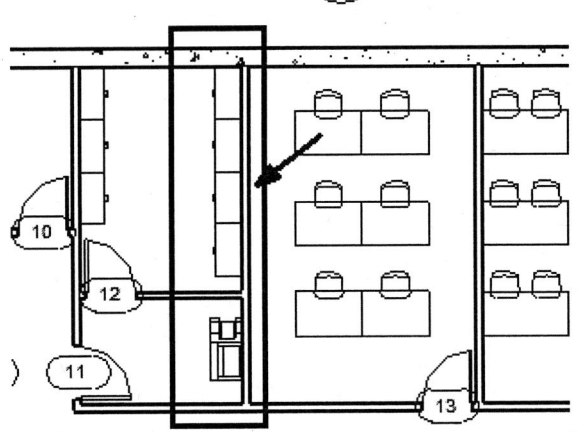

14. Select the wall as well as the cabinets and copier next to the wall.

15. Select the **Move** tool on the Modify ribbon.

5-14

Dimensions and Constraints

16. 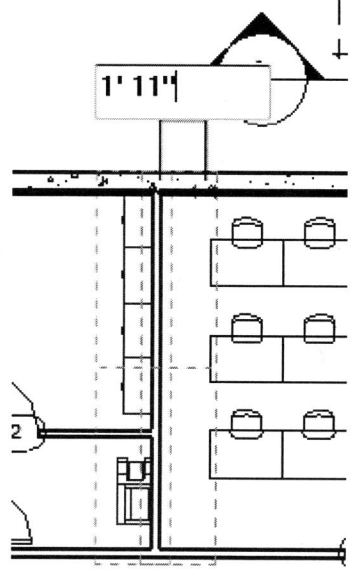 Move the selected elements to the right **1′ 11″**.

17. 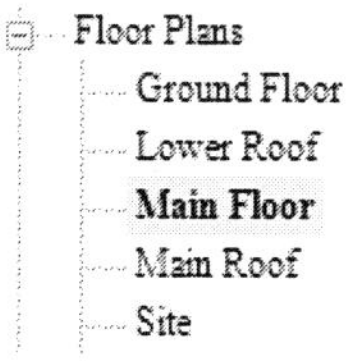 Activate the **Main Floor** floor plan.

18. 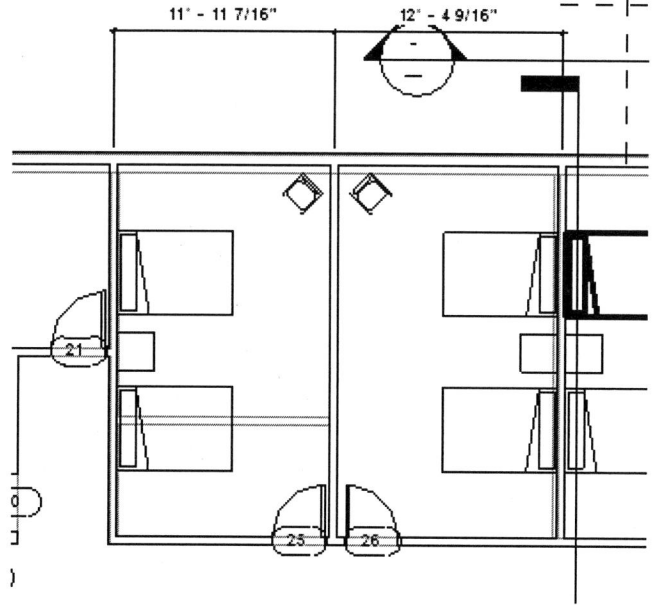 Note that the main floor interior wall has also shifted and the dimension has updated.

19. Close without saving.

5-15

The Unofficial Revit 2012 Certification Exam Guide

Practice Associate Exam

1. Constraints can be used to:
   - A. Prevent other users from moving an element in a shared project.
   - B. Lock two elements at a fixed distance.
   - C. Keep two elements equally spaced.
   - D. Alert the user when someone changes or moves an element.

2. To change a dimension's value:
   - A. Use the Change Dimension tool.
   - B. Click on Edit Witness Line.
   - C. Select the element to be re-dimensioned.
   - D. Click on the dimension.

3. True or False: You can override a dimension value with a new dimension value.

4. Select the TWO types of dimensions:
   - A. PERMANENT
   - B. TEMPORARY
   - C. PERPETUAL
   - D. INVISIBLE

5. To create a dimension using feet and inches, you can use this keystroke to separate the feet and inches values:
   - A. COMMA
   - B. SEMI-COLON
   - C. SPACE
   - D. COLON

6. A _____ allows you to locate elements equidistant from one another.
   - A. multi-segmented dimension
   - B. single-segmented dimension
   - C. scope box
   - D. reference plane

Answers:
1) B; 2) C; 3) False; 4) A & B; 5) C; 6) A

Lesson Six

Developing the Building Model

This lesson addresses the following Associate and Professional exam questions:

- Floors
- Ceilings
- Ceiling Lighting Fixtures
- Stairs
- Railings
- Roofs

Floors are level-based system families. A floor is added on the active level. The top of the floor is aligned to the level with its thickness projected downwards. You can also offset the floor so it is above or below a level using Element Properties.

Floors can be sloped. Floors can also be created by creating a mass element and selecting a face on the mass element.

Openings can be added to floors either by modifying the floor sketch or adding an opening. Railings can be added to either sloped or flat floors.

Ceilings are level-based system families. Ceilings can be controlled in a similar manner as floors using element properties.

Both ceilings and floors are Model elements.

Roofs are also level-based system families.

Stairs and railings are system families. They use profiles, which can be loaded. When you click the starting point of the stairs in plan view, the number of treads is calculated based on the distance between the floors and the maximum riser height. You can adjust the maximum riser height in the stairs element properties.

Railings consist of rails and balusters.

Stairs are automatically created assuming that they are going up from the level where they are placed. You can change the direction of the stairs (flip from going up to going down) by using the control arrow.

The Unofficial Revit 2012 Certification Exam Guide

Command Exercise
Exercise 6-1 – Modifying a Floor Perimeter

Drawing Name: **i_floors.rvt**
Estimated Time to Completion: 15 Minutes

Scope

Modify a floor.
Determine the floor's perimeter.

Solution

1. Activate **the Main Floor Admin Wing** floor plan.

2. Window around the entire view.

3. Select the **Filter** tool located in the lower right corner of the window.

4. Select **Check None** to disable all the checks.

    Then check only the **Floors**.

    Press **OK**.

6-2

Developing the Building Model

5. 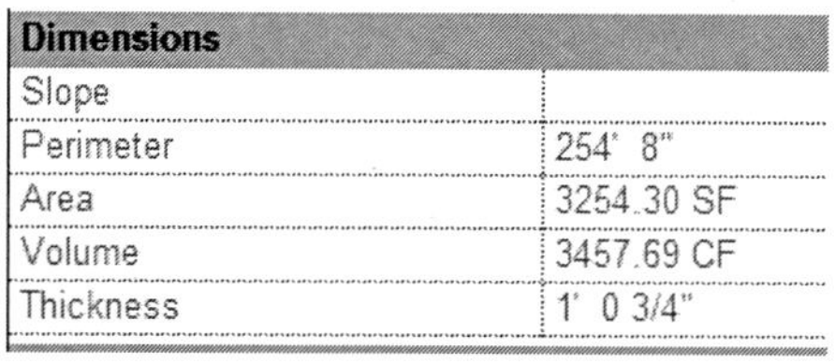 In the Properties pane:

Dimensions	
Slope	
Perimeter	254' 8"
Area	3254.30 SF
Volume	3457.69 CF
Thickness	1' 0 3/4"

   Note that the floor has a perimeter of 254' 8".

   Press **OK** to close the dialog.

6. 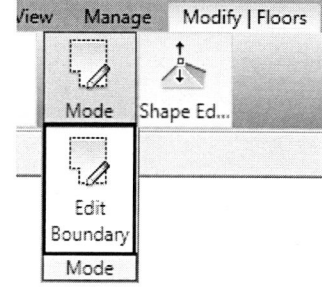 Select **Edit Boundary** under the Mode panel.

7. 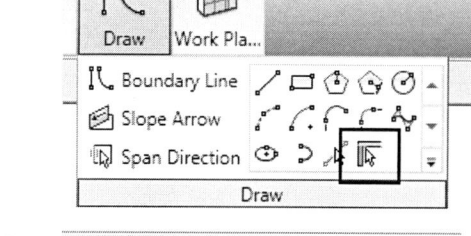 Select **Pick Walls** mode under the Draw panel.

8. 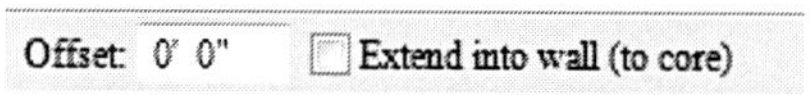 Uncheck the Extend into wall (to core) option.

9. 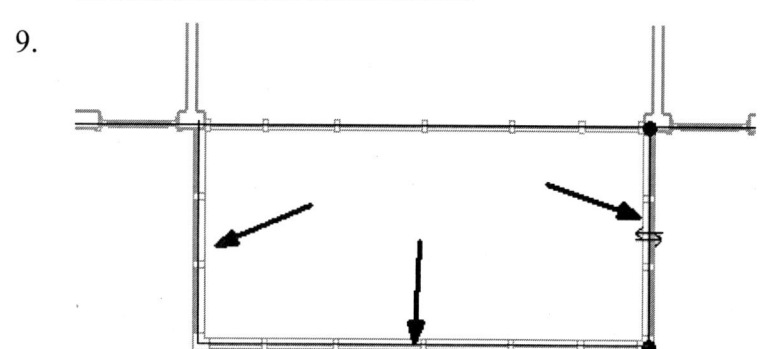 Select the three walls indicated.

10. 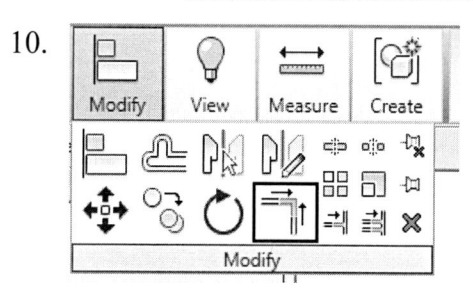 Select the **Trim** tool on the Modify panel from the ribbon.

6-3

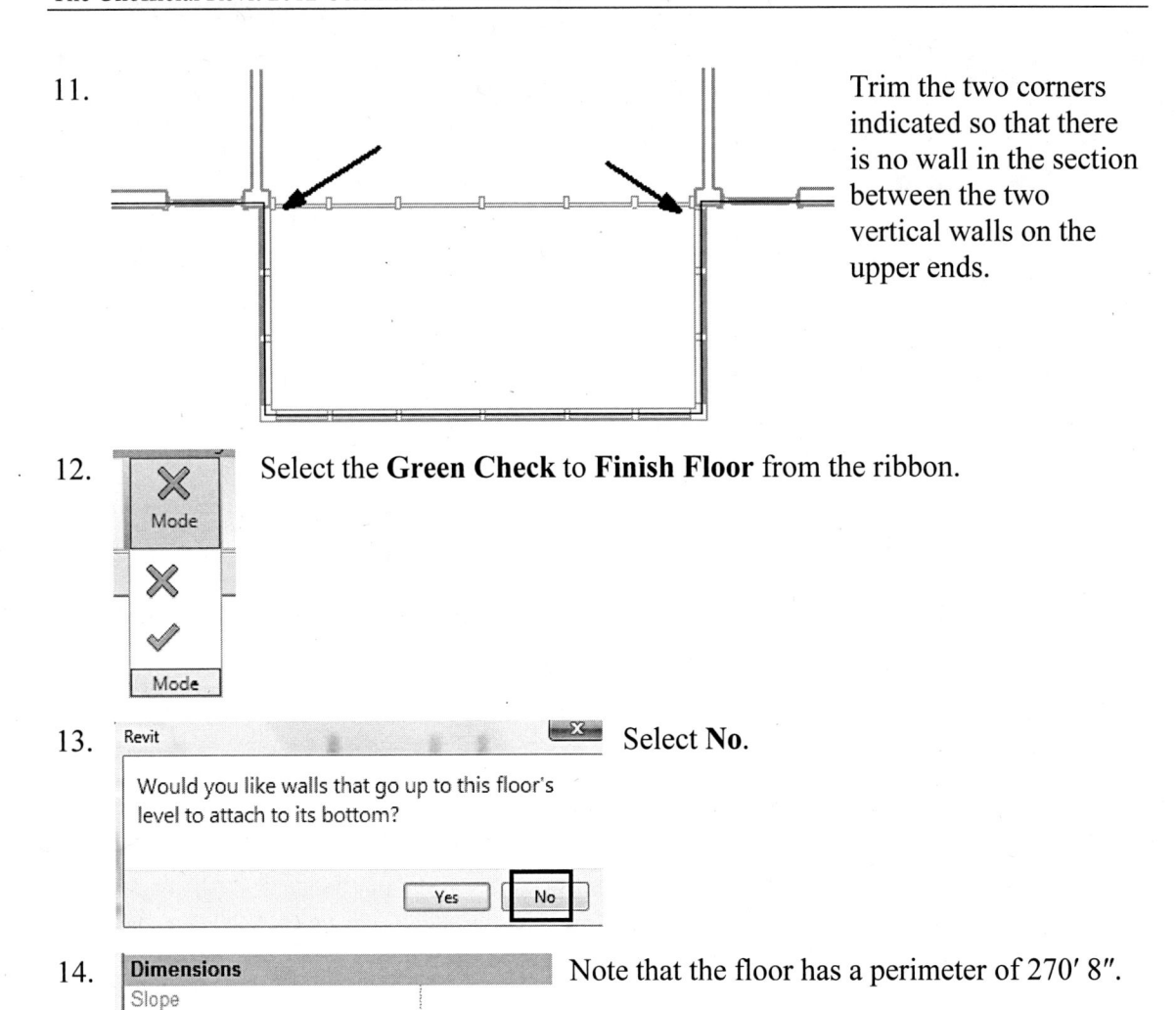

11. Trim the two corners indicated so that there is no wall in the section between the two vertical walls on the upper ends.

12. Select the **Green Check** to **Finish Floor** from the ribbon.

13. Select **No**.

14. Note that the floor has a perimeter of 270' 8".

    Press **OK** to close the dialog.

Dimensions	
Slope	
Perimeter	270' 8"
Area	3390.71 SF
Volume	3602.63 CF
Thickness	1' 0 3/4"

15. Close without saving.

In the Professional exam, you may be asked to modify a floor's sketch and then enter the resulting area, perimeter, or volume. Practice this exercise until you can get the correct perimeter value and feel comfortable using the tools.

Command Exercise

Exercise 6-2 – Modifying a Ceiling

Drawing Name: **i_ceilings.rvt**
Estimated Time to Completion: 15 Minutes

Scope

Modify a ceiling.
Rotate a ceiling grid.
Determine the ceiling's elevation.

Solution

1. Activate the **Ground Floor Admin Wing** ceiling plan.

2. Zoom into the area where the ceiling grid and lighting fixtures are placed.

3. Window around the ceiling and lighting fixtures to select.

4. Select the **Filter** tool.

5. Verify that only the ceiling and lighting fixtures are selected.

    Press **OK**.

6. Select the **Rotate** tool from Modify panel on the ribbon.

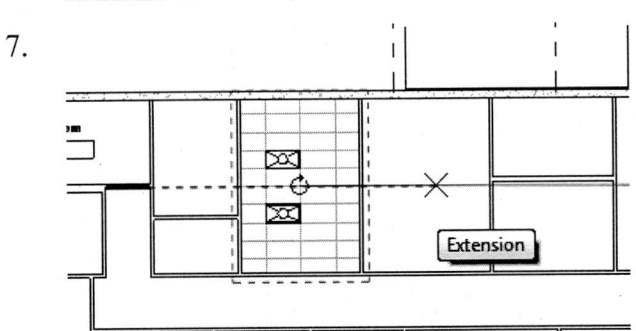

7. Select a base point that is horizontal and to the right of the selected elements.

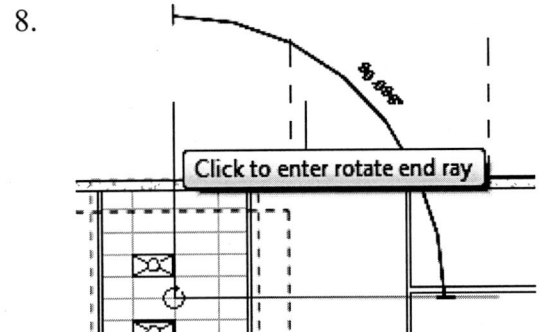

8. Move the cursor above the selected elements.

   Enter **90** to ensure a 90-degree rotation.

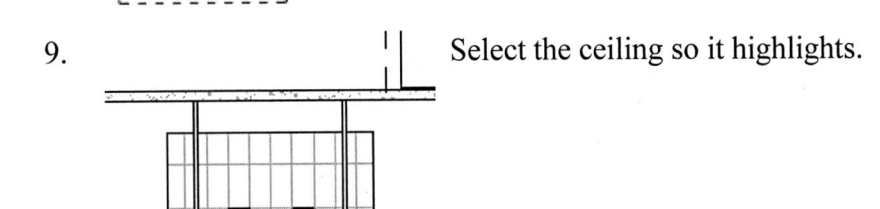

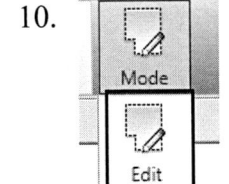

9. Select the ceiling so it highlights.

10. Select **Edit Boundary** from the Mode panel.

Developing the Building Model

11. Select the **Align** tool from the Modify panel on the ribbon.

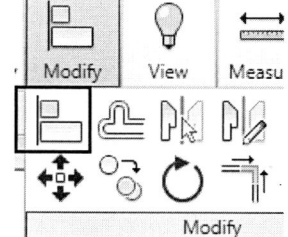

12. Align the ceiling boundary to the inner face of the walls.

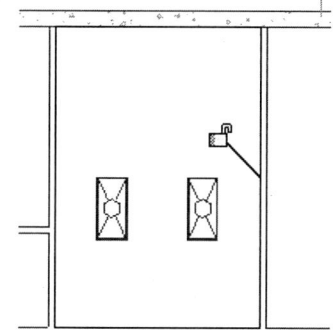

13. Select the **green check** to **Finish Ceiling**.

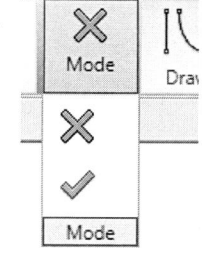

14. The grid updates.

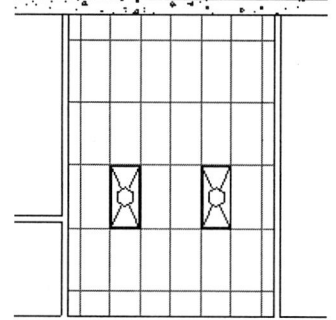

15. Select the **Align** tool from the Modify panel on the ribbon.

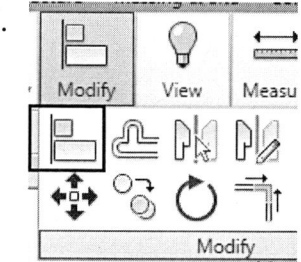

16. Select the inner face of the upper wall with the top horizontal gridline.

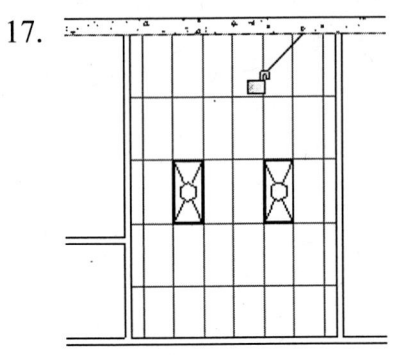

17. The ceiling grid updates so that all the grid tiles are whole in the vertical direction.

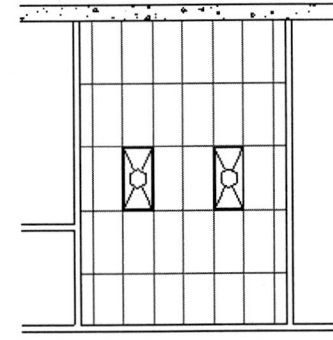

18. Select the ceiling ONLY using Filter or the TAB functions.

19. In the Properties pane:

Constraints	
Level	Ground Floor
Height Offset From Level	8' 0"
Room Bounding	✓

    Note that the user can control the height offset from the level where the ceiling is placed.

    Note the perimeter, area, and volume values.

20. Close without saving.

The Professional exam will ask the user to either place or modify a ceiling and then identify one of the element parameters, such as perimeter, area, or volume. Users should practice this exercise until they are comfortable with the tools.

Command Exercise

Exercise 6-3 – Creating Stairs

Drawing Name: **i_stairs.rvt**
Estimated Time to Completion: 20 Minutes

Scope

Place stairs using reference work planes.

Solution

1. Activate **the Ground Floor** floor plan.

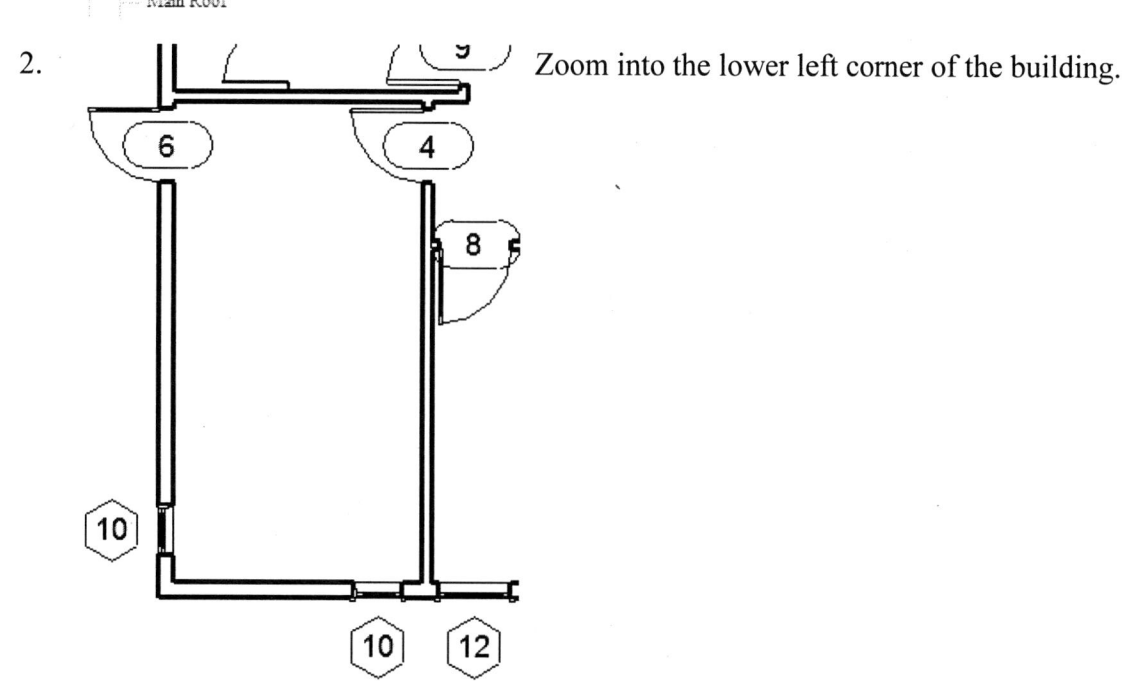

2. Zoom into the lower left corner of the building.

3. Select the **Reference Plane** tool from the Work Plane panel on the Home ribbon.

4. Set the Offset to **2' 4"** on the Options bar.

6-9

5. Select the **Pick Lines** tool from the Draw panel.

6. Place a vertical reference plane 2' 4" to the left of the wall where Door 4 is placed.

7. Place a vertical reference plane 2' 4" to the right of the wall where Door 6 is placed.

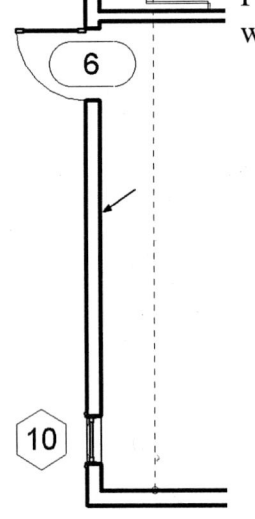

8. Set the Offset to **4' 4"** on the Options bar.

9. Place a horizontal reference plane 4' 4" above the wall where Window 10 is located.

10. Set the Offset to **7' 4"** on the Options bar.

6-10

11. Place a horizontal reference plane 7' 4" above the first horizontal reference plane.

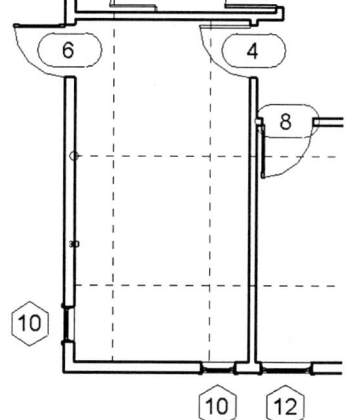

Four reference planes – two horizontal and two vertical should be placed in the room.

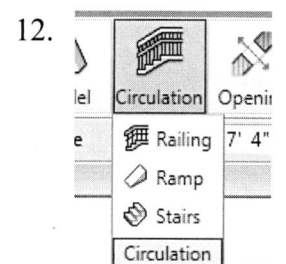

12. Activate the Home ribbon.

Select the **Stairs** tool from the Circulation panel.

13. Select **Edit Type** from the Properties pane.

14. Change the Maximum Riser Height to **8"**.

Press **OK**.

15. Note that the stair width is set to 4' 0".
Set the desired number of risers to **16**.

16. Select the **Run** tool from the Draw panel on the ribbon.

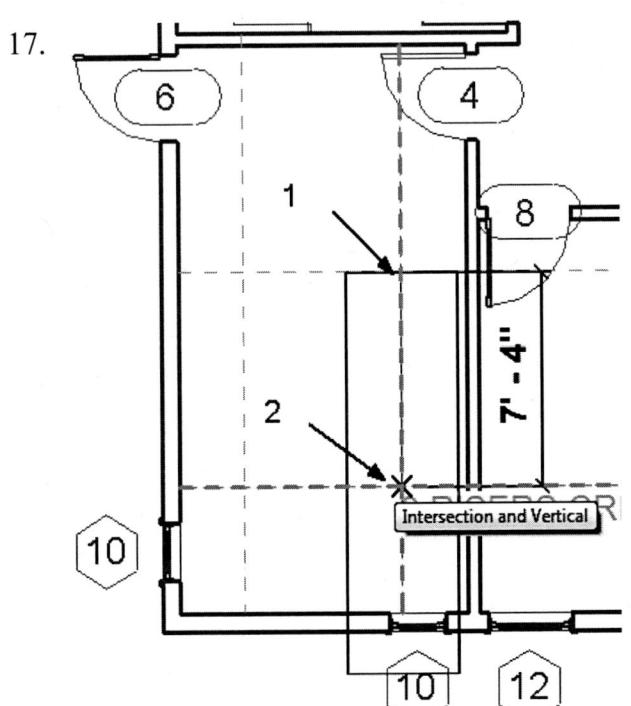

17. Pick the first intersection point indicated for the start of the run.

    Pick the second point indicated.

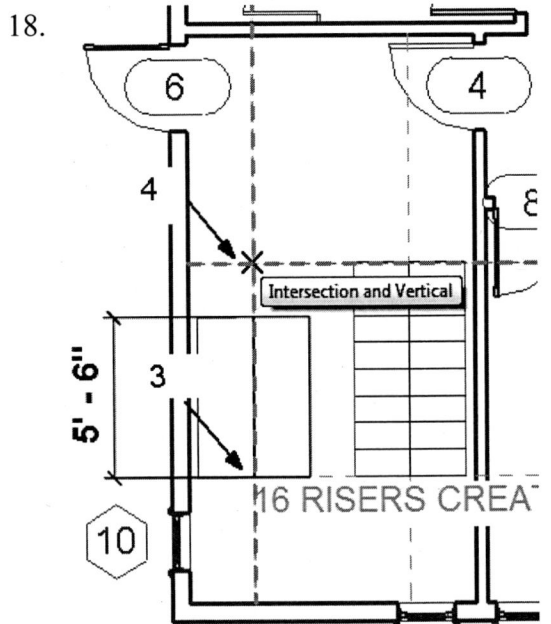

18. Moving clockwise, select the lower intersection point #3 and then the upper intersection point #4.

19. A U-shaped stairs is placed.

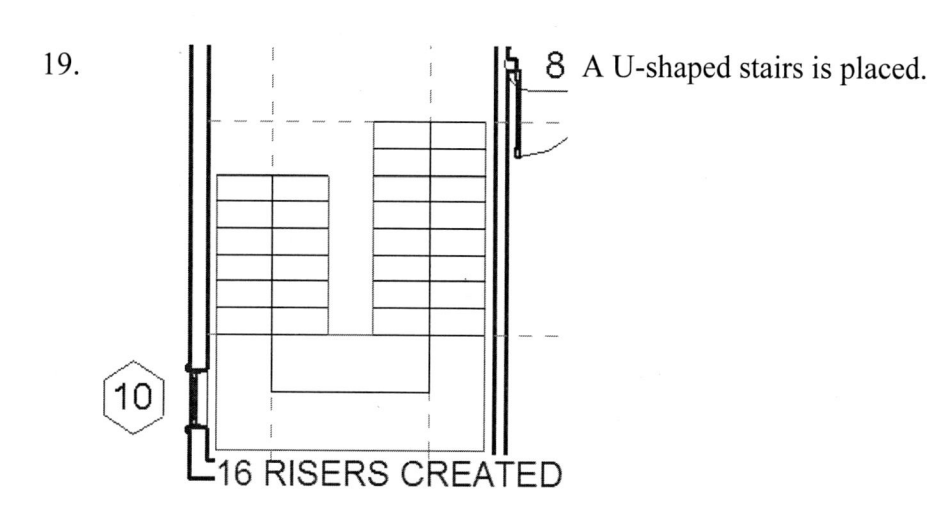

20. Select the **Green Check** on the Mode panel to **Finish Stairs**.

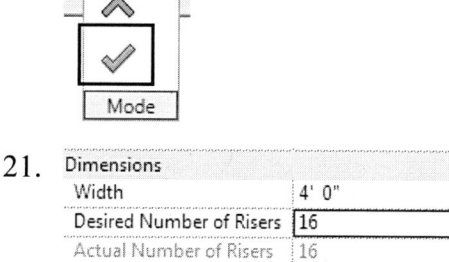

21. Select the stairs.

    On the Properties pane:
    Locate the value for the Actual Tread Depth.

    Locate the value for the Actual Riser Height.

22. Close without saving.

Command Exercise

Exercise 6-4 – Creating a Roof by Footprint

Drawing Name: **i_roofs.rvt**
Estimated Time to Completion: 15 Minutes

Scope

Create a roof.
Determine the roof's volume.

Solution

1. Activate the **Lower Roof** floor plan.

2. Select **Roof by Footprint** from the ribbon.

3. Select **Edit Type** from the Properties panel.

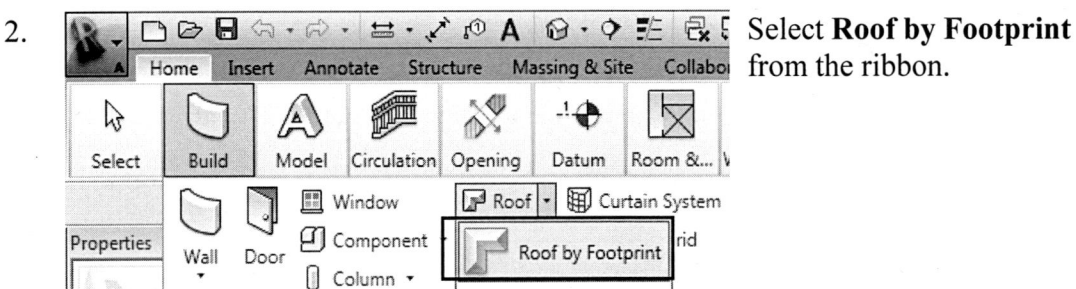

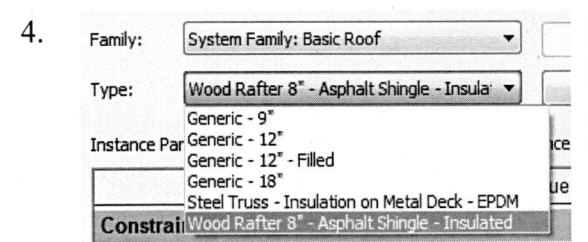

4. Select the **Wood Rafter 8″ Asphalt Shingle Roof** type.

   Press **OK** to close the dialog.

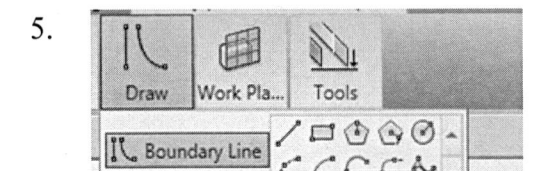

5. Select **Pick Walls** mode.

Developing the Building Model

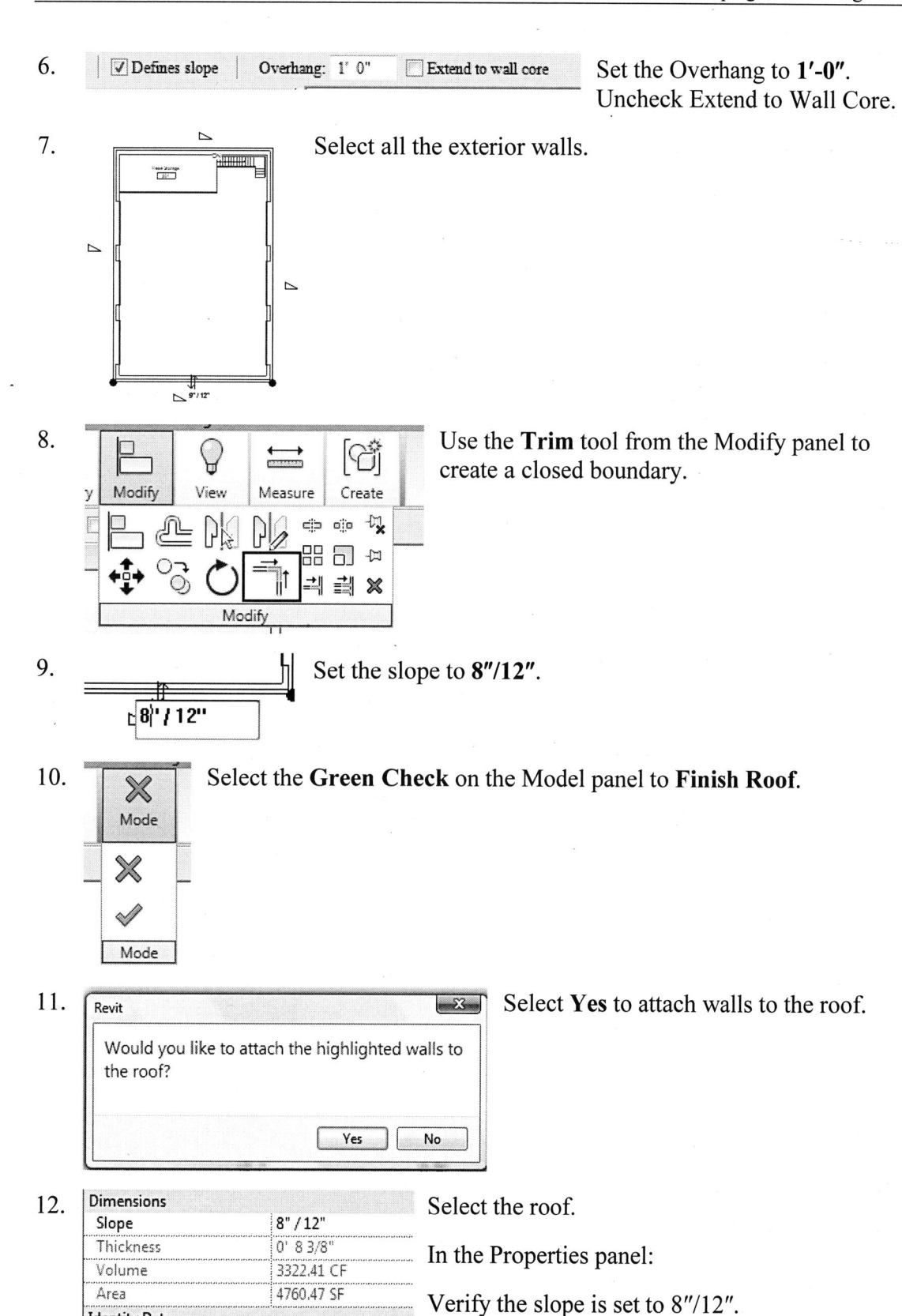

6. Set the Overhang to **1′-0″**.
   Uncheck Extend to Wall Core.

7. Select all the exterior walls.

8. Use the **Trim** tool from the Modify panel to create a closed boundary.

9. Set the slope to **8″/12″**.

10. Select the **Green Check** on the Model panel to **Finish Roof**.

11. Select **Yes** to attach walls to the roof.

12. Select the roof.

    In the Properties panel:

    Verify the slope is set to 8″/12″.

    Note the volume of the roof.

13. Close without saving.

6-15

Command Exercise

Exercise 6-5 – Creating a Roof by Extrusion

Drawing Name: **i_roofs_extrusion.rvt**
Estimated Time to Completion: 30 Minutes

Scope

Create a roof by extrusion.
Modify a roof.

Solution

1. Activate the **3D view.**

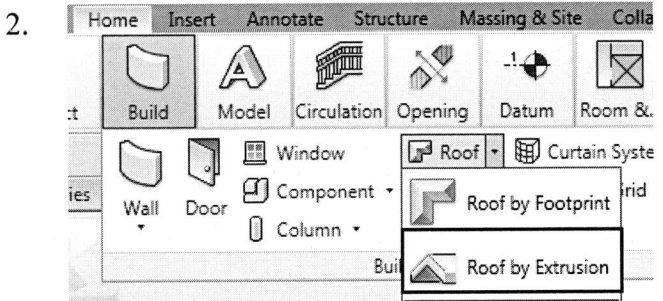

2. Activate the Home ribbon.

    Select **Roof by Extrusion** under the Build panel.

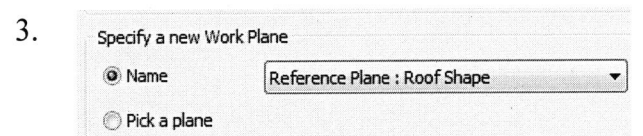

3. Enable **Name**.
    Select **Roof Shape** from the list of reference planes.
    Press **OK**.

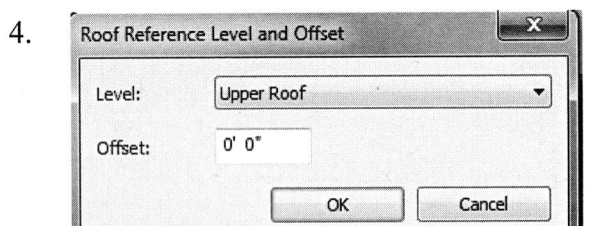

4. Select **Upper Roof** from the list.
    Press **OK**.

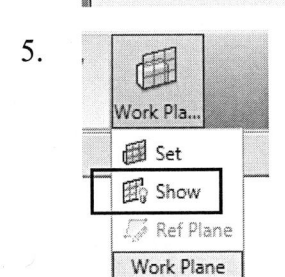

5. Select the **Show** tool from the Work Plane panel.

    This will display the active work plane.

Developing the Building Model

6. Right click on the ViewCube's ring.

   Select **Orient to a Plane**.

7. Enable **Name**.
   Select **Roof Shape** from the list of reference planes.
   Press **OK**.

8. Select the **Start-End-Radius Arc** tool from the Draw panel.

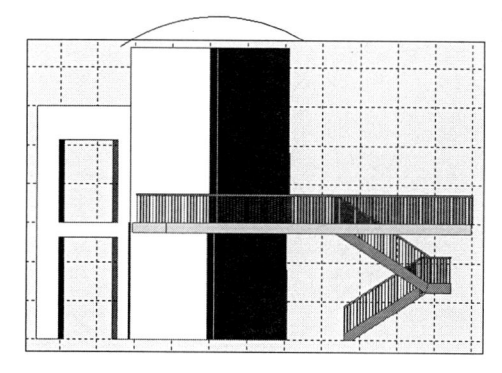

9. Draw an arc over the building as shown.

10. Select the **Green Check** under the Mode panel to finish the roof.

11. Switch to a 3D view.

6-17

12. Select the wall below the roof.

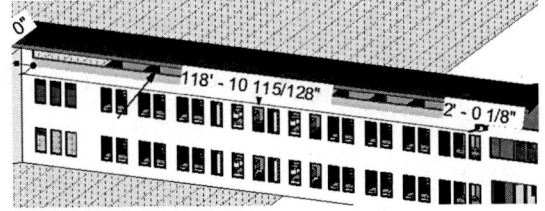

13. Select **Attach Top/Base** from the Modify Wall panel.

    Then select the roof.

    The wall will adjust to meet the roof.

    Go around the building and attach the appropriate remaining walls.

14. Activate the **Level 3** floor plan.

15. Activate the Home ribbon.

    Select the **Roof By Footprint** tool from the Build panel.

16. Select the **Pick Walls** tool from the Draw panel.

17. On the Options bar:

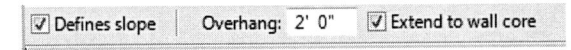

    Enable **Defines slope**.
    Set the Overhang to **2' 0"**.
    Enable **Extend to wall core**.

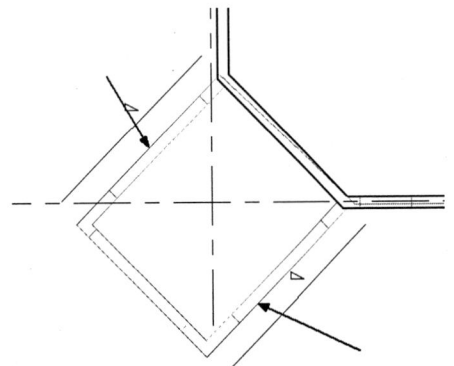

18. Select the outside of edge of the two walls indicated.

Developing the Building Model

19. Disable **Defines slope**.

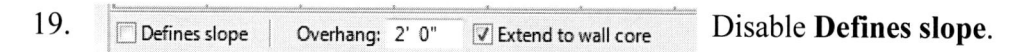

20. Select the outside edge of the wall indicated.

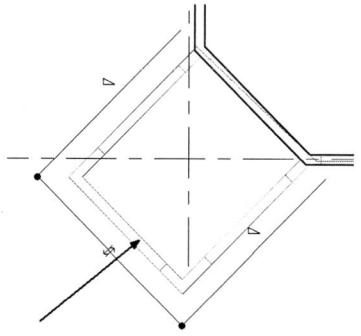

21. Set the Overhang to **0′ 0″**.

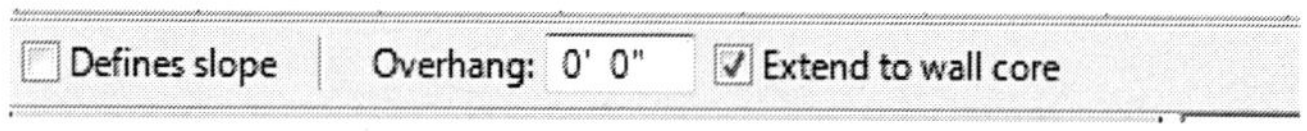

22. Select the **Pick Line** tool from the Draw panel.

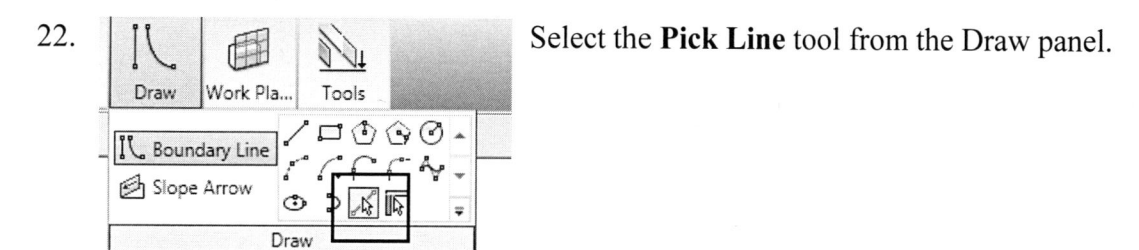

23. Pick the exterior side of the wall indicated.

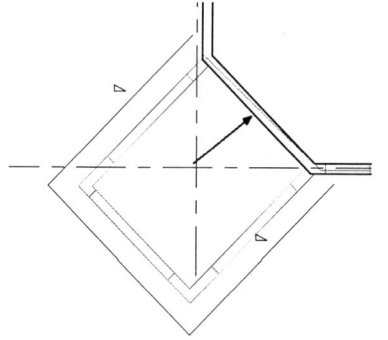

24. Select the **Trim** tool from the Modify panel.

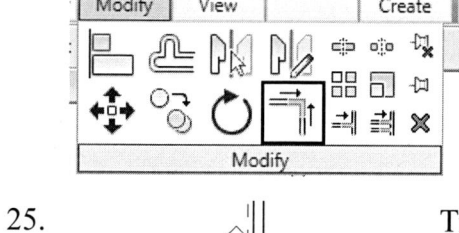

25. Trim the roof boundaries so they form a closed polygon.

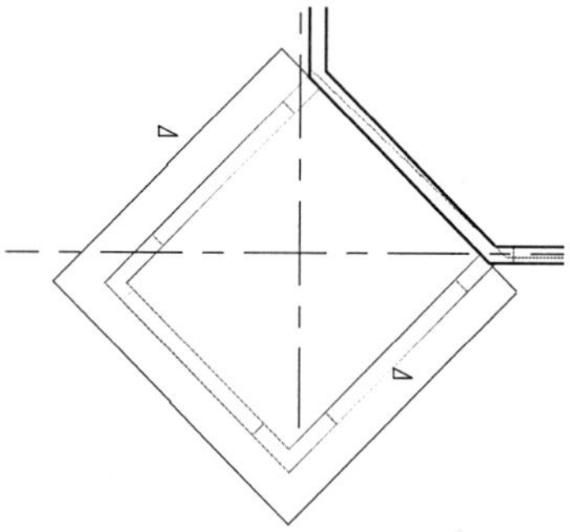

6-19

26. Select **Edit Type** in the Properties pane.

27. Set the Type to **Generic- 9"**.
    Press **OK**.

28. Set the Slope to 6"/12".

29. Once the sketch is closed and trimmed properly, select the **Green Check** on the Mode panel.

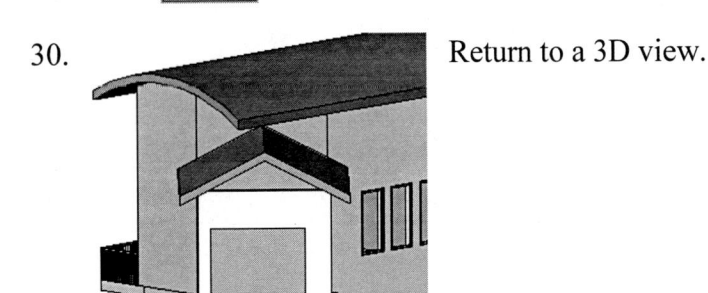

30. Return to a 3D view.

31. Select the front wall.

32. Select Attach Top/Base from the Modify Wall panel.

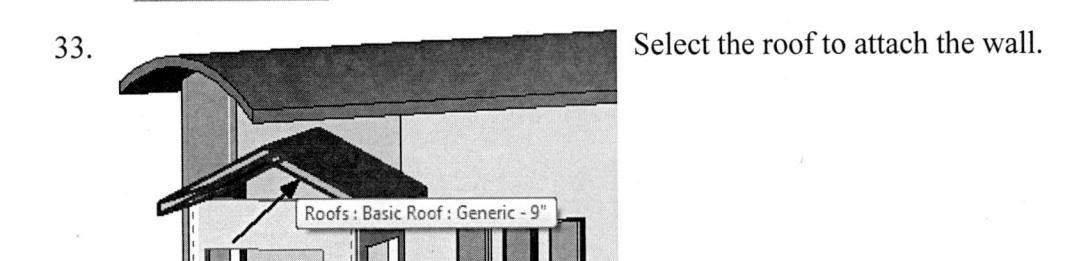

33. Select the roof to attach the wall.

34. Close without saving.

Command Exercise

Exercise 6-6 – Creating a Sloped Ceiling

Drawing Name: **i_ceilings.rvt**
Estimated Time to Completion: 30 Minutes

Scope

Create a sloped ceiling.

Solution

1. Activate the **Ground Floor Admin Wing** ceiling plan.

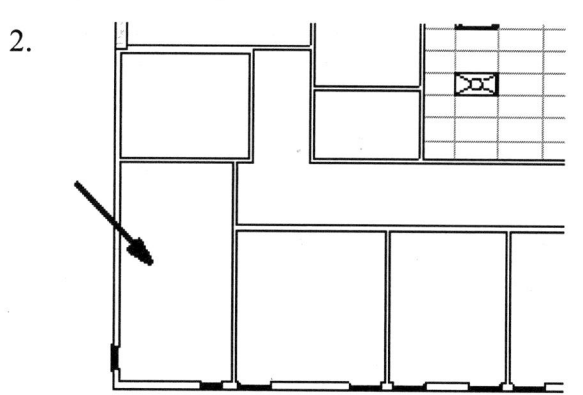

2. A sloped ceiling will be placed in the room indicated.

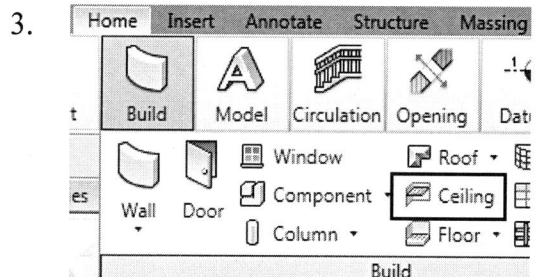

3. Select the **Ceiling** tool from the Build panel on the Home ribbon.

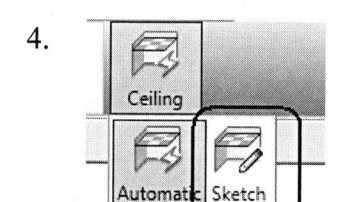

4. Select **Sketch Ceiling** from the Ceiling panel.

6-21

5. Select the **Rectangle** tool from the Draw panel.

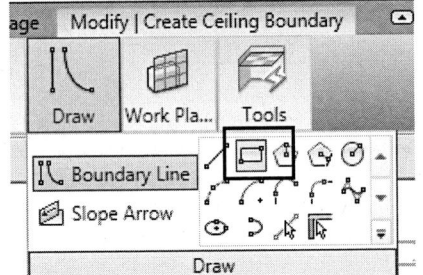

6. Draw a rectangle inside the room by selecting opposing corners.

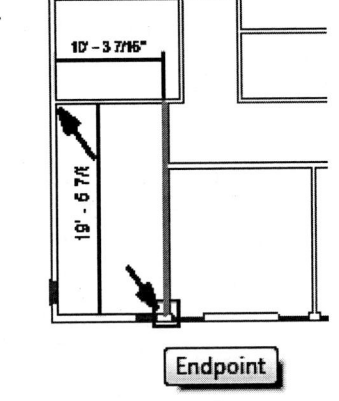

7. Select the **Slope Arrow** tool from the Draw panel to place a slope.

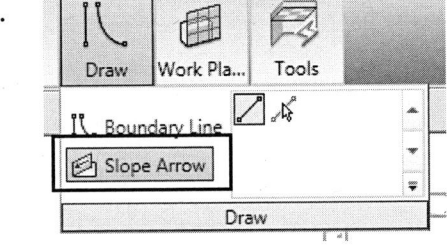

8. Select the Midpoint at the top of the rectangle.

9. Bring the arrow down to indicate the direction of the slope.

   Pick to place the endpoint so it is coincident with the lower wall.

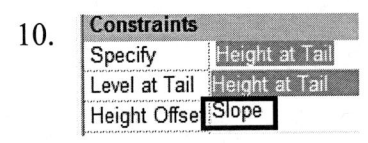

10. On the Properties pane:

    Under Specify: Select **Slope**.

Developing the Building Model

11. 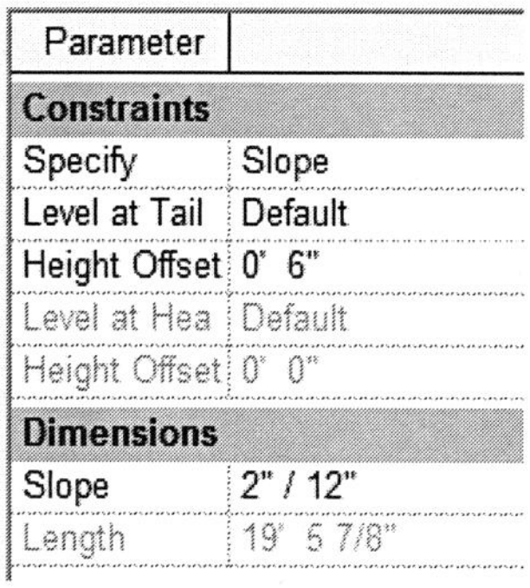 Set the Height Offset to **6″**.

   Set the Slope to **2″/12″**.

   Left click in the drawing window to release the selection.

Parameter	
Constraints	
Specify	Slope
Level at Tail	Default
Height Offset	0' 6"
Level at Hea	Default
Height Offset	0' 0"
Dimensions	
Slope	2" / 12"
Length	19' 5 7/8"

12. 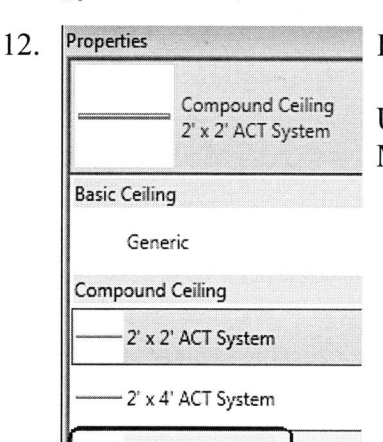 In the Properties pane:

   Use the Type Selector to set the ceiling type to **GWB on Mtl. Stud**.

13. 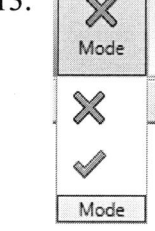 Select the **Green Check** on the Mode panel to **Finish Ceiling**.

14. 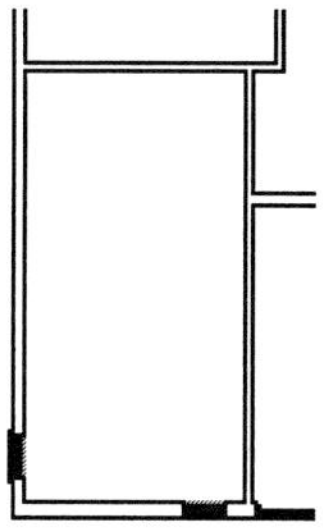 The ceiling does not display a hatch pattern by default.

15. 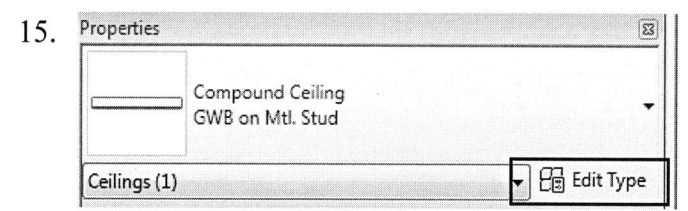 Select the ceiling.

   Select **Edit Type** in the Properties pane.

6-23

16. Under Structure, select **Edit**.

17. Select the Material definition for the Finish material Gypsum.

18. No Surface Pattern has been assigned. Select the down arrow.

19. Select **Gypsum-Plaster** from the list.

    Press **Apply**.

20. Move the dialog over to see how the ceiling appears.

    Close the dialogs.

21. Activate the **Ground Floor** floor plan.

6-24

Developing the Building Model

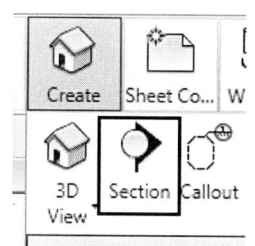

22. Select the **Section** tool from the Create panel on the View menu.

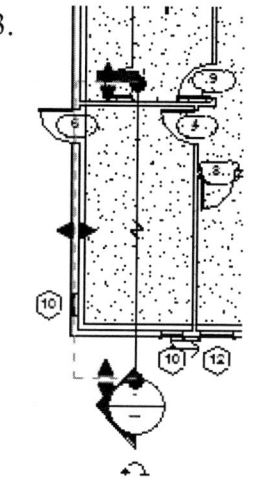

23. Place the section so it intersects the room with the sloped ceiling.

    Double click on the section head bubble to activate the section view.

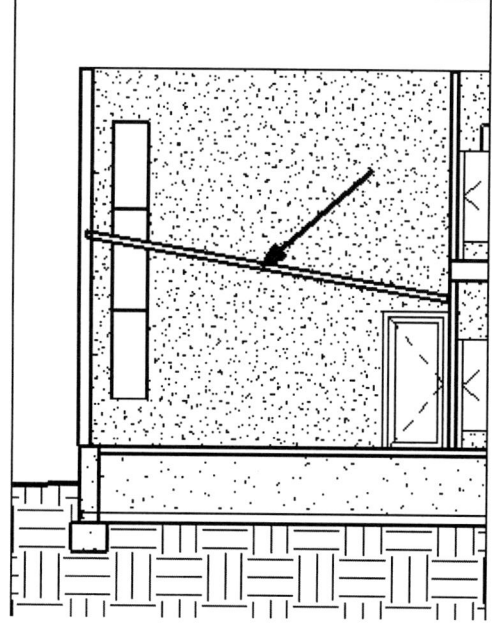

24. The sloped ceiling is shown.

    Select the ceiling.

25.

Constraints	
Level	Ground Floor
Height Offset From Level	7' 0"
Room Bounding	✓
Dimensions	
Slope	1/4" / 12"
Perimeter	59' 6 5/8"
Area	200.52 SF
Volume	71.02 CF
Identity Data	
Comments	
Mark	
Phasing	
Phase Created	New Construction
Phase Demolished	None

In the Properties pane:

Set the Height Offset to **7' 0"**.

Set the Slope to **1/4"/12"**.

Press **OK**.

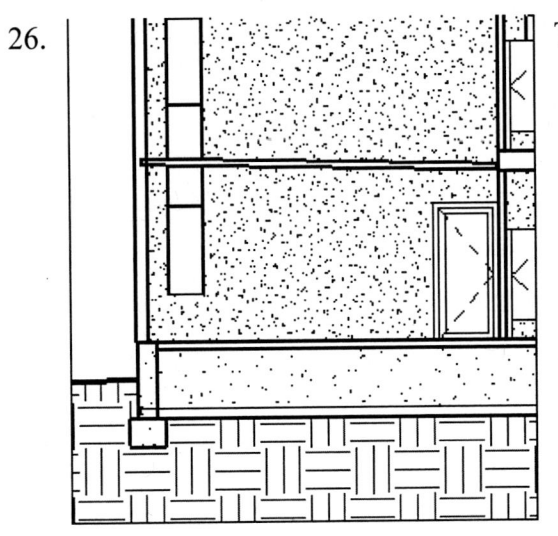

26. The ceiling updates with the new values.

27. Close without saving.

Practice Associate Exam

1. To create a partial ceiling:
    A. Use a sketch
    B. Create an area first
    C. Use the partial ceiling tool
    D. Create modified ceiling

2. The boundary of a floor is defined by:
    A. Model Lines
    B. Reference Lines
    C. Slab Edges
    D. Sketch Lines
    E. Drafting Lines

3. For the stairs shown, the vertical green lines represent:
    A. Risers
    B. Boundary Lines
    C. Stringers
    D. Run
    E. Railings

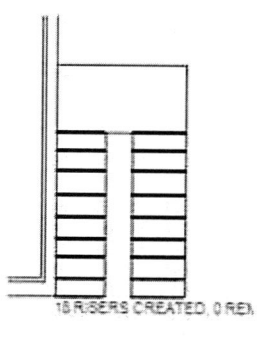

4. True or False: Stairs can be placed on multiple levels at a time.

5. True or False: You can change the direction of stairs using the flip arrows.

6. Identify the type of roof:
    A. Gable
    B. Hip
    C. Tar and Gravel
    D. Flat
    E. Shingled

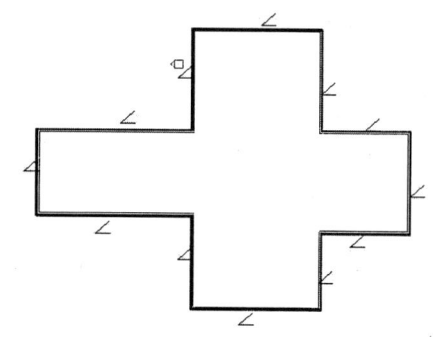

7. Name the three methods used to place a roof:
    A. By face
    B. By profile
    C. By footprint
    D. By extrusion
    E. By sketch

8. True or False: The extrusion of a roof can extend only in a positive direction from the selected work plane.

9. True or False: When attaching a wall to a roof, the profile of the wall does not change.

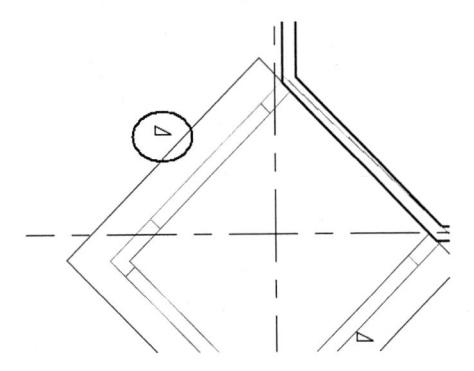

10. The symbol circled indicates:

    A. Slope
    B. Top Constraint
    C. Roof Boundary
    D. Gutter

11. To place a railing:

    A. Draw a path
    B. Select a host element
    C. Click to place
    D. Work in section view

12. You can change a Generic 12" Floor to a Wood Joist 10" Floor using the:

    A. Properties filter
    B. Options Bar
    C. Type Selector
    D. Modify ribbon

13. To create a stair landing, use the _____ tool.

    A. Run
    B. Boundary
    C. Riser
    D. Landing

14. To attach the top of a wall to a roof:

    A. Drag the top of the wall by grips
    B. Select the wall, check on Attach Top/Base and select roof
    C. Define wall attachments in instance properties
    D. Use the ALIGN tool

Answers:
1) A; 2) D; 3) B; 4) True; 5) True; 6) B; 7) A, C & D; 8) False; 9) False; 10) A) Slope; 11) B; 12) C; 13) B; 14) B

Lesson Seven

Detailing and Drafting

This lesson addresses the following Associate and Professional exam questions:

- Callouts
- Tags
- Detail Views
- Text
- Callout view of a Section
- Drafting View
- Revision Clouds
- Revision Schedules
- Grid Guides

A callout is a view that is placed in a plan, section, detail or elevation view to create a more detailed view of part of the building model. The area that the callout defines in the view is called the callout bubble. The callout bubble has a leader or connecting line to a callout head which displays the detail number and sheet number. All these parts – callout bubble, callout head, and callout leader – are referred to as a callout tag.

When you create a callout, a new view is automatically created. There are two types of callout views: Callout in Parent View and Callout in Detail View.

A detail view is a view of a specific area of a plan, elevation or section view. This view provides a greater level of detail at a larger scale than the parent view. Detail views can be linked to callouts.

Drafting views are 2D views that depict a small area of the building model. These views do not contain any model elements at all. Users can create a library of drafting views to depict foundation work, stairs and railings, wall framing, etc., and use them across multiple projects.

Revision clouds and revision schedules are used to track changes to a project. Users can enter the changes into a project and then issue the changes to a sheet once the changes are made.

The Unofficial Revit 2012 Certification Exam Guide

Command Exercise
Exercise 7-1 – Creating Drafting Views

Drawing Name: **c_libraries_and_details.rvt**
Estimated Time to Completion: 30 Minutes

Scope

*Use an existing AutoCAD detail drawing and convert it into a Revit drafting view.
Add a callout to a section view.
Add a section view with callout to a sheet.
Add a drafting view to a sheet.*

Solution

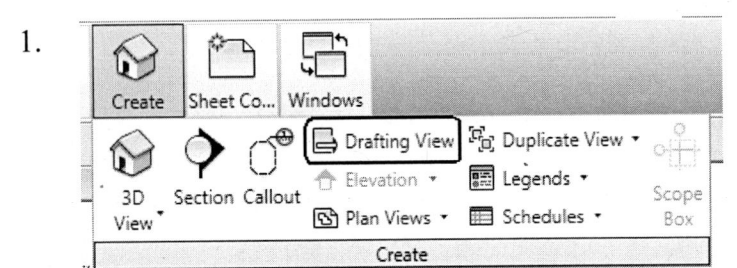

1. Activate the **View** ribbon.

   Select **Drafting View** from the Create panel.

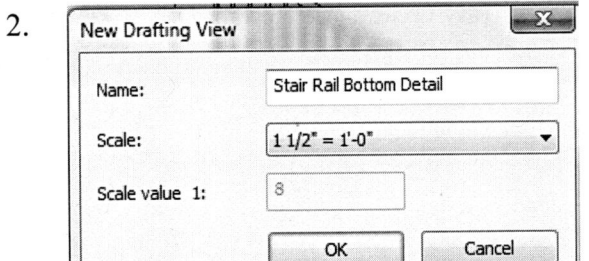

2. Name the new Drafting View: **Stair Rail Bottom Detail**.
   Set the scale to 1 ½" = 1'-0"

   Press **OK**.

3. In the Project Browser, note that the Drafting Views category has been added and the new view is listed.
   The window will open to the new view which is empty.

4. Activate the **Insert** ribbon.

   Select **Import CAD** from the Import panel.

7-2

Detailing and Drafting

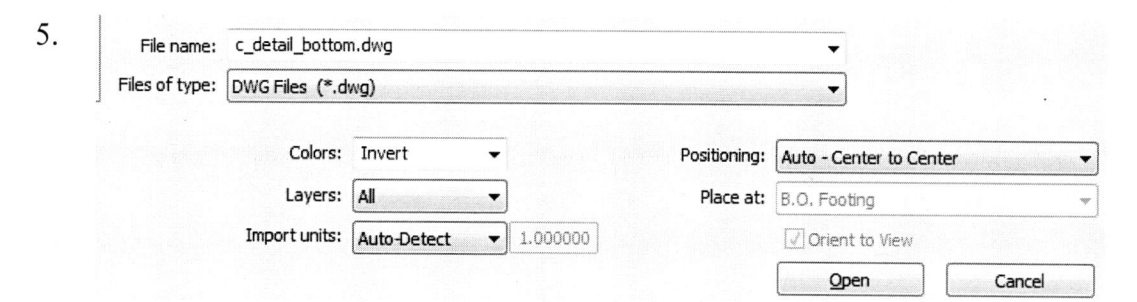

5. Locate the *c_detail_bottom.dwg* file.
   Set Colors to **Invert**.
   Press **Open**.

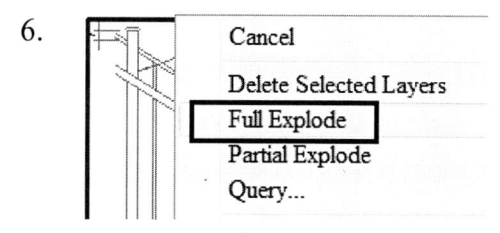

6. Select the CAD data. It is a single image.

   Right click and select **Full Explode**.

   This will convert the data to Revit entities.

   You can also do a Full Explode from the ribbon.

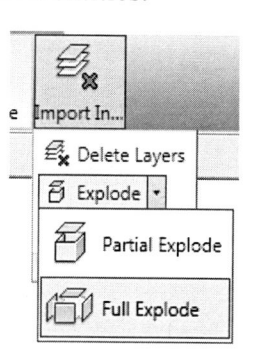

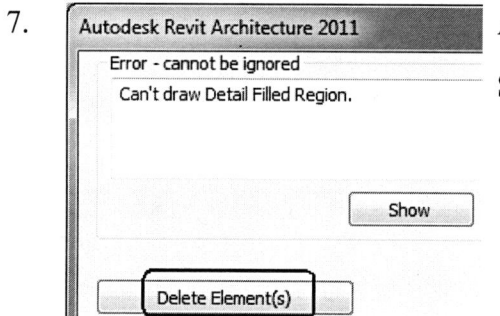

7. An error message may appear.

   Select **Delete Element(s)**.

   Revit was unable to convert the detail filled region, but you can add that later.

8. Next we add a callout for the drafting view.
   Activate the **Stair Section** under Sections.

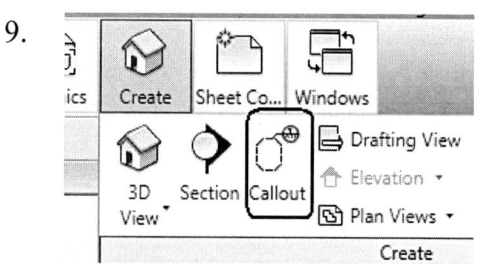

9. Activate the **View** ribbon.

   Select the **Callout** tool from the Create panel.

10.

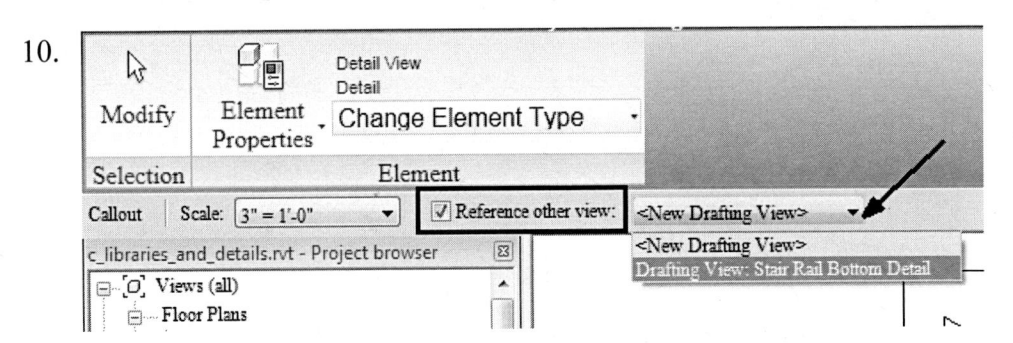

Place a check on the **Reference other view** box.

In the drop-down list, select the **Stair Rail Bottom Detail** for the view to be referenced.

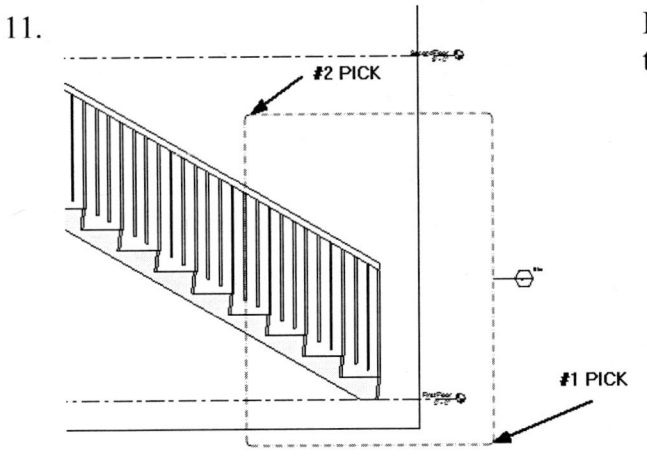

11. Place the callout outline by picking in the two locations indicated.

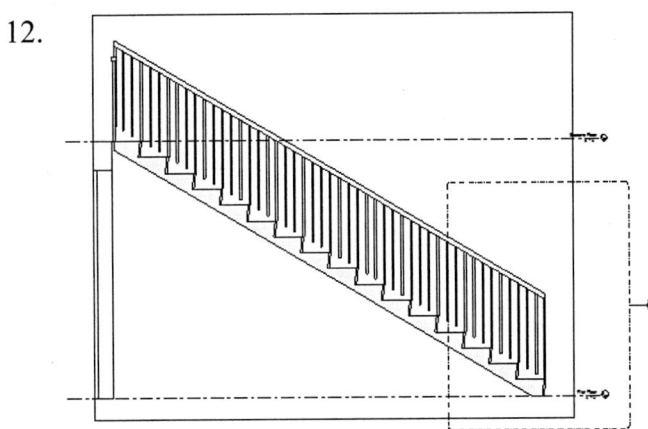

12. Some users don't like to see the viewport outline. This is the rectangle around the view.

Use the **Hide Crop Region** toggle on the View Control bar to hide the viewport outline.

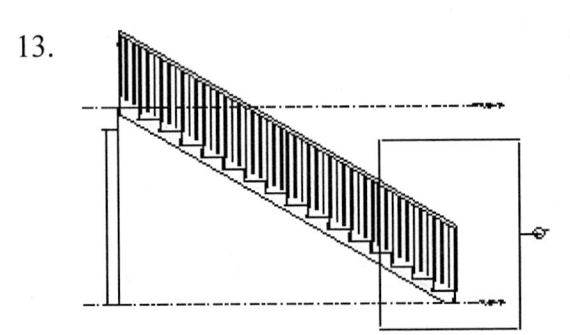

13. The rectangular viewport is no longer visible.

Detailing and Drafting

14. Zoom into the callout bubble.
The bubble data is blank until the drafting view is added to a sheet.

15. Activate the **Stair Section** sheet.

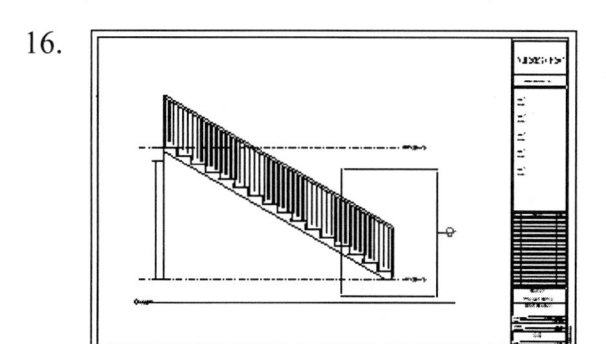

16. Drag and drop the Stair Section from the browser onto the sheet.

17. Activate the **Stair Details** sheet.

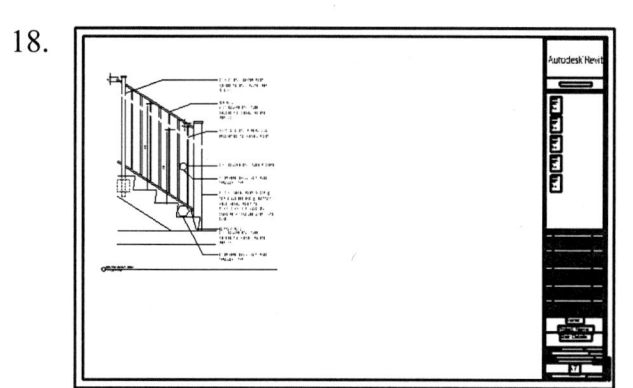

18. Drag and drop the Drafting View for the bottom of the stairs onto the sheet.

19. Activate the **Stair Section** view under Sections.

20. Zoom into the callout bubble.

    Note that the callout is now filled in with the sheet information.

    Double left click on the bubble.

21. **Drafting Views (Detail)** / **Stair Rail Bottom Detail** — This navigates the user to the drafting view.

22. **Sections (Building Section)** / **Stair Section** — Activate the **Stair Section** view under Sections.

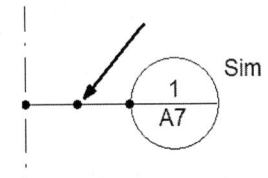

23. Select the callout handle.

24. **Edit Type** — Select **Edit Type** in the Properties pane.

25. Delete the word **Sim** in the Reference Label field.

    Press **OK**.

Parameter	Value
Graphics	
Callout Tag	Callout Head w 1/8" Corner Radi
Section Tag	Section Head - No Arrow, Secti
Reference Label	Sim

26. Activate the **Stair Rail Bottom Detail** view.

    In the Properties pane:

    Note that the Referencing Sheet is listed under the Identity Data

Identity Data	
View Name	Stair Rail Bottom Detail
Dependency	Independent
Title on Sheet	
Sheet Number	A7
Sheet Name	Stair Details
Referencing Sheet	
Referencing Detail	

    None of the data is editable in this dialog.

27. Save as *ex7-1.rvt*.

Extra Challenge:

Create a callout for the top of the stairs using c_detail_top.dwg as the drafting view.

Add the new drafting view to the Stair Details sheet.

1. Create a new drafting view.
2. Import the CAD file.
3. Add the callout to the top of the stairs on the section view.
4. Drag the new drafting view to the Stair Details sheet.

Detailing and Drafting

Command Exercise

Exercise 7-2 – Save and Re-Use a Drafting View

Drawing Name: **c_ details.rvt**
Estimated Time to Completion: 10 Minutes

Scope

Save a drafting view for re-use.
Insert the saved file into a project.

Solution

1. 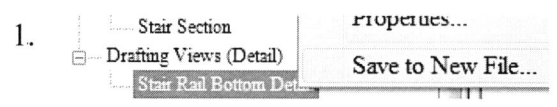 Highlight the **Stair Rail Bottom Detail** in the Drafting Views (Detail) category in the Project Browser.

2. Right click and select **Save to New File**.

3. 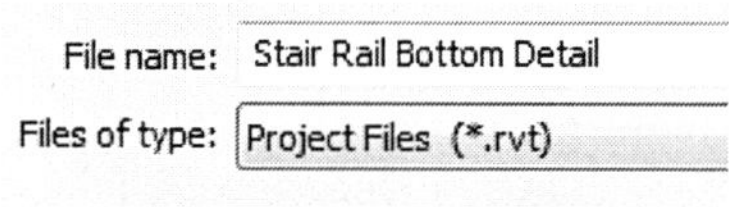 Browse to your work folder and select **Save**.

4. 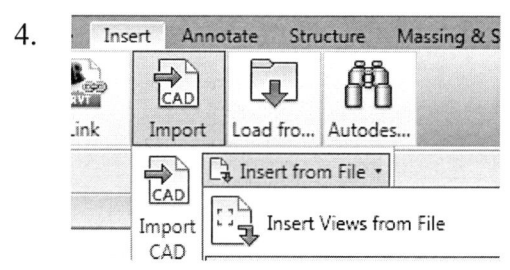 Activate the **Insert** ribbon.

   Select **Insert from File→Insert Views from File** from the Import panel.

5. 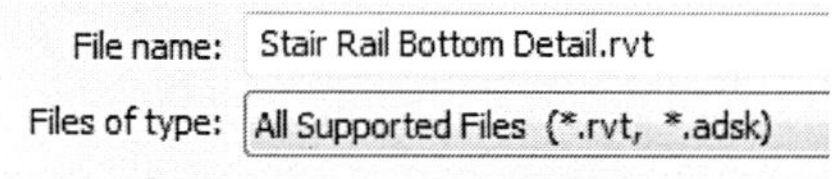 Locate the file you just saved.

   Press **Open**.

6. [Insert Views dialog]

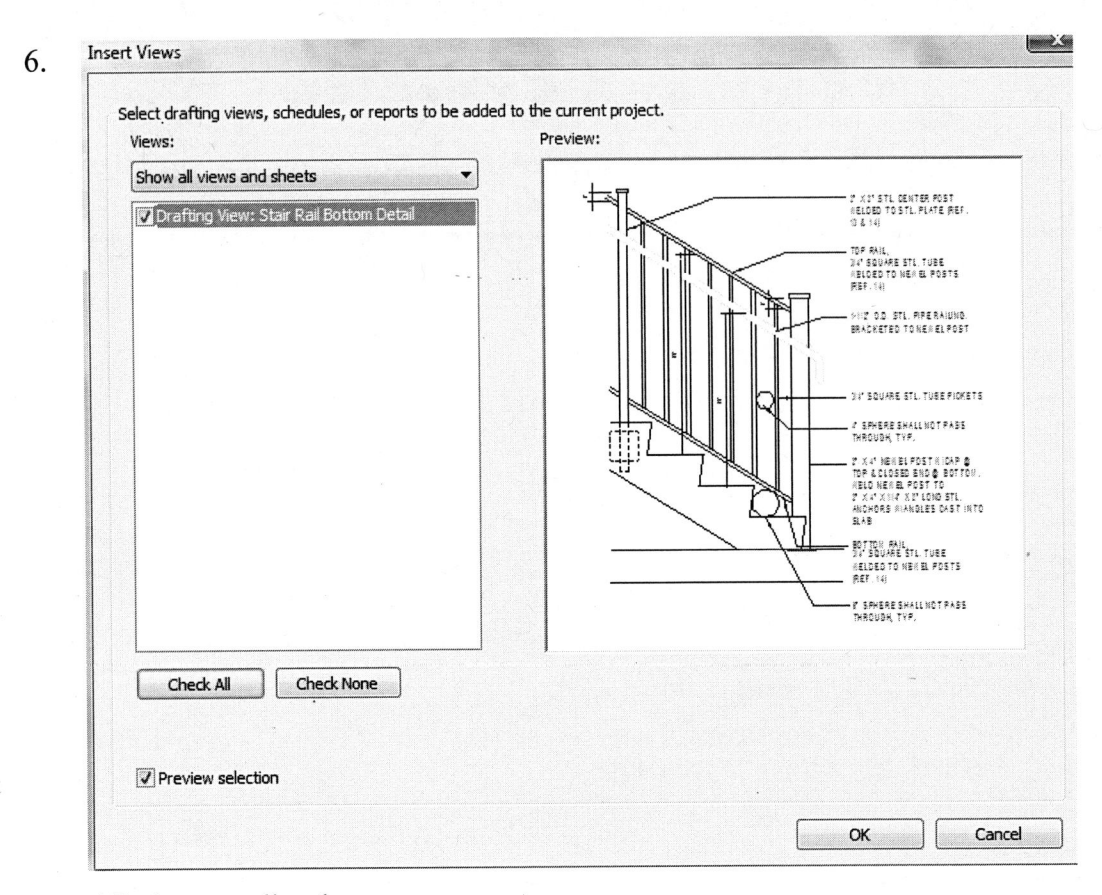

   All views are listed.

   Only one view is available for import – the view you saved.

   Press **OK**.

7. [Duplicate Types dialog]

   You may see this dialog having to do with sun settings.

   Press **OK**.

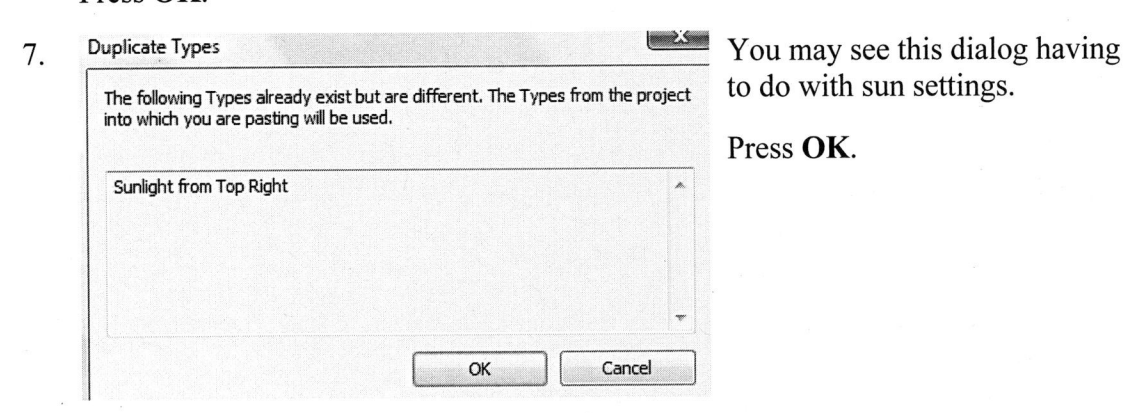

8. [Drafting Views (Detail) browser showing Stair Rail Bottom Detail and Stair Rail Bottom Detail1]   The new view is listed in the browser and is activated.

9. Close the files without saving.

Command Exercise

Exercise 7-3 – Adding Tags

Drawing Name: **i_dimensions.rvt**
Estimated Time to Completion: 15 Minutes

Scope

Add room tags to a view.
Duplicate view with Detailing
Duplicate view as dependent
Change the room tags assigned type.

Solution

1. Activate the **Ground Floor Admin Wing**.

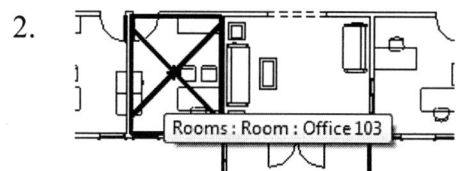

2. Mouse over the different rooms and note that room elements have been placed in each room.

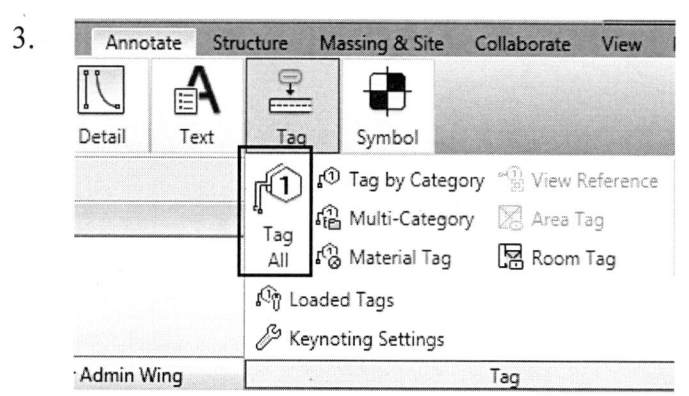

3. Activate the **Annotate** ribbon. Select the **Tag All** tool from the Tag panel.

4. Select the **Room Tag**.

   Press **OK**.

7-9

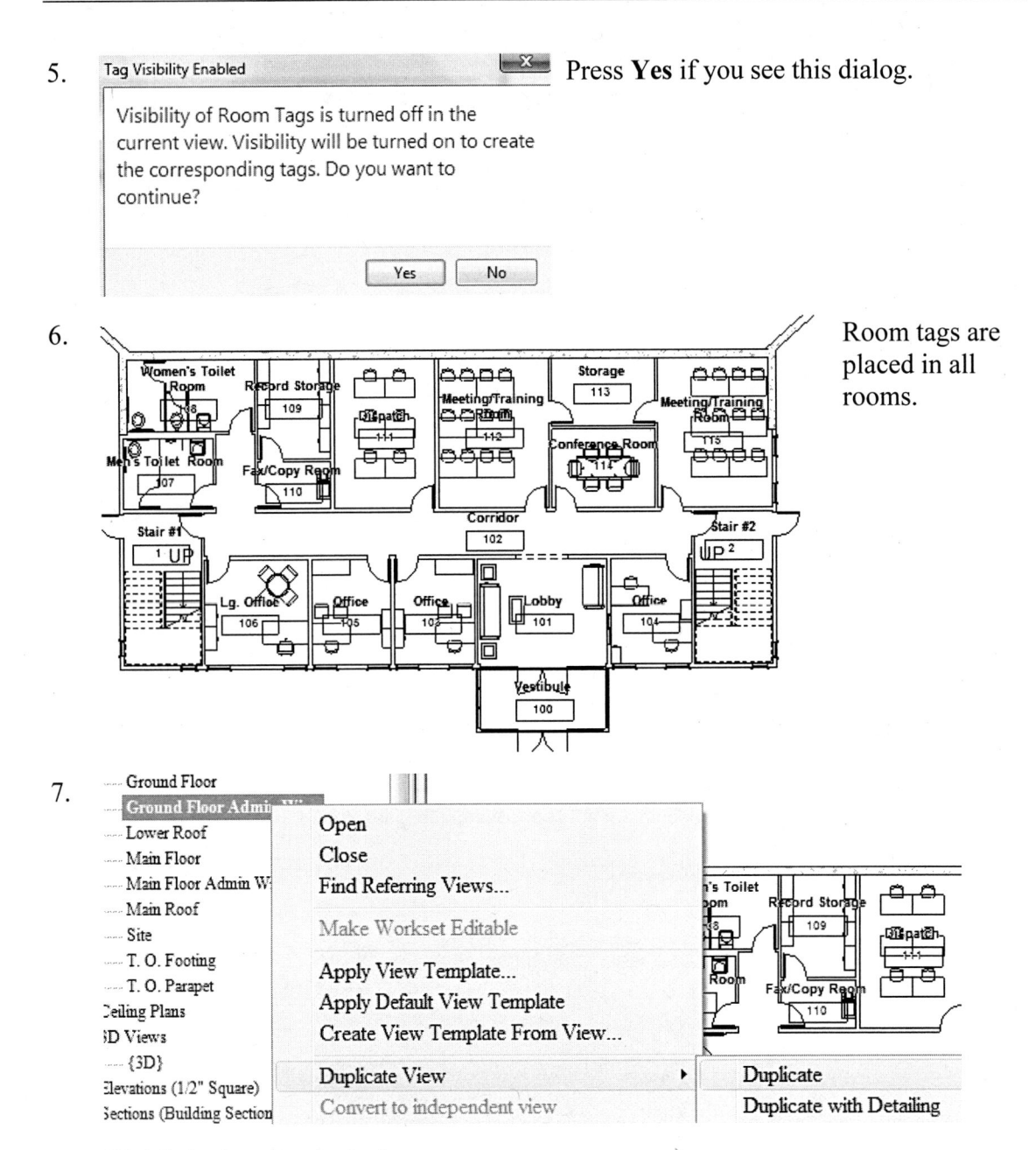

The Unofficial Revit 2012 Certification Exam Guide

5. Press **Yes** if you see this dialog.

   Tag Visibility Enabled dialog: Visibility of Room Tags is turned off in the current view. Visibility will be turned on to create the corresponding tags. Do you want to continue?

6. Room tags are placed in all rooms.

7. Highlight the view in the browser.

   Right click and select **Duplicate View→Duplicate**.

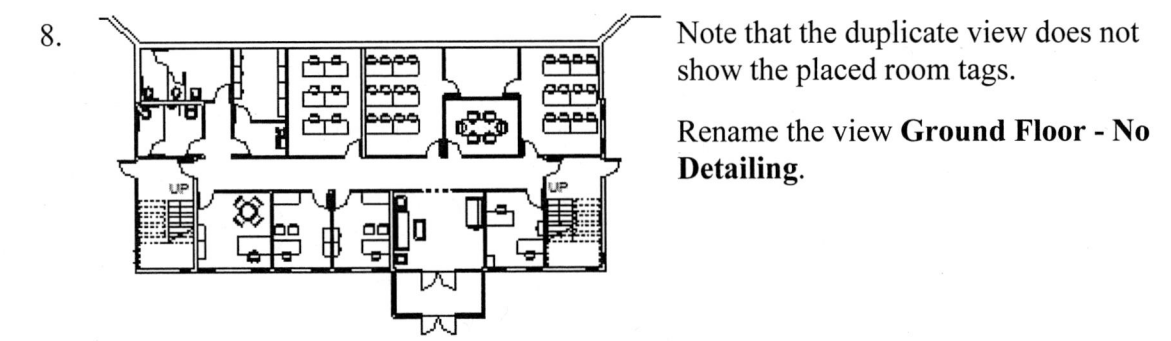

8. Note that the duplicate view does not show the placed room tags.

   Rename the view **Ground Floor - No Detailing**.

Detailing and Drafting

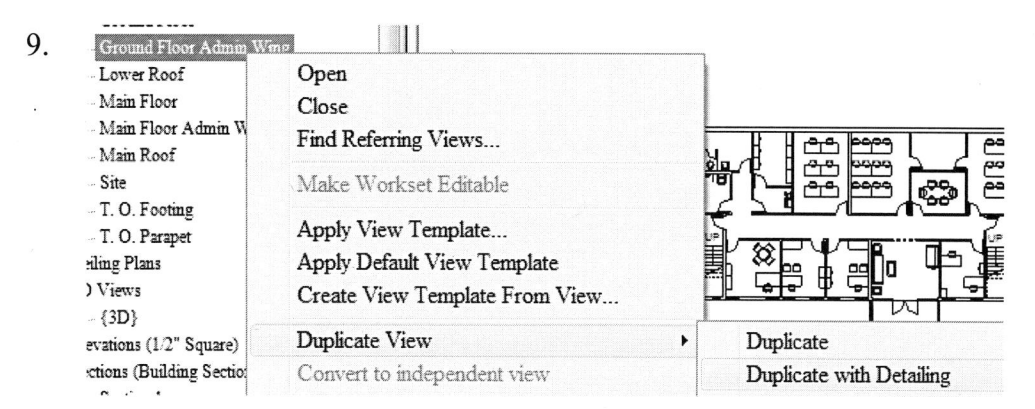

9. Highlight the Ground Floor Admin Wing floor plan view in the browser.

Right click and select **Duplicate View→Duplicate with Detailing**.

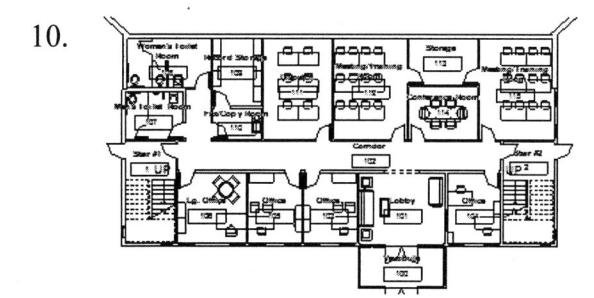

10. Note that the new view includes the room tags.

Rename the view - **Ground Floor - Detailing**

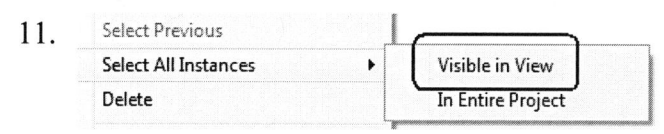

11. Select one of the room tags.

Right click and select **Select All Instances→Visible in View**.

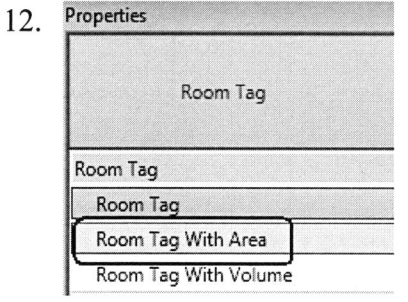

12. In the Type drop-down on the Properties pane, select **Room Tag with Area**.

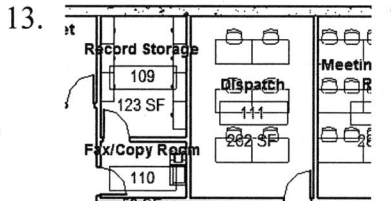

13. The room tags update.

14. Switch back to the original Ground Floor Admin Wing.

Note that the room tags for that view did not update.

15. Close without saving.

7-11

Command Exercise

Exercise 7-4 – Creating a Detail View

Drawing Name: **i_detail.rvt**
Estimated Time to Completion: 40 Minutes

Scope

Add detail components to a detail view.

Solution

1. Activate the **Main Roof** floor plan.

2. Double click on the section head indicated to activate that section view.

3. Note the name of the active section view in the browser.

4. Double click on the callout bubble to activate the callout view.

5. Note the name of the active callout section view in the browser.

Detailing and Drafting

6. Click on the crop window to activate the grips.

   The grips allow you to change the extents of the view.

7. Drag the crop region up using the drip bubble so that the roof parapet is shown.

8. Highlight the active Callout view in the browser.

   Right click and select **Rename**.

9. Change the name to **Roof Detail**.

   Press **OK**.

10. In the Properties pane:

    Under Extents:
    Set the Far Clip Settings to **Independent**.

7-13

11. Select the roof.

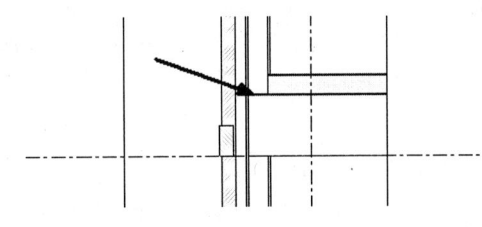

    If the roof is selected, it should be listed in the Options bar.

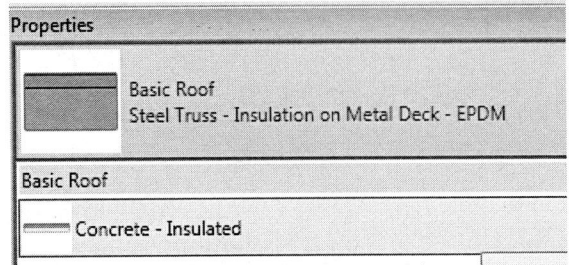

12. Change the Roof type to **Concrete - Insulated** on the Properties pane.

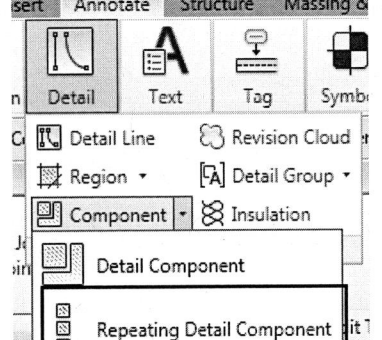

13. Select the **Repeating Detail** tool from the Detail panel on the Annotate ribbon.

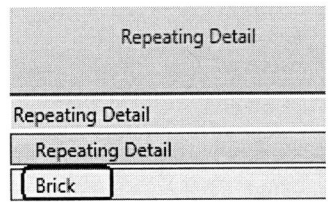

14. Set the repeating detail as **Brick**.

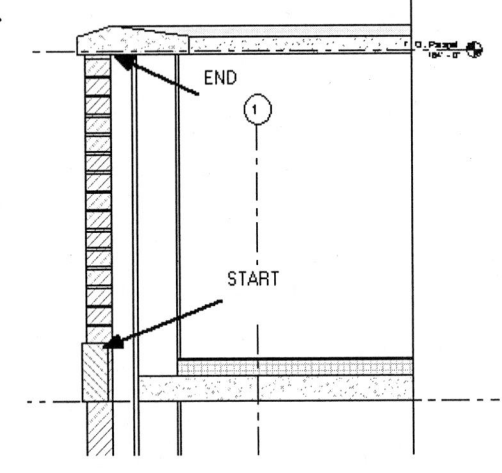

15. Pick the two points indicated to place the brick detail.

16. Select the brick repeating detail just placed.

    Select the **Edit Type** on the Properties pane.

17.

Parameter	Value
Pattern	
Detail	Brick Standard : Running Secti
Layout	Fixed Distance
Inside	Fill Available Space
Spacing	Fixed Distance
Detail Rotation	Fixed Number
	Maximum Spacing

Note that the detail was placed using a **Fixed Distance** layout.

18.

Pattern	
Detail	Brick Standard : Running
Layout	Fixed Distance
Inside	✓
Spacing	0' 2 5/8"
Detail Rotation	None

None
90° Clockwise
90° Counterclockwise
180°

Note that the detail can be rotated.

Note the spacing is set to **2 5/8"**.

Press **OK** to close the Type Properties dialog.

19. Select the **Detail Component** tool from the Annotate ribbon.

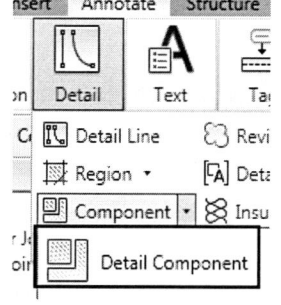

20. Note that the loaded component is a Brick Mortar Joint.

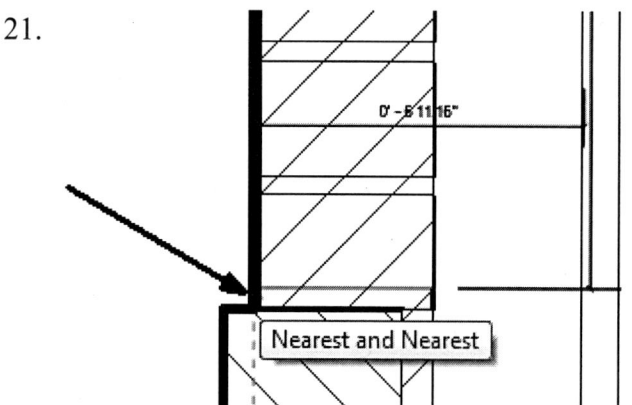

21. Place the joint at the bottom of the repeating detail.

Right click and select Cancel to exit the command.

22. 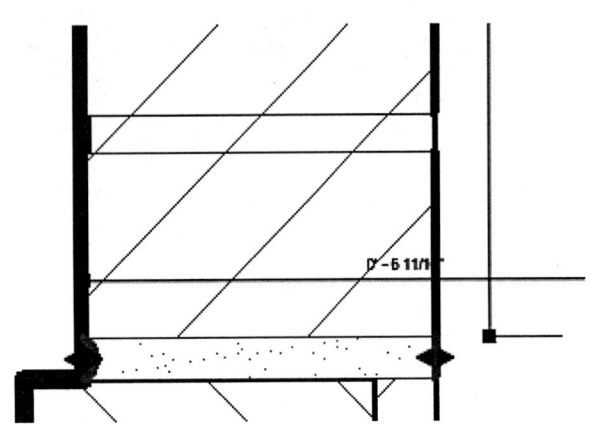 Select the mortar joint detail that was just placed.

23.  Select **Copy**.

24. 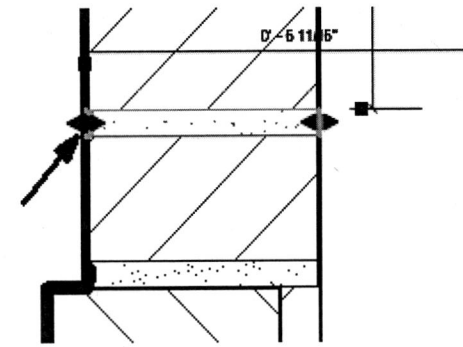 Place a copy of the mortar joint detail in the next mortar joint section on the repeating detail.

25. Select the copied mortar joint.

26. 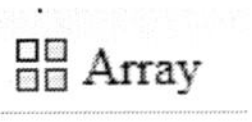 Select the **Array** tool.

27. 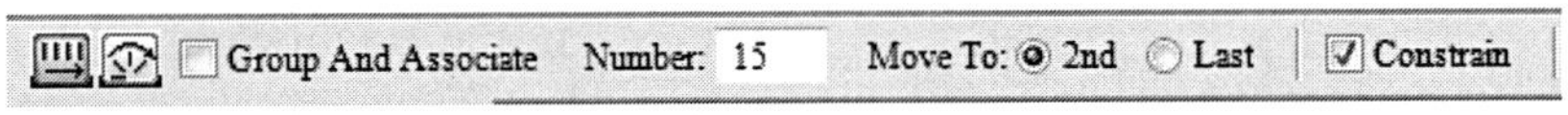 Enable **Linear**.
Uncheck **Group and Associate**.
Set the Number to **15**.
Enable **2ⁿᵈ**.
Check **Constrain**.

28. 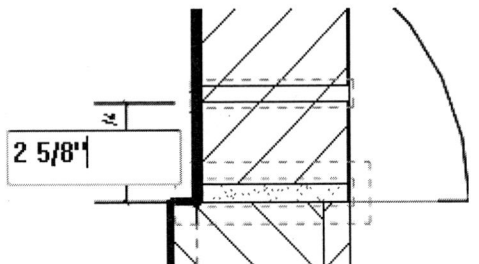 Set the spacing distance to **2 5/8″**.

Detailing and Drafting

29. Select the **Detail Component** tool from the Annotate ribbon.

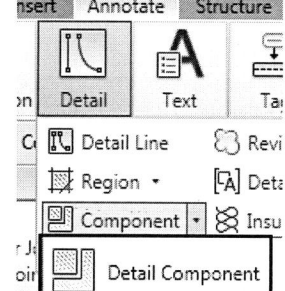

30. Select the **3″ x 3″ Cant Strip** from the drop-down list.

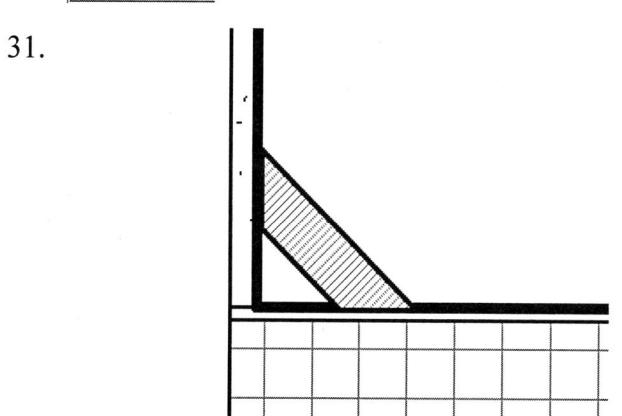

31. Place the cant strip as shown.

32. Select the **Detail Line** tool from the Annotate ribbon.

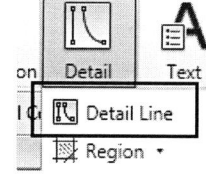

33. Select **Medium Lines** from the options drop-down list.

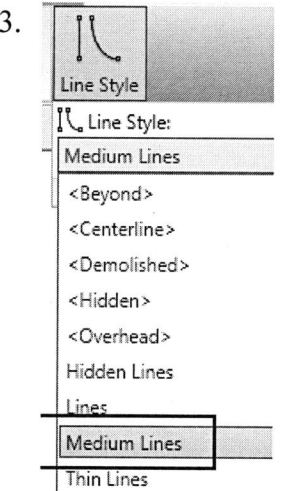

34. Enable **Chain**.
    Enter **1/4″** in the Offset box.

35. Select **Pick Lines** mode from the Draw panel.

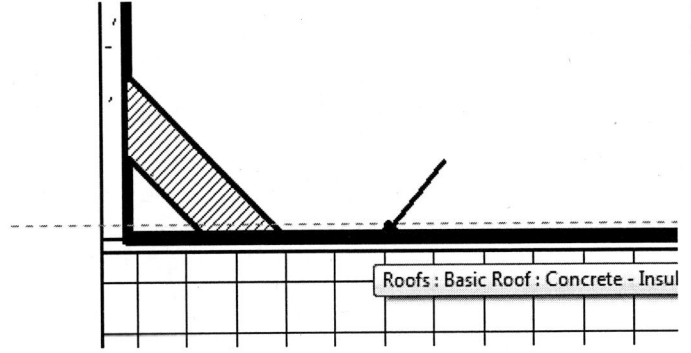

36. Pick the top of the roof to place the first offset line.

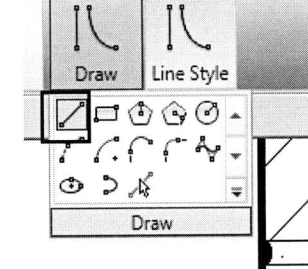

37. Switch to **Draw Line** mode.

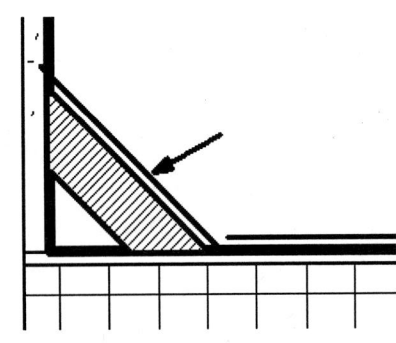

38. Place a line parallel to the Cant Strip.

    Set the offset to 1/4" and start the line at the top of the cant strip. This will orient the line above the can strip.

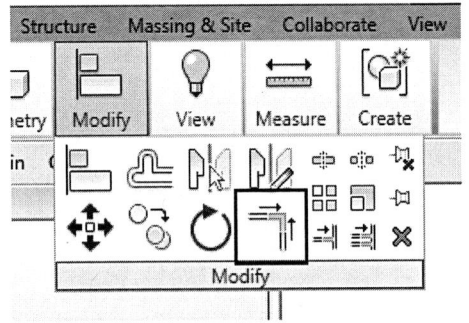

39. Use the **Trim** tool to clean up the detail lines.

40. Go to **File→Save As**.
    Save the file as *ex7-4.rvt*.

Command Exercise

Exercise 7-5 – Creating a Detail Group

Drawing Name: **i_detail_groups.rvt**
Estimated Time to Completion: 20 Minutes

Scope

> Add hidden lines.
> Add a steel plate using Detail Component.
> Add bolts to a plate.
> Create a detail group.
> Mirror a detail group.

Solution

1. Activate the **Beam-Column Connection** section view.

2. Activate the Annotate ribbon.

   Select the **Detail Component** tool from the Detail panel.

3. Select **Load Family** from the Mode panel.

4. Browse to the *Metal Fastenings* folder under *Detail Components Div 05 - Metals\ 050500 - Common Work Results for Metals*.

5. Open the *Steel Shear Plate - Face* family.

6. Press the SPACE bar to rotate the component prior to placing.

   Place on the left side of the column.

7. Activate the Annotate ribbon.

   Select the **Repeating Detail Component** tool from the Detail panel.

8. Select the **A325 - 5/8"** Plan detail.

9. Select **Edit Type** in the Properties pane.

10. Set the Layout to **Maximum Spacing**.
    Set the Spacing to **3 11/256"**.

    Press **OK**.

Detailing and Drafting

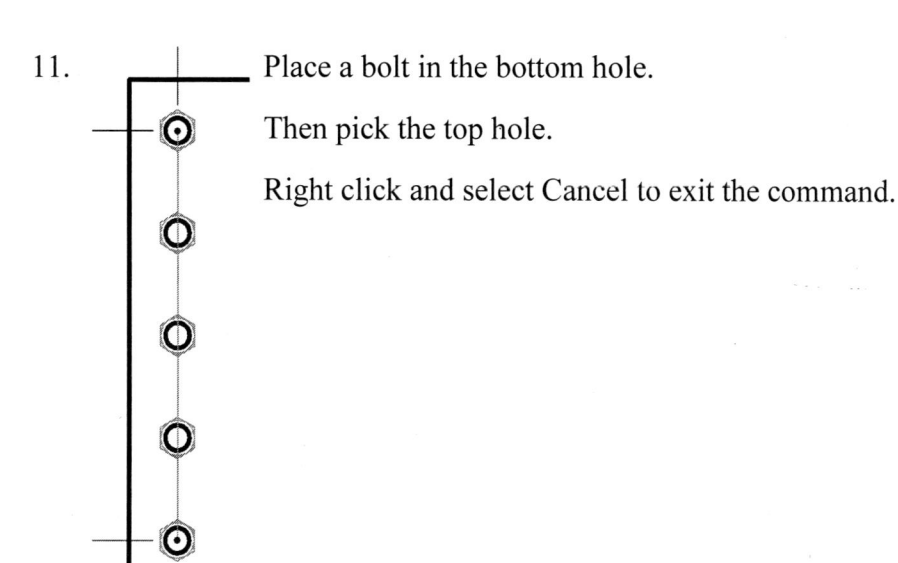

11. Place a bolt in the bottom hole.

Then pick the top hole.

Right click and select Cancel to exit the command.

12. 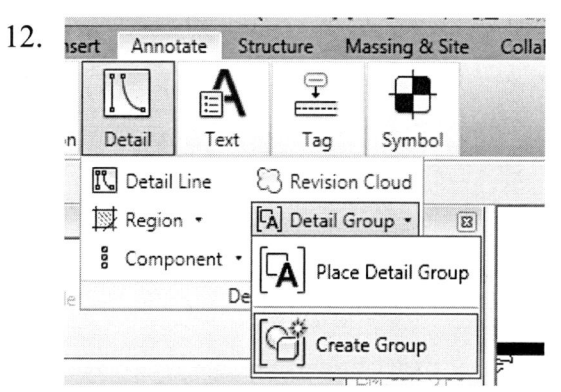 Window around the steel plate and the placed bolts to select them.

Select **Detail Group→Create Group** from the Detail panel on the Annotate ribbon.

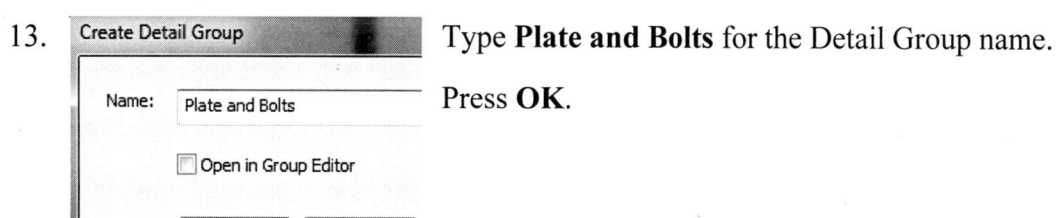

13. Type **Plate and Bolts** for the Detail Group name.

Press **OK**.

14. 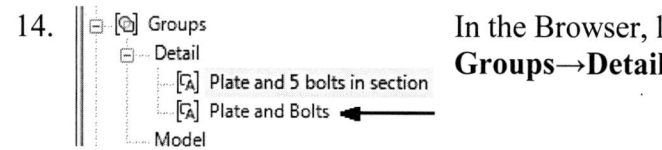 In the Browser, locate the detail group created under **Groups→Detail**.

15. 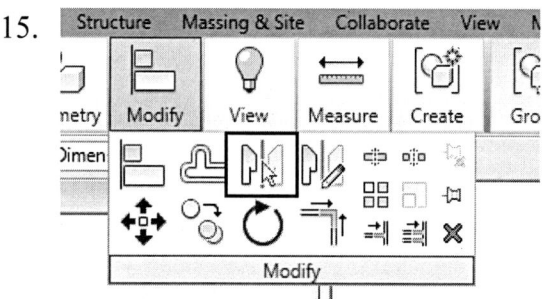 Select the steel plate and bolts detail group in the display window. The group should highlight.

Select **Mirror→Pick Axis** from the Modify panel.

7-21

16. Select the grid centered on the column as the axis.

   Click anywhere in the window to release the selection and complete the mirror command.

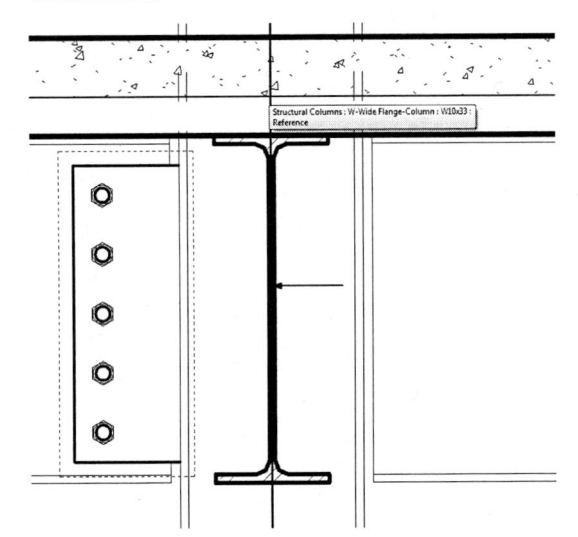

17. Locate the **Plate and 5 bolts in section** in the Project Browser.

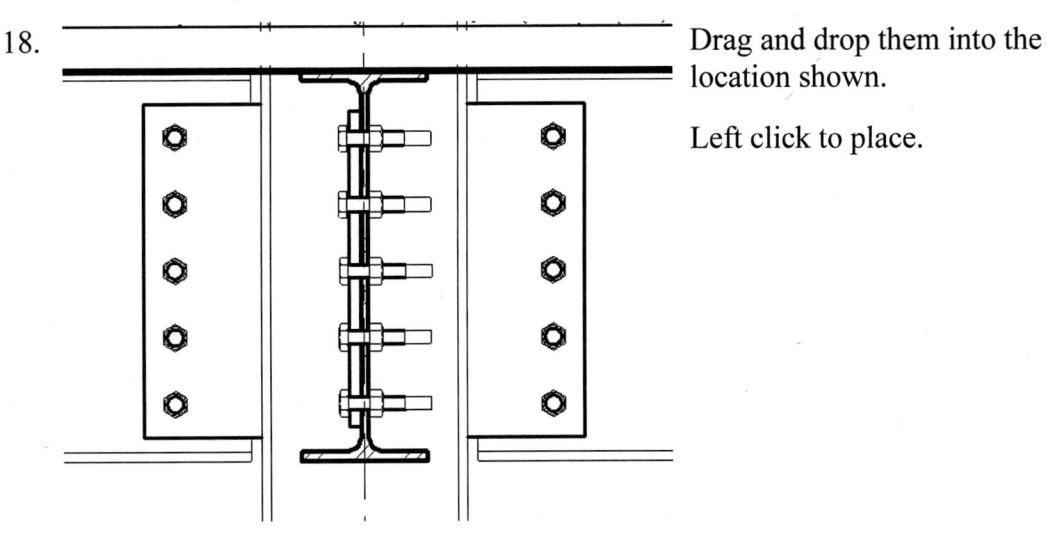

18. Drag and drop them into the location shown.

   Left click to place.

19. Close without saving.

Command Exercise

Exercise 7-6 – Import and Edit DWG Details

Drawing Name: **i_dwg_detail.rvt**
Estimated Time to Completion: 20 Minutes

Scope

Import a DWG file.
Edit the DWG details.
Modify the display of DWG layers.

Color Numbering Systems

Name	RGB	HSL	EGA	HTML	DGN	AutoCAD
Black	0,0,0	0,0,0	0	#000000	255	0
Blue	0,0,255	170,255,128	1	#0000FF	1	5
Green	0,255,0	85,255,128	2	#00FF00	2	3
Cyan	0,255,255	128,255,128	3	#00FFFF	7	4
Red	255,0,0	0,255,128	4	#FF0000	3	1
Magenta (pink)	255,0,255	213,255,128	5	#FF00FF	5	6
Yellow	255,255,0	43,255,128	6	#FFFF00	4	2
White	255,255,255	0,0,255	7	#FFFFFF	0	7
Gray	128,128,128	0,0,128	8	#808080	9	8
Light Blue	128,128,255	170,255,192	9	#8080FF		13
Light Green	128,255,128	85,255,192	10	#80FF80		11
Light Cyan	128,255,255	28,255,192	11	#80FFFF		12
Light Red	255,128,128	0,255,128	12	#FF8080		9
Light Magenta	255,128,255	213,255,192	13	#FF80EE		14
Light Yellow	255,255,128	42,255,92	14	#FFFF80		10
Light Gray	192,192,192	0,0,192	15	#C0C0C0		15

Solution

1. Activate the **View** ribbon.

   Select the **Drafting View** tool from the Create panel.

The Unofficial Revit 2012 Certification Exam Guide

2. Type **Gable Truss**.

   Press **OK**.

3. The drafting view is now listed in the Project Browser.

4. Activate the **Insert** ribbon.

   Select the small down arrow located on the Import panel.

5. Change the Lineweight for Color Number 1 to 3.
   Change the Lineweight for Color Number 2 to 2.
   Change the Lineweight for Color Number 5 to 4.

   Refer to the chart at the top of this exercise to find which colors are assigned which numbers.

6. Click **Save As**.

   By default, the lineweight settings are stored in a Read Only text file named *importlineweights-dwg-default.txt*.

   The file is located in the *C:\Program Files\Autodesk\Revit Architecture 2012\Data* folder.

7. Browse to your exercise folder.
   Name the file *Custom DWG Import*.

   Press **Save**.

Detailing and Drafting

8. 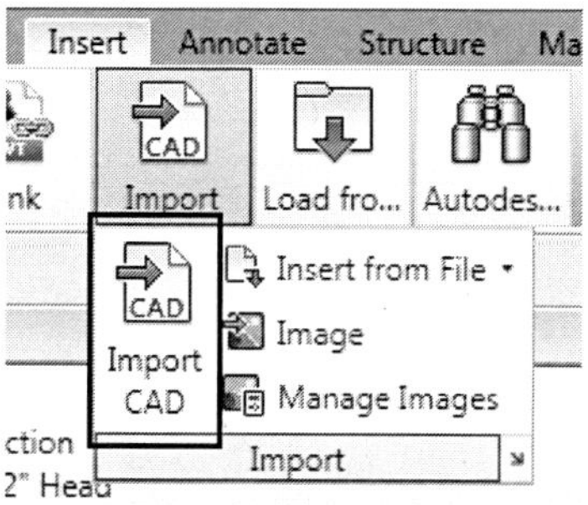 Activate the **Insert** ribbon.

   Select **Import CAD** from the Import panel.

9. 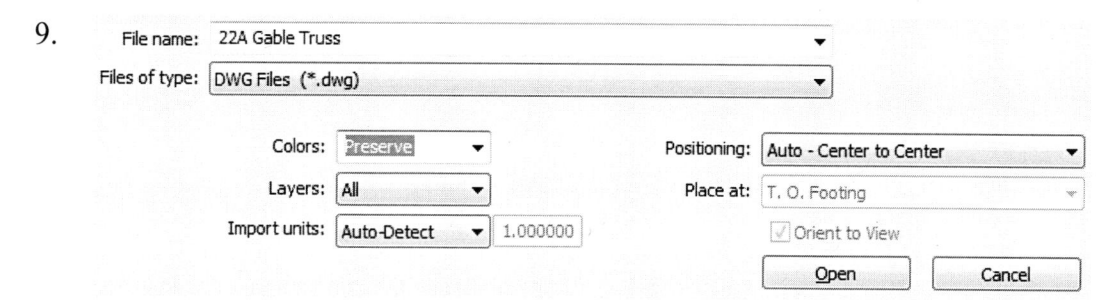 Locate the *22A Gable Truss dwg* file.

   Set Colors to **Preserve**.
   Set Layers to **All**.
   Set Import Units to **Auto-Detect**.
   Set Positioning to **Auto- Center to Center**.

10. Press **Open**.

11. 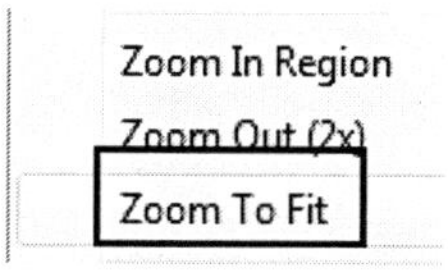 Right click in the drawing window.
    Select **Zoom to Fit**.

    You can also type ZF as a shortcut key.

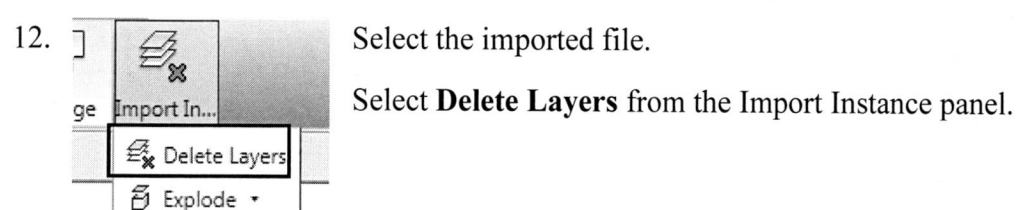

12. Select the imported file.

    Select **Delete Layers** from the Import Instance panel.

13. 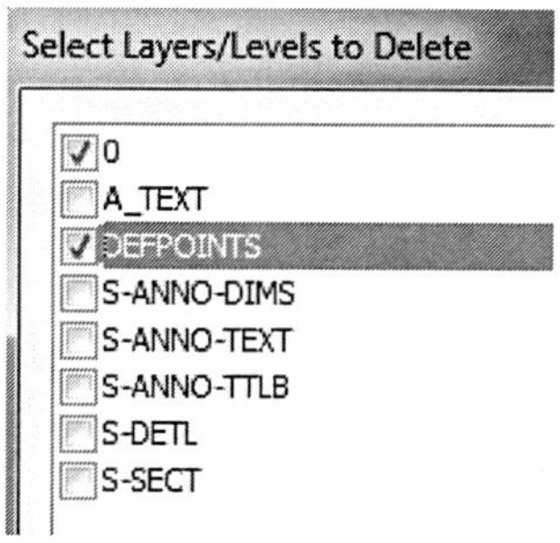 Enable **0** and **DEFPOINTS** as layers to delete.

    Press **OK**.

7-25

14. Left pick in the window to release the selection.

The Properties pane now shows the view properties.

Select **Edit** next to Visibility/Graphics Overrides.

15. Activate the Imported Categories tab.

Disable **A_TEXT** so that the layer is no longer visible.

Press **Apply** to see how the drawing changes.

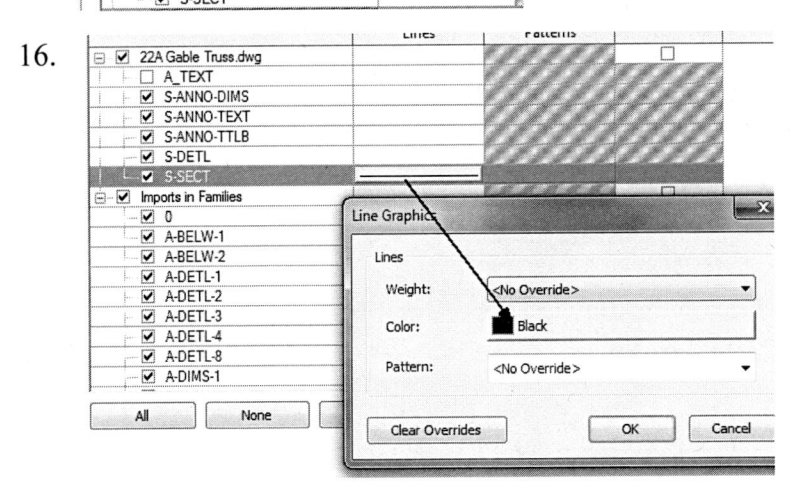

16. Select the Lines overrides for S-SECT layer.
Set the color to Black.

Press **OK**.

Press **Apply** to see how the drawing changes.

17. Select the imported drawing so it highlights.

Select **Partial Explode** from the Import Instance panel.

7-26

18. Select **Delete Element(s)**.

19. Window around the entire object.
    Select **Filter**.

20. Select **Check None** to uncheck all the categories.
    Then check only **Text Notes**.
    Press **OK**.

21. Set the Text to use **1/4″ Arial** in the Properties pane.

22. Select **Edit Type**.

23. Select **Duplicate**.

24. Enter **1/2″ RomanS**.
    Press **OK**.

25. Set the Color to **Red**.

26. Set the Text Font to **RomanS**.
    Set the Text Size to **1/2″**.
    Press **OK**.

27. Close without saving.

Command Exercise

Exercise 7-7 – Creating a Drafting View

Drawing Name: i_drview.rvt
Estimated Time to Completion: 50 Minutes

Scope
Create a drafting view.

Solution

1. 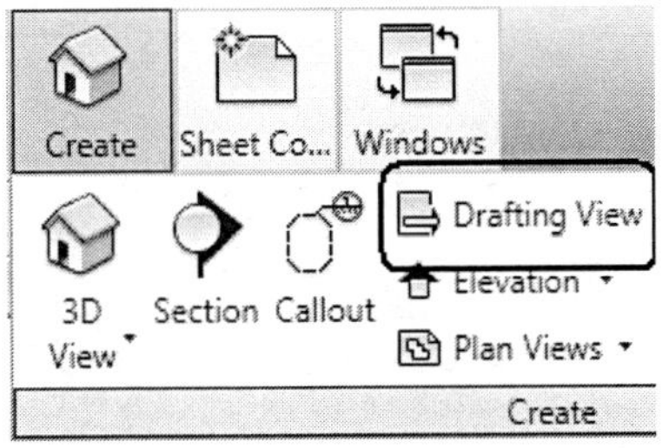 Activate the **View** ribbon.

   Select the **Drafting View** tool from the Create panel.

2. 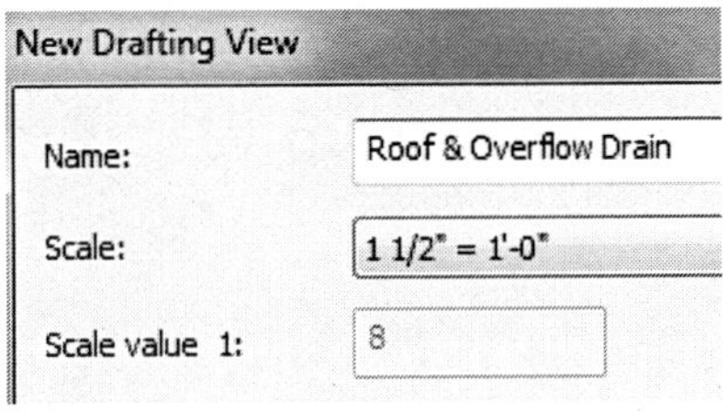 Enter **Roof & Overflow Drain** for the Name.
   Set the Scale to **1 ½″ = 1′0″**.

   Press **OK**.

3. A blank view opens.
   Note in the browser that we are in an active drafting view.

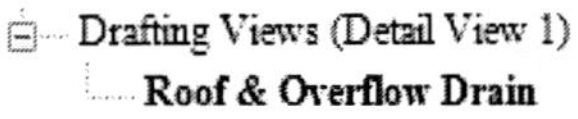

4. 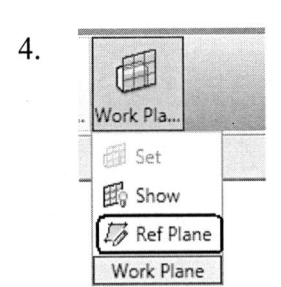 Select the **Reference Plane** tool from the Work Plane panel on the Home ribbon.

7-28

Detailing and Drafting

5. Place a vertical reference plane in the middle of the blank view.

6. Select the **Detail Component** tool from the Detail panel on the Annotate ribbon.

7. Select **Roof Drain** from the Type Selector list on the Properties pane.

8. Place the roof drain **1'-3"** to the left of the reference plane.

   Right click and select Cancel to exit the command.

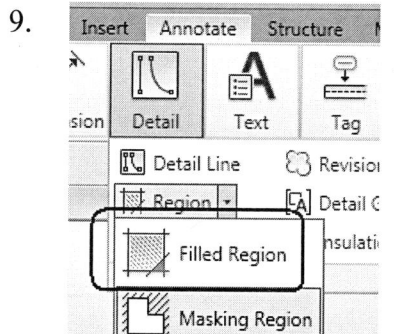

9. Select the **Filled Region** tool from the Detail panel on the Annotate ribbon.

7-29

The Unofficial Revit 2012 Certification Exam Guide

10. 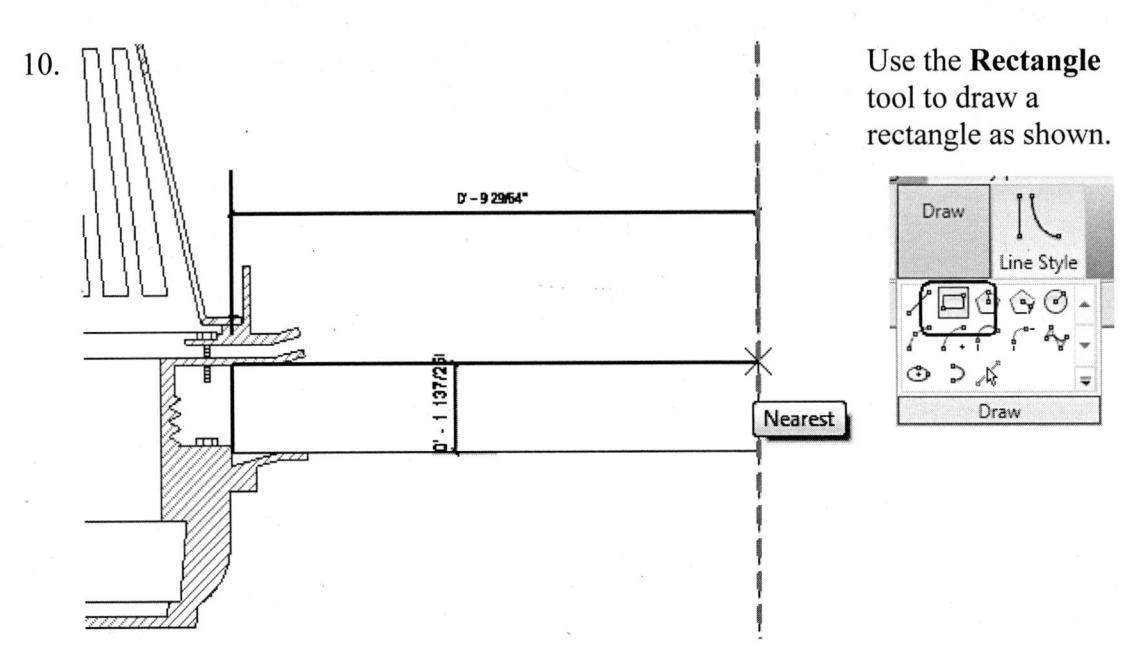 Use the **Rectangle** tool to draw a rectangle as shown.

11. 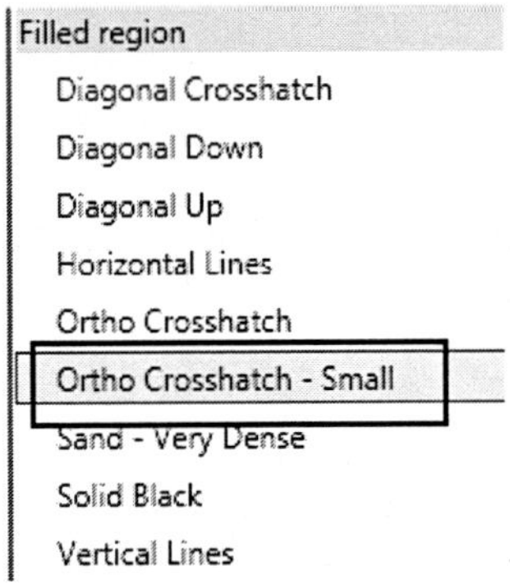 In the Properties pane:

    Select the Filled Region type to **Ortho Crosshatch – Small**.

12. 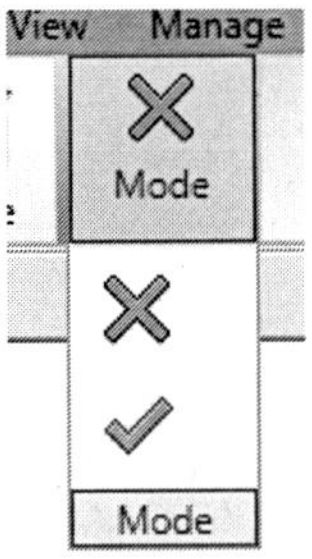 Select the **Green Check** under Mode to **Finish Region**.

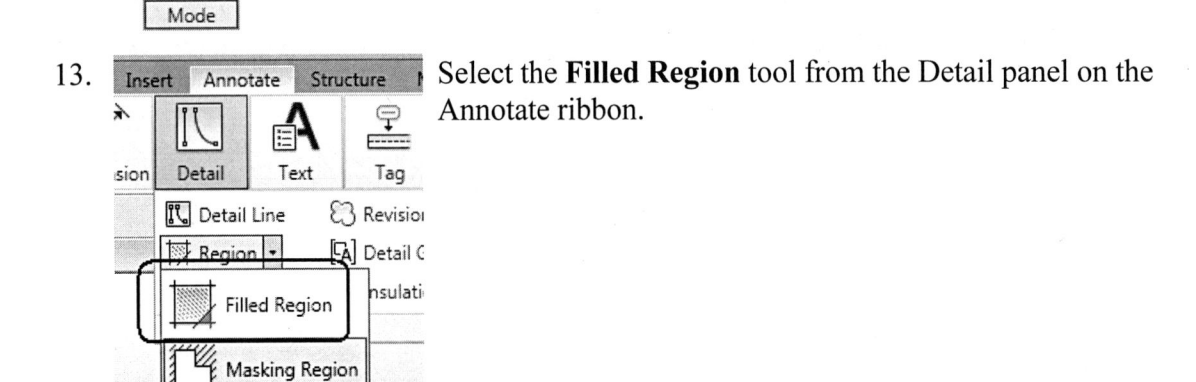

13. Select the **Filled Region** tool from the Detail panel on the Annotate ribbon.

Detailing and Drafting

14. Use the **Rectangle** tool to draw a rectangle as shown.

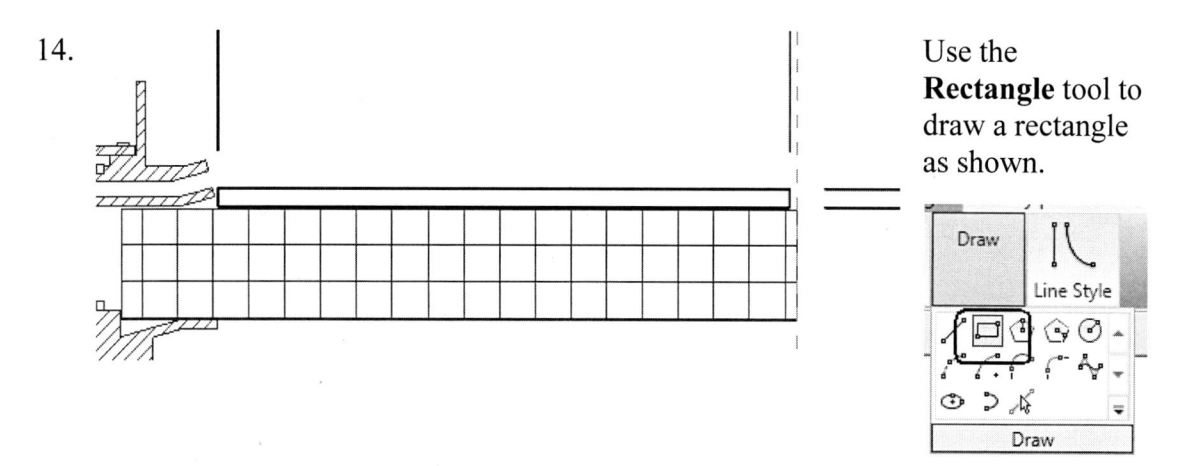

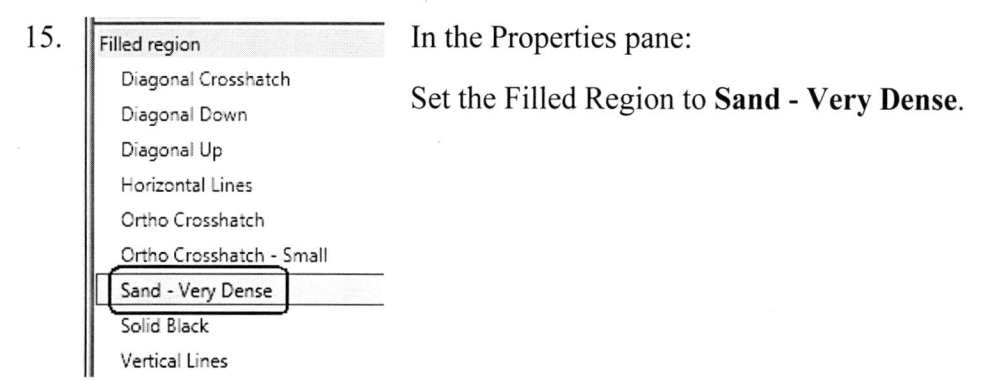

15. In the Properties pane:

    Set the Filled Region to **Sand - Very Dense**.

16. Select the **Green Check** under Mode to **Finish Region**.

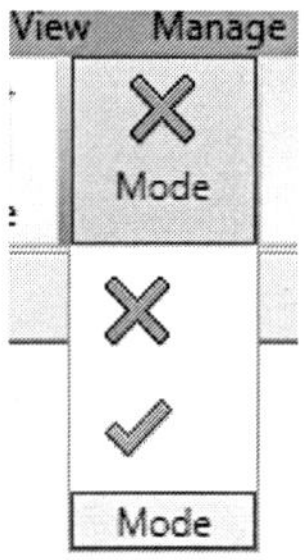

17. Select the **Detail Line** tool from the Detail panel.

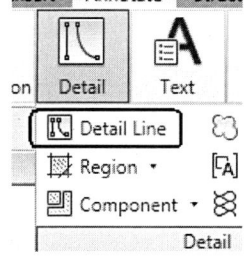

18. Select **Thin Lines** on the Line Style.

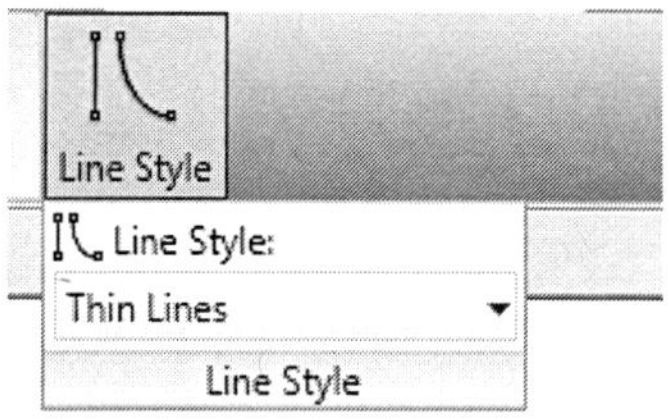

7-31

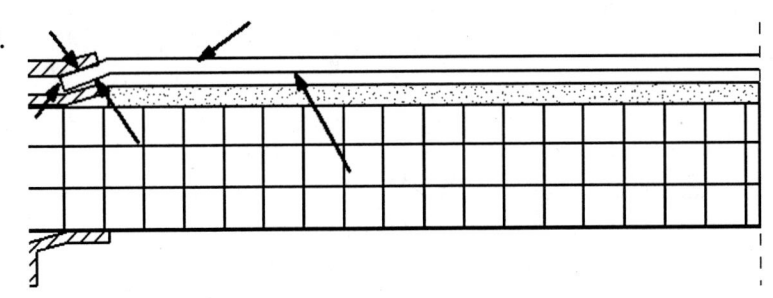

19. Draw the outline indicated with arrows.

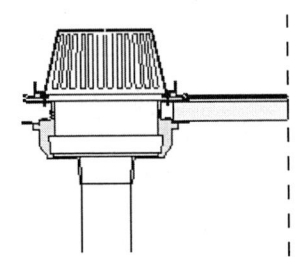

20. Window around the elements to select everything except the reference plane.

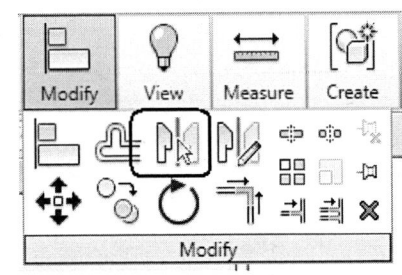

21. Select the **Mirror** tool using the **Mirror Pick Axis** option.
Select the reference plane to use as the axis.

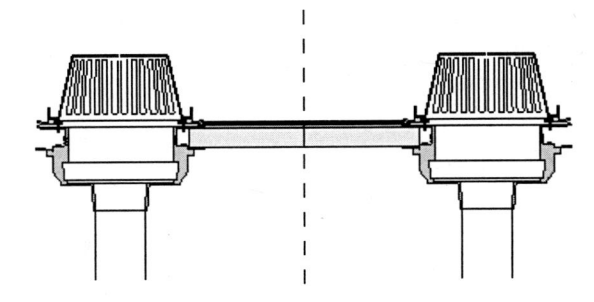

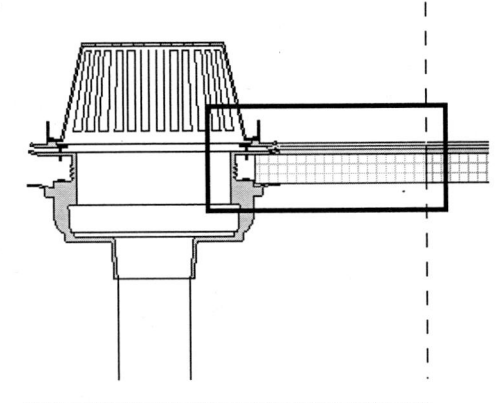

22. Window around the filled regions and detail lines to select.

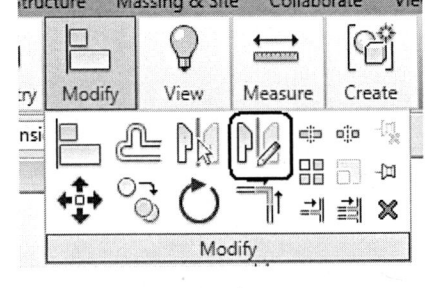

23. Select the **Mirror** tool using the **Draw Mirror Axis** option.
Select the reference plane to use as the axis.

7-32

24. 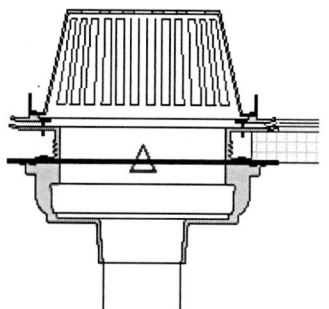 Select the midpoint of the roof drain to draw the axis.

25. 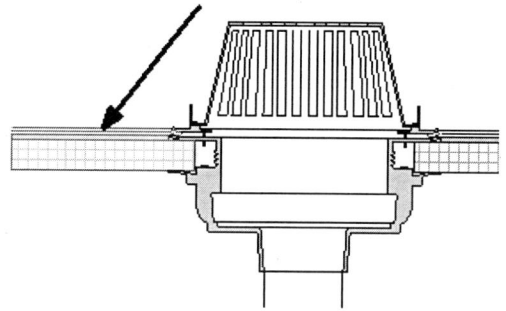 The elements are mirrored to the other side.

26. 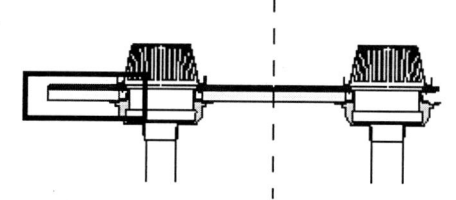 Select the mirrored elements.

27. 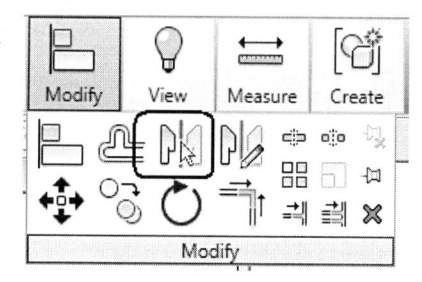 Select **Mirror → Pick Mirror Axis** from the ribbon.

28. 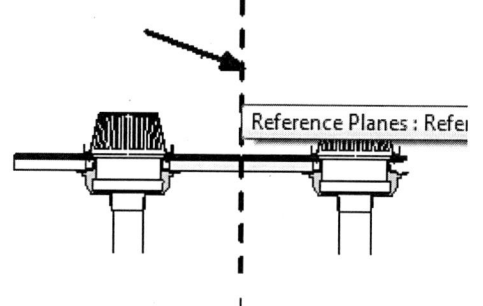 Select the reference plane to use as the mirror axis.

29. 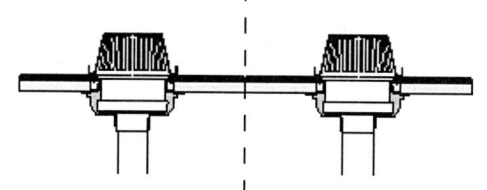 The elements are mirrored.

7-33

30. Select the **Detail Component** tool from the Annotate ribbon.

31. Select **Break Line** from the Type Selector drop-down list on the Properties pane.

32. Position the cursor to the left of the detail view.

    Press the SPACEBAR to rotate the break line.

33. Place the break line so it is coincident with the vertical line at the end of the filled region element.

    Repeat for the right side.

34. On the Properties Pane:

    Change the Ring Height to **2"**.

    Press **OK**.

35. Select the **Aligned** dimension tool on the Annotate ribbon.

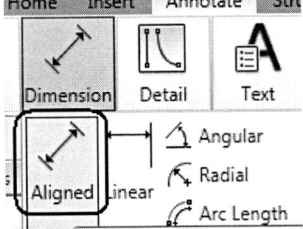

7-34

Detailing and Drafting

36. Place a dimension from center to center distance between the roof drains.

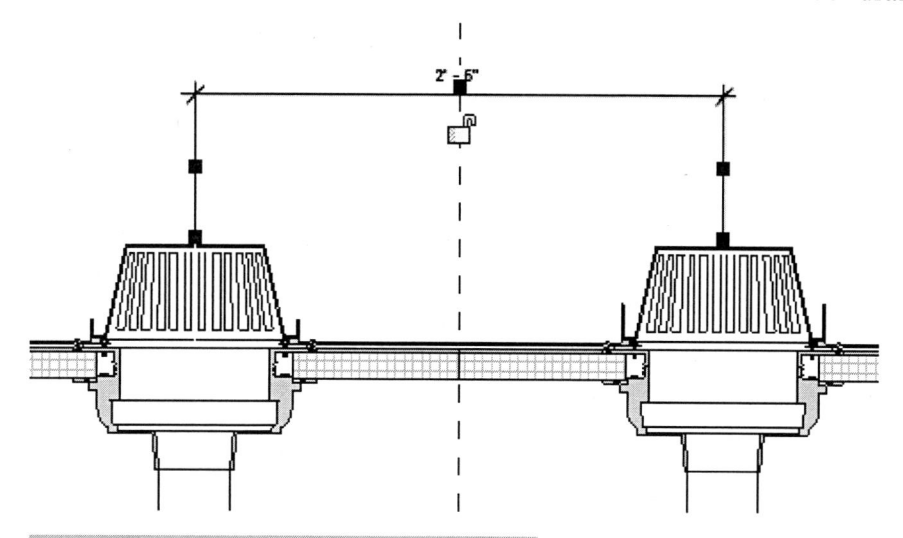

37. With the dimension selected, select **Linear w Center - 3/32" Arial** from the Type Selector drop-down list on the Properties pane.

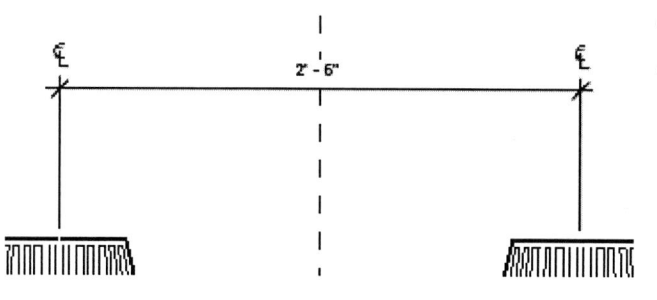

38. The dimension changes to display centerline symbols.

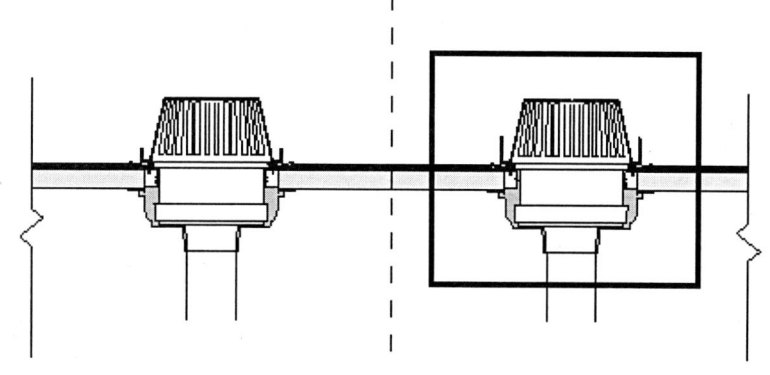

39. Zoom into the right roof drain.

7-35

40. Select the **Text** tool from the Annotate ribbon.

41. Enable the **Two Segments** leader option on the Format panel.

42. Place the text as shown.

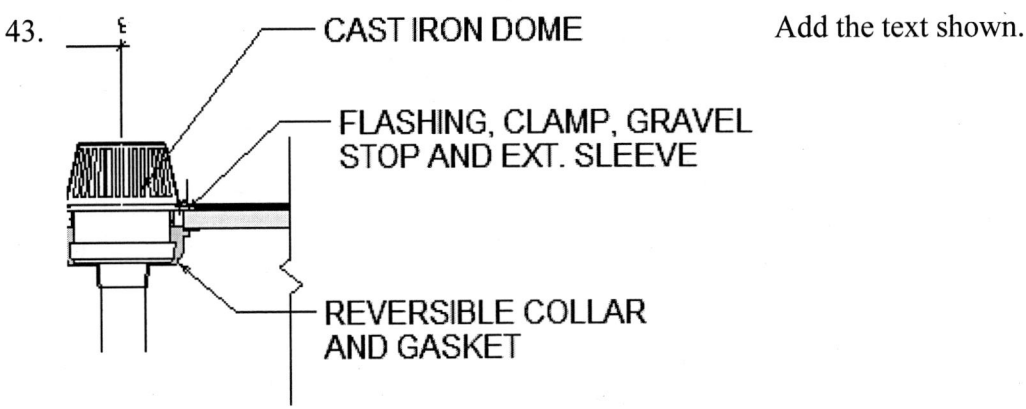

43. Add the text shown.

44. Close without saving.

Command Exercise

Exercise 7-8 – Revision Control

Drawing Name: **i_Revisions.rvt**
Estimated Time to Completion: 15 Minutes

Scope

Add a sheet.
Add a view to a sheet.
Setting up Revision Control in a project.

Solution

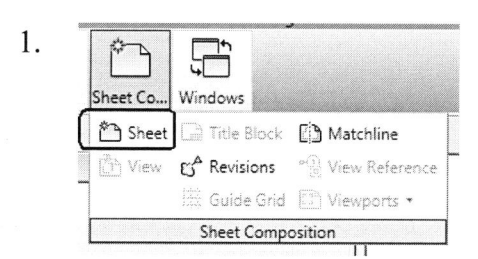

1. Activate the **View** ribbon.

   Select the **New Sheet** tool on the Sheet Composition panel.

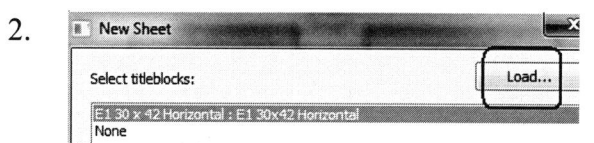

2. Select the **Load** button.

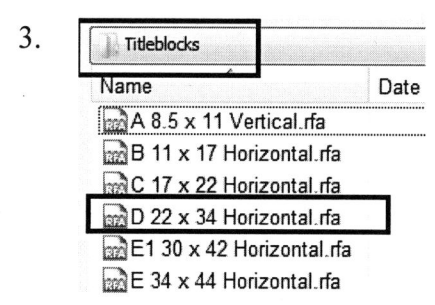

3. Locate the *Titleblocks* folder.

   Locate the **D 22 x 34 Horizontal** titleblock.

   Press **Open**.

4. Highlight the **D 22 x 34 Horizontal** titleblock.

   Press **OK**.

The Unofficial Revit 2012 Certification Exam Guide

5. Drag and drop the **Level 1** floor plan onto the sheet.

6. Select the view.

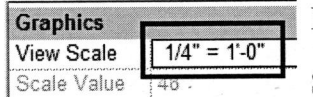

   In the Properties pane:

   Set the View Scale to **1/4″ = 1′-0″**.

7. Position the view on the sheet.

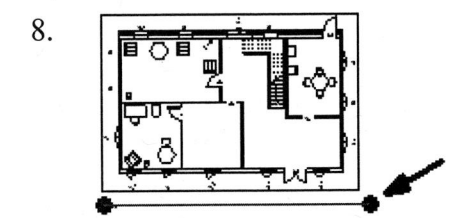

8. To adjust the view title bar, select the view and the grips will become activated.

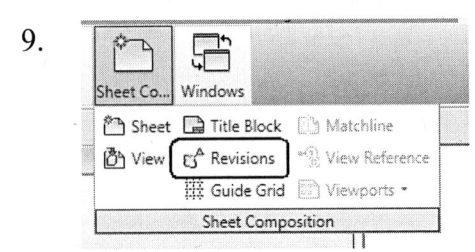

9. Activate the **View** ribbon.

   Select **Revisions** on the **Sheet Composition** panel.

10. This dialog manages revision control settings and history.

Numbering can be controlled per project or per sheet. The setting used depends on your company's standards.

Enable **Per Project**.

One Revision is available by default. Additional revisions are added using the **Add** button.

11. The visibility of revisions can be set to **None**, **Tag** or **Cloud and Tag**. Use the **None** setting for older revisions which are no longer applicable so as not to confuse the contractors.

Set the revision to show **Cloud and Tag**.

12. Select the **Options** button.

13. Change the sequence to remove the letters **I** and **O**.

Press **OK**.

Revit only allows numeric or alphabetic revisions – no combinations.

14. Set the Numbering to **Alphabetic**.

15. Enter the three revision changes shown.

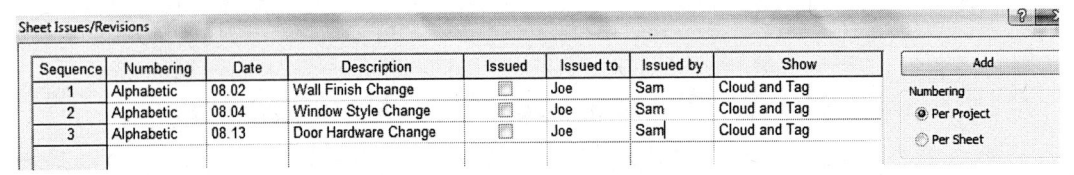

Sequence	Numbering	Date	Description	Issued	Issued to	Issued by	Show
1	Alphabetic	08.02	Wall Finish Change	☐	Joe	Sam	Cloud and Tag
2	Alphabetic	08.04	Window Style Change	☐	Joe	Sam	Cloud and Tag
3	Alphabetic	08.13	Door Hardware Change	☐	Joe	Sam	Cloud and Tag

Numbering:
- ● Per Project
- ○ Per Sheet

16. Press **OK** to close the dialog.

17. Save project as *ex7-8.rvt*.

Detailing and Drafting

Command Exercise

Exercise 7-9 – Modify a Revision Schedule

Drawing Name: **ex7-8.rvt**
Estimated Time to Completion: 20 Minutes

Scope

Modify a revision schedule in a title block.

Solution

1. 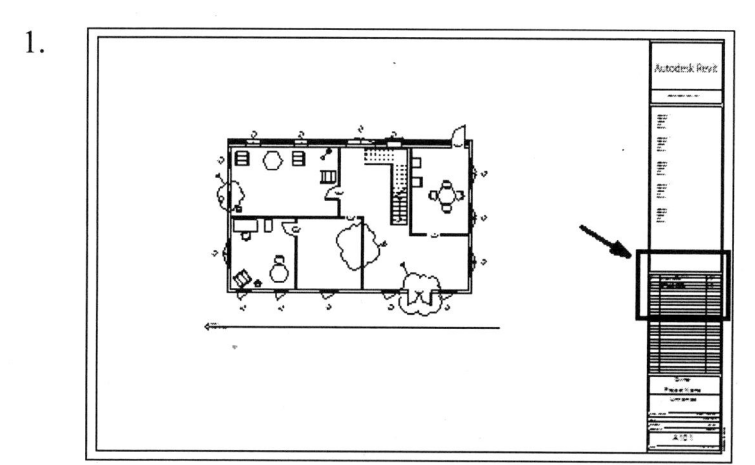 Zoom in to the **Revision Block** area on the sheet.

2. 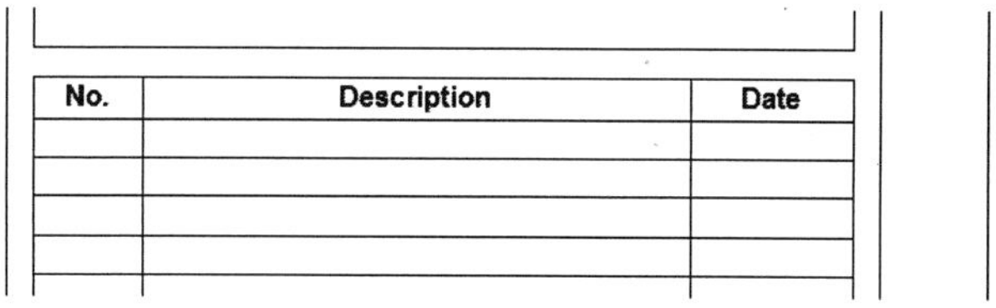 Note that the title block includes a revision schedule by default.

3. 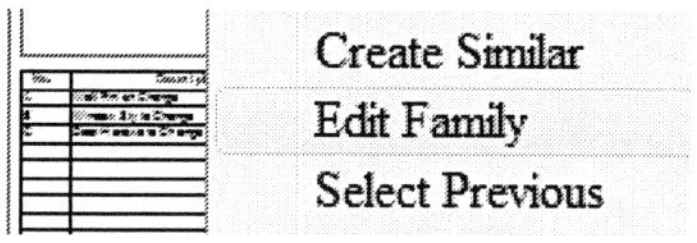 Select the title block.

   Right click and select **Edit Family**.

4. 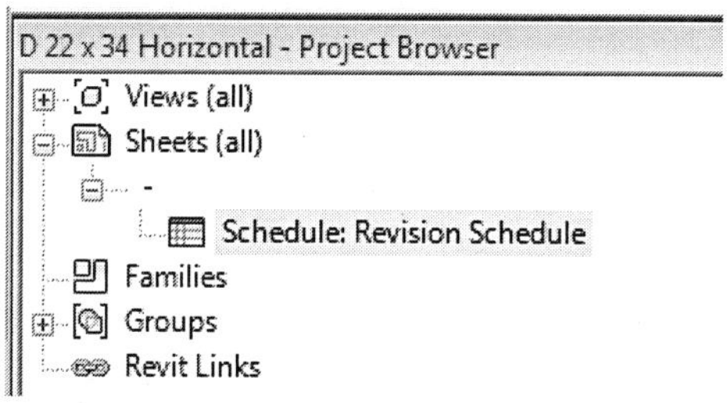 Select the **Revision Schedule** in the Project Browser.

5. 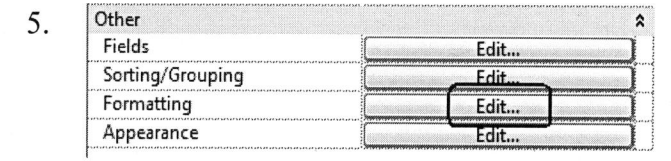 Select **Edit** next to Formatting in the Properties pane.

7-41

6. Change the First Column Header to **Rev**.

7. Select the Fields tab.

   Add the **Issued By** field.

8. Do **NOT** remove the Revision Sequence field. This is a hidden field.

   Note that the Hidden field control is located on the Formatting tab. This is a possible question on the Associate exam.

9. Order the fields as shown.

   Press **OK**.

10. The Revision Schedule updates.

11. Adjust the column width of the schedule so it fits properly in the title block.

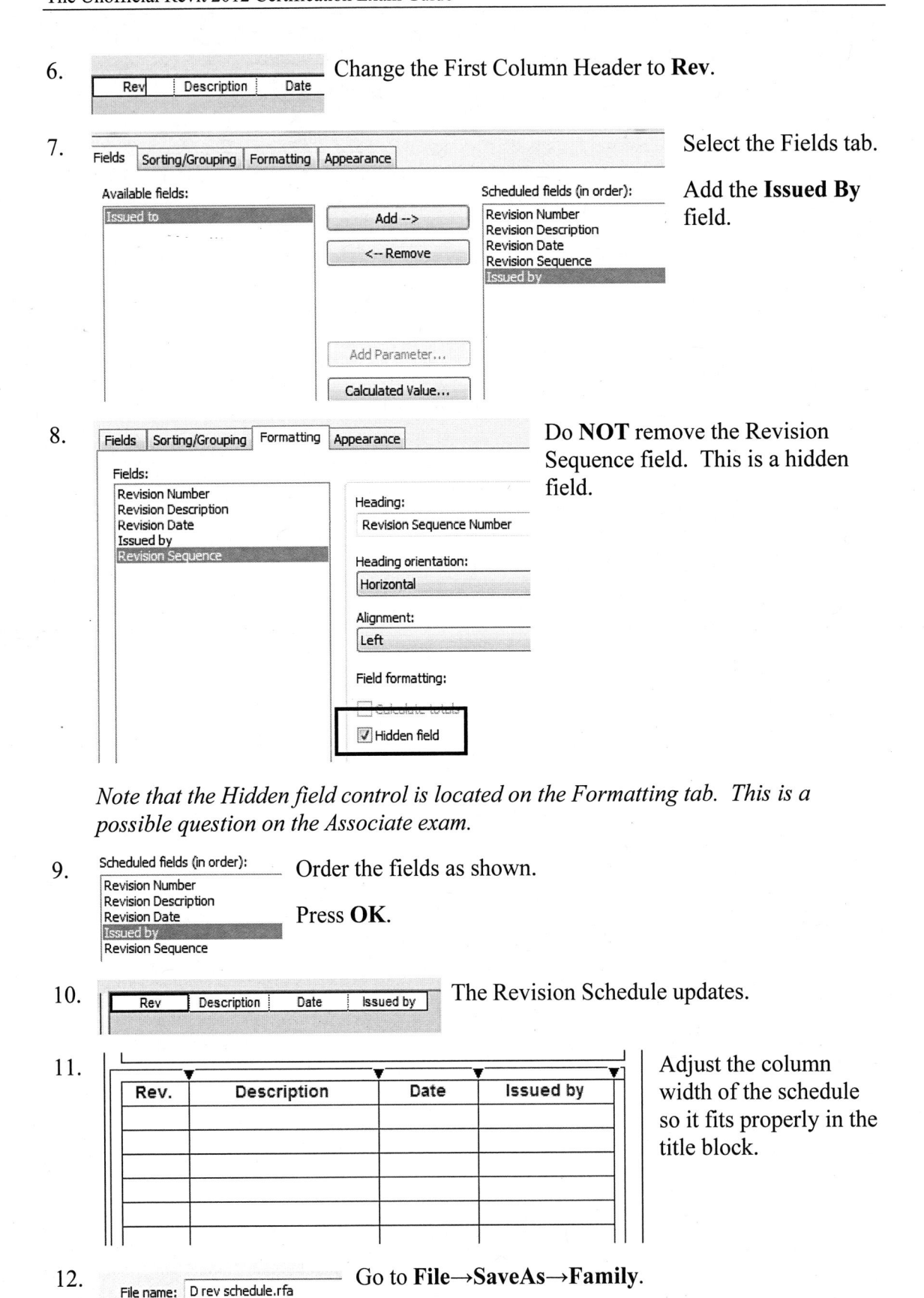

12. Go to **File→SaveAs→Family**.

    Save as *D rev schedule.rfa*.

7-42

Detailing and Drafting

13. Select **Load into Project** on the Family Editor panel on the ribbon.

14. If you have more than one project open:

    Place a check next to *ex7-8.rvt*.

    Press **OK**.

15. Select **Overwrite the existing version** if this dialog appears.

    You will only see this dialog if you have already loaded the new title block in the project.

16. Select the title block so it is highlighted.

    Locate the **D rev schedule** title block in the pull-down list on the Properties pane and select.

17. Note the title block updates with the new revision schedule format.

18. Save as *ex7-9.rvt*.

7-43

The Unofficial Revit 2012 Certification Exam Guide

Command Exercise
Exercise 7-10 – Add Revision Clouds

Drawing Name: **ex7-9.rvt**
Estimated Time to Completion: 30 Minutes

Scope

Add revision clouds to a view.
Tag revision clouds.

Solution

1. Activate the sheet with the **Level 1** floor plan.

2. Activate the **Annotate** ribbon.

    Select **Revision Cloud** from the Detail panel.

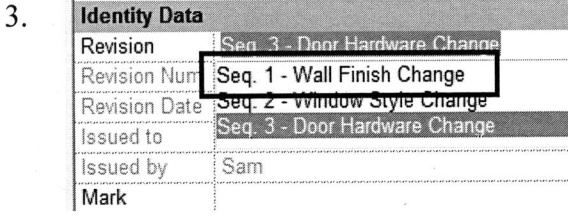

3. On the Properties pane:

    Select the Revision that is tied to the revision cloud – **Wall Finish Change**.

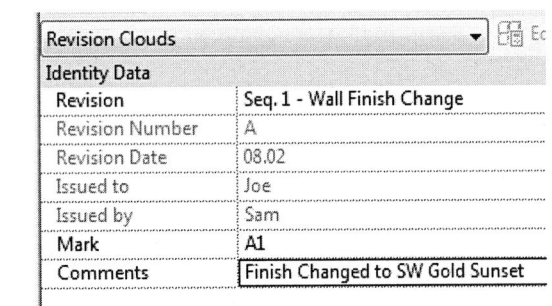

4. Under Mark: Enter **A1**.

    Under Comments: Enter **Finish Changed to SW Gold Sunset**.

Detailing and Drafting

5. 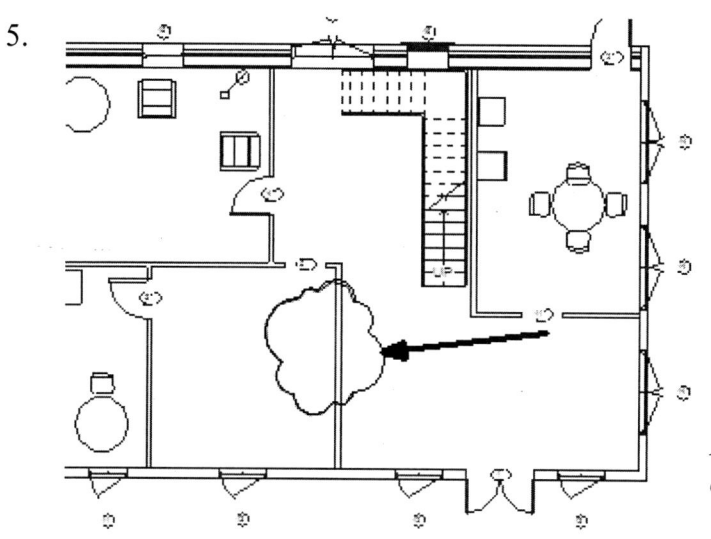 Draw the Revision Cloud on the wall indicated.

   Note that clouds are drawn clockwise.

6. 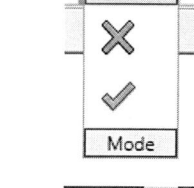 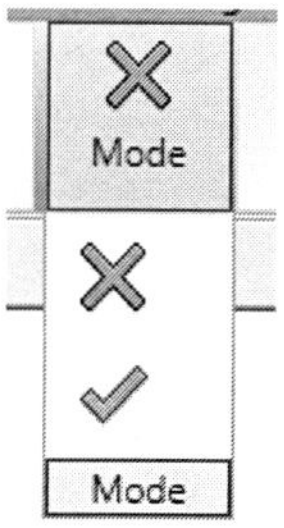 Select the **Green Check** on the Mode panel to **Finish Cloud**.

7. 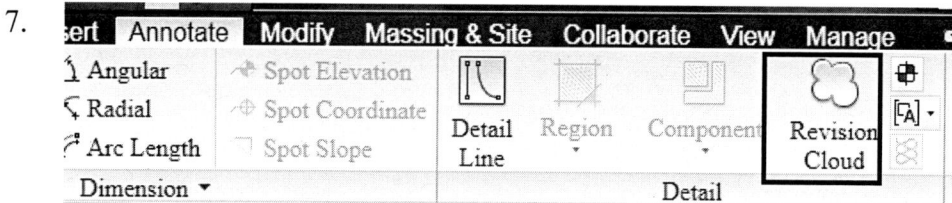 Activate the **Annotate** ribbon.

   Select **Revision Cloud**.

8. 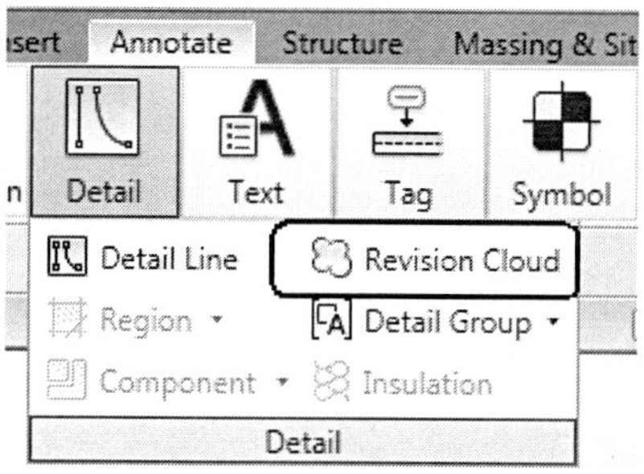 Activate the **Annotate** ribbon.

   Select **Revision Cloud** from the Detail panel.

9. Select the Revision that is tied to the revision cloud – **Window Style Change**.

7-45

10. | Parameter | Value |
|---|---|
| **Identity Data** | |
| Revision | Seq. 2 - Window Style Change |
| Revision Number | B |
| Revision Date | 08.04 |
| Issued to | Joe |
| Issued by | Sam |
| Mark | B1 |
| Comments | Use Assy Code 301 |

Under Mark: Enter **B1**.

Under Comments: Enter **Use Assy Code 301**.

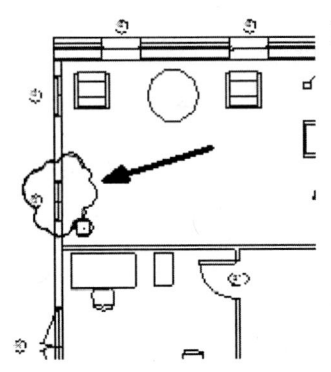

11. Draw the Revision Cloud on the window indicated.

12. Select the **Green Check** on the Mode panel to **Finish Cloud**.

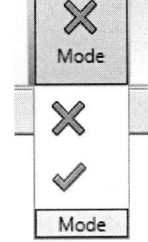

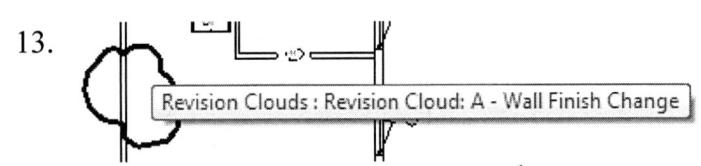

13. If you mouse over the revision cloud, you will see a tooltip to indicate what the revision is.

    (Revision Clouds : Revision Cloud: A - Wall Finish Change)

14. Activate the **Annotate** ribbon.

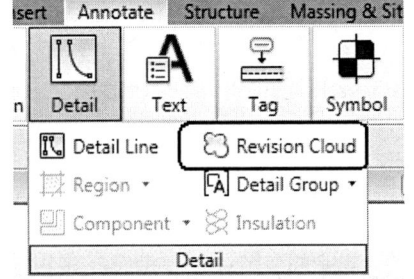

    Select **Revision Cloud** from the Detail panel.

15. On the Properties pane:

    Select the Revision that is tied to the revision cloud – **Door Hardware Change**.

Detailing and Drafting

16. Under Mark: Enter **C1**.

    Under Comments: Enter **Use Hardware Set #230**.

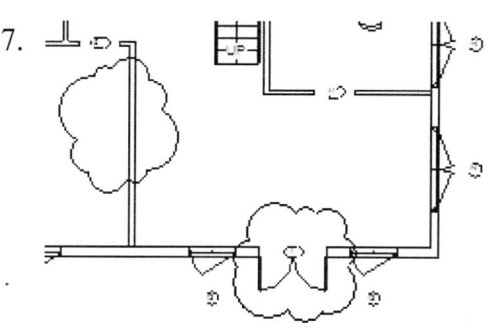

17. Draw the Revision Cloud on the door indicated.

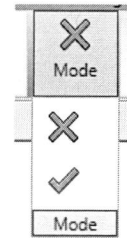

18. Select the **Green Check** on the Mode panel to **Finish Cloud**.

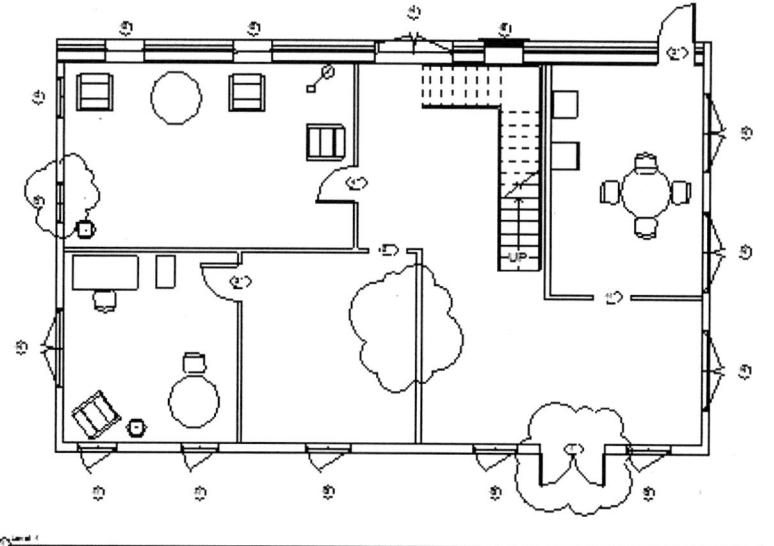

19. Three revision clouds have been placed in the view.

20. Zoom into the title block and note that the revision block has updated with the revisions that have been issued.

7-47

21. Select the **Tag by Category** tool from the Tag panel on the Annotate ribbon.

22. Pick one of the revision clouds to identify the category to be tagged.

23. Press **Yes**.

24. Select the *Annotations* folder.

    Locate the **Revision Tag**.

    Press **Open**.

25. Select the revision cloud to add the tag.

26. The tag is placed.

27. Repeat to add tags to the other two revision clouds.

28. Save as *ex7-10.rvt*.

7-48

Detailing and Drafting

Command Exercise

Exercise 7-11 – Aligning Views between Sheets

Drawing Name: **aligning_views.rvt**
Estimated Time to Completion: 30 Minutes

Scope

Using Grid Guides

Solution

1. Activate the sheet with the sheet with **Level 1** floor plan.

2. In the Properties pane:

   Scroll down and note that Grid Guide is set to <None>.

3. Activate the **View** ribbon.

   Select **Guide Grid** on the Sheet Composition panel.

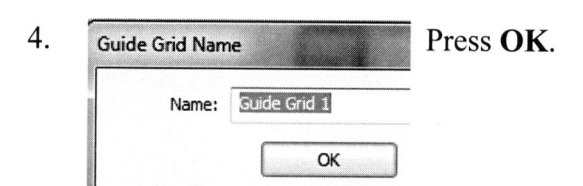

4. Press **OK**.

5. Select the Guide Grid.

   In the Properties pane:
   Set the Guide Spacing to **2"**.

7-49

The Unofficial Revit 2012 Certification Exam Guide

6. The grid updates.

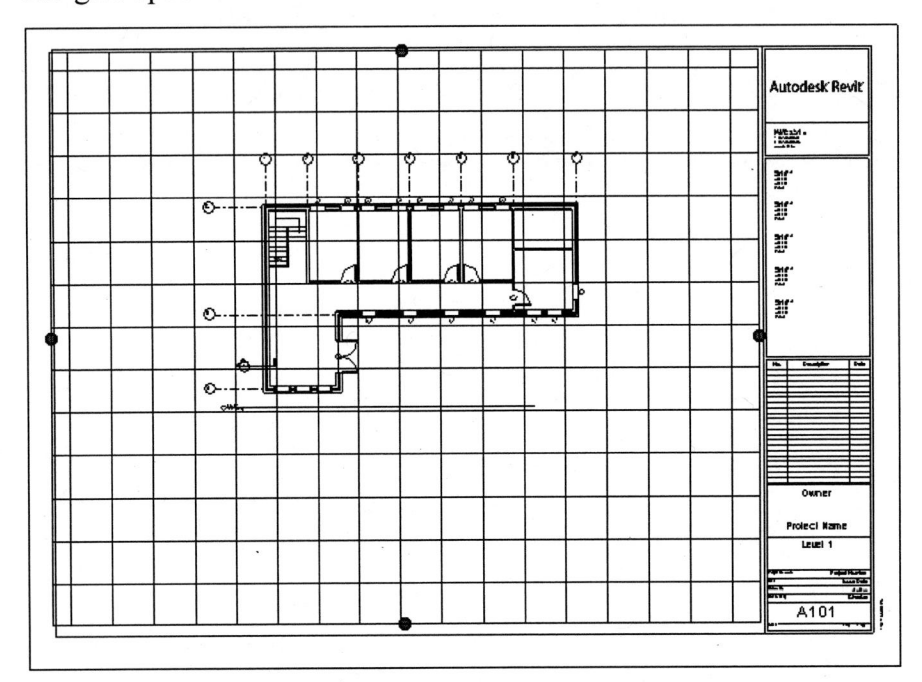

Use the blue grips to adjust the grid so it lies entirely inside the title block.

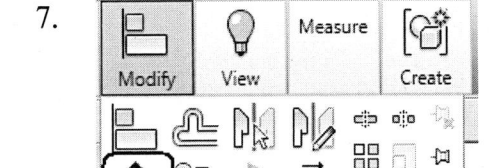

7. Select the viewport.

   Select the **Move** tool from the Modify Panel.

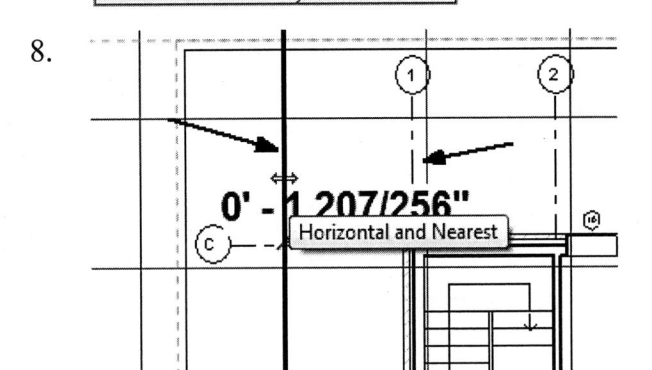

8. Select on the grid line 1 in the view.

   Then select the guide grid.

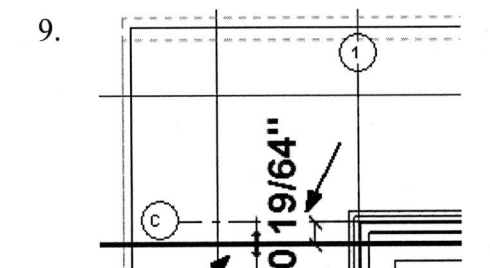

9. Repeat to shift grid line C into alignment with the grid guide.

7-50

Detailing and Drafting

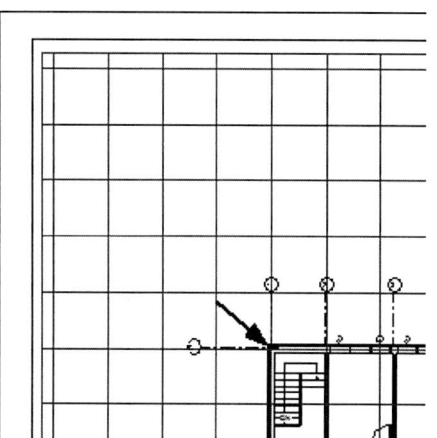

10. Zoom out and note which grid the view is aligned to.

11. Activate the sheet named **High Roof**.

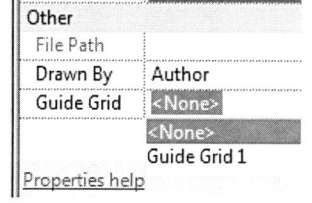

12. In the Properties pane:

    Set the Guide Grid to **Guide Grid 1**.

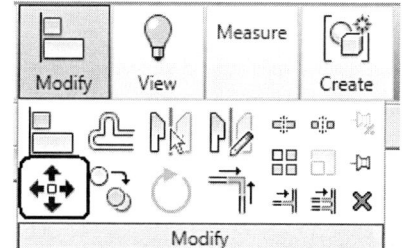

13. Select the viewport.

    Select the **Move** tool from the Modify Panel.

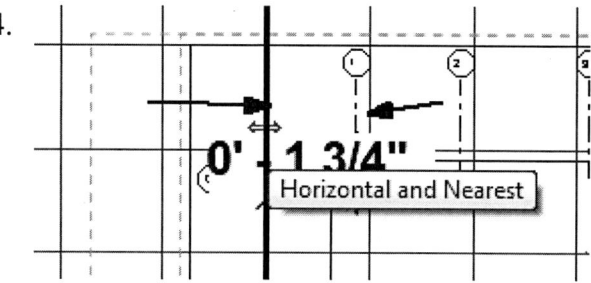

14. Select on the grid line 1 in the view.

    Then select the guide grid.

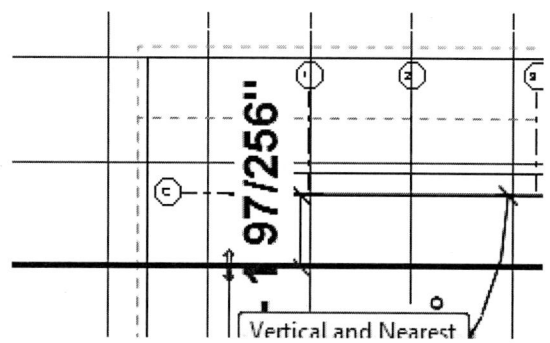

15. Repeat to shift grid line C into alignment with the grid guide.

7-51

16. Select the view title and adjust the position.

17. Type **VV**.
    Select the **Annotation Categories** tab.
    Disable visibility of the **Guide Grid**.
    Press **OK**.

18. Select the viewport.
    Select **Pin** from the Modify panel.

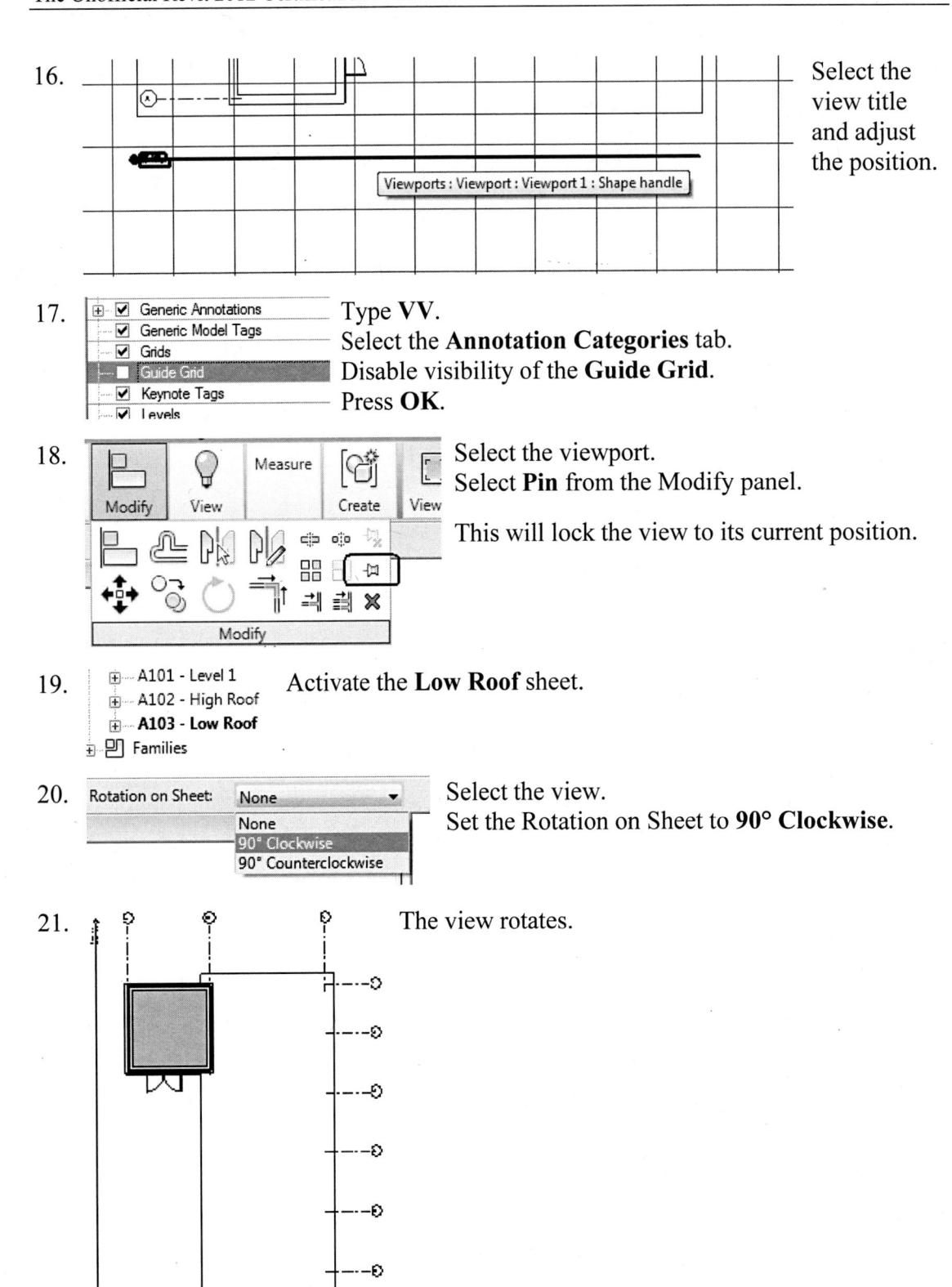

    This will lock the view to its current position.

19. Activate the **Low Roof** sheet.

20. Select the view.
    Set the Rotation on Sheet to **90° Clockwise**.

21. The view rotates.

22. Close the file without saving.

7-52

Practice Associate Exam

1. Select the element which is NOT considered an annotation:
   A. Callout
   B. Elevation Marker
   C. Aligned Dimension
   D. Door Tag
   E. Text

2. Tags:
   A. Are View-specific
   B. Cannot be placed in an elevation view
   C. Are added or modified using the Text tool
   D. Display Parametric Information
   E. Scale with a view

3. True – False: After you place a revision cloud, you can add a tag to it.

4. True – False: A revision schedule displays information derived from revision clouds.

5. A callout:
   A. Crops a 3D view
   B. Tags Elements in a building model
   C. Shows enlarged details of camera views
   D. Generates separate views of elements of existing views

6. A detail view can be placed in which of the following:
   A. 3D View
   B. Plan View
   C. Elevation View
   D. Section View
   E. Camera View

7. Drafting Views can contain (select all that apply):
   A. Model elements
   B. Detail Lines
   C. Detail Components
   D. Filled Region
   E. Model Lines

8. A view title on a sheet can be moved independently from the view portion of the viewport, if you:
   A. Select only the view title.
   B. Enable Move View Title Independently on the Properties pane.
   C. Disable Move Title with View on the Properties pane.
   D. Modify the Viewport's Type parameters.

9. To rotate a view on a sheet:

    A. Select the view and then use the Rotate tool on the Modify panel.
    B. Set the view rotation in the Properties pane.
    C. Select the view and then set the view rotation on the Options bar.
    D. Change the Project North.

10. You can place Detail Components in all views EXCEPT:

    A. Plan
    B. Sections
    C. Sheets
    D. Legends

11. A Filled Region allows you to define its:

    A. Function
    B. Level Offset
    C. Boundary
    D. Phase

12. _____ can be used to align elements within and between sheets.

    A. Guide Grid
    B. Align
    C. Underlay
    D. Aligned Dimension

13. To lock a viewport's position:

    A. Right click and select Lock Position.
    B. Select the viewport, then Enable Lock Position on the Properties pane.
    C. Change the viewport's properties to lock position.
    D. Select the viewport, then use Pin from the Modify panel to lock position.

Answers
 1) B; 2) A; 3) True; 4) False; 5) C; 6) B, C & D; 7) B, C & D; 8) D; 9) C; 10) C; 11) C; 12) A; 13) D

Lesson Eight

Construction Documentation

This lesson addresses the following Associate and Professional exam questions:

- Schedules
- Legends
- Rooms and Areas

A schedule is a type of view. It is a tabular display of information using element properties. Each element property is represented as a column field in the schedule.

The Schedules and Legends tools are located on the View ribbon.

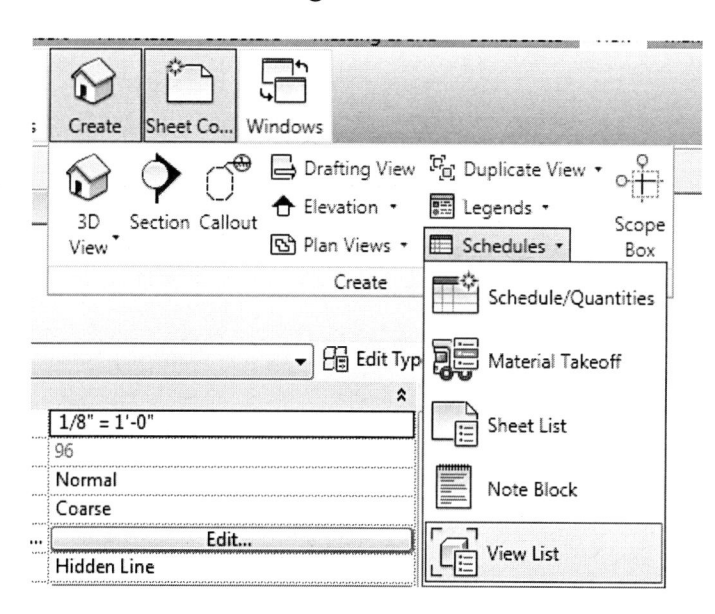

The **Schedule/Quantities** tool is used to create component schedules. Components are elements such as doors, windows, and rooms.

The **Material Takeoff** schedule lists the materials of any family used in the project.

A **Sheet List** is usually placed on the first sheet of the documentation set. It is a schedule of all sheets used in the project.

Note Blocks are useful for listing notes applied to elements in a project. For example, a user may have attached a note to several walls, which might have a description of the finish applied to each wall.

A **View List** is used to sort and itemize the views available in a project.

Command Exercise

Exercise 8-1 – Creating a Door Schedule

Drawing Name: **i_schedules.rvt**
Estimated Time to Completion: 5 Minutes

Scope

Create a door schedule.
Use the sort and group feature to determine how many doors of a specific type are on a level.

Solution

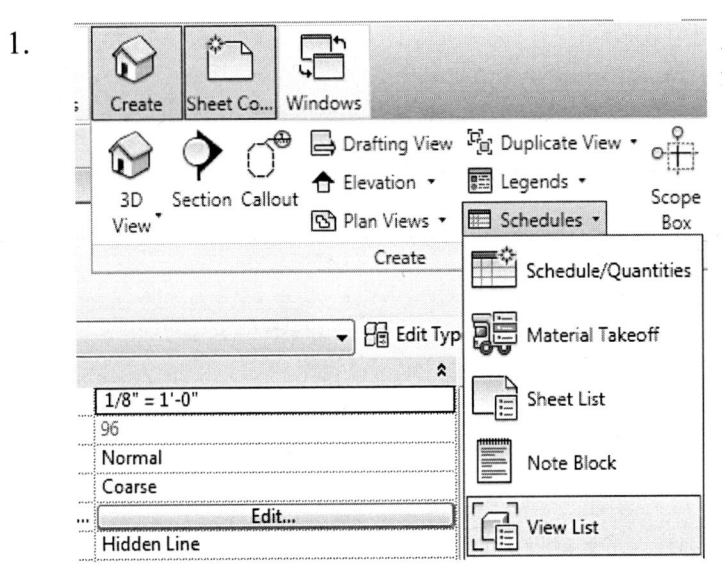

1. Activate the **View** tab on the ribbon.

   Select **Schedule/Quantities** from the Create panel.

2. Highlight the **Doors** category.

   Enable **Schedule building components**.

   Set the Phase to **New Construction**.

   Press **OK**.

8-2

3.

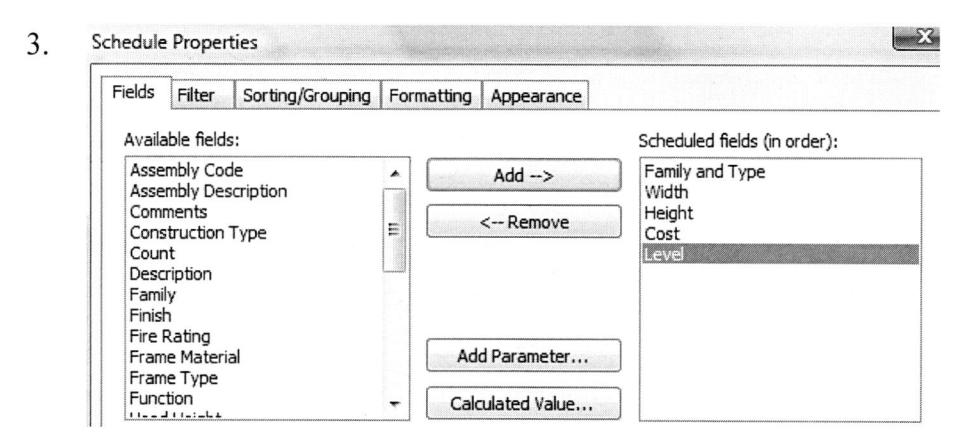

Add the following fields:

   Family and Type
   Width
   Height
   Cost
   Level

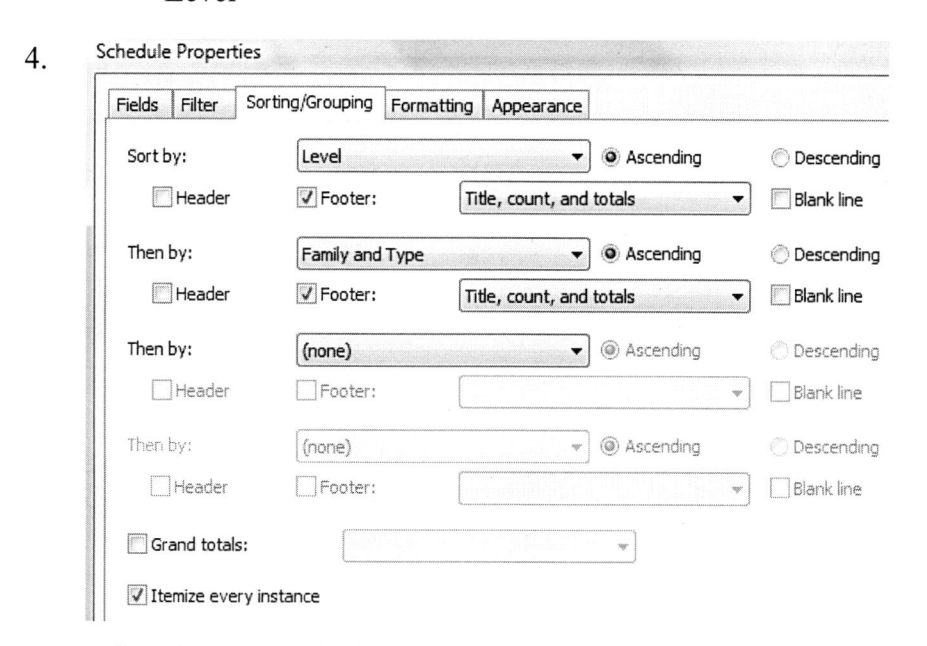

4.

Select the **Sorting/ Grouping** tab.

Set Sort by: **Level**

Enable **Footer**: **Title, count, and totals**

Then by: **Family and Type**

Enable **Footer**: **Title, count, and totals**

5. Select the **Formatting** tab.

   Highlight **Cost**.

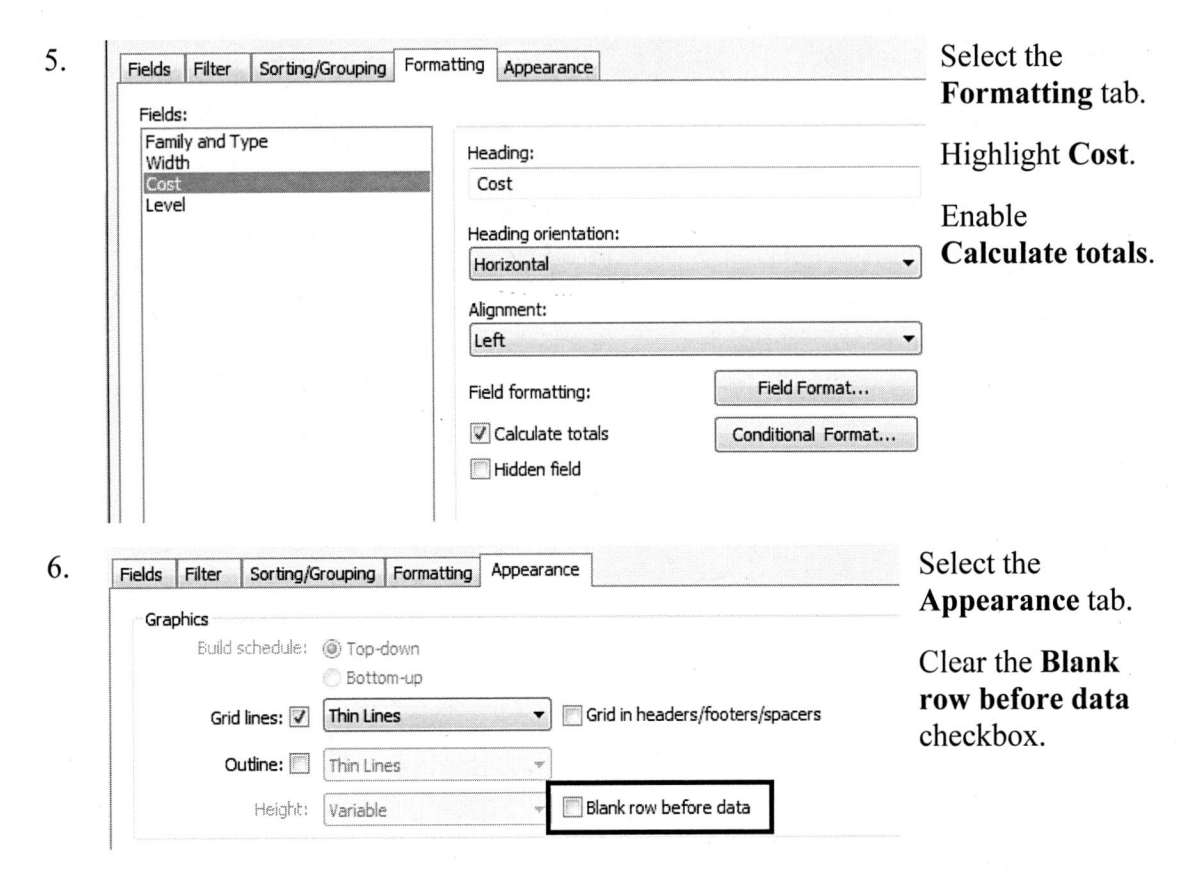

   Enable **Calculate totals**.

6. Select the **Appearance** tab.

   Clear the **Blank row before data** checkbox.

7. Press **OK**.

8. Locate how many **Single-Flush Vision: 36" x 84"** doors are placed on the Main Floor level.

   On the Professional exam, there may be one question where you will be asked how many doors or windows of a specific type are located on a level. Repeat this exercise until you are comfortable with getting the correct answer.

9. Close without saving.

Construction Documentation

Command Exercise

Exercise 8-2 – Creating a Legend

Drawing Name: **i_Legends.rvt**
Estimated Time to Completion: 30 Minutes

Scope

*Create a Legend.
Add to a sheet.
Export Legend.*

Solution

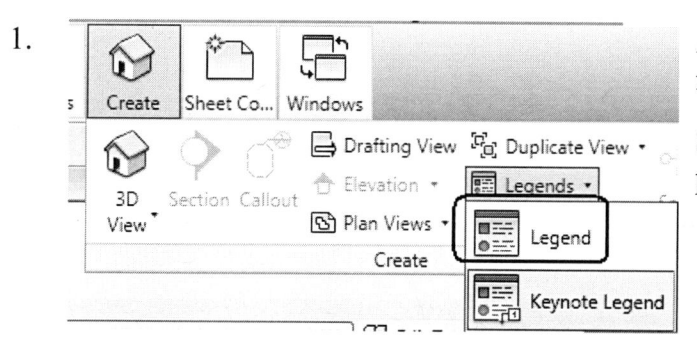

1. Activate the **View** tab on the ribbon.

   Select **Legend** from the Create panel.

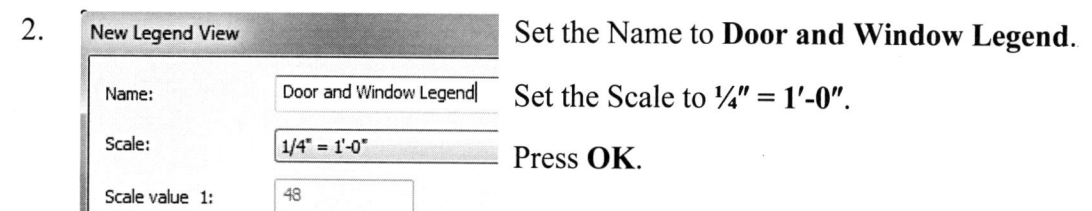

2. Set the Name to **Door and Window Legend**.

   Set the Scale to ¼" = 1'-0".

   Press **OK**.

3. The Legend is listed in the browser.

   An empty view window is opened.

4. In the browser, locate all the door families.

8-5

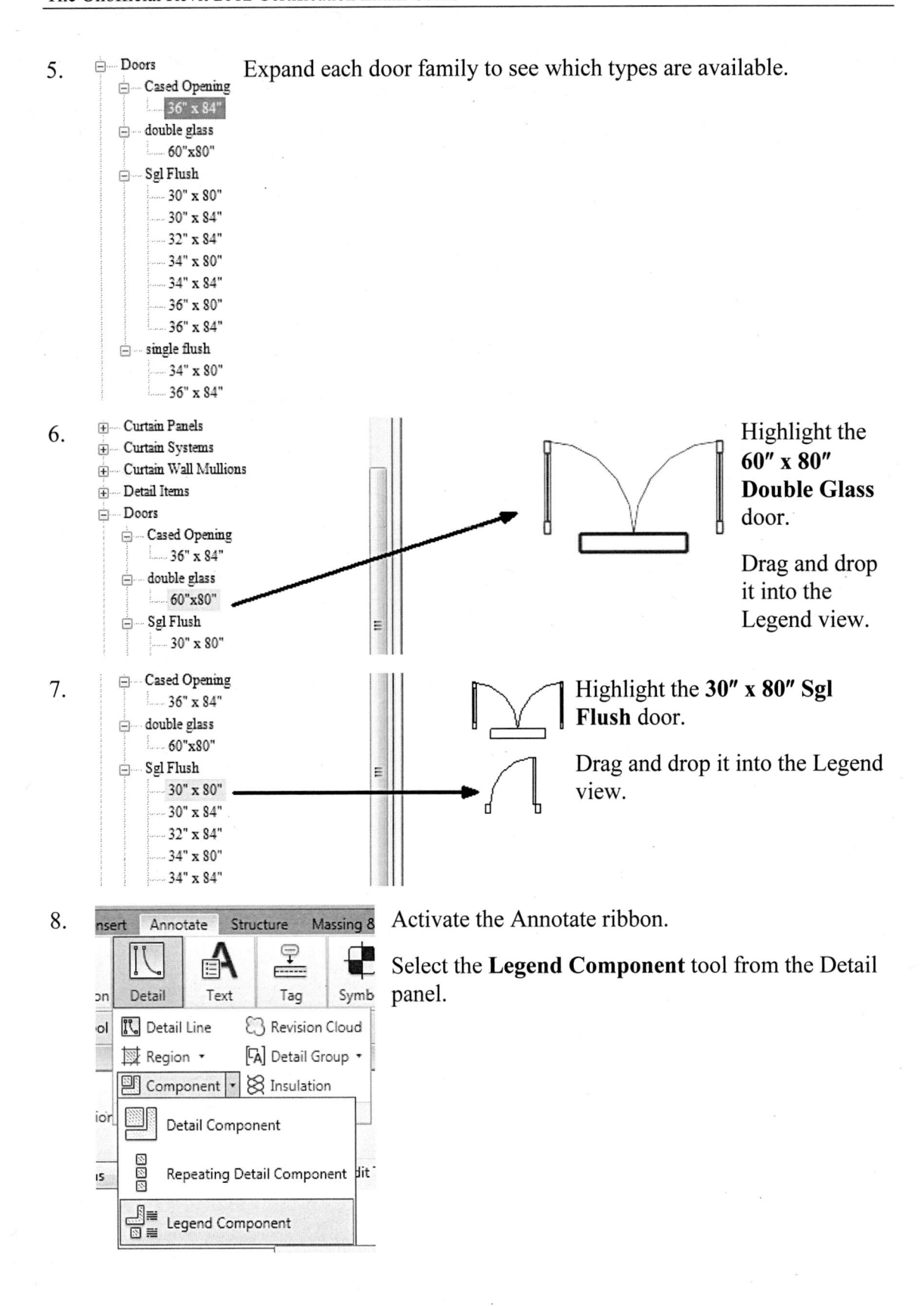

5. Expand each door family to see which types are available.

6. Highlight the **60″ x 80″ Double Glass** door.

   Drag and drop it into the Legend view.

7. Highlight the **30″ x 80″ Sgl Flush** door.

   Drag and drop it into the Legend view.

8. Activate the Annotate ribbon.

   Select the **Legend Component** tool from the Detail panel.

Construction Documentation

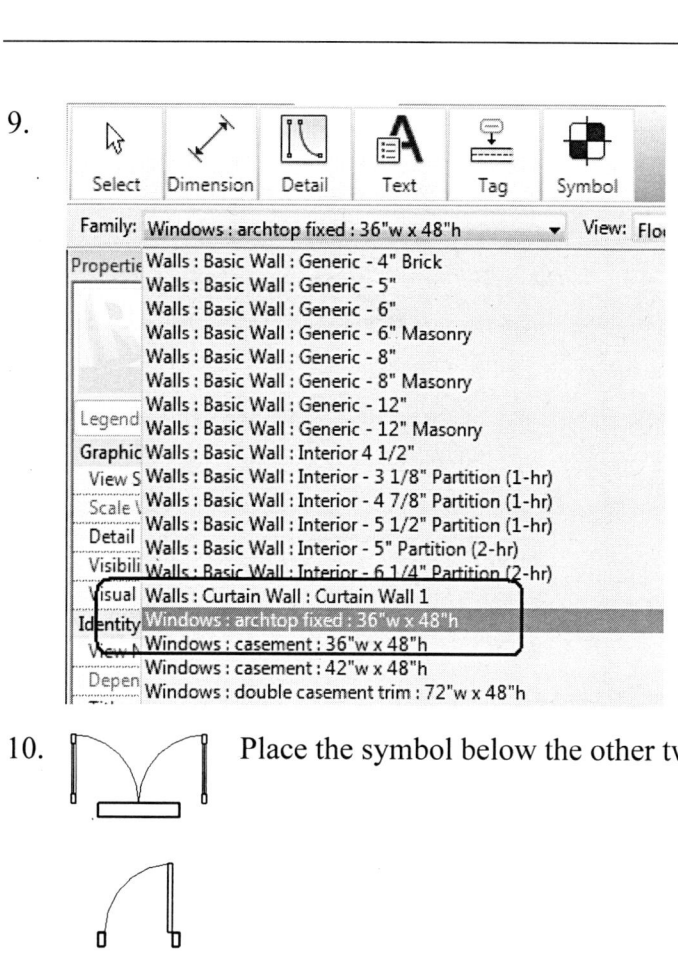

9. On the Options bar:

Select the **Windows : archtop fixed : 36″ w x 48″ h** from the list.

10. Place the symbol below the other two symbols.

11. Drag and drop each window symbol into the Legend view.

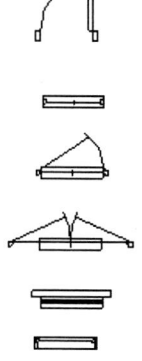

12. Activate the **Annotate** ribbon.

Select the **Text** tool.

8-7

13. DOUBLE GLASS DOOR Add text next to each symbol.

    SINGLE FLUSH DOOR

14. *Legend Components : Legend Component - Windows : archtop fixed : 36"w x 48"h (Floor Plan)*

    Mouse over a symbol to see what family type it is, if needed.

15. DOUBLE GLASS DOOR   Add text as shown.

    SINGLE FLUSH DOOR

    ARCHTOP FIXED

    CASEMENT

    DOUBLE CASEMENT WITH TRIM

    DOUBLE HUNG WITH TRIM

    FIXED

16. Select the **Detail Line** tool from the Detail panel on the Annotate ribbon.

17. DOOR AND WINDOW LEGEND

SYMBOL	DESCRIPTION
	DOUBLE GLASS DOOR
	SINGLE FLUSH DOOR
	ARCHTOP FIXED
	CASEMENT
	DOUBLE CASEMENT WITH TRIM
	DOUBLE HUNG WITH TRIM
	FIXED

    Add a rectangle.

    Add a vertical and horizontal line as shown.

    Add the header text.

18. Locate the **Sheets** category in the browser.

    Right click and select **New Sheet**.

Construction Documentation

19. [Load...] Select **Load**.

20. [Titleblocks folder image] Locate the *Titleblocks* folder.

    Locate the **D 22 x 34 Horizontal** title block.

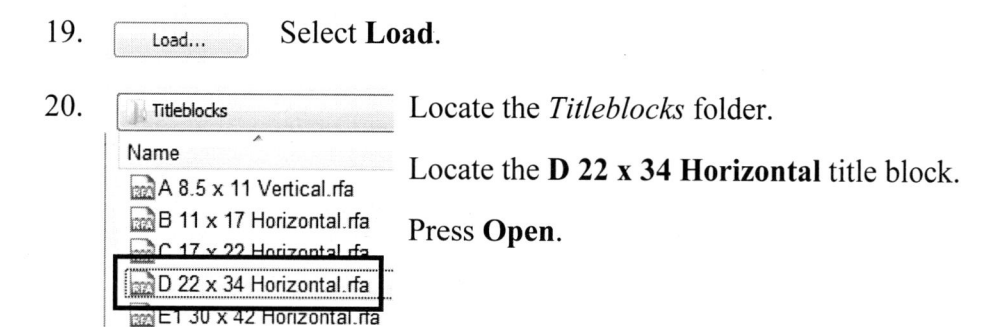

    Press **Open**.

21. Select a titleblock Highlight the **D 22 x 34 Horizontal** title block.

    Press **OK**.

22. Drag and drop the Level 1 floor plan on to the sheet.

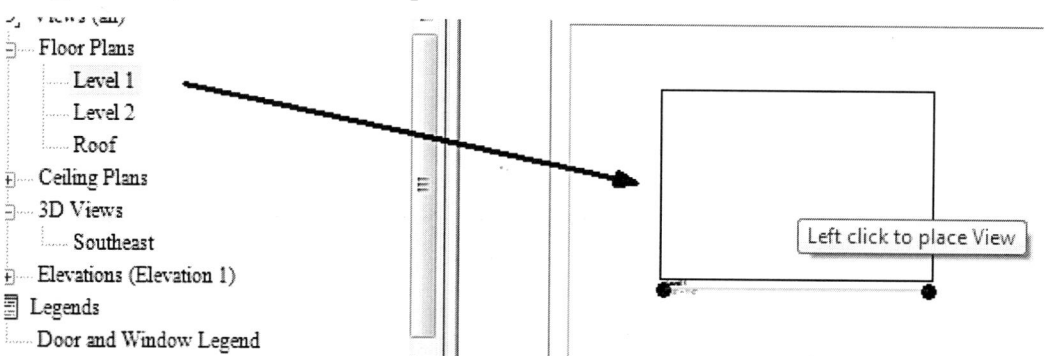

23. Graphics / View Scale 1/4" = 1'-0"   In the Properties pane:

    Change the View Scale to ¼" = 1'-0".

24. Drag and drop the Door and Window Legend onto the sheet.

    Place to the right of the view.

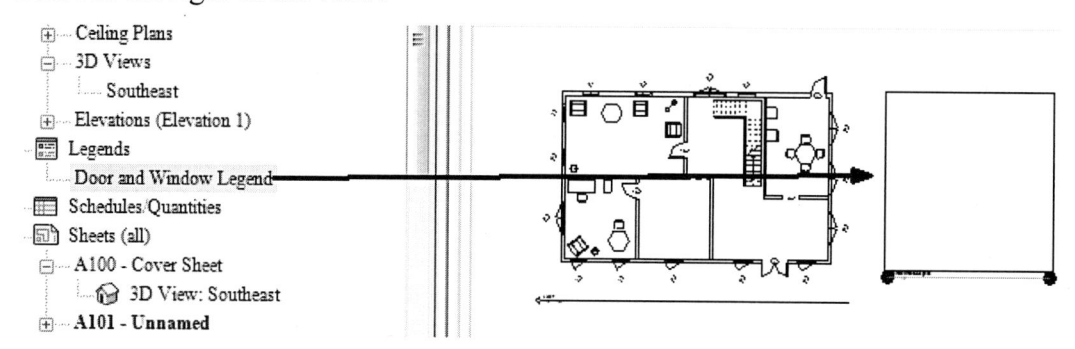

25. Select the legend so it highlights.

    [Edit Type] Select **Edit Type** on the Properties pane.

26. [Duplicate...] Select **Duplicate**.

8-9

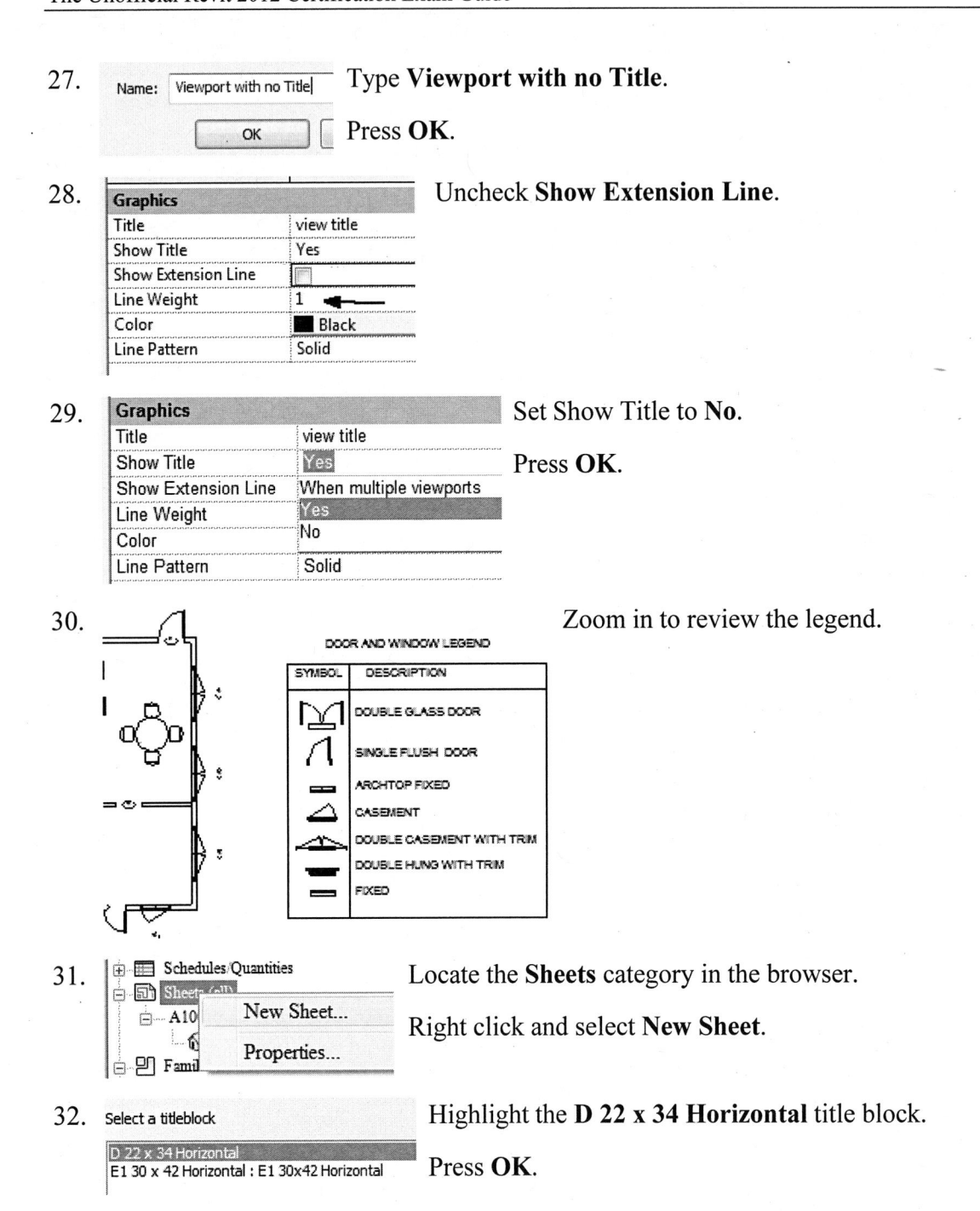

27. Type **Viewport with no Title**.

    Press **OK**.

28. Uncheck **Show Extension Line**.

29. Set Show Title to **No**.

    Press **OK**.

30. Zoom in to review the legend.

31. Locate the **Sheets** category in the browser.

    Right click and select **New Sheet**.

32. Highlight the **D 22 x 34 Horizontal** title block.

    Press **OK**.

33. Drag and drop the **Level 2** floor plan on to the sheet.

Construction Documentation

34. In the Properties pane:

    Change the View Scale to ¼" = **1'-0"**.

35. Drag and drop the Door and Window Legend onto the sheet.

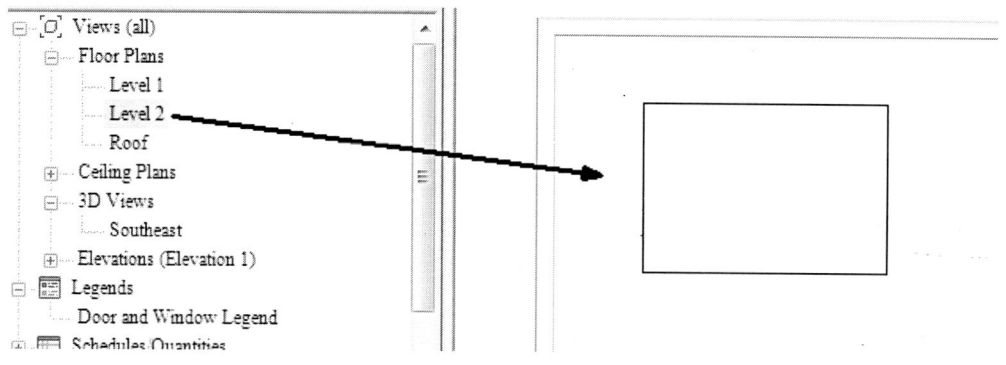

    Place to the right of the view.

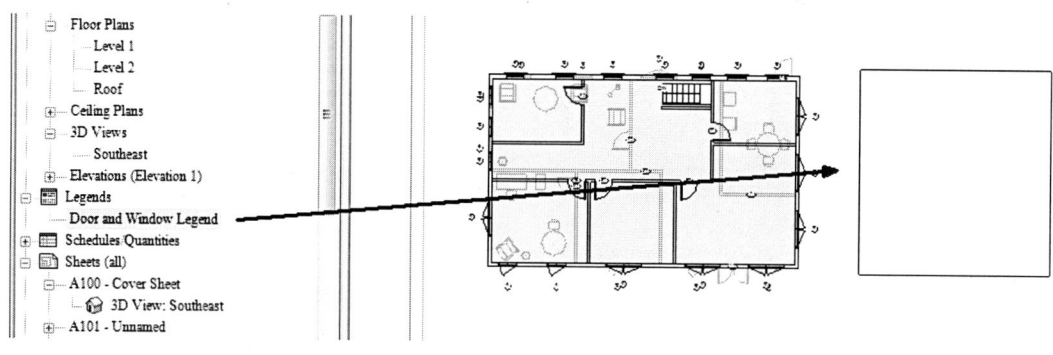

36. Select a view and then use the type selector in the Properties pane to set whether the view should have a title or not.

    Note that legends can be placed on more than one sheet.

37. Save as *ex8-2.rvt*.

Command Exercise

Exercise 8-3 – Adding Rooms to a Floor Plan

Drawing Name: **i_rooms.rvt**
Estimated Time to Completion: 10 Minutes

Scope

Add rooms to a floor plan.

Solution

1. Activate the **2nd Floor** floor plan.

2. Select the **Room** tool from the Room & Area panel on the Home ribbon.

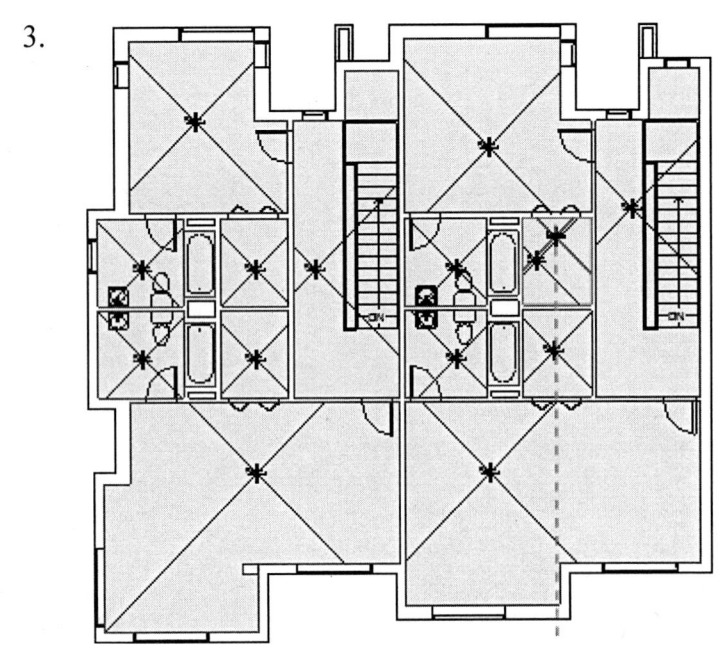

3. Place a room in each enclosed boundary.

Construction Documentation

4. Select the room in the upper left corner.

5.
Identity Data	
Number	8
Name	Master Bedroom
Comments	
Occupancy	2
Department	
Base Finish	
Ceiling Finish	Gypsum - Paint
Wall Finish	Gypsum - Paint
Floor Finish	Carpet

In the Properties pane:

Enter the data as shown.

Press **Apply**.

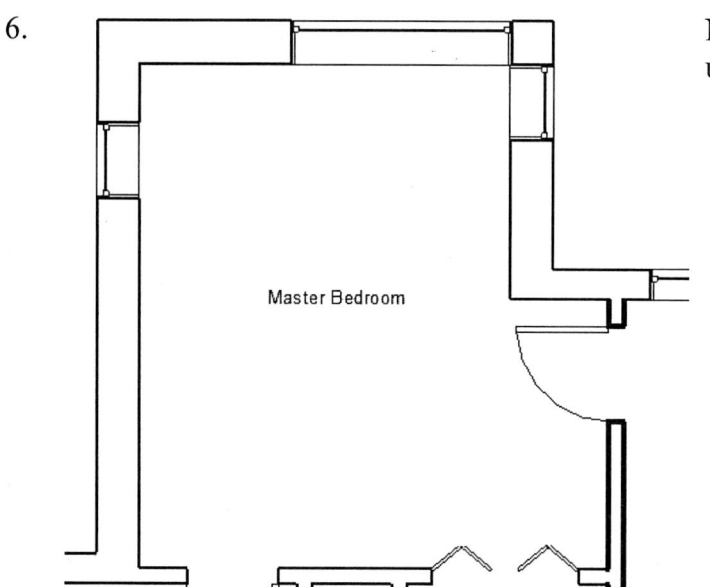

6. Note that the Room Name updates to the name assigned.

Master Bedroom

7. Add the room names shown.

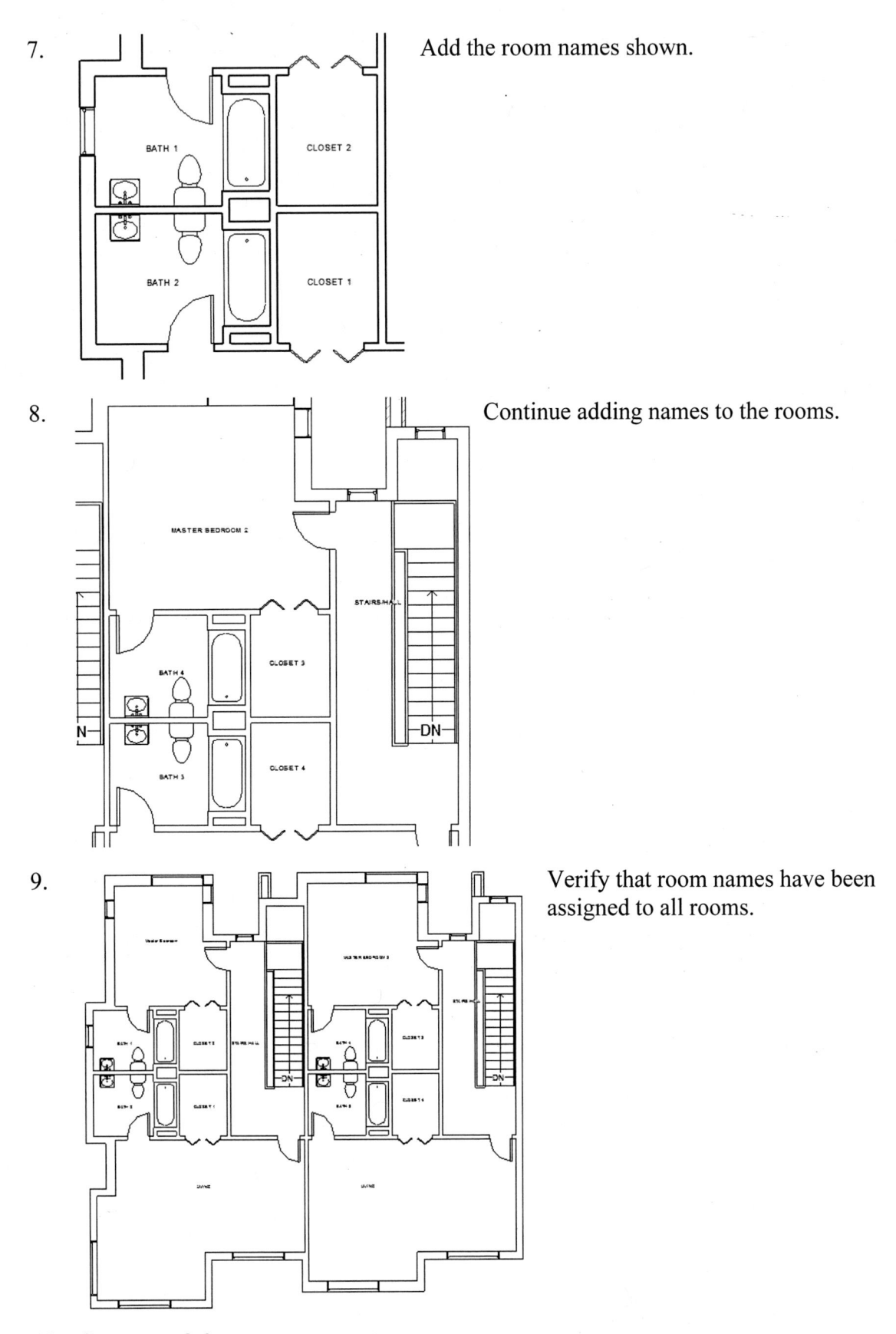

8. Continue adding names to the rooms.

9. Verify that room names have been assigned to all rooms.

10. Save as *ex8-3.rvt*.

Command Exercise

Exercise 8-4 – Creating an Area Scheme

Drawing Name: **i_Color_Scheme.rvt**
Estimated Time to Completion: 10 Minutes

Scope:

Create an area plan using a color scheme.
Place a color scheme legend.

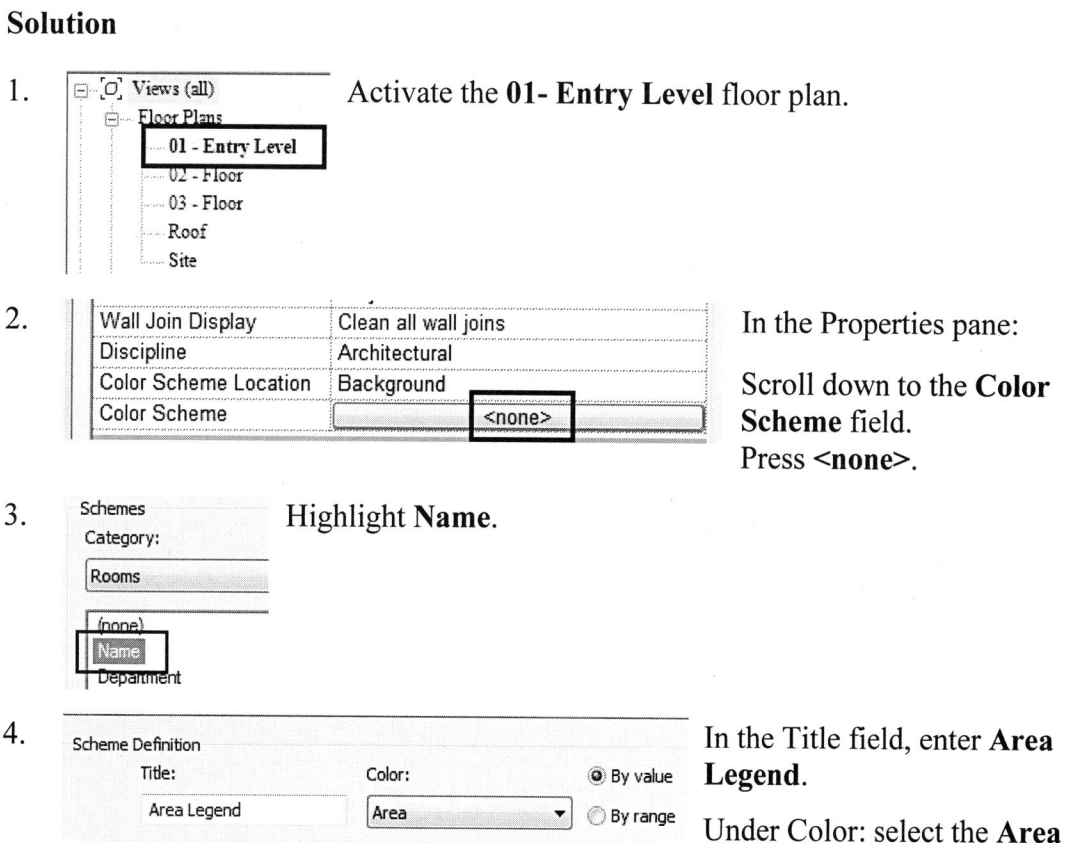

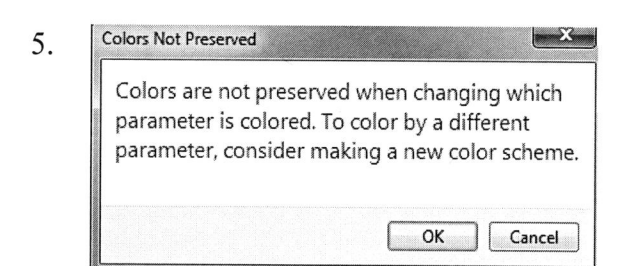

Solution

1. Activate the **01- Entry Level** floor plan.

2. In the Properties pane:

   Scroll down to the **Color Scheme** field.
   Press **<none>**.

3. Highlight **Name**.

4. In the Title field, enter **Area Legend**.

   Under Color: select the **Area** scheme.

5. Press **OK**.

The Unofficial Revit 2012 Certification Exam Guide

6.

	Value	Visible	Color	Fill Pattern	Preview
1	47 SF	✓	RGB 156-1	Solid fill	
2	58 SF	✓	PANTONE	Solid fill	
3	64 SF	✓	PANTONE	Solid fill	
4	76 SF	✓	RGB 139-1	Solid fill	
5	90 SF	✓	PANTONE	Solid fill	
6	94 SF	✓	RGB 096-1	Solid fill	
7	95 SF	✓	RGB 209-2	Solid fill	
8	133 SF	✓	RGB 173-1	Solid fill	
9	168 SF	✓	RGB 194-1	Solid fill	
10	177 SF	✓	PANTONE	Solid fill	
11	187 SF	✓	RGB 192-0	Solid fill	
12	198 SF	✓	RGB 064-0	Solid fill	
13	204 SF	✓	RGB 064-1	Solid fill	
14	208 SF	✓	RGB 064-0	Solid fill	
15	209 SF	✓	RGB 096-2	Solid fill	

Note that different colors are applied depending on the square footage of the rooms.

Press **OK**.

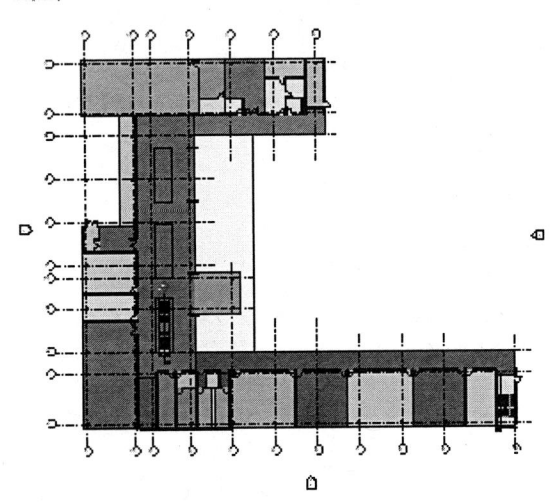

7. The rooms fill in according to the square footage.

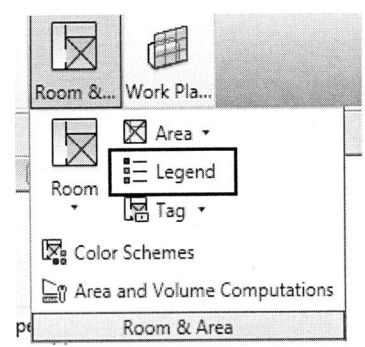

8. Activate the **Home** ribbon.

Select the **Legend** tool on the Room & Area panel.

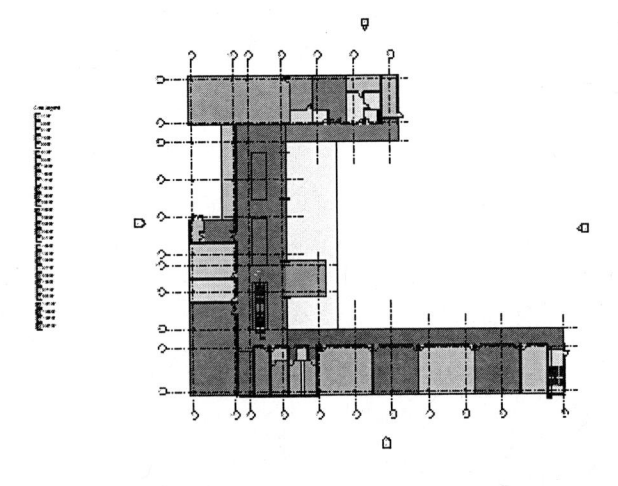

9. Place the legend in the view.

8-16

Construction Documentation

10. Select the legend that was placed in the display window.

Select **Edit Scheme** from the Scheme panel on the ribbon.

11.

	Value	Visible	Color	Fill Pattern	Preview	In Use
1	47 SF	✓	RGB 156-18	Crosshatch-small		Yes
2	58 SF	✓	PANTONE	Solid fill		Yes
3	64 SF	✓	PANTONE	Solid fill		Yes
4	76 SF	✓	RGB 139-16	Solid fill		Yes

Change the Fill Pattern for 47 SF **to Crosshatch- Small**.

12.

	Value	Visible	Color	Fill Pattern	Preview
1	47 SF	✓	RGB 156-18	Crosshatch-small	
2	58 SF	✓	PANTONE	Diagonal down	
3	64 SF	✓	PANTONE	Diagonal up	
4	76 SF	✓	RGB 139-16	Earth	
5	90 SF	✓	PANTONE	Solid fill	
6	94 SF	✓	RGB 096-17	Solid fill	
7	95 SF	✓	RGB 209-20	Solid fill	
8	133 SF	✓	RGB 173-11	Diagonal crosshatch	
9	168 SF	✓	RGB 194-16	Solid fill	

Change the hatch patterns for the next few rows.

Press **OK**.

13. **Area Legend** Note that the legend updates.

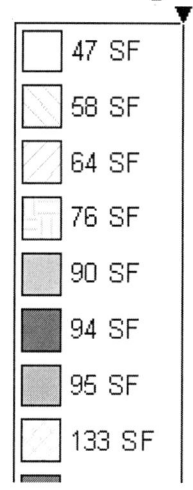

47 SF
58 SF
64 SF
76 SF
90 SF
94 SF
95 SF
133 SF

14. Close without saving.

8-17

Command Exercise

Exercise 8-5 – Creating an Area Plan

Drawing Name: **i_Area_Plan.rvt**
Estimated Time to Completion: 30 Minutes

Scope:
Create an area plan.
Add areas to a floor plan.

Solution

1. Activate the **01- Entry Level** floor plan.

2. Select the **Area Plan** tool from the Room & Area panel on the **Home** ribbon.

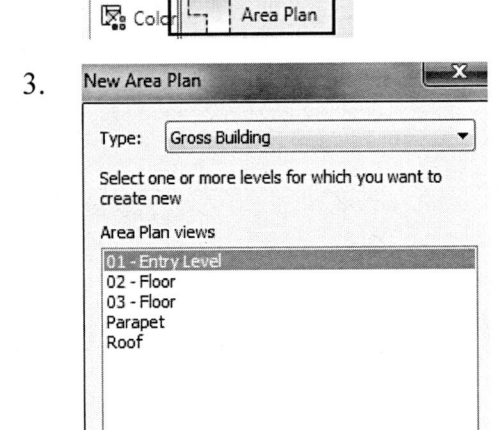

3. Select **Gross Building** under the Type drop-down.

   Select **01- Entry Level**.

   Enable **Do not duplicate existing views**.

   Set the Scale to **1/8″ = 1′-0″**.

   Press **OK**.

8-18

Construction Documentation

4. 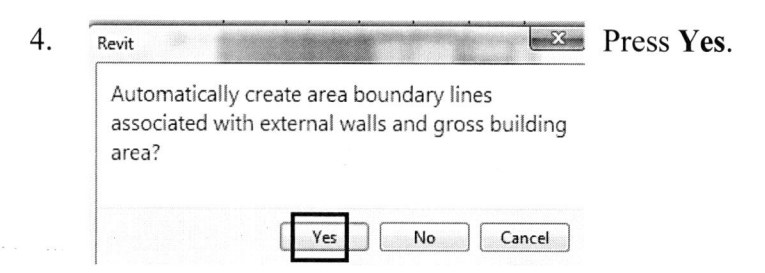 Press **Yes**.

   Automatically create area boundary lines associated with external walls and gross building area?

5. 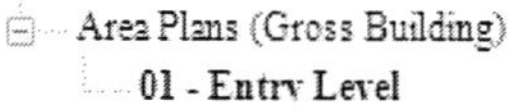 A new area plan will be listed in the Project Browser.

   Area Plans (Gross Building)
   01 - Entry Level

6. 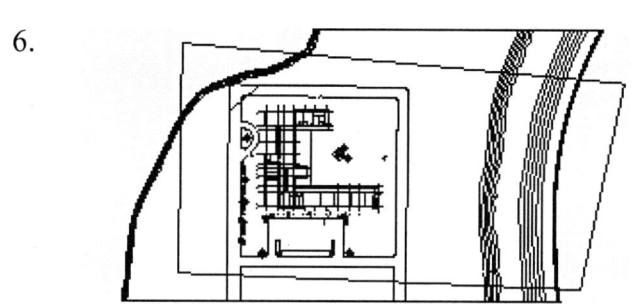 A new view will open in the graphics window.

7. Type **VV** to launch the Visibility/Graphics dialog.

8. 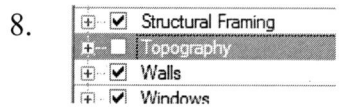 Clear the **Topography** box to turn off the visibility.

9. 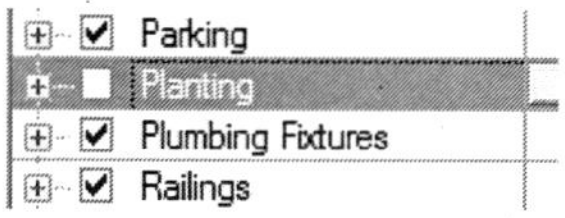 Clear the **Planting** box to turn off the visibility.

   Press **OK** to close the dialog.

10. Select the property line in the graphics window.

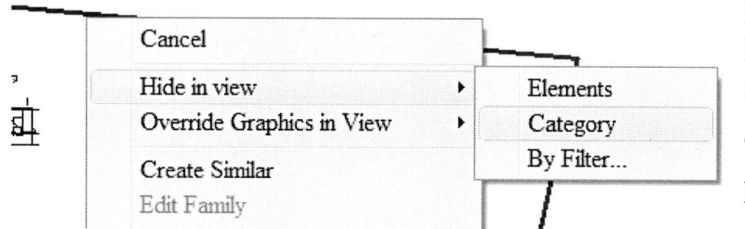

    Right click and select **Hide in view→Category**.

    This will hide all property lines.

11. 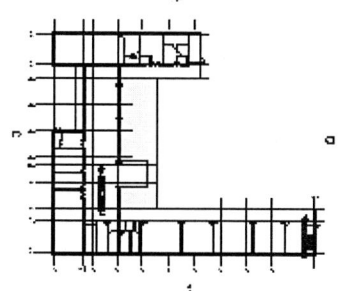 The view now shows just the building with grid lines.

8-19

12. Activate the **Modify** ribbon.

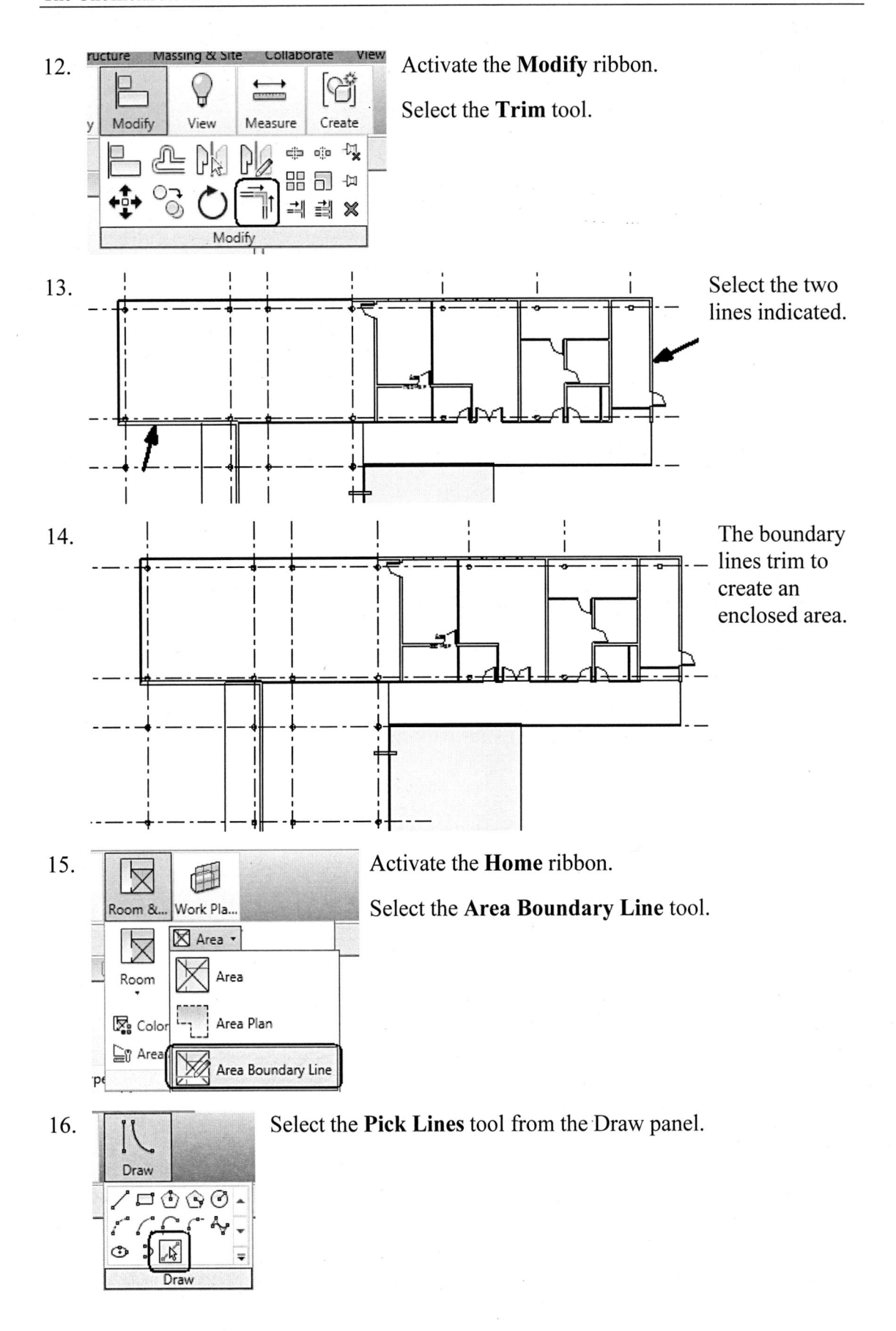

    Select the **Trim** tool.

13. Select the two lines indicated.

14. The boundary lines trim to create an enclosed area.

15. Activate the **Home** ribbon.

    Select the **Area Boundary Line** tool.

16. Select the **Pick Lines** tool from the Draw panel.

Construction Documentation

17. Select the wall indicated to place an area boundary line.

    This divides the area into two different sections.

18. Activate the **Home** ribbon.

    Select the **Area** tool.

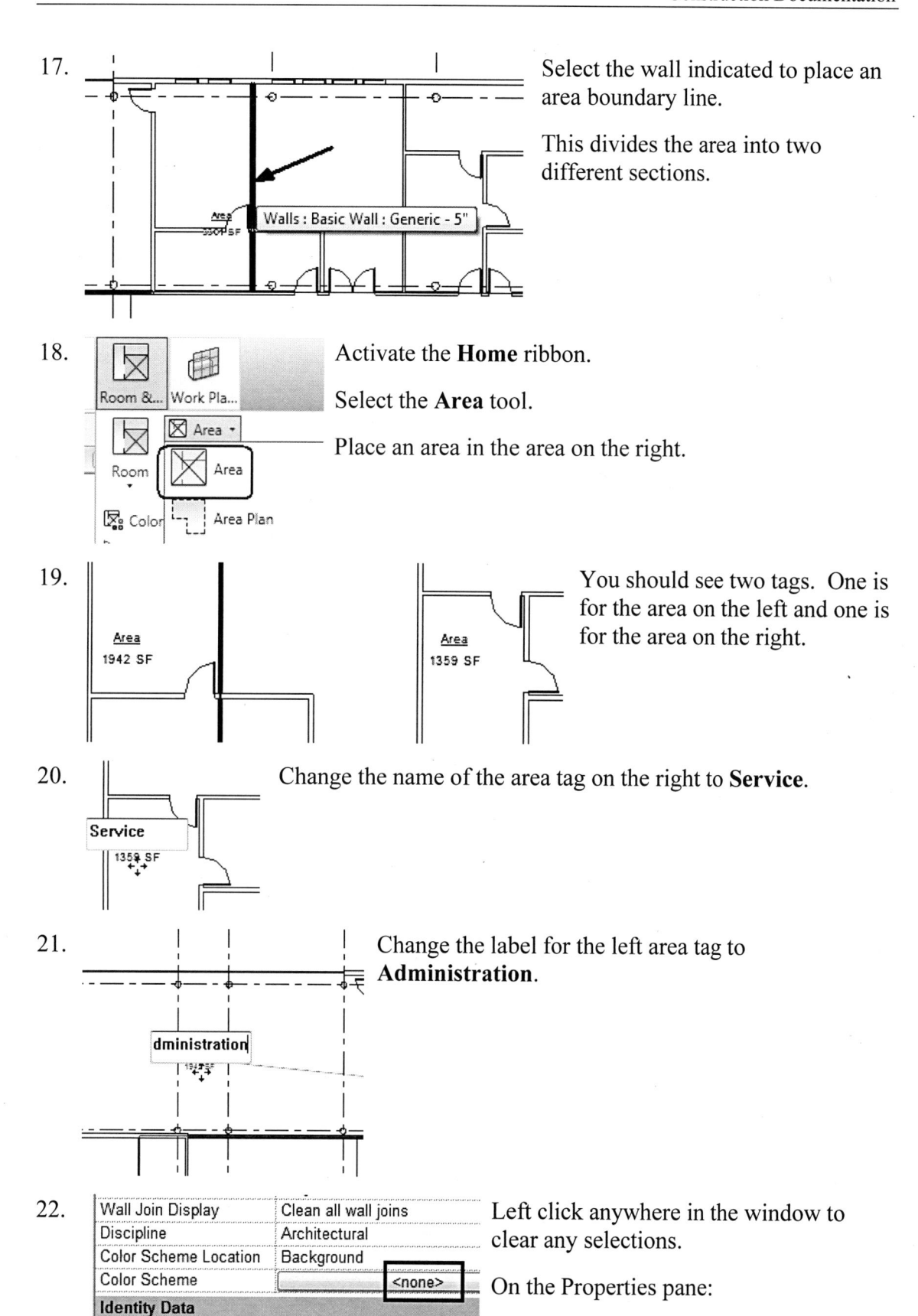

    Place an area in the area on the right.

19. You should see two tags. One is for the area on the left and one is for the area on the right.

20. Change the name of the area tag on the right to **Service**.

21. Change the label for the left area tag to **Administration**.

22. Left click anywhere in the window to clear any selections.

    On the Properties pane:

    Click on **<none>** next to Color Scheme.

8-21

23. Select **Gross Building Area** under Category.

24. Under Color: select **Name**.

25. Press **OK**.

26. The two named areas are listed.

    Colors are automatically assigned.

27. Press **OK**.

28. Save as *ex8-5.rvt*.

Construction Documentation

Command Exercise

Exercise 8-6 – Creating a Room Schedule

Drawing Name: **i_Finish_Schedule.rvt**
Estimated Time to Completion: 10 Minutes

Scope

Create a room finish schedule.

Solution

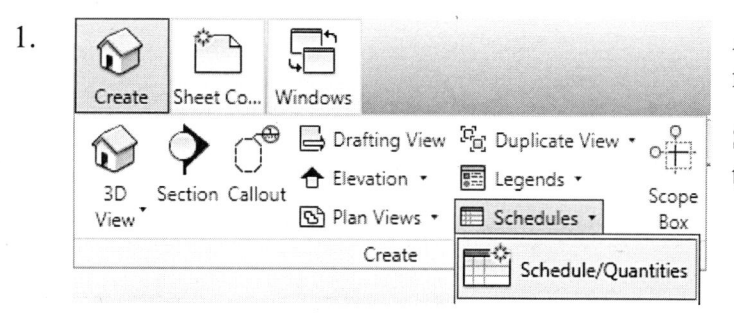

1. Activate the **View** tab on the ribbon.

   Select the **Schedule/Quantities** tool from the Create panel.

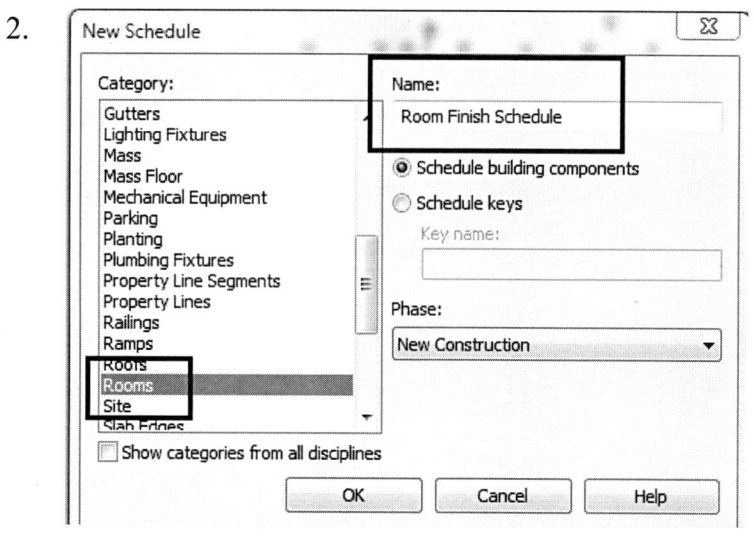

2. Select **Rooms** in the Category list box.

   Change the Name to **Room Finish Schedule**.

   Press **OK**.

3. Add the fields shown to the schedule.

   Scheduled fields (in order):
   - Number
   - Name
   - Base Finish
   - Floor Finish
   - Wall Finish
   - Ceiling Finish
   - Area
   - Comments
   - Level

4. Select the **Sorting/ Grouping** tab.

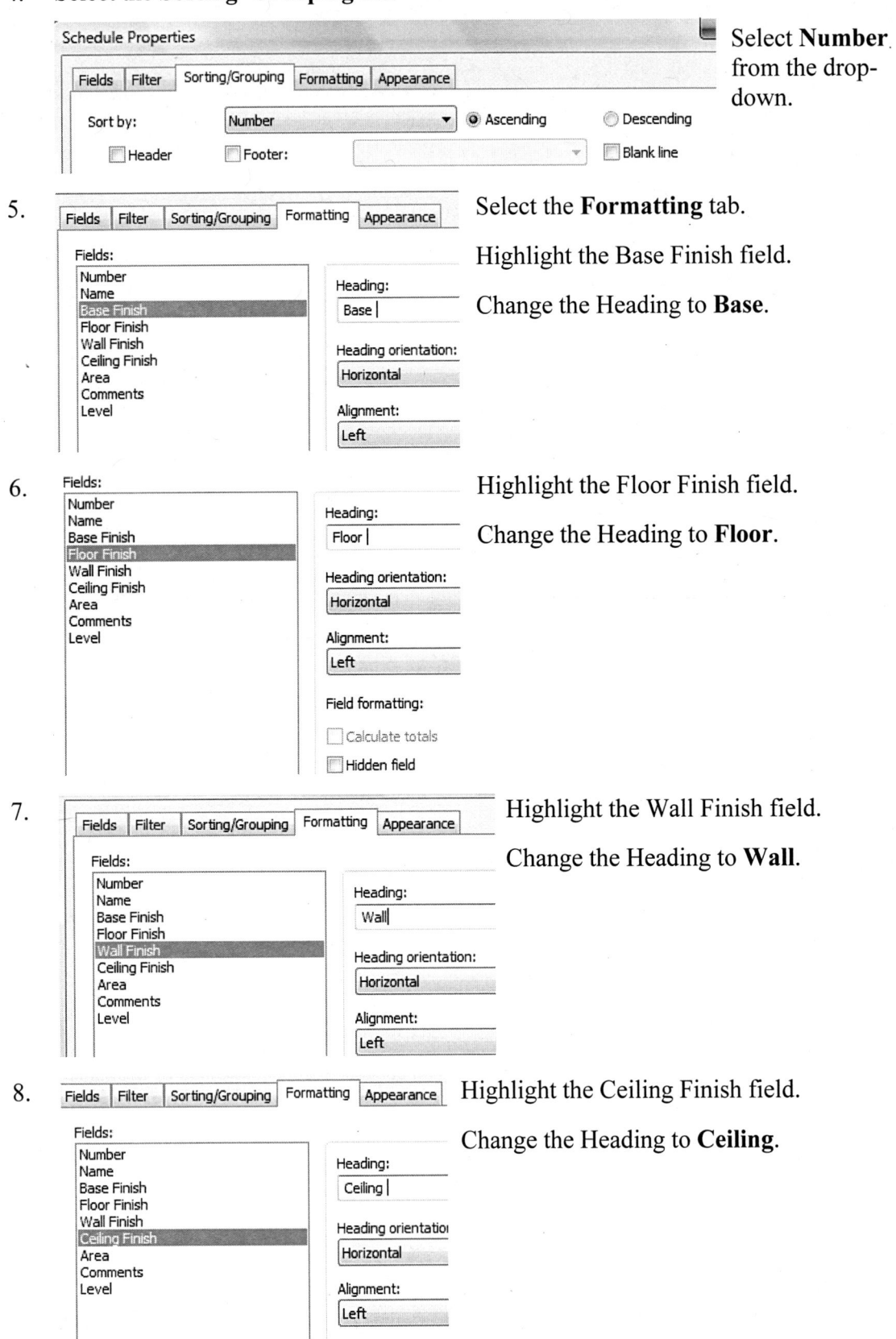

Select **Number** from the drop-down.

5. Select the **Formatting** tab.

Highlight the Base Finish field.

Change the Heading to **Base**.

6. Highlight the Floor Finish field.

Change the Heading to **Floor**.

7. Highlight the Wall Finish field.

Change the Heading to **Wall**.

8. Highlight the Ceiling Finish field.

Change the Heading to **Ceiling**.

9. Press **OK** to finish the schedule.

10. The schedule view opens.

Room Finish Schedule								
Number	Name	Base	Floor	Wall	Ceiling	Area	Comments	Level
102	Lobby					3537 SF		01 - Entry Level
121	Caferteria					1557 SF		01 - Entry Level
122	Prep/Dish					233 SF		01 - Entry Level
124	Dry Stora					97 SF		01 - Entry Level
125	Electrical					65 SF		01 - Entry Level
123	Conferen					440 SF		01 - Entry Level
127	Office					169 SF		01 - Entry Level
126	Admin					178 SF		01 - Entry Level
128	Storage					91 SF		01 - Entry Level
129	Toilet					58 SF		01 - Entry Level
130	Stair					204 SF		01 - Entry Level
119	Sprinkler					97 SF		01 - Entry Level
118	Electrical					206 SF		01 - Entry Level
117	Instructio					518 SF		01 - Entry Level

11. Drag your cursor to select the Base, Floor, Wall, and Ceiling headers.

    Select the **Group** tool.

12. Add the word **FINISH** above the grouped fields.

13. Close the file without saving.

The Unofficial Revit 2012 Certification Exam Guide

Command Exercise

Exercise 8-7 – Creating a Drawing List

Drawing Name: **i_sheets.rvt**
Estimated Time to Completion: 15 Minutes

Scope

Create a sheet list schedule.
Add to a sheet.

Solution

1. Highlight **Sheets** in the Project Browser.

   Right click and select **New Sheet**.

2. Select **Load**.

3. Browse to the *Titleblocks* folder.

   Select the *B 11 x 17 Horizontal Titleblock* and press **Open**.

4. The B size Titleblock is listed in the dialog list.

   Highlight and press **OK**.

5. Select the title block.
   In the Properties pane:

   Rename the sheet **Cover Sheet**.

   Press **OK**.

8-26

Construction Documentation

6. Activate the View ribbon.

Select the **Sheet List** tool under Schedules on the Create panel.

8. Add the following fields to the schedule:

Sheet Number
Sheet Name
Current Revision
Sheet Issue Date

9. Select the Sorting/Grouping tab.
Sort by **Sheet Number**.

10. Press **OK** to create the schedule.

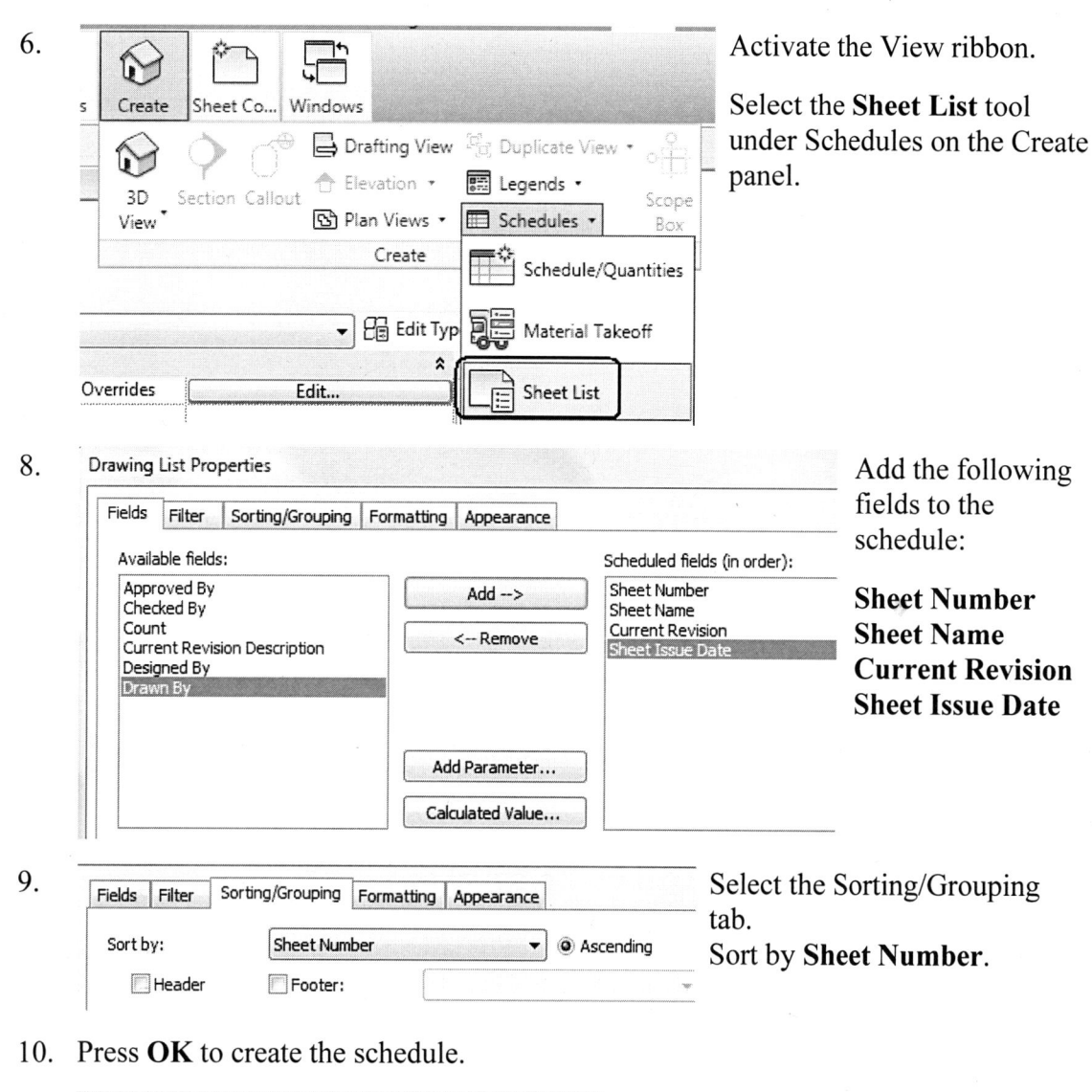

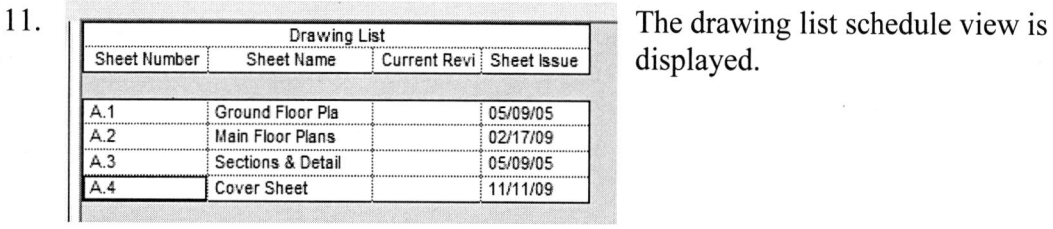

11. The drawing list schedule view is displayed.

12. Activate the **A.4- Cover Sheet**.

8-27

13. Drag and drop the drawing list onto the cover sheet.

14. Activate the Cover Sheet.

15. In the Properties pane:

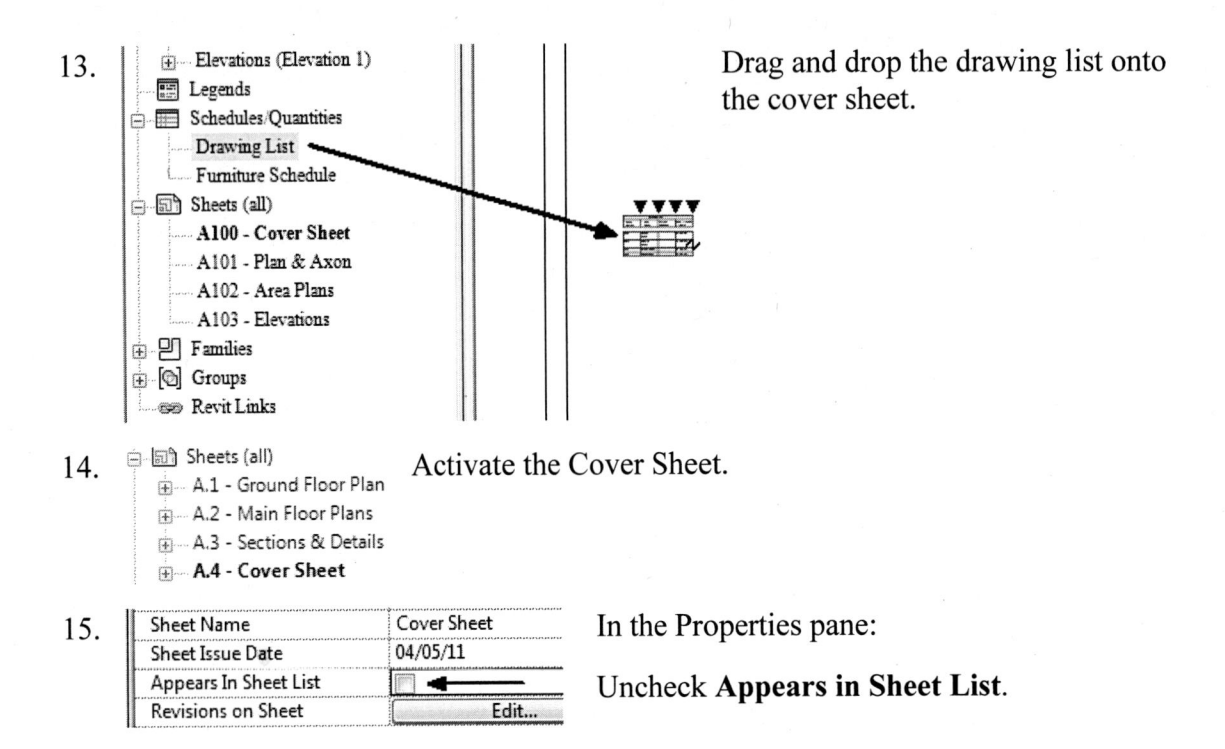

    Uncheck **Appears in Sheet List**.

Sheet Number	Sheet Name	Current Revision	Sheet Issue Date
A.1	Ground Floor Plan		05/09/05
A.2	Main Floor Plans		02/17/09
A.3	Sections & Details		05/09/05

16. The schedule will automatically update.

    Close without saving.

Construction Documentation

Command Exercise

Exercise 8-8 – Create a Note Symbol

Drawing Name: **notes.doc**
Estimated Time to Completion: 30 Minutes

Scope

Create Note Symbol.

Solution

1. Go to **New→Annotation Symbol** on the Applications Menu.

2. Select *Generic Annotation*.
   Press **Open**.

3. Select the **Text** tool from the Text panel.

4. Locate the Word document titled *Notes* in the exercise folder and open it.

8-29

5. Highlight the Floor Plan Notes.
   Use Ctl-C to copy.

6.

   Switch to Revit.
   Place your cursor inside the text box.
   Enter Ctl-V to paste.

7. Use the Format settings to add an underline and bold the heading for the notes.

8. Left click anywhere in the drawing window to exit the Text command.
   Right click and select **Cancel**.

9. Select the note.
   Right click and select **Delete**.

10. Save the family as *Floor Plan Notes - Embry Home*.

11. Close the file.

Construction Documentation

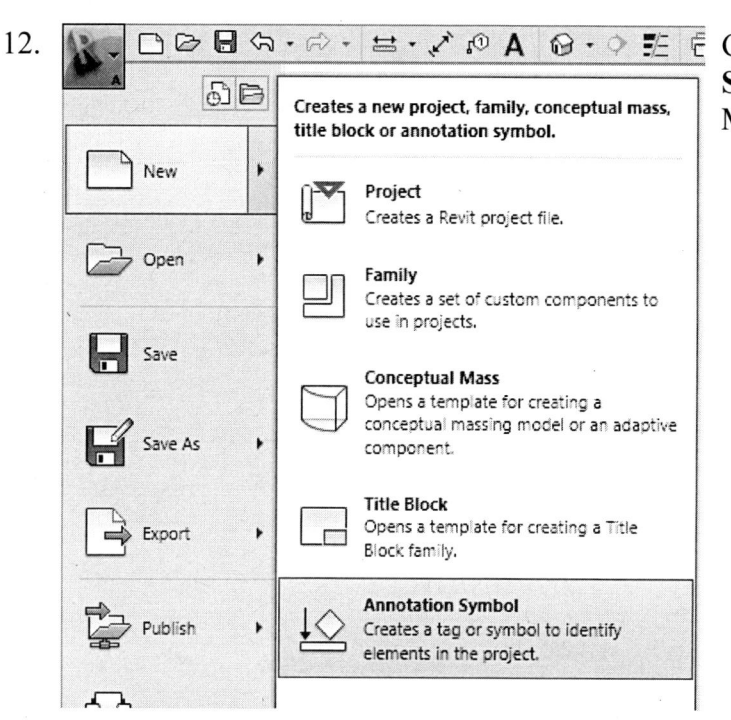

12. Go to **New→Annotation Symbol** on the Applications Menu.

13. Select *Generic Annotation*.

    Press **Open**.

14. Select the **Text** tool from the Text panel.

15. Locate the Word document titled *Notes* in the exercise folder and open it.

16. Highlight the General Project Notes.

    Use Ctl-C to copy.

17. Switch to Revit.
    Place your cursor inside the text box.
    Enter Ctl-V to paste.

8-31

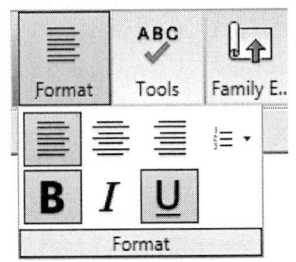

18. Use the Format settings to add an underline and bold the heading for the notes.

19. Left click anywhere in the drawing window to exit the Text command. Right click and select **Cancel**.

20. Use the grips on the sides to resize the text box.

    GENERAL PROJECT NOTES:
    1. PROVIDE AN ALLOWANCE FOR ADA COMPLIANT SIGNAGE AT TOILET.
    2. CONTRACTOR SHALL OBTAIN AND PAY FOR ALL BUILDING PERMITS.
    3. PROVIDE AN ALLOWANCE FOR AN UNDERGROUND UTILITY SURVEY TO BE PERFORMED PRIOR TO THE START OF CONSTRUCTION.
    4. ALL CONSTRUCTION SHALL BE IN COMPIANCE WITH INTERNATIONAL BUILDING CODE, THE AMERICAN'S WITH DISABILITIES ACT, AND ALL OTHER APPLICABLE REGULATIONS.
    5. APPLICATIONS FOR PAYMENT SHALL BE MADE MONTHLY ON AIA FROM G702/G703, CORRESPONDING TO CONTRACTOR'S SCHEDULE OF VALUES PROVIDED TO THE OWNER AT THE START OF THE PROJECT. PAYMENTS WILL BE MADE BASED ON THE OWNER'S ACCEPTANCE OF WORK. APPLICATIONS FOR PAYMENT MUST BE ACCOMPANIED BY APPROPRIATE DOCUMENTATION FROM SUBCONTRACTORS AND MATERIAL SUPPLIERS INDICATING ACTUAL PROJECT EXPENDITURES.
    6. SUBMIT SHOP DRAWINGS AND SAMPLES OF ALL CONSTRUCTION MATERIALS PRIOR TO THEIR ORDER. ALLOW ONE WEEK FOR OWNER/ARCHITECTURE REVIEW OF ALL SUBMITTALS. PROVIDE CONSTRUCTION SCHEDULE OF VALUES PRIOR TO THE FIRST APPLICATION FOR PAYMENT.
    7. CONTRACTOR SHALL PROVIDE ADEQUATE PERSONNEL ON SITE TO SUPERVISE CONSTRUCTION AND MAINTAIN PROGRESS SCHEDULE. ALL MATERIALS PROVIDED SHALL BE NEW AND INSTALLED IN ACCORDANCE WITH MANUFACTURER'S WRITTEN INSTRUCTIONS AND THE CONSTRUCTION DOCUMENTS.
    8. PROVIDE TEMPORARY FIRE PROTECTION, TRASH REMOVAL, SECURITY, ELECTRICAL, AND WATER SERVICES. PROVIDE PORTABLE TEMPORARY TOILET FACILITIES.
    9. CONTRACTORS MAY PROPOSE APPROVED EQUIVALENT PRODUCTS BY OTHER MANUFACTURERS FOR SUBSTITUTION IN LIEU OF SPECIFIED HEREIN.
    10. PRIOR TO SUBSTANTIAL COMPLETION, THOROUGHLY CLEAN ALL BUILDING ELEMENTS AND SURFACES WITHIN THE AREA OF CONSTRUCTION. FOLLOWING A SUBSTANTIAL COMPLETION, PROVIDE A WRITTEN PUNCHLIST OF ITEMS TO THE OWNER TO BE COMPLETED WITHIN 15 DAYS.
    11. PROVIDE SUBSTRATE SOIL TREATMENT EQUIVALENT TO AN EPA-REGISTERED TERMITICIDE. PROVIDE A PROPOSAL FOR CONTINUING SERVICE INCLUDING MONITORING INSPECTION AND RETREATMENT.

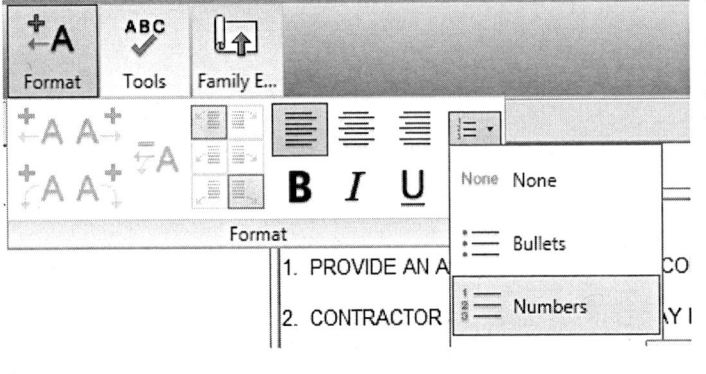

21. Use the **Numbers** formatting tool on the Format panel to clean up the notes.

8-32

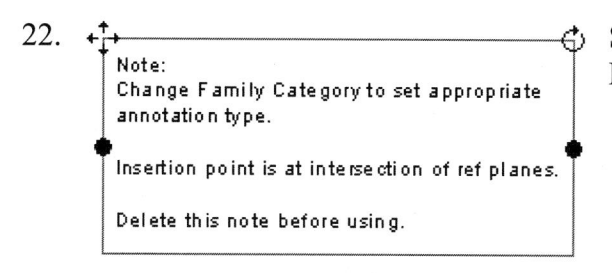

Construction Documentation

22. [Note box:]
    Note:
    Change Family Category to set appropriate annotation type.

    Insertion point is at intersection of ref planes.

    Delete this note before using.

    Select the note. Right click and select **Delete**.

23. The notes should look like this.

    GENERAL PROJECT NOTES:
    1. PROVIDE AN ALLOWANCE FOR ADA COMPLIANT SIGNAGE AT TOILET.
    2. CONTRACTOR SHALL OBTAIN AND PAY FOR ALL BUILDING PERMITS.
    3. PROVIDE AN ALLOWANCE FOR AN UNDERGROUND UTILITY SURVEY TO BE PERFORMED PRIOR TO THE START OF CONSTRUCTION.
    4. ALL CONSTRUCTION SHALL BE IN COMPIANCE WITH INTERNATIONAL BUILDING CODE, THE AMERICAN'S WITH DISABILITIES ACT, AND ALL OTHER APPLICABLE REGULATIONS.
    5. APPLICATIONS FOR PAYMENT SHALL BE MADE MONTHLY ON AIA FROM G702/G703, CORRESPONDING TO CONTRACTOR'S SCHEDULE OF VALUES PROVIDED TO THE OWNER AT THE START OF THE PROJECT. PAYMENTS WILL BE MADE BASED ON THE OWNER'S ACCEPTANCE OF WORK. APPLICATIONS FOR PAYMENT MUST BE ACCOMPANIED BY APPROPRIATE DOCUMENTATION FROM SUBCONTRACTORS AND MATERIAL SUPPLIERS INDICATING ACTUAL PROJECT EXPENDITURES.
    6. SUBMIT SHOP DRAWINGS AND SAMPLES OF ALL CONSTRUCTION MATERIALS PRIOR TO THEIR ORDER. ALLOW ONE WEEK FOR OWNER/ARCHITECTURE REVIEW OF ALL SUBMITTALS. PROVIDE CONSTRUCTION SCHEDULE OF VALUES PRIOR TO THE FIRST APPLICATION FOR PAYMENT.
    7. CONTRACTOR SHALL PROVIDE ADEQUATE PERSONNEL ON SITE TO SUPERVISE CONSTRUCTION AND MAINTAIN PROGRESS SCHEDULE. ALL MATERIALS PROVIDED SHALL BE NEW AND INSTALLED IN ACCORDANCE WITH MANUFACTURER'S WRITTEN INSTRUCTIONS AND THE CONSTRUCTION DOCUMENTS.
    8. PROVIDE TEMPORARY FIRE PROTECTION, TRASH REMOVAL, SECURITY, ELECTRICAL, AND WATER SERVICES. PROVIDE PORTABLE TEMPORARY TOILET FACILITIES.
    9. CONTRACTORS MAY PROPOSE APPROVED EQUIVALENT PRODUCTS BY OTHER MANUFACTURERS FOR SUBSTITUTION IN LIEU OF SPECIFIED HEREIN.
    10. PRIOR TO SUBSTANTIAL COMPLETION, THOROUGHLY CLEAN ALL BUILDING ELEMENTS AND SURFACES WITHIN THE AREA OF CONSTRUCTION. FOLLOWING A SUBSTANTIAL COMPLETION, PROVIDE A WRITTEN PUNCHLIST OF ITEMS TO THE OWNER TO BE COMPLETED WITHIN 15 DAYS.
    11. PROVIDE SUBSTRATE SOIL TREATMENT EQUIVALENT TO AN EPA-REGISTERED TERMITICIDE. PROVIDE A PROPOSAL FOR CONTINUING SERVICE INCLUDING MONITORING INSPECTION AND RETREATMENT.

    The width of the note should be no more than 5" in order to fit properly in the title block.

24. [File name: Floor Plan Notes | Embry Home / Files of type: Family Files (*.rfa)] Save the family as *General Project Notes*.

25. Close the file.

The Unofficial Revit 2012 Certification Exam Guide

Command Exercise

Exercise 8-9 – Add Notes

Drawing Name: **i_notes.rvt**
Estimated Time to Completion: 10 Minutes

Scope

Use Annotation Symbols.

Solution

1. Activate the **Insert** ribbon.

   Select **Load Family** from the Load from Library panel.

2. Hold down the Control key to select both files.

3. Locate the two annotation symbols created called *General Project Notes* and *Floor Plan Notes - Embry Home*.

   Press **Open**.

4. Activate the **Ground Floor Plan** sheet.

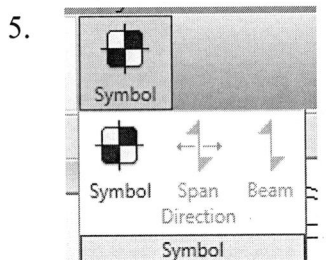

5. Activate the **Annotate** ribbon.

   Select the **Symbol** tool on the Symbol panel.

8-34

Construction Documentation

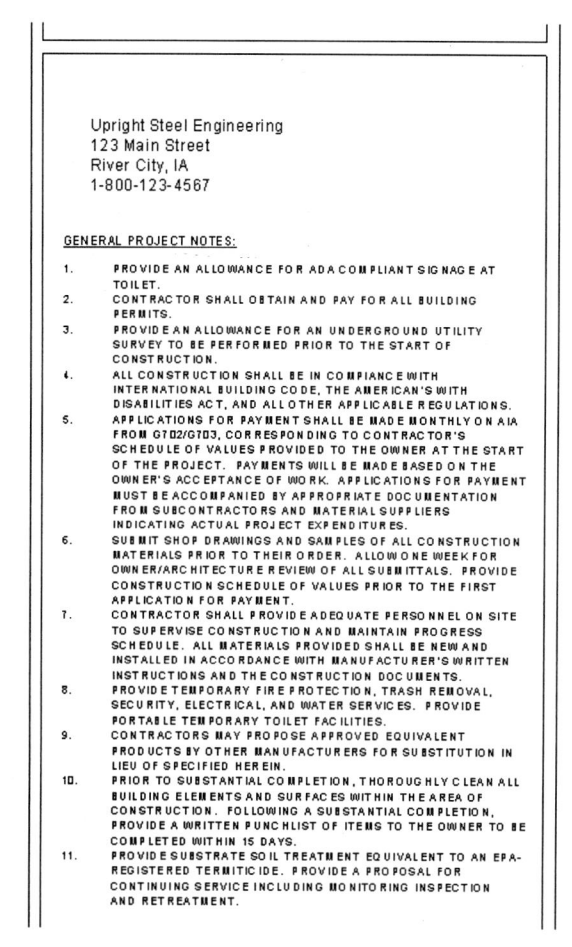

6. Select the **General Project Notes** from the Properties pane.

Place in the title block.

Right click and select **Cancel**.

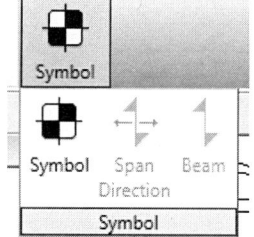

7. Activate the **Annotate** ribbon.

Select the **Symbol** tool on the Symbol panel.

8. Select the **Floor Plan Notes** from the Properties pane.

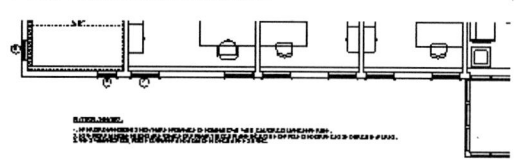

9. Place on the sheet above the title mark.

10. Close without saving.

8-35

Command Exercise

Exercise 8-10 – Create a Material TakeOff Schedule

Drawing Name: **i_materials.rvt**
Estimated Time to Completion: 10 Minutes

Scope

Create a material takeoff schedule

Solution

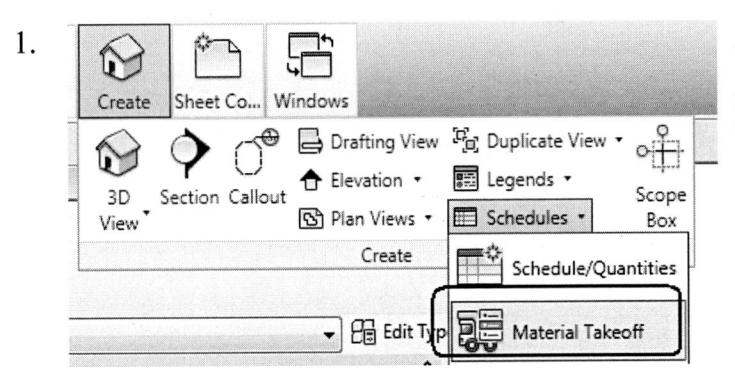

1. Activate the View ribbon.

   Select **Schedules→Material Takeoff** from the Create panel.

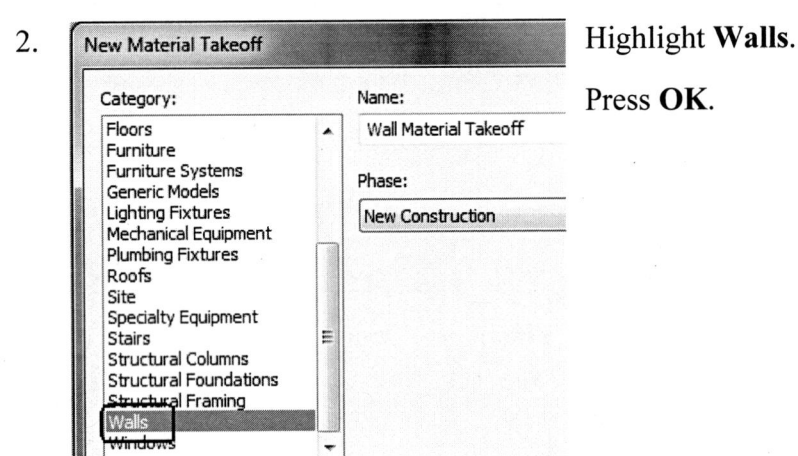

2. Highlight **Walls**.

   Press **OK**.

3. On the **Fields** tab:

   Add the following fields:

   Family and Type
   Material: Name
   Material: Area

8-36

Construction Documentation

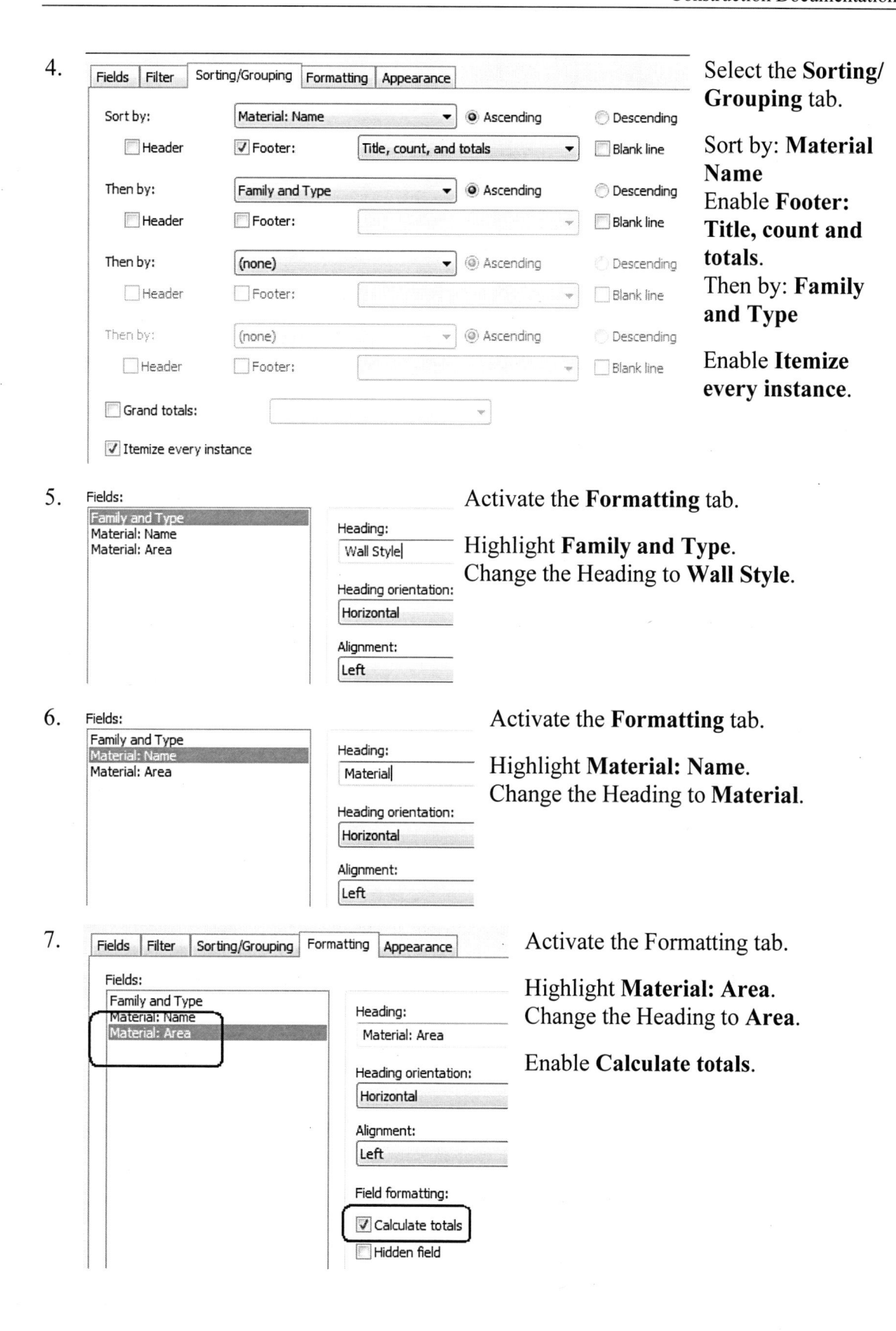

4. Select the **Sorting/Grouping** tab.

   Sort by: **Material Name**

   Enable **Footer: Title, count and totals**.

   Then by: **Family and Type**

   Enable **Itemize every instance**.

5. Activate the **Formatting** tab.

   Highlight **Family and Type**.
   Change the Heading to **Wall Style**.

6. Activate the **Formatting** tab.

   Highlight **Material: Name**.
   Change the Heading to **Material**.

7. Activate the Formatting tab.

   Highlight **Material: Area**.
   Change the Heading to **Area**.

   Enable **Calculate totals**.

8-37

8. Activate the **Appearance** tab.

   Disable **Blank row before data**.

   Set the Header Text to **1/4″ Bold**.

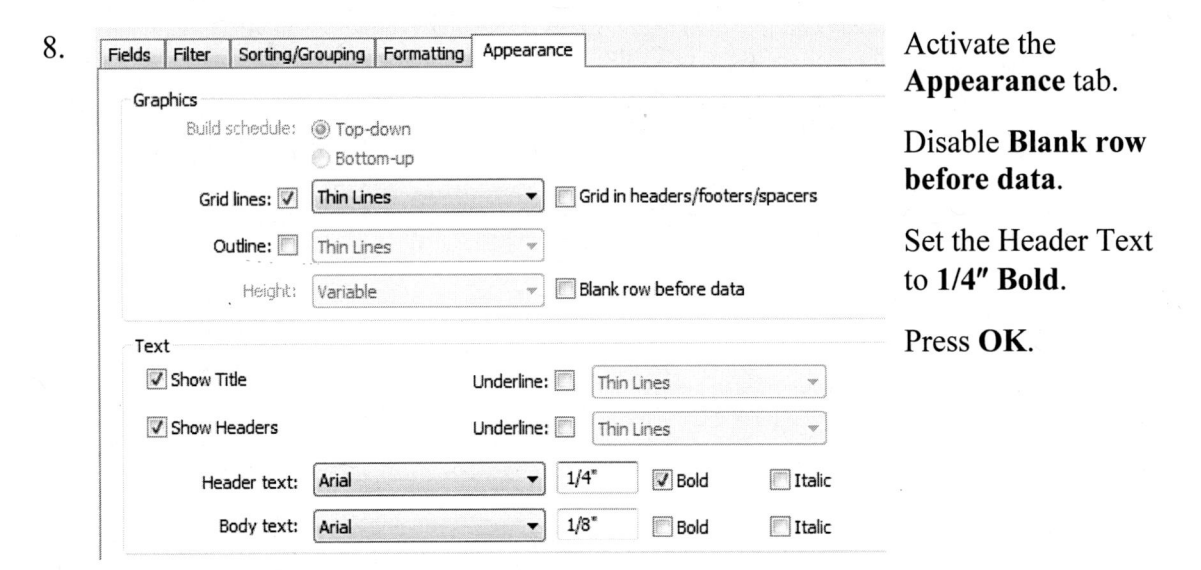

   Press **OK**.

9. A window opens with the new schedule.

10. Close without saving.

Construction Documentation

Command Exercise

Exercise 8-11 – Create a Mass Floor Schedule

Drawing Name: **mass_schedule.rvt**
Estimated Time to Completion: 10 Minutes

Scope

    Create a mass floor schedule

Solution

1. Activate the **View** ribbon.

   Select **Schedules→Schedule/Quantities** from the Create panel.

2. Highlight **Mass**.
   Press **OK**.

3. Add the following fields:

   Family and Type
   Gross Floor Area
   Gross Volume
   Description

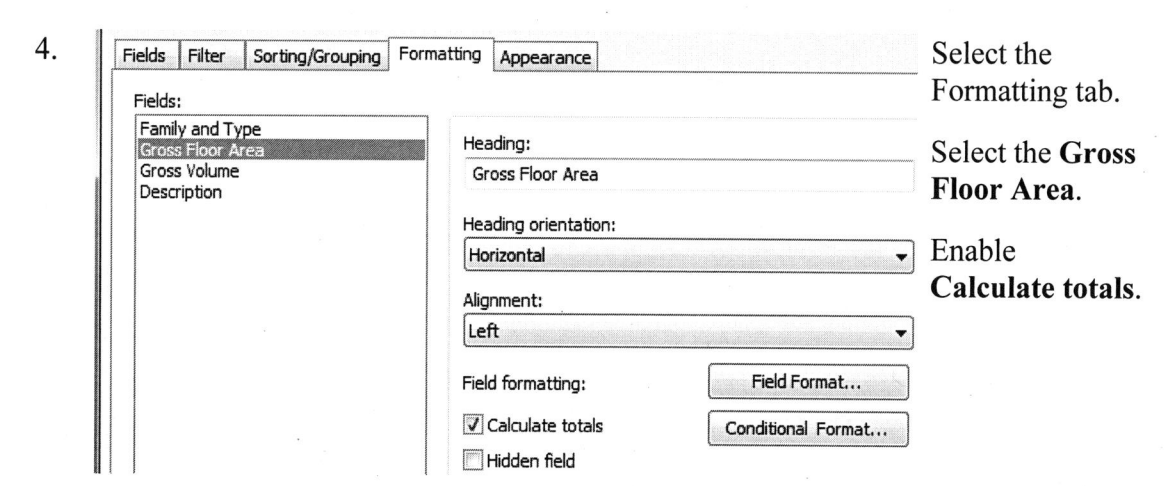

4. Select the Formatting tab.

   Select the **Gross Floor Area**.

   Enable **Calculate totals**.

8-39

5. ☐ Blank row before data   Select the Appearance tab.
   Disable **Blank row before data**.

   Press **OK**.

6. | Mass Schedule ||||
    |---|---|---|---|
    | Family and T | Gross Floor | Gross Volum | Description |
    | Building 1 | | 475111.08 C | |
    | Building 2 | | 58017.48 CF | |
    | Building 3 | | 846350.11 C | |
    | Building 4 | 63900 SF | 730950.20 C | |
    | Tower 1: | | 331007.33 C | |
    | Building 5 | | 174509.62 C | |

    You will only see floor area for the mass where mass floors exist.

7. Close the file without saving.

Practice Associate Exam

1. Legend views:

    A. Are placed on only one sheet at a time
    B. Contain model and annotation elements
    C. Have model components tagged
    D. Have dimensions added to system families

2. To add or remove fields from a revision schedule:

    A. Select the revision schedule in the browser, right click and select Properties
    B. Select the Schedules tool on the View ribbon.
    C. First you must open the title block family for editing
    D. Select the Revision Table in the graphics window, right click and select Element Properties

3. To add revisions to the Sheet Issues/Revisions dialog, you must access this ribbon:

    A. View
    B. Manage
    C. Annotate
    D. Insert

4. On which tab of the Schedule Properties dialog can hidden fields be enabled?

    A. Fields
    B. Filter
    C. Formatting
    D. Appearance
    E. Sorting/Grouping

5. Color Schemes can be placed in the following views (Select 3):

    A. Floor plan
    B. Ceiling Plan
    C. Section
    D. Elevation
    E. 3D

6. To define the colors and fill patterns used in a color scheme legend, select the legend, and Click Edit Scheme on the:

    A. Properties palette
    B. View Control Bar
    C. Ribbon
    D. Options Bar

Room Schedule			
Number	Name	Area	Level
4	Accounting	49.29	Level 1
3	CEO	117.84	Level 1
9	Common Area	391.84	Level 1
6	Conference Room	146.21	Level 1
7	Copy/Mail Room	71.73	Level 1
1	Engineering	136.75	Level 1
8	Lobby	236.81	Level 1
5	Operations	49.29	Level 1
2	Sales/Marketing	119.02	Level 1
Grand total: 9		1318.77	

7. The Room Schedule shown sorts by Level and by _____.

   A. Name
   B. Area
   C. Number
   D. Total

8. A legend is a view that can be placed on:

   A. A plan view
   B. A drafting view
   C. Multiple Plan Regions
   D. Multiple Sheets

9. The calculated total for a mass floor area can be displayed in:

   A. Project Browser
   B. Properties pane
   C. Mass Floor Schedule
   D. Floors Schedule

10. To compute the total cost of a material in a schedule, you need to create a _____.

    A. Project parameter for cost
    B. Shared Parameter
    C. Calculated Value
    D. Project Filter

11. A _____ is a view that displays information about a building project in tabular form.

    A. Schedule
    B. Graph
    C. Legend
    D. Chart

Answers
1) B; 2) C; 3) A; 4) C; 5) A, C, D; 6) C; 7) A; 8) D; 9) C; 10) C; 11) A

Lesson Nine

Presenting the Building Model

This lesson addresses the following Associate and Professional exam questions:

- Sun and Shadow Settings
- Rendering
- Decals

Revit Architecture can create photorealistic images of both exterior and interior views of your model. Users can create lighting, plants, decals, and place people in their model.

If you need to monitor how much memory the rendering process is using in the Windows Task Manager, the rendering process is named fbxooprender.exe. When you render an image, the rendering process may use up to 4 CPUs.

Because rendering can use up system resources, turn off active screen savers, and shut down any non-essential processes. (For example, close your email program and don't browse the internet during rendering.) By closing applications, more CPU capacity will be made available to the rendering process and can reduce render time. Many users will have two workstations: one for rendering and one for regular office work if they create a lot of renderings.

If you experience long delays when rendering, use the Windows Task Manager to monitor processes. If fbxooprender.exe is not using close to 99% of processor power, other active processes may be interfering with the rendering process. Shut down non-essential tasks to make more processor power available for the rendering process.

Command Exercise

Exercise 9-1 – Creating a Toposurface

Drawing Name: **C_Condo_complex.rvt**
Estimated Time to Completion: 40 Minutes

Scope

Create a toposurface.
Add site components.
Add entourage.

Solution

1. Activate the **Site** view.
   Turn off the visibility of grids, elevations, and sections.

2. Activate the **Massing & Site** ribbon.

3. Select the **Toposurface** tool.

4. Use the **Place Point** tool to create an outline of a lawn surface.

Presenting the Building Model

5. Pick the points indicated to create a lawn expanse.

   You can grab the points and drag to move into the correct position.

6. Click on the **Select** tool on the ribbon to exit out of the add points mode.

7. Left click in the **Material** column on the Properties pane.

8. In the search field, type site.

   Site materials will then be listed.

   Highlight **Site - Grass**.

9. Enable **Use Render Appearance for Shading**.

   Press **OK**.

10. Select the **Green Check** on the Surface panel to **Finish Surface**.

9-3

The Unofficial Revit 2012 Certification Exam Guide

11. 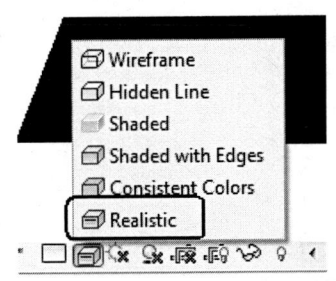 Switch to **Realistic** to see the grass material.

12. 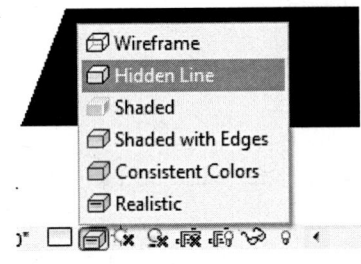 Switch the display to **Hidden Line** to make it easier to place the building pad.

13.  Activate the **Massing & Site** ribbon.

14. 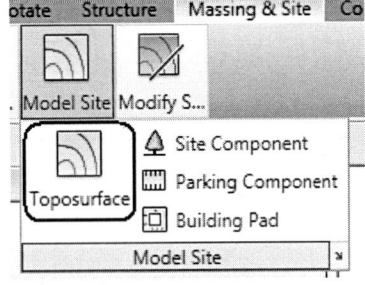 Select the **Toposurface** tool.

15. 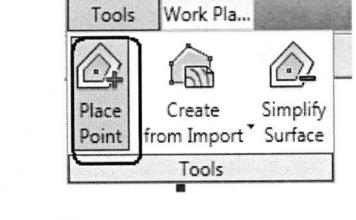 Use the **Place Point** tool to create an outline of a lawn surface.

16. 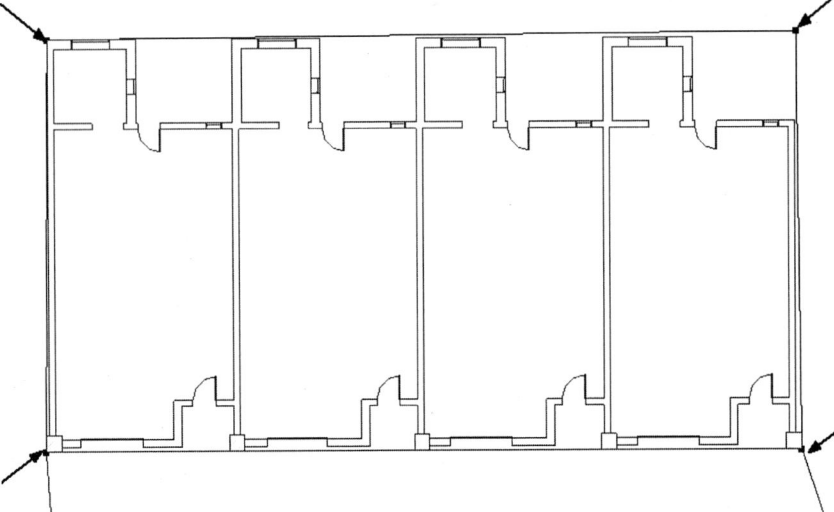 Select the four corners of the building to form a rough rectangle.

Presenting the Building Model

17. Click on the **Select** tool on the ribbon to exit out of the add points mode.

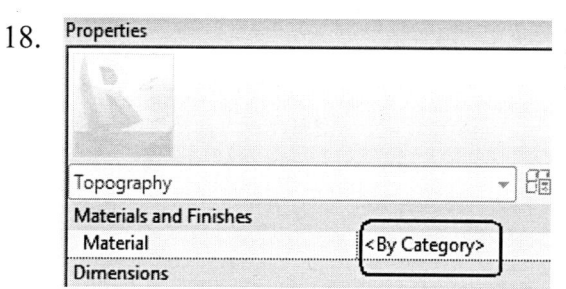

18. Left click in the **Material** column on the Properties pane.

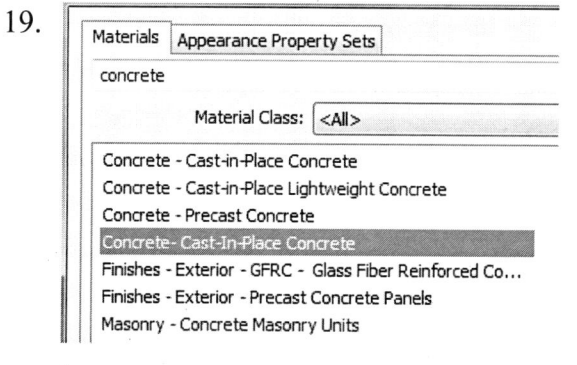

19. On the Materials tab on the left side:

    In the search field, type concrete.

    Site materials will then be listed.

    Highlight **Concrete - Cast In-Place Concrete**.

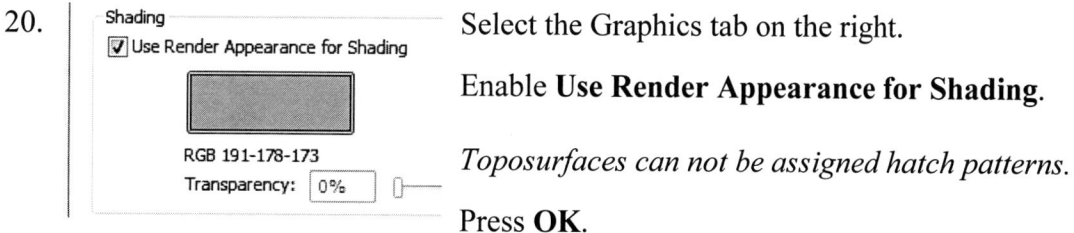

20. Select the Graphics tab on the right.

    Enable **Use Render Appearance for Shading**.

    Toposurfaces can not be assigned hatch patterns.

    Press **OK**.

21. Select the **Green Check** on the Surface panel to **Finish Surface**.

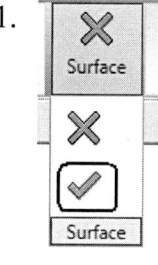

22. Select the **Building Pad** tool from the Model Site panel.

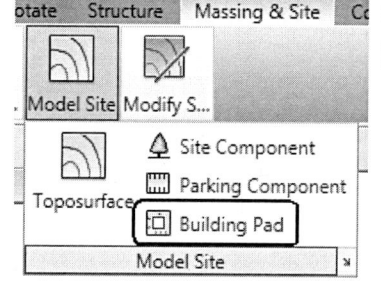

9-5

23. Select the **Rectangle** tool from the Draw panel

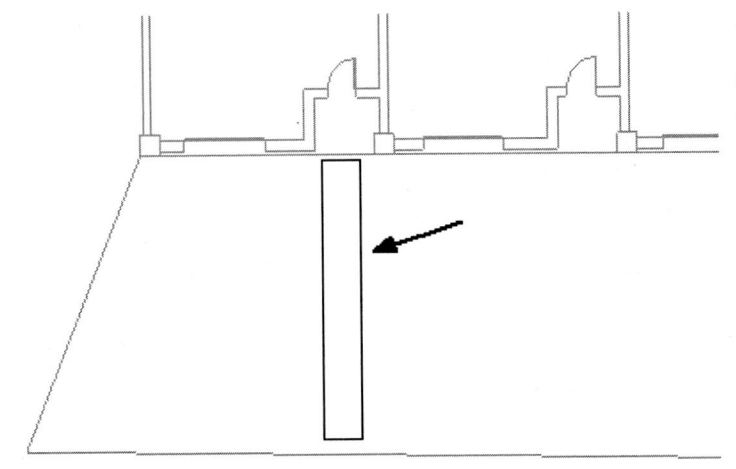

24. Use **Rectangle** to create a sidewalk up to the left entrance of the building.

   The rectangle must be entirely within the toposurface or you will get an error message.

25. On the Properties pane:

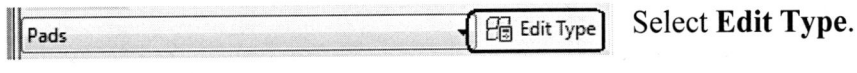

   Pads — Select **Edit Type**.

26. Duplicate... Select **Duplicate**.

27. Name: Walkway — Enter **Walkway** in the Name field. Press **OK**.

28. Select **Edit** under Structure.

Parameter	Value
Construction	
Structure	Edit...
Thickness	1' 0"
Graphics	
Coarse Scale Fill Patt	
Coarse Scale Fill Colo	Black

29. In the Material dialog for Structure [1], select **Masonry - Brick**. Press **OK**.

#	Function	Material	Thick
1	Core Boundary	Layers Above Wra	0' 0"
2	Structure [1]	Masonry - Brick	1' 0"
3	Core Boundary	Layers Below Wra	0' 0"

Presenting the Building Model

30. Enable **Use Render Appearance for Shading**.

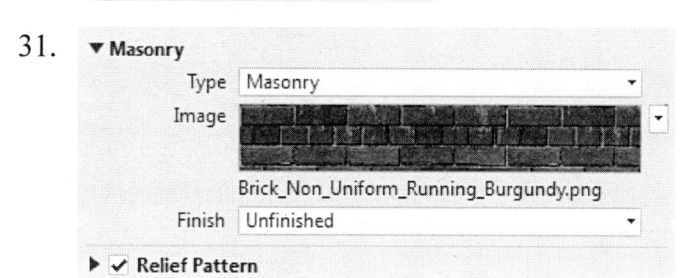

31. Select the **Appearance** tab and there will be a preview of how the walkway should appear in the rendering.

   Press **OK** multiple times to close all dialogs.

32. In the Properties pane:

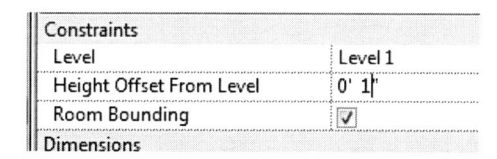

   Set the Height Offset from Level to **1″**.

   This protrudes the walkway 1″ above the toposurface so it appears better.

33. Select the **Green Check** on the Mode panel to **Finish Building Pad**.

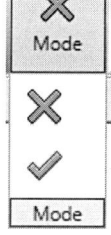

34. Switch to a **3D** view.

35. Use View Properties (VP) to set the style to **Shaded**.

   Rotate the view so you can see the topo surface.

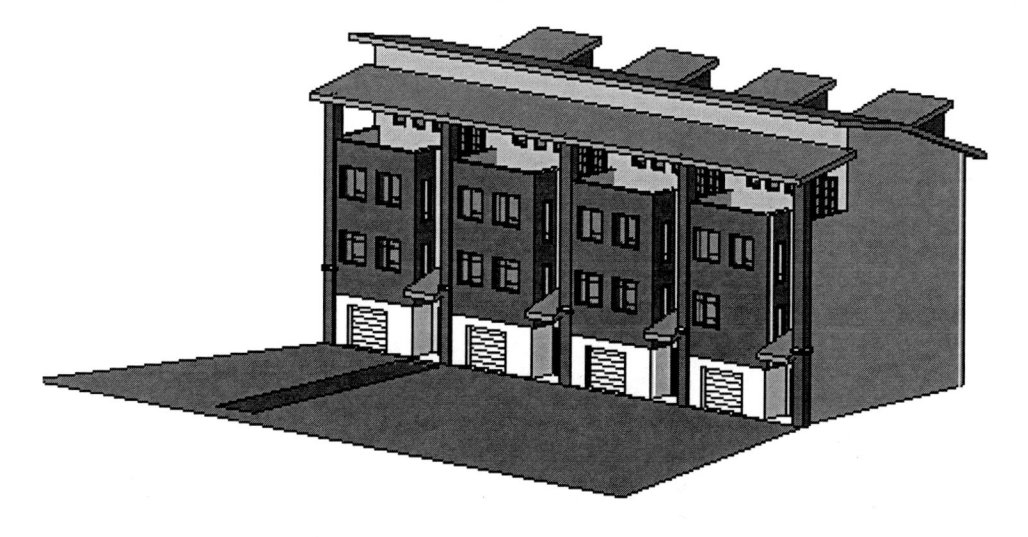

The Unofficial Revit 2012 Certification Exam Guide

36. Switch to the **Site** view.

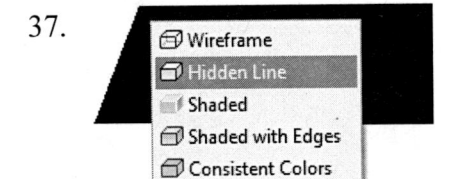

37. Switch the display to **Hidden Line**.

38. Activate the **Massing & Site** ribbon.

39. Select the **Site Component** tool on the Model Site panel.

40. Select the **Load Family** tool from the Mode panel.

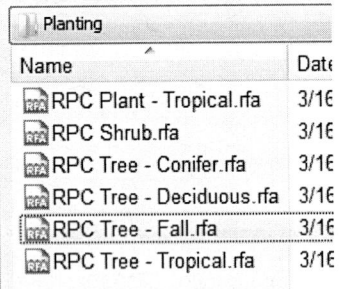

41. Select the *Planting* folder.

42. Select the *RPC Tree – Fall.rfa*.

    Press **Open**.

Presenting the Building Model

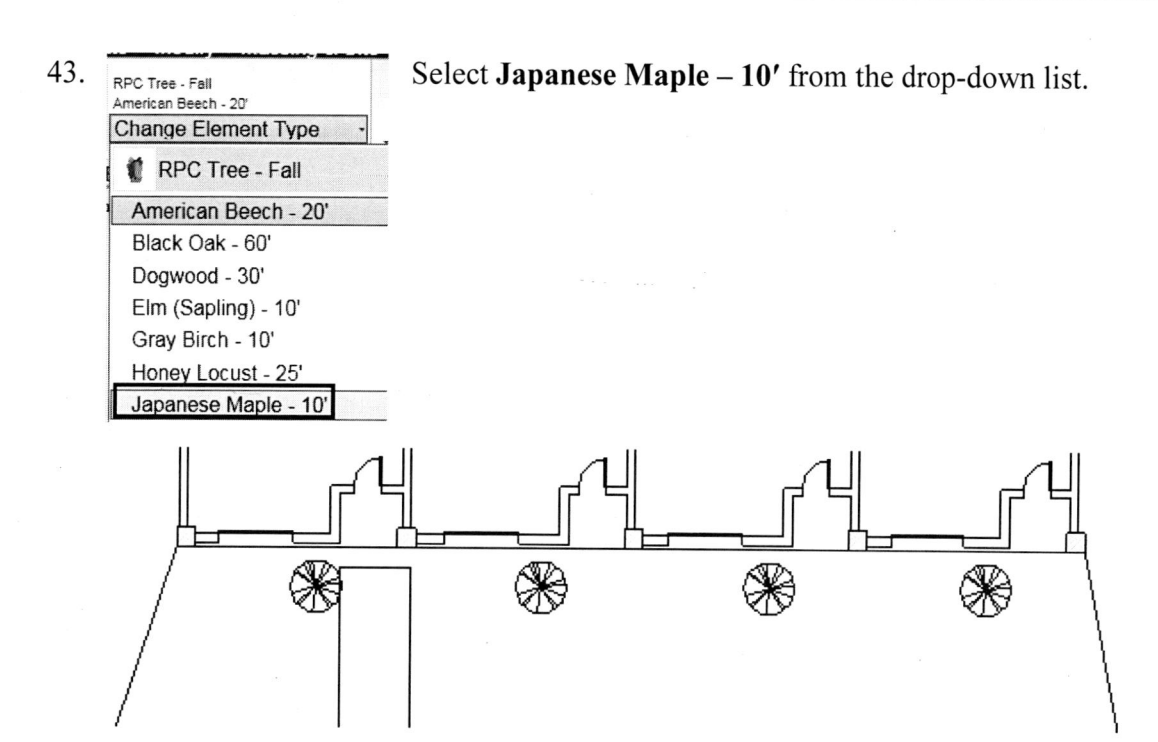

43. Select **Japanese Maple – 10'** from the drop-down list.

44. Place a tree at each entrance.

45. Select the **Site Component** tool on the Model Site panel.

46. Select the **Load Family** tool from the Mode panel.

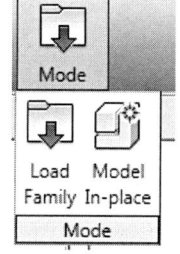

47. Browse to the *Entourage* folder.

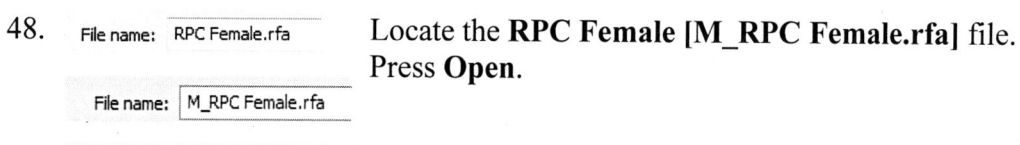

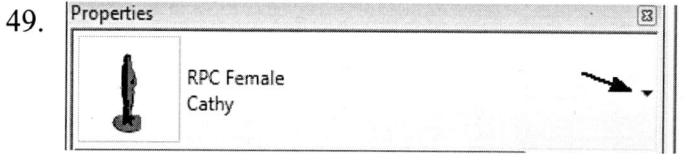

48. Locate the **RPC Female [M_RPC Female.rfa]** file. Press **Open**.

49. Set the Female to **Cathy** in the Properties pane.

9-9

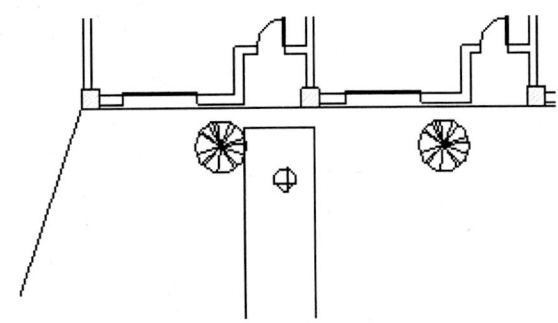

50. Place the person on the walkway.

51. If you zoom in on the person, you only see a symbol – you don't see the real person until you perform a Render. You may need to switch to Hidden Line view to see the symbol for the person.

The point indicates the direction the person is facing.

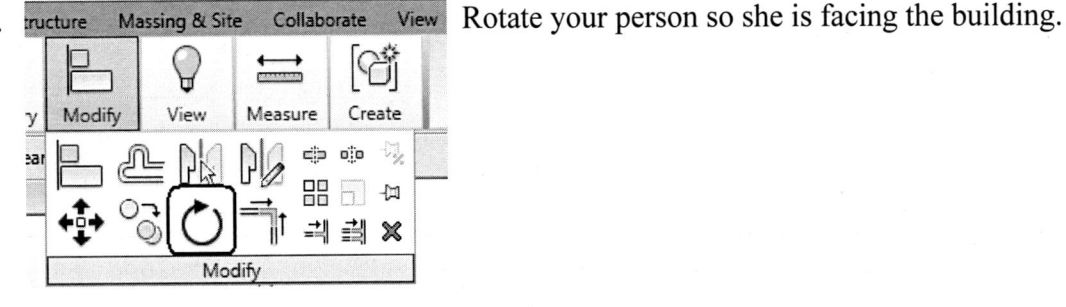

52. Rotate your person so she is facing the building.

53. Save the file as *ex9-1.rvt*.

> **TIP:** Make sure **Level 1** or **Site** is active, or your trees could be placed on Level 2 (and be elevated in the air). If you mistakenly placed your trees on the wrong level, you can pick the trees, right click, select Properties, and change the level.

Command Exercise

Exercise 9-2 – Defining Camera Views

Drawing Name: **ex9-1.rvt**
Estimated Time to Completion: 10 Minutes

Scope

Create a camera view.
Rename the view.
Set view properties.

Solution

1. Activate the **Site** floor plan.

2. Activate the **View** ribbon.

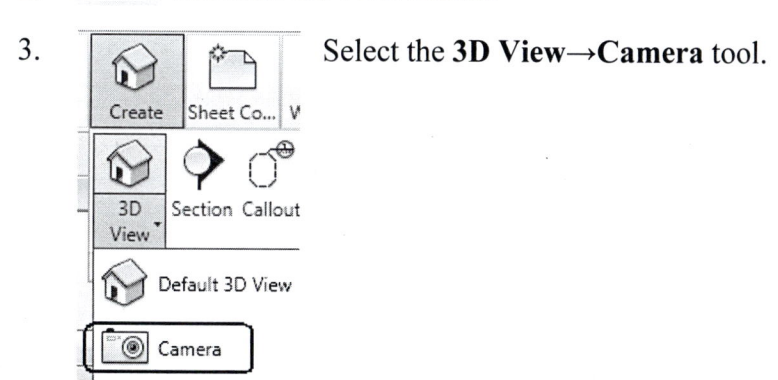

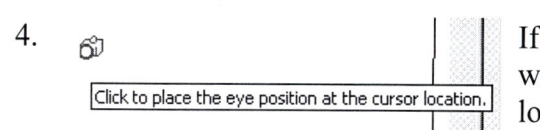

3. Select the **3D View→Camera** tool.

4. If you move your mouse in the graphics window, you will see a tooltip to pick the location for the camera.

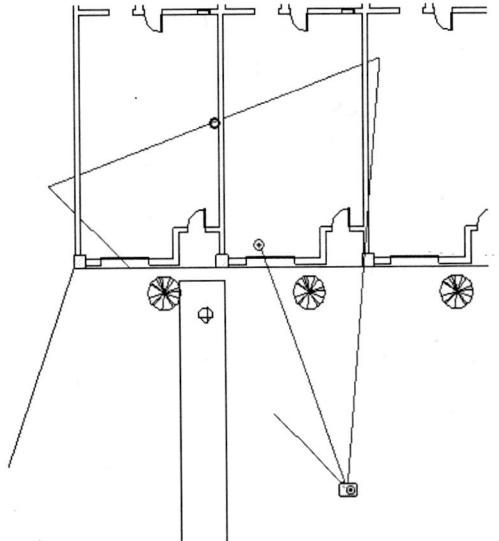

5. Aim the camera towards the front entrance to the building.

6. A window opens with the camera view of your model.

   The person and the tree appear as stick figures because the view is not rendered yet.

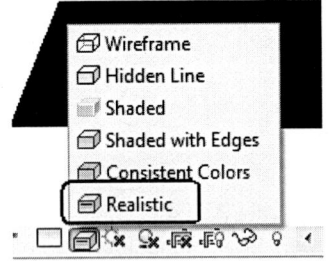

7. Switch to a **Realistic** display.

8. Our view changes to a colored view.

9-12

Presenting the Building Model

9. If you look in the browser, you see that a view has been added to the 3D Views list.

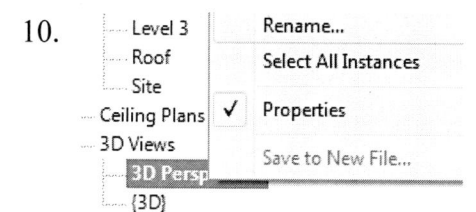

10. Highlight the **3D View 1**.

   Right click and select **Rename**.

   Rename to **3D Perspective**.

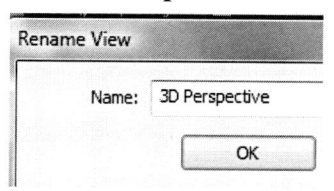

The view we have is a perspective view – not an isometric view. Isometrics are true scale drawings. The Camera View is a perspective view with vanishing points. Isometric views have no vanishing points. Vanishing points are the points at which two parallel lines appear to meet in perspective.

11. In the Properties pane:

   Change the Eye Elevation to **4′6″ [1370 mm]**.

   Change the Target Elevation to **5′ 10″ [3200 mm]**.

12. Press **Apply**.

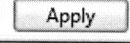

   Your view shifts slightly.

13. Save the file as *ex9-2.rvt*.

TIP: Additional material libraries can be added to Revit. You may store your material libraries on a server to allow multiple users access to the same libraries. You must add a path under Settings → Options to point to the location of your material libraries. There are many online sources for photorealistic materials; www.accustudio.com is a good place to start.

Command Exercise

Exercise 9-3 – Graphic Display Options

Drawing Name: **ex9-2.rvt**
Estimated Time to Completion: 15 Minutes

Scope

Graphic Display Options

Solution

1. Activate the **3D Perspective** view.

2. Select **Graphic Display Options** on the View Display toolbar.

Presenting the Building Model

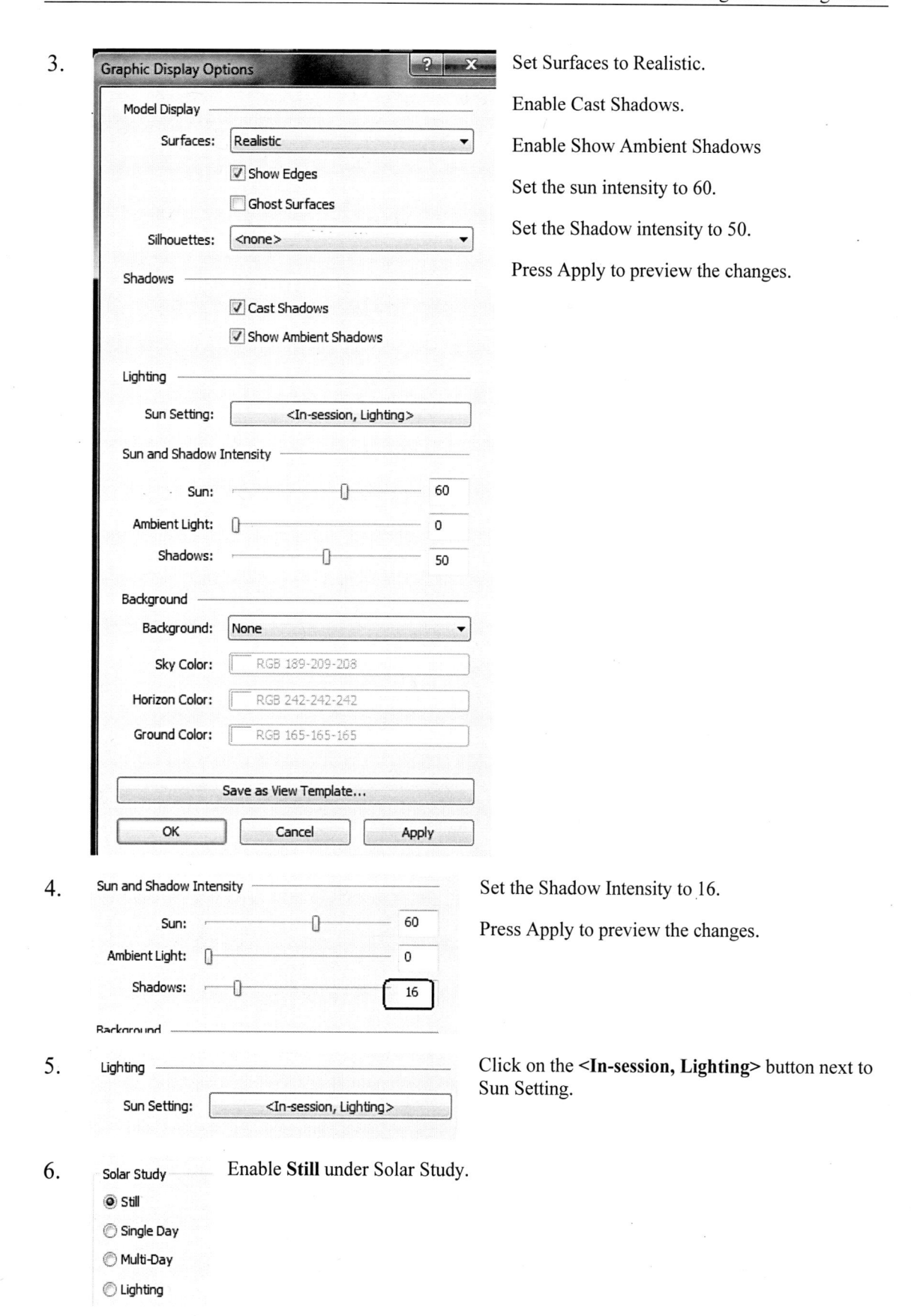

3. Set Surfaces to Realistic.

   Enable Cast Shadows.

   Enable Show Ambient Shadows

   Set the sun intensity to 60.

   Set the Shadow intensity to 50.

   Press Apply to preview the changes.

4. Set the Shadow Intensity to 16.

   Press Apply to preview the changes.

5. Click on the **<In-session, Lighting>** button next to Sun Setting.

6. Enable **Still** under Solar Study.

7. Select the browse button next to Location.

8. Enter an address into the Project Address field.

   Press **Search** to locate the address.

   Enable **Use Daylight Savings time**.

   Press **OK**.

9. Enable **Ground Plane at Level: Level 1**.

   Press **OK**.

10. Close the Graphics Options dialog.

11. Save as *ex9-3.rvt*.

Command Exercise

Exercise 9-4 – Assigning Settings

Drawing Name: **ex9-3.rvt**
Estimated Time to Completion: 15 Minutes

Scope

Create a rendering.
Control rendering options.
Save a rendering to the project.

Solution

1. 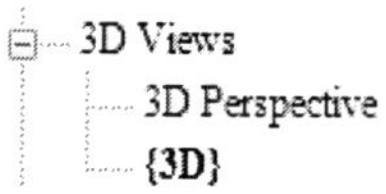 Activate the **3D Perspective** view.

2. On the Properties pane:

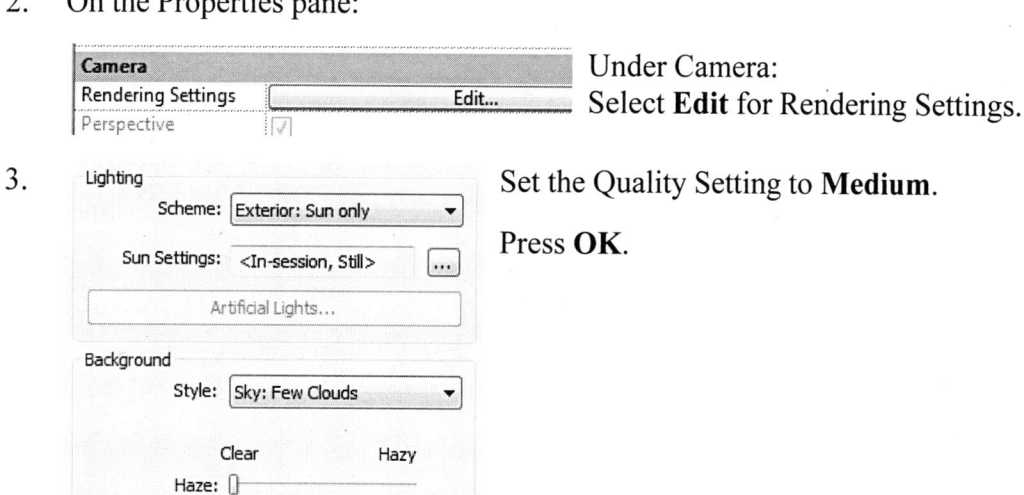

    Under Camera:
    Select **Edit** for Rendering Settings.

3. Set the Quality Setting to **Medium**.

    Press **OK**.

4. 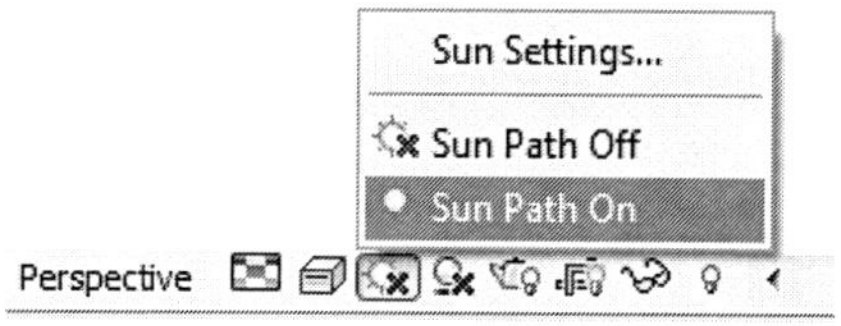 Set **Sun Path On** using the Display Control bar.

5. 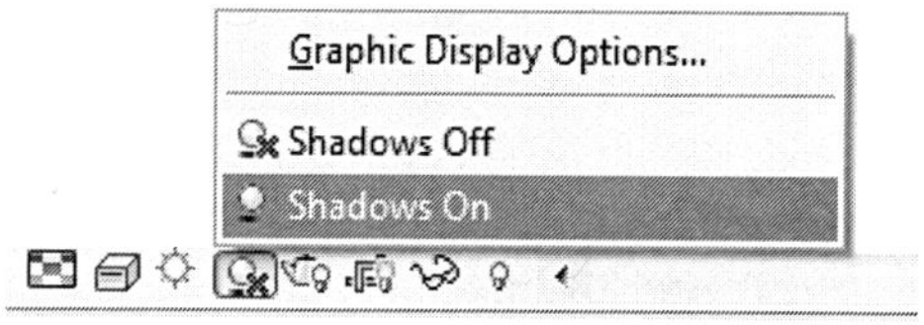 Set **Shadows On** using the Display Control bar.

The Unofficial Revit 2012 Certification Exam Guide

6. Select **Sun Settings** from the Display Control bar.

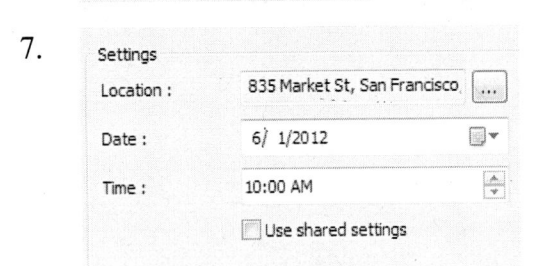

7. This is the same dialog we brought up using the Graphic Display Settings.

   Press **OK** to close the dialog.

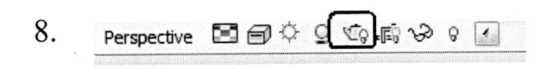

8. Select the **Rendering** tool located on the Display Control bar.

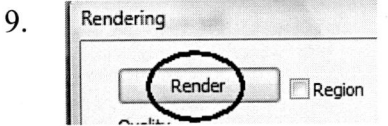

9. Select the **Render** button.

10. Your window will be rendered.

11. Select **Save to Project**.

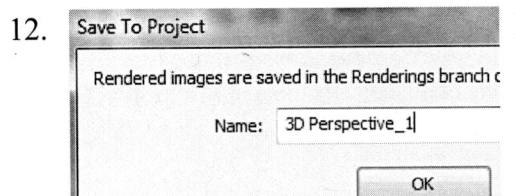

12. Press **OK** to accept the default name.

13. Under Renderings, we now have a view called **3D Perspective_1**.

14. Select the **Show the model** button.
    Close the Rendering dialog.

    Our window changes to – not Rendered – mode.

15. Save the file as *ex9-4.rvt*.

Command Exercise

Exercise 9-5 – Place a Decal

Drawing Name: **ex9-4.rvt**
Estimated Time to Completion: 30 Minutes

Scope

Create a decal type.
Place a decal.
Add model text.
Join Geometry
Render.

Solution

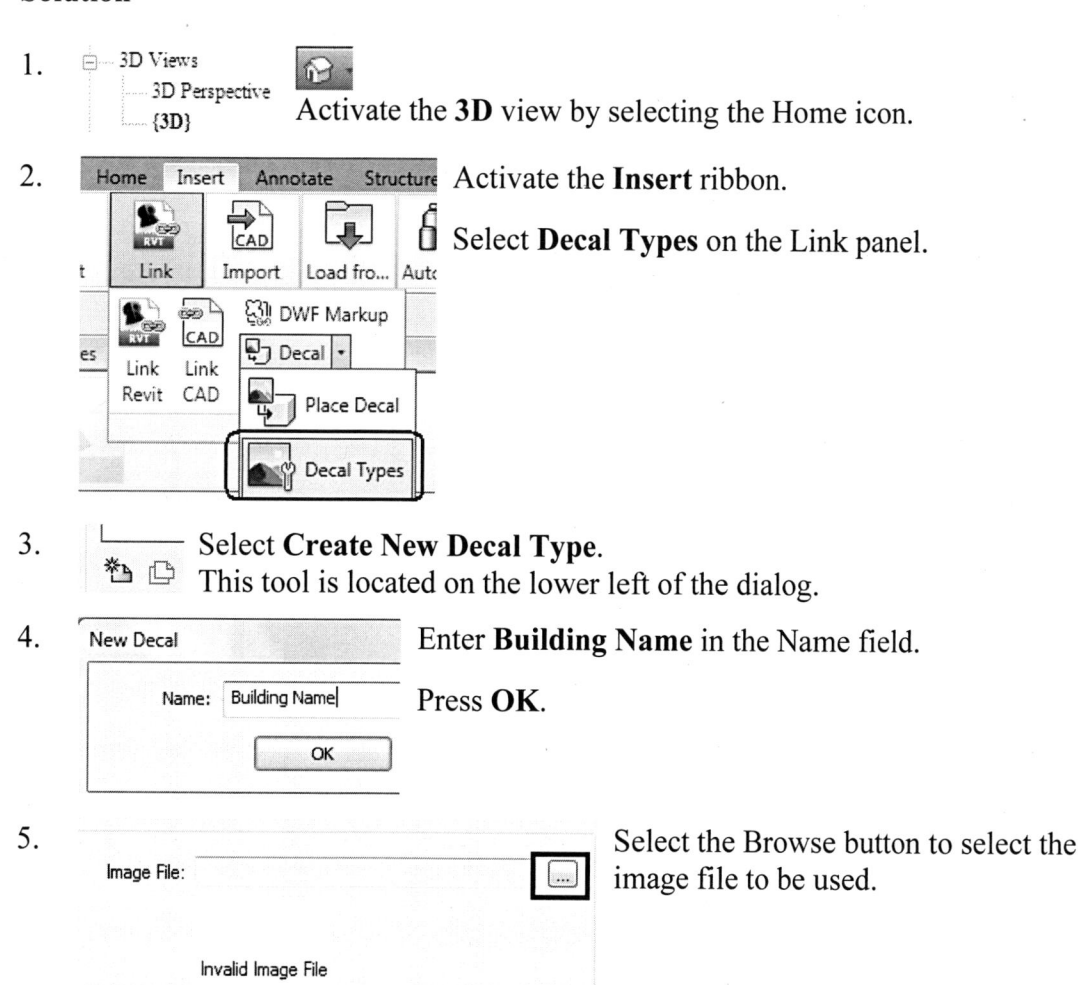

1. Activate the **3D** view by selecting the Home icon.

2. Activate the **Insert** ribbon.

   Select **Decal Types** on the Link panel.

3. Select **Create New Decal Type**.
   This tool is located on the lower left of the dialog.

4. Enter **Building Name** in the Name field.

   Press **OK**.

5. Select the Browse button to select the image file to be used.

The Unofficial Revit 2012 Certification Exam Guide

6. 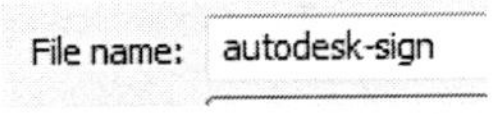 Locate the *autodesk-sign.jpg* file.
   You can use a different image file if you prefer.
   Press **Open**.

7.  You will see a preview of the image file.
   Press **OK**.

8. 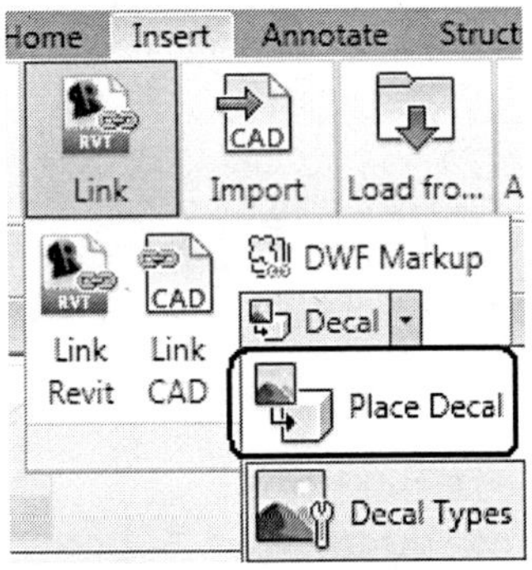 Select the **Place Decal** tool from the Link panel

9. 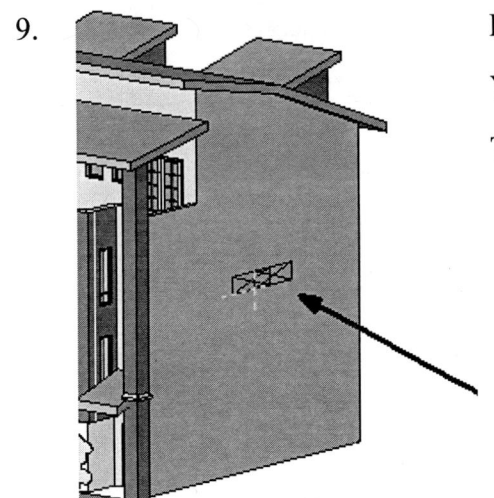 Place the decal on the side of the building.

   You will not see the image, only a placeholder.

   This is to conserve memory resources.

10.  Select the Modify tool and then pick the decal that was placed.

11. 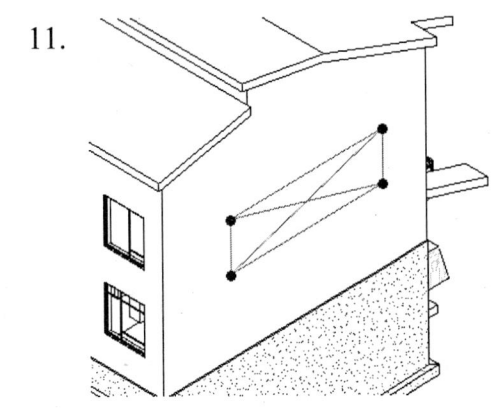 Use the grips located on the corners to enlarge the decal.

    The grips can also be used to move the decal into the desired position.

9-20

Presenting the Building Model

12.  Activate the **Home** ribbon.

13. 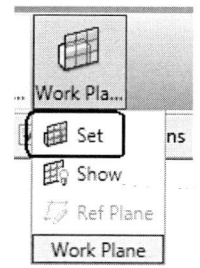 Select the **Set Work plane** tool from the Work Plane panel.

14. 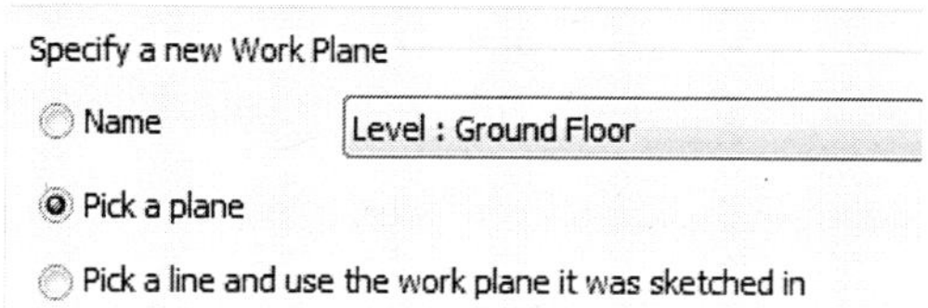 Enable **Pick a plane**.

    Press **OK**.

15. 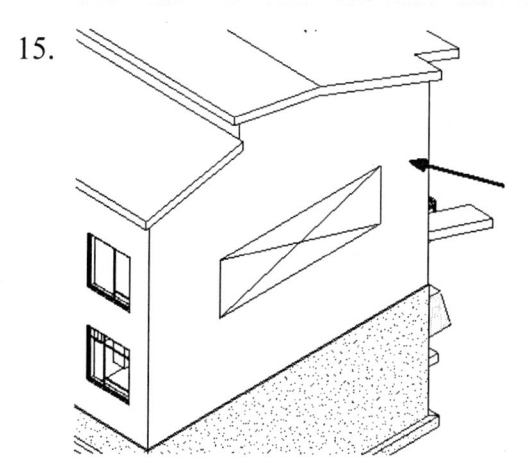 Select the wall where the decal is placed.

    If you wish to verify that you have selected the correct work plane, use the Show Work Plane tool.

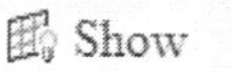

16. 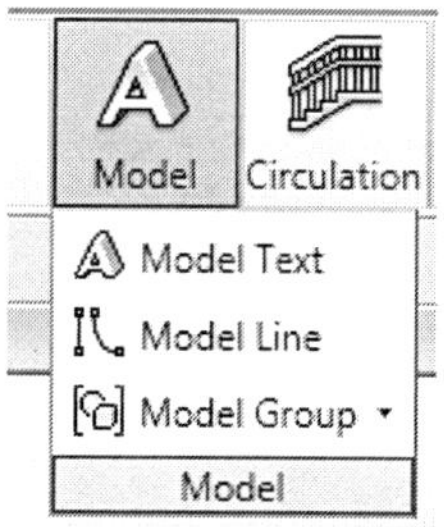 Select the **Model Text** tool from the Model panel on the Home ribbon.

17. 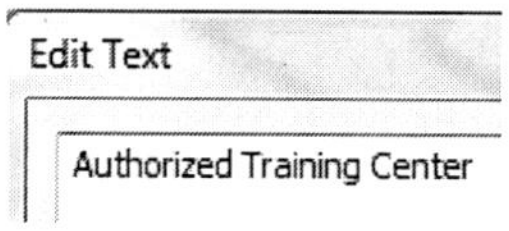 Enter **Authorized Training Center** into the Edit Text dialog.

    Press **OK**.

18. 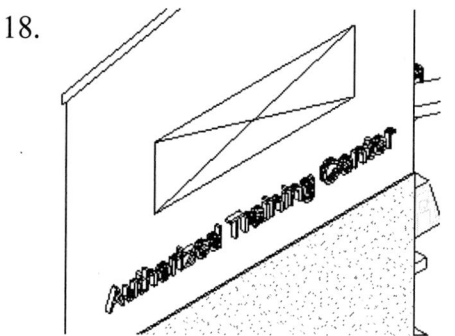 Place it on the wall beneath the decal.

9-21

19. Set the display to **Realistic.**

20. Decals are displayed in Realistic mode.

21. Select the model text you just placed.

    In the Properties pane:

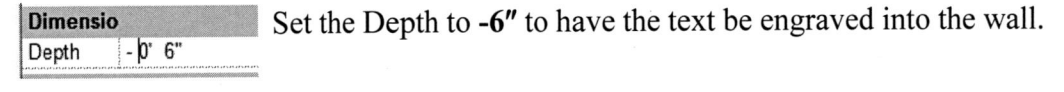

    Set the Depth to **-6″** to have the text be engraved into the wall.

22. Select the Materials field to set the material.

23. Highlight **Finishes - Interior - Paints and Coatings**.

24. Select **New Material** to create a new material.

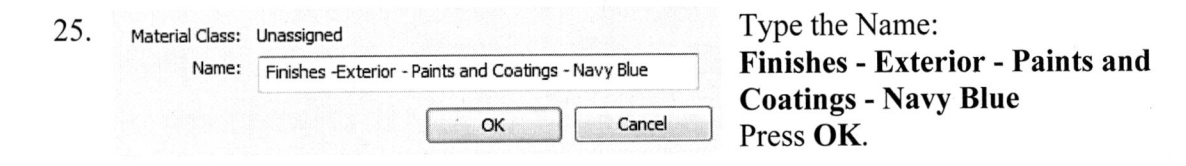

25. Type the Name:
    Finishes - Exterior - Paints and Coatings - Navy Blue
    Press **OK**.

Presenting the Building Model

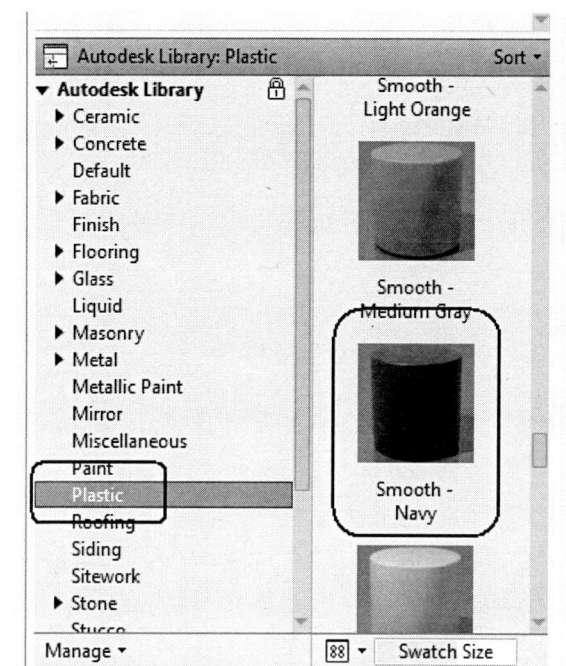

26. Activate the Appearance tab.

Activate the Appearance Property Sets tab.

Highlight **Plastic** in the left pane.

Select the **Smooth - Navy** color in the right pane.

27. Press **OK**.

28. Activate the **Modify** ribbon.

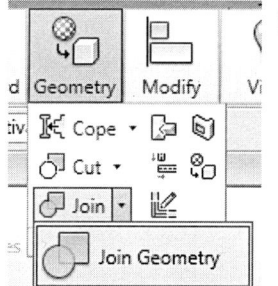

29. Select **Join Geometry** from the Geometry panel.

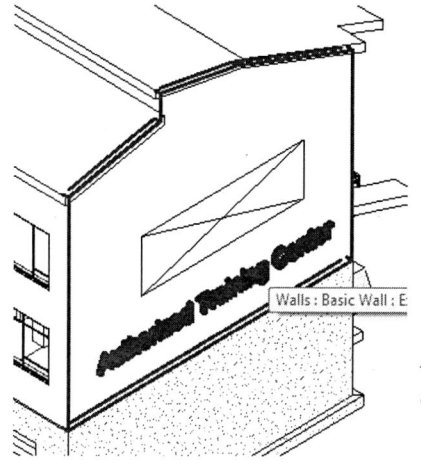

30. Select the model text and the wall to join them.

If you mouse over the wall, you should see the wall and text highlight if the join was done correctly.

9-23

31. Select the **Rendering** tool located on the Display Control bar.

32. Enable **Region**.
Set the Quality Setting to **Medium**.
Select the **Render** button.

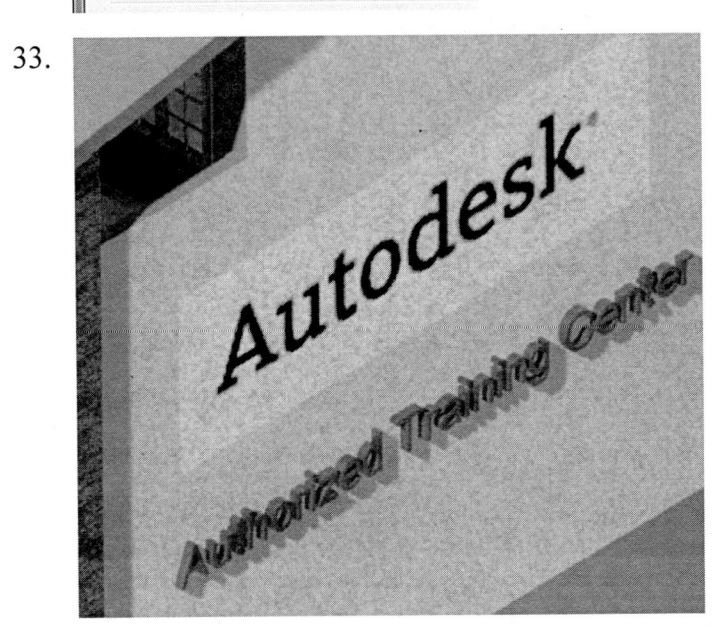

33. Your window will be rendered with the decal.

34. Save the file as *ex9-5.rvt*.

Presenting the Building Model

Command Exercise

Exercise 9-6 – Custom Render Settings

Drawing Name: **custom_rendering.rvt**
Estimated Time to Completion: 30 Minutes

Scope

Create custom rendering settings

Solution

1. Activate the **Lobby 3D** view.

2. Select the **Render** tool from the View Control bar.

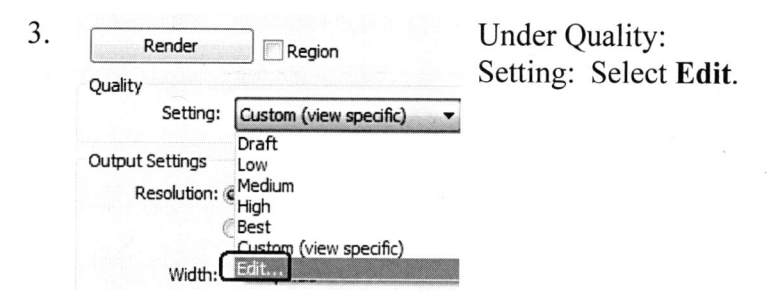

3. Under Quality:
   Setting: Select **Edit**.

4. Set the Setting to **Custom**.

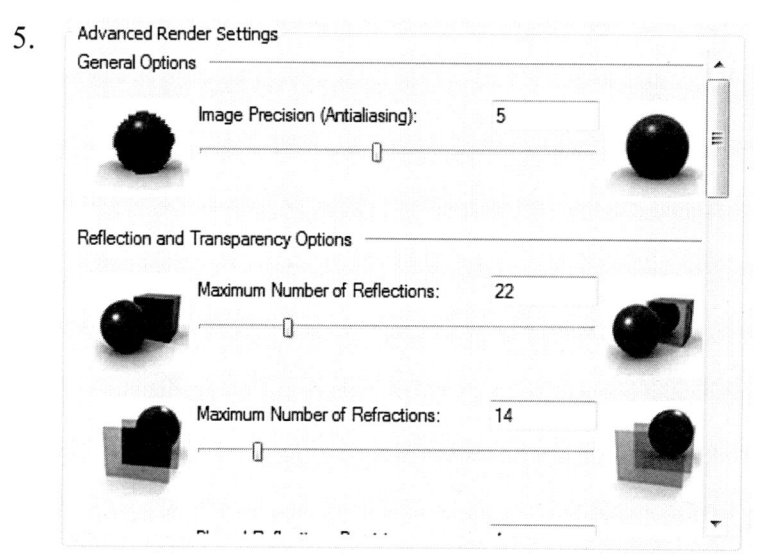

5. Set Image Precision to **5**.

   Set Maximum Number of Reflections to **22**.

   Set Maximum Number of Refractions to **14**.

9-25

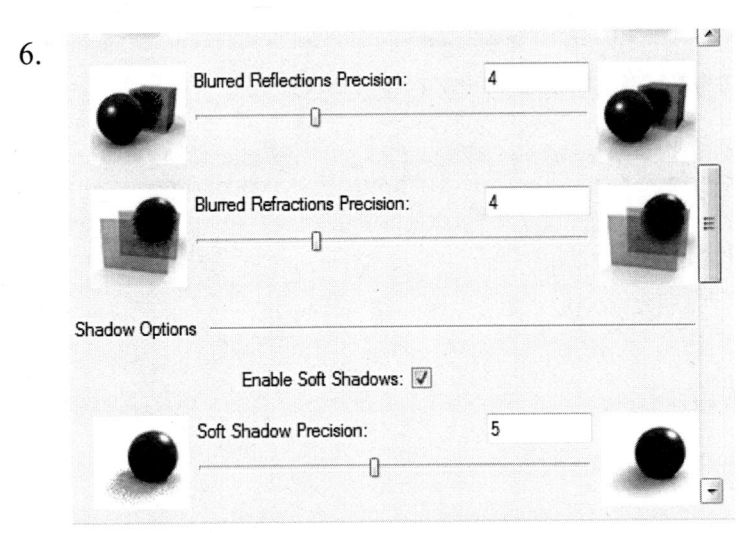

6. Scroll down.
   Set Blurred Reflection Precision to **4**.
   Set Blurred Refraction Precision to **4**.
   Enable **Soft Shadows**.
   Set Soft Shadow Precision to **5**.

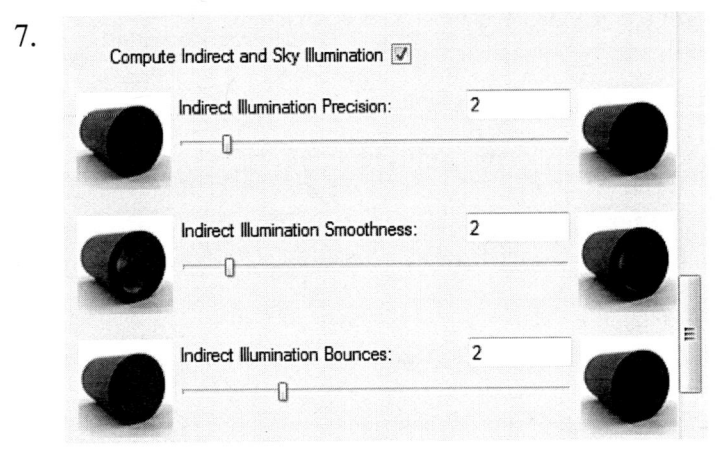

7. Enable **Indirect and Sky Illumination**.
   Set Indirect Illumination Precision to **2**.
   Set Indirect Illumination Smoothness to **2**.
   Set Indirect Illumination Bounces to **2**.

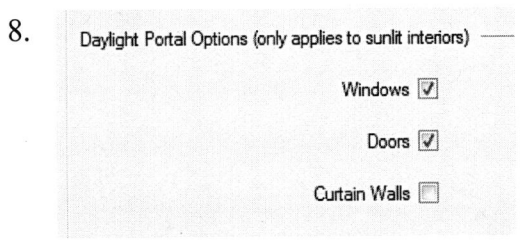

8. Enable **Windows** and **Doors** under Daylight Portal Options.
   Press **OK**.

9. Press **Render**.

10. Close the file without saving.

Practice Associate Exam

1. Renderings can be created in which TWO view types:
    A. Elevation
    B. Plan
    C. Section
    D. 3D
    E. Camera

2. THREE items important for accurate shadow studies:
    A. Shared parameters
    B. Toposurface
    C. Color fill schemes
    D. Project location
    E. Sun position (date and time)

3. In the *default.rte* template, what level is the Ground Plane set in the Sun and Shadow Settings?
    A. Site
    B. Level 1
    C. Level 2

4. The Place Decal tool is located on which ribbon:
    A. Home
    B. Insert
    C. Modify
    D. Annotations

5. Before you add a building pad, you need a:
    A. floor
    B. toposurface
    C. wall
    D. isolated foundation

6. You can create a toposurface by placing points OR:
    A. creating from import
    B. drawing contour lines
    C. drawing a path
    D. picking points

7. When creating a rendering, you can control the Maximum Number of Reflections by adjusting the _____ settings.

   A. Image
   B. Lighting
   C. Quality
   D. Output

8. Select the display setting that allows you to preview a decal.

   A. Wireframe
   B. Hidden line
   C. Consistent Colors
   D. Realistic

Answers
1) D & E; 2) B, D & E; 3) B; 4) B; 5) B; 6) A; 7) C; 8) D

Lesson Ten

Collaboration

This lesson addresses the following Associate and Professional exam questions:

- Demonstrate how to copy and monitor elements in a linked file
- Apply interference checking in Revit
- Using Shared Coordinates
- Worksets
- Linked files

In most building projects, you need to collaborate with outside contractors and with other team members. A mechanical engineer uses an architect's building model to layout the HVAC (heating and air conditioning) system. Proper coordination and monitoring ensures that the mechanical layout is synchronized with the changes that the architect makes as the building develops. Effective change monitoring reduces errors and keeps a project on schedule.

Worksets are used in a team environment when you have many people working on the same project file. The project file is located on a server (a central file). Each team member downloads a copy of the project to their local machine. The person is assigned a workset consisting of building elements which they can change. If you need to change an element that belongs to another team member, you issue an Editing Request which can be granted or denied. Workers check in and check out the project, updating both the local and server versions of the file upon each check in/out.

Project sharing is the process of linking projects across disciplines. You can share a Revit Structure model with an MEP engineer.

You can link different file formats in a Revit project, including other Revit files (Revit Architecture, Revit Structure, Revit MEP), CAD formats (DWG, DXF, DGN, SAT, SKP), and DWF markup files. Linked files act similarly as external references (XREFs) in AutoCAD. You can also use file linking if you have a project which involves multiple buildings.

It is recommended to use linked Revit models for

- Separate buildings on a site or campus

- Parts of buildings which are being designed by different design teams or designed for different drawing sets

- Coordination across different disciplines (for example, an architectural model and a structural model)

Linked models may also be appropriate for the following situations:

- Townhouse design when there is little geometric interactivity between the townhouses

- Repeating floors of buildings at early stages in the design, where improved Revit model performance (for example, quick change propagation) is more important than full geometric interactivity or complete detailing

You can select a linked project and bind it within the host project. Binding converts the linked file to a group in the host project. You can also convert a model group into a link which saves the group as an external file.

I have included a portion of the worksets exercise I do in my classroom. This exercise requires that there is a shared location on a server where students have read/write access. In many classroom settings, the IT department only provides students with read access and they can only write to a local flash drive. This is to prevent file corruption and minimize exposures to computer viruses. Instructors and users should keep this in mind during the workset exercise.

Command Exercise

Exercise 10-1 – Monitoring a Linked File

Drawing Name: **i_multiple_disciplines.rvt**
Estimated Time to Completion: 40 Minutes

Scope

Link a Revit Structure file
Monitor the levels in the linked file
Reload the modified Structure file
Perform a coordination review
Create a Coordination Review report

Solution

1. Activate the **Insert** ribbon.

   Select the **Link Revit** tool on the Link panel.

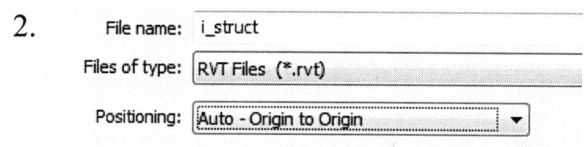

2. Locate the *i_struct* file.

   Set the Positioning to **Auto-Origin to Origin**.

   Press **Open**.

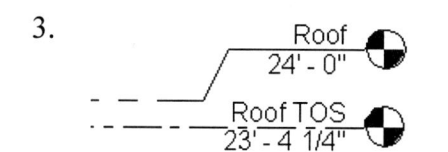

3. Zoom into the left side of the screen where the level markers are.

   There are two sets of level lines. One is part of the original file and the other is from the linked file.

4. Activate the Collaborate ribbon.

   Select **Copy/Monitor→Select Link** from the Coordinate panel.

   Pick in the window to select the linked file.

10-3

5. 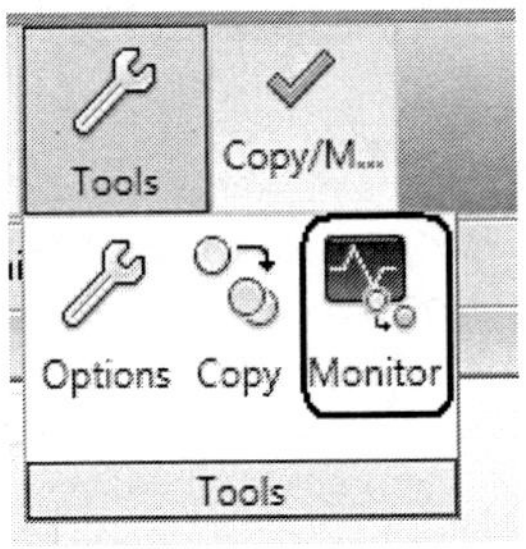 Select the **Monitor** tool from the Tools panel.

6. 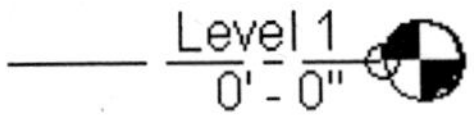 Select the Level 1 level line twice.
   The first selection will be the host file.
   The second selection will be the linked file.
   This is because the level lines overlap.

7. 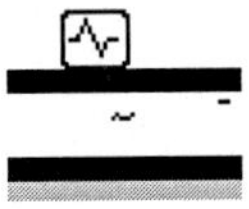 You should see a symbol on Level 1 indicating that Level 1 is currently being monitored for changes.

8. 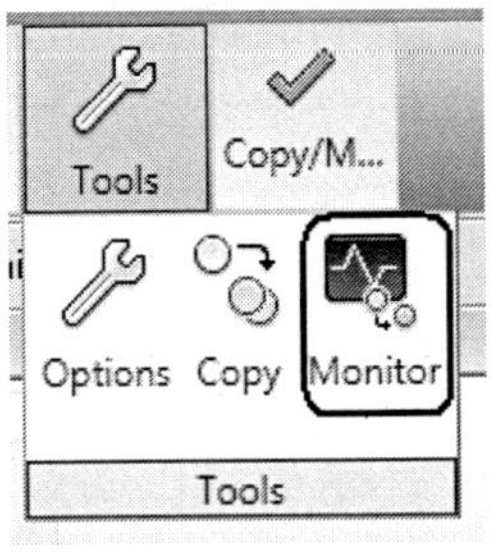 Select the **Monitor** tool from the Tools panel.

9. 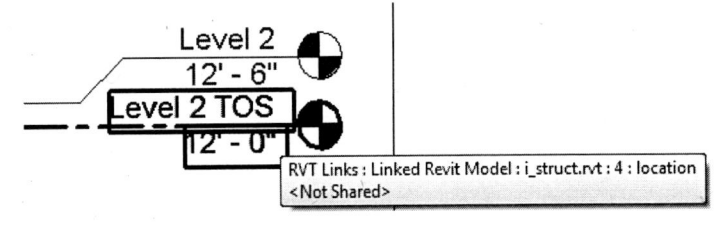 Select the Level 2 level line.
   The first selection will be the host file.
   The second selection will be the linked file.
   You should see a tool tip indicating a linked file is being selected.

10. 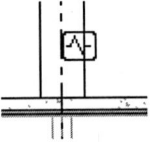 Zoom out.

    You should see a symbol on Level 2 indicating that Level 2 is currently being monitored for changes.

11. 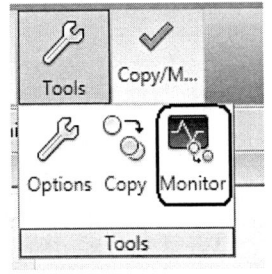 Select the **Monitor** tool from the Tools panel.

10-4

Collaboration

12. Select the Roof level line.
The first selection will be the host file.
The second selection will be the linked file.
You should see a tool tip indicating a linked file is being selected.

13. Zoom out.

You should see a symbol on the Roof level indicating that it is currently being monitored for changes.

14. If you try to select elements which have already been set to be monitored, you will see a warning dialog.
Simply close the dialog and move on.

15. Select **Finish** on the Copy/Monitor panel.

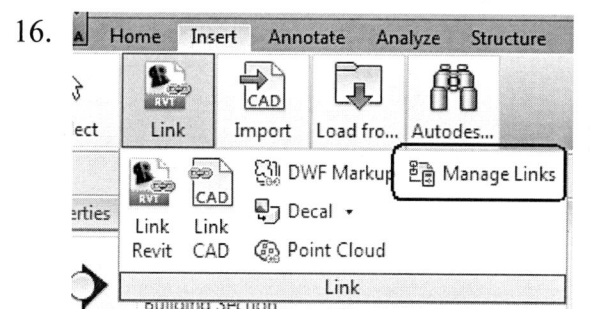

16. Activate the **Insert** ribbon.

Select **Manage Links** from the Link panel.

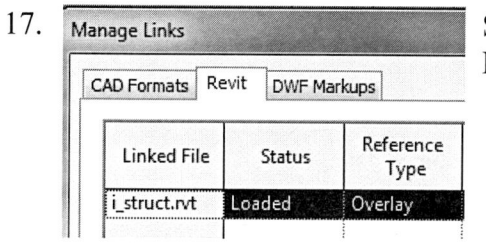

17. Select the **Revit** tab.
Highlight the *i_struct.rvt* file.

18. Select **Reload From**.

19. Locate the *i_struct_revised* file.
Press **Open**.

10-5

20. A dialog will appear indicating that the revised file requires Coordination Review.

    Press **OK**.

21. Note that the revised file has replaced the previous link.

    This is similar to when a sub-contractor or other consultant emails you an updated file for use in a project.

    Press **OK**.

22. Activate the **Collaborate** ribbon.

    Select **Coordination Review→Select Link** from the Coordinate panel.

    Select the linked file in the drawing window.

23. A dialog appears.

    Expand the notations so you can see what was changed.

24. Highlight first change.

    Select **Move Level Roof**.

Collaboration

25. Select the **Add Comment** button.

26. Type **Approved [your initials] [Date]**.

    Press **OK**.

27. Highlight the second change change.

    Select **Move Level Level 2**.

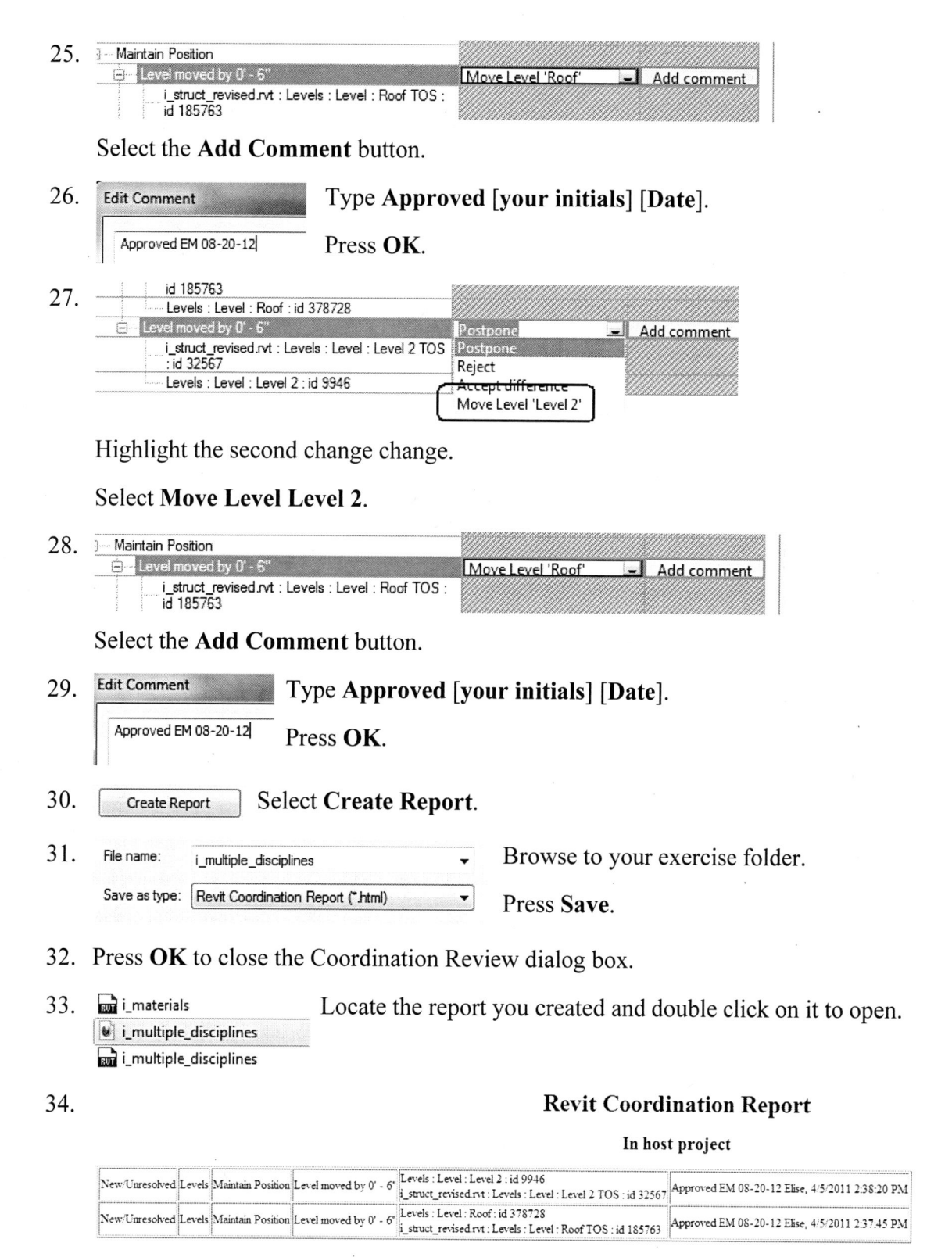

28. Select the **Add Comment** button.

29. Type **Approved [your initials] [Date]**.

    Press **OK**.

30. Select **Create Report**.

31. Browse to your exercise folder.

    Press **Save**.

32. Press **OK** to close the Coordination Review dialog box.

33. Locate the report you created and double click on it to open.

34. **Revit Coordination Report**

    In host project

    This report can be emailed or used as part of the submittal process.

35. Close the file without saving.

10-7

Command Exercise
Exercise 10-2 – Interference Checking

Drawing Name: **c_interference_checking.rvt**
Estimated Time to Completion: 40 Minutes

Scope

Describe Interference Checks
Check and fix interference conditions in a building model
Generate an interference report

Solution

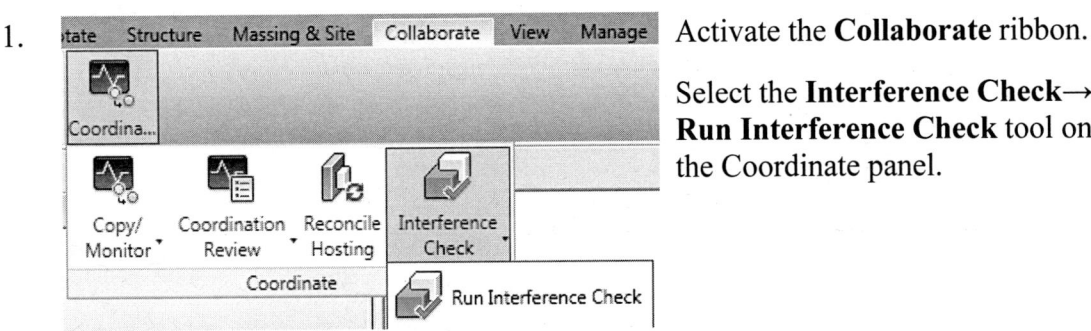

1. Activate the **Collaborate** ribbon.

   Select the **Interference Check→ Run Interference Check** tool on the Coordinate panel.

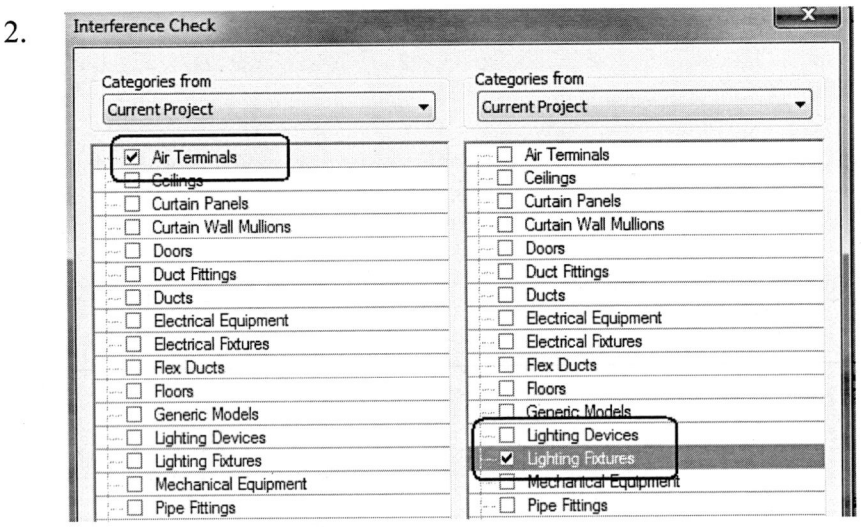

2. Enable Air Terminals in the left panel.

   Enable Lighting Fixtures in the right panel.

   If you select all in both panels, the check can take a substantial amount of time depending on the project and the results you get may not be very meaningful.

3. Press **OK**.

4.
```
⊟─ Air Terminals
    ⊟─ Lighting Fixtures
        ├─ Air Terminals : Supply Diffuser - Rectangular Face Round Neck : 24x24 - 8 Neck - Mark 359 : id 728098
        └─ Lighting Fixtures : Recessed Parabolic Light : 2'x4'(2 Lamp) - 120V - Mark 636 : id 808190
    ⊟─ Lighting Fixtures
        ├─ Air Terminals : Supply Diffuser - Rectangular Face Round Neck : 24x24 - 8 Neck - Mark 358 : id 728040
        └─ Lighting Fixtures : Recessed Parabolic Light : 2'x4'(2 Lamp) - 120V - Mark 638 : id 808320
```

Highlight the Lighting Fixture in the first error.

Press the **Show** button.

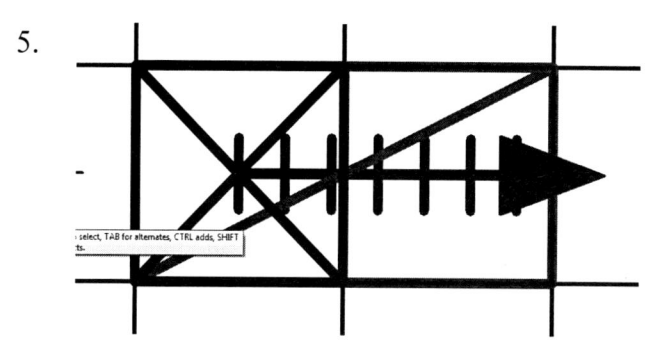

5. The display will update to show the interference between the two elements.

6. Select **Export**.

7. Browse to your exercise folder.

   Press **Save**.

8. Press **Close** to close the dialog box.

9. Locate the report you created and double click on it to open.

10. **Interference Report**

    Interference Report Project File: E:\Schroff\Revit 2011 Exam Guide\exercise files\c_interference_checking.rvt
    Created: Friday, August 20, 2010 4:27:08 PM
    Last Update:

A	B
1 Air Terminals : Supply Diffuser - Rectangular Face Round Neck : 24x24 - 8 Neck - Mark 358 : id 728040	Lighting Fixtures : Recessed Parabolic Light : 2'x4'(2 Lamp) - 120V - Mark 638 : id 808320
2 Air Terminals : Supply Diffuser - Rectangular Face Round Neck : 24x24 - 8 Neck - Mark 359 : id 728098	Lighting Fixtures : Recessed Parabolic Light : 2'x4'(2 Lamp) - 120V - Mark 636 : id 808190

    End of Interference Report

    This report can be emailed or used as part of the submittal process.

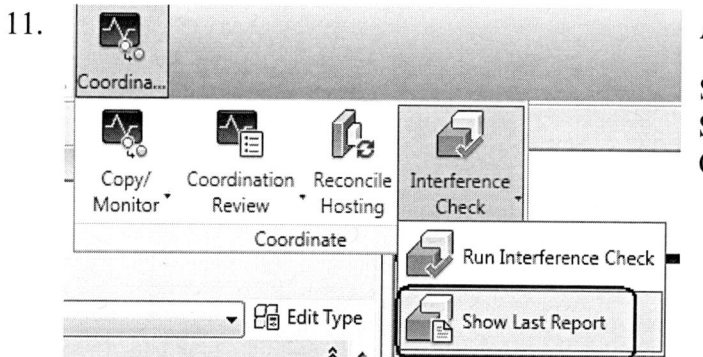

11. Activate the **Collaborate** ribbon.

    Select the **Interference Check→Show Last Report** tool on the Coordinate panel.

10-9

12.

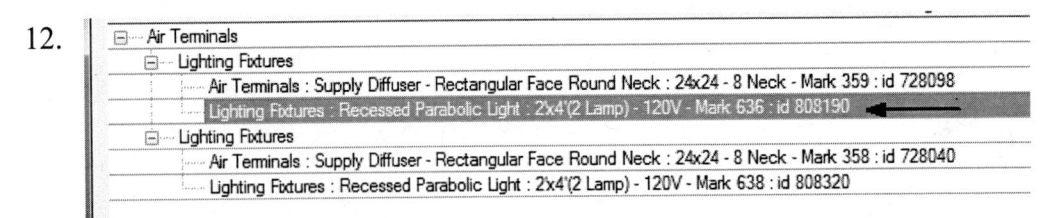

```
Air Terminals
    Lighting Fixtures
        Air Terminals : Supply Diffuser - Rectangular Face Round Neck : 24x24 - 8 Neck - Mark 359 : id 728098
        Lighting Fixtures : Recessed Parabolic Light : 2'x4'(2 Lamp) - 120V - Mark 636 : id 808190
    Lighting Fixtures
        Air Terminals : Supply Diffuser - Rectangular Face Round Neck : 24x24 - 8 Neck - Mark 358 : id 728040
        Lighting Fixtures : Recessed Parabolic Light : 2'x4'(2 Lamp) - 120V - Mark 638 : id 808320
```

Highlight the first lighting fixture.

Close the dialog.

13. 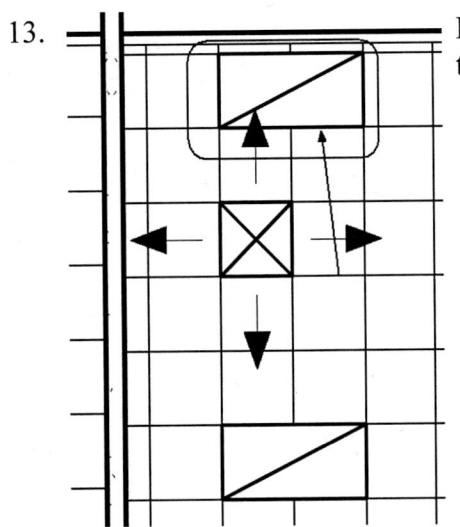 Move the lighting fixture to a position above the air terminal.

14. 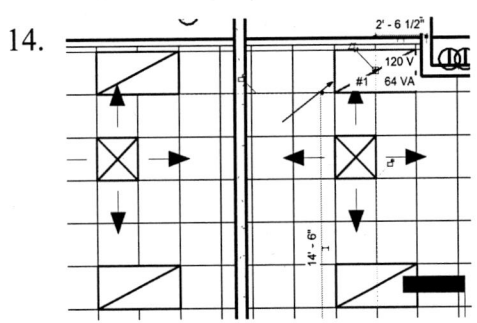 Move the second lighting fixture on the right so it is no longer on top of the air terminal.

15. 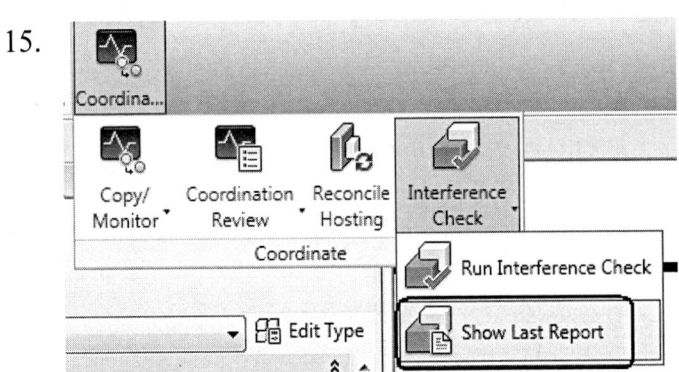 Activate the **Collaborate** ribbon.

Select the **Interference Check→ Show Last Report** tool on the Coordinate panel.

16. 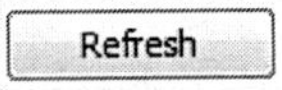 Select **Refresh**.

17. The message list is now empty.
    Close the dialog box.

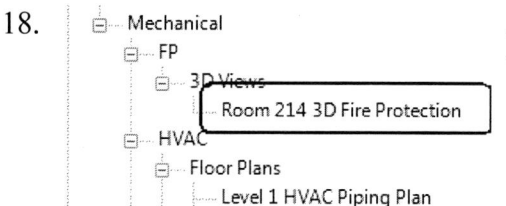

18. Activate the **Room 214 3D Fire Protection view** located under Mechanical.

19. Zoom in so you can see the room.

    Window around the entire room so everything is selected.

20. Activate the **Collaborate** ribbon.

    Select the **Interference Check→ Run Interference Check** tool on the Coordinate panel.

21. Press **OK**.

22. Review the report.

    Press **Close**.

23. Close all files without saving.

10-11

Command Exercise

Exercise 10-3 – Using Shared Coordinates

Drawing Name: **Import Site.Dwg**
Estimated Time to Completion: 40 Minutes

Scope

Link an AutoCAD file
Set Shared Coordinates
Set Project North

Every project has a project base point ⊗ and a survey point △, although they might not be visible in all views, because of visibility settings and view clippings. They cannot be deleted.

The project base point defines the origin (0,0,0) of the project coordinate system. It also can be used to position the building on the site and for locating the design elements of a building during construction. Spot coordinates and spot elevations that reference the project coordinate system are displayed relative to this point.

The survey point represents a known point in the physical world, such as a geodetic survey marker. The survey point is used to correctly orient the building geometry in another coordinate system, such as the coordinate system used in a civil engineering application.

Solution

1. Start a new project file.

2. Activate the **Site** floor plan.

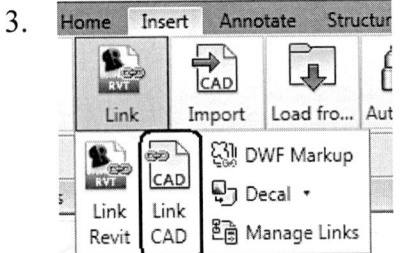

3. Activate the **Insert** ribbon.

   Select the **Link CAD** tool on the Link panel.

4.

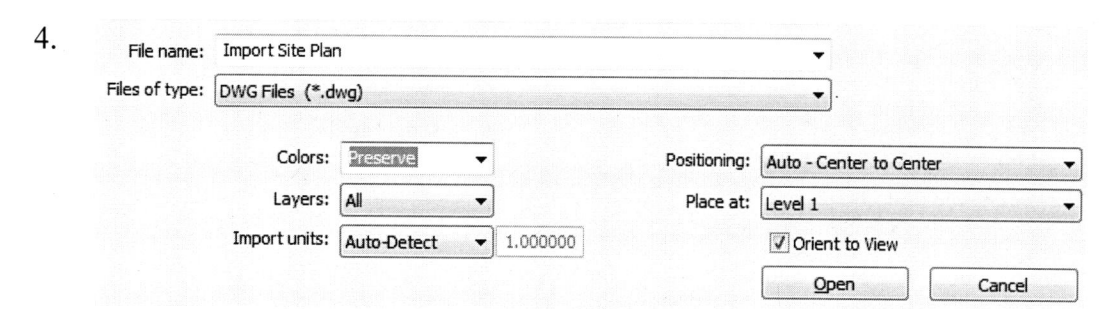

Select the *Import Site Plan*.

Set Colors to **Preserve**.
Set Import Units to **Auto-Detect**.
Set Positioning to **Auto - Center to Center**.
Press **Open**.

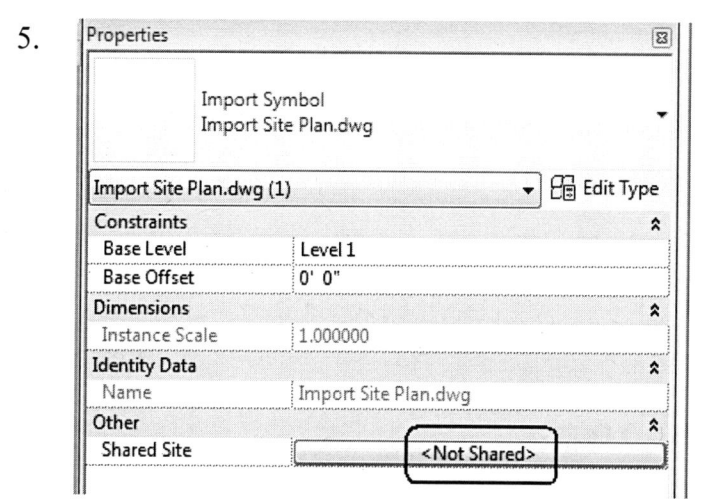

5.

Select the imported site plan.

In the Properties pane:

Select the Shared Site button.

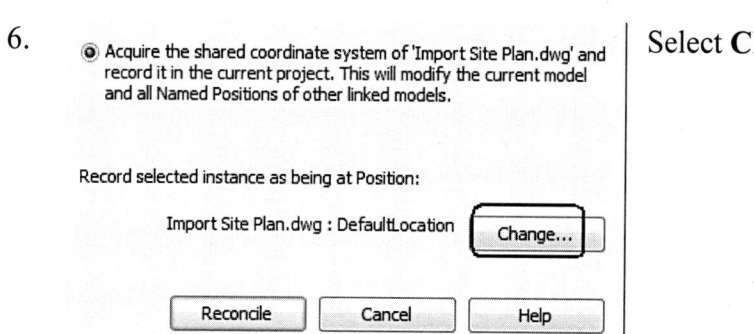

6.

Select **Change**.

7.

Activate the Location tab.

Enter the Project Address.

Press **Search**.
Then, press **OK**.

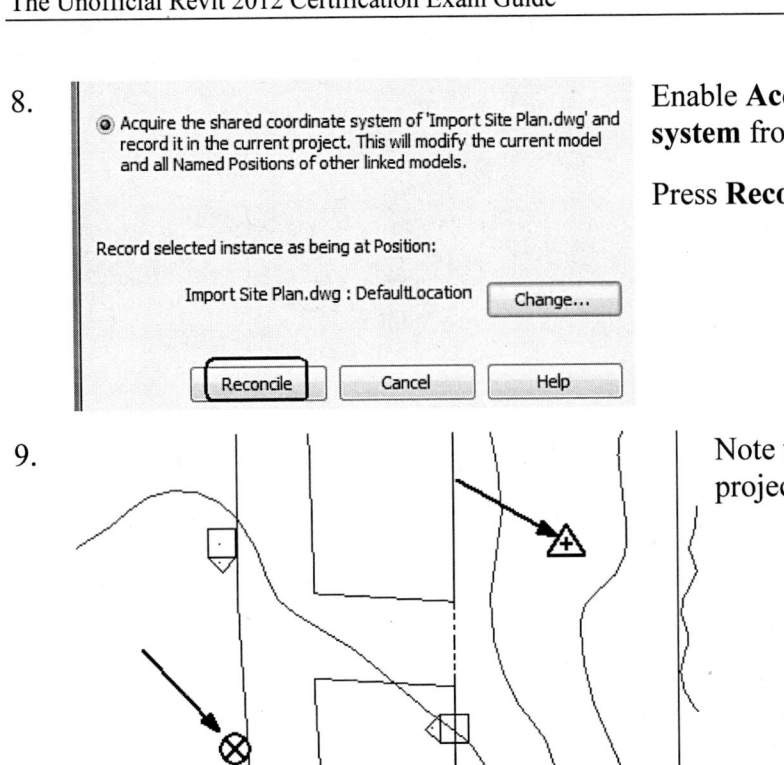

8. Enable **Acquire Shared coordinate system** from the drawing.

   Press **Reconcile**.

9. Note that the survey point and project base point shift position.

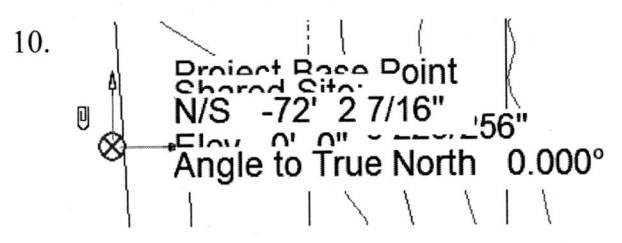

10. Select the Project Base point.

    This is the symbol that is a circle with an X inside.

11. Change the Elev to **126' 0"**.
    Change the Angle to Truth North to **90.00**.
    Press **Apply**.
    The site plan will rotate 90 degrees.

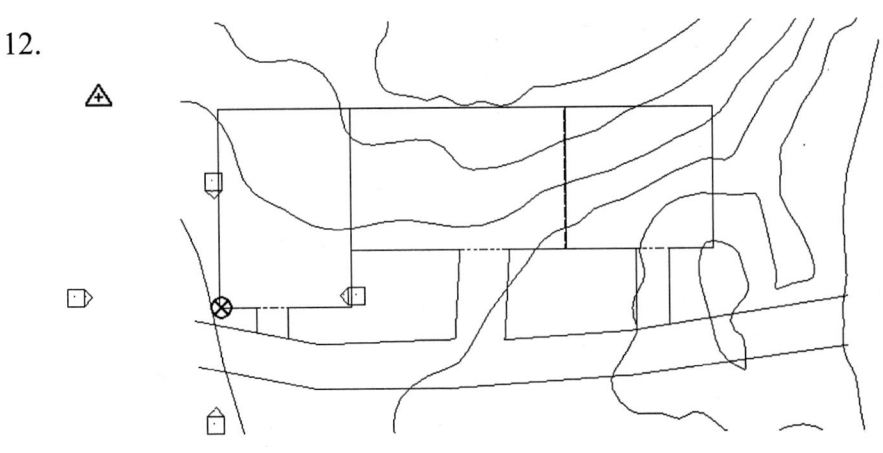

12. Move the import site plan so that the corner of the rectangle is coincident with the project base point.

Collaboration

13. Activate the Insert ribbon.

    Select **Link Revit** from the Link panel.

14. Select the *i_shared_coords* file.
    Set the Positioning to: **Manual - Base point**.
    Press **Open**.

15. Place the Revit file to the left of the site plan.

16. Select the **Align** tool on the Modify panel on the Modify ribbon.

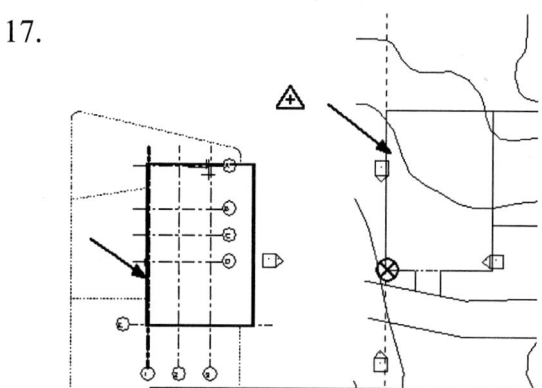

17. Select the vertical line above the project base point.

    Then select Grid line 1.

10-15

18. Change the display to wireframe, if necessary.

    Select the horizontal line on the project base point. Then select Grid line E.

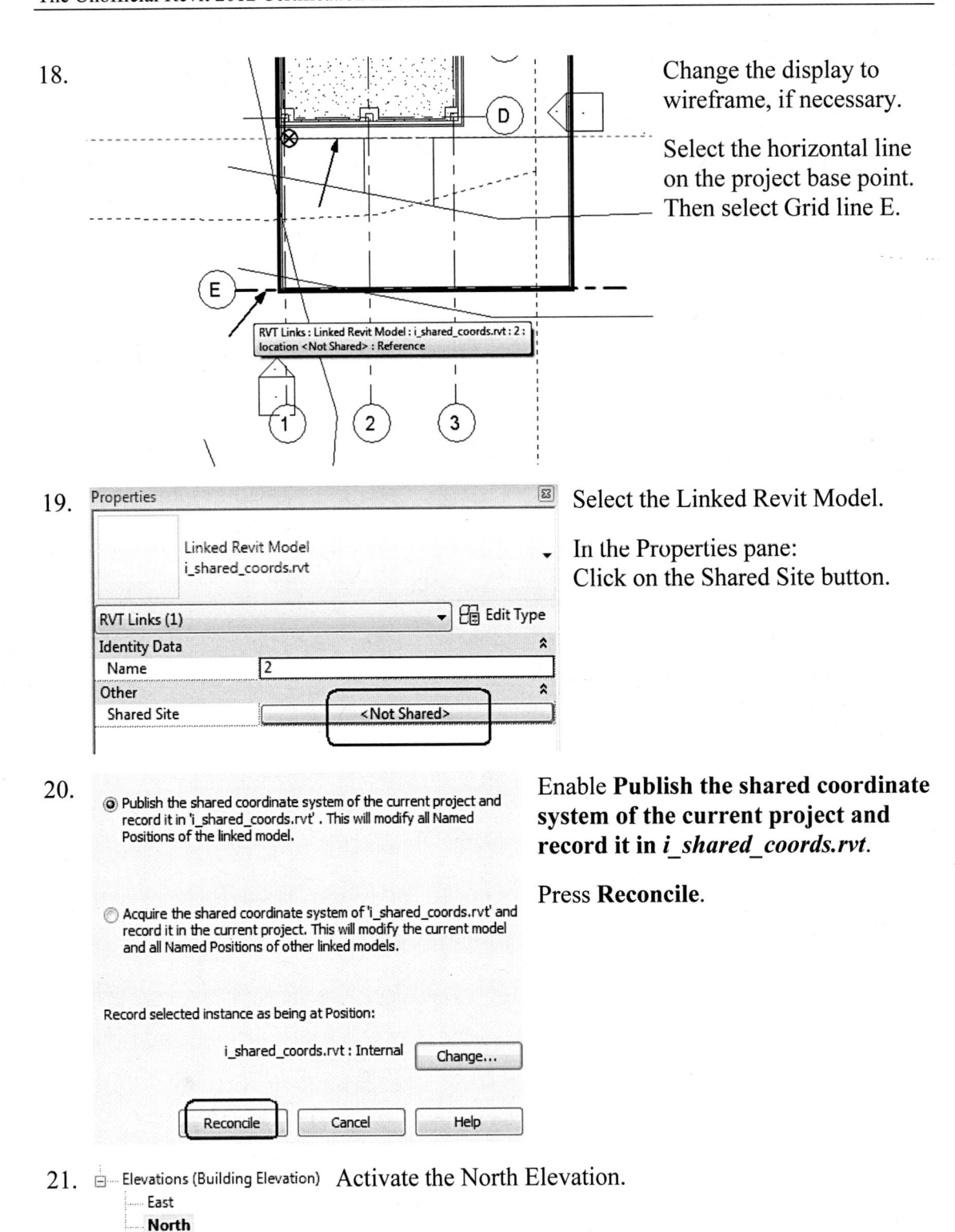

19. Select the Linked Revit Model.

    In the Properties pane:
    Click on the Shared Site button.

20. Enable **Publish the shared coordinate system of the current project and record it in *i_shared_coords.rvt*.**

    Press **Reconcile**.

21. Activate the North Elevation.

22.

Level 1 and Level 2 are in the host project.

The other levels shown are in the Linked Revit model.

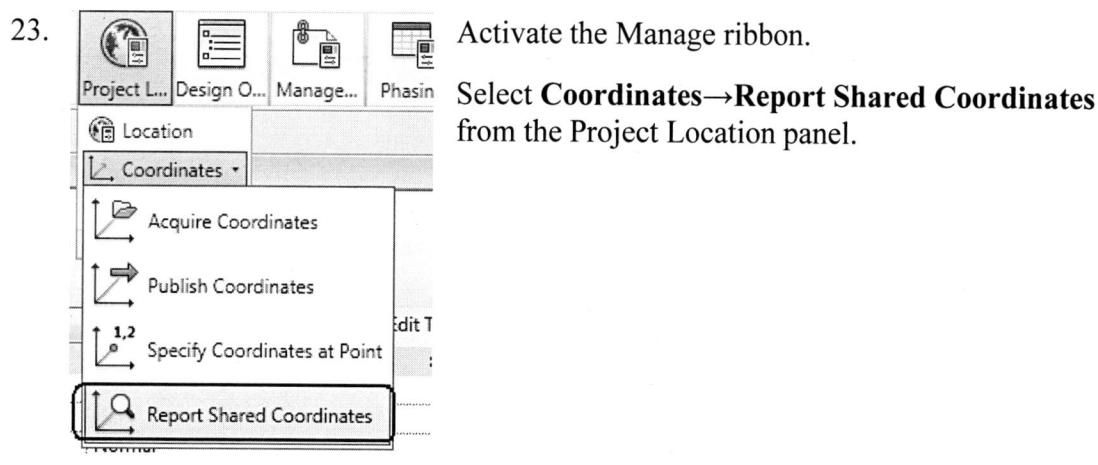

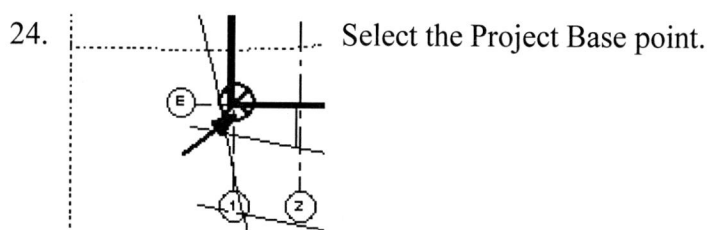

23. Activate the Manage ribbon.

Select **Coordinates→Report Shared Coordinates** from the Project Location panel.

24. Select the Project Base point.

25. E/W: -122' 5 225/256"   N/S: -72' 2 7/16"   Elevation: 126' 0"   The coordinate information will display.

26. Close without saving.

Command Exercise
Exercise 10-4 – Point Clouds

Drawing Name: **point_clouds.rvt**
Estimated Time to Completion: 15 Minutes

Scope

Import point cloud

A point cloud is a set of vertices with three-dimensional coordinates created by 3D scanners. The new feature allows Revit to read .PCG files to visualize volumetric data of existing buildings or manufactured parts. In this exercise, you can check if the floor layout created fits inside the scanned building.

Solution

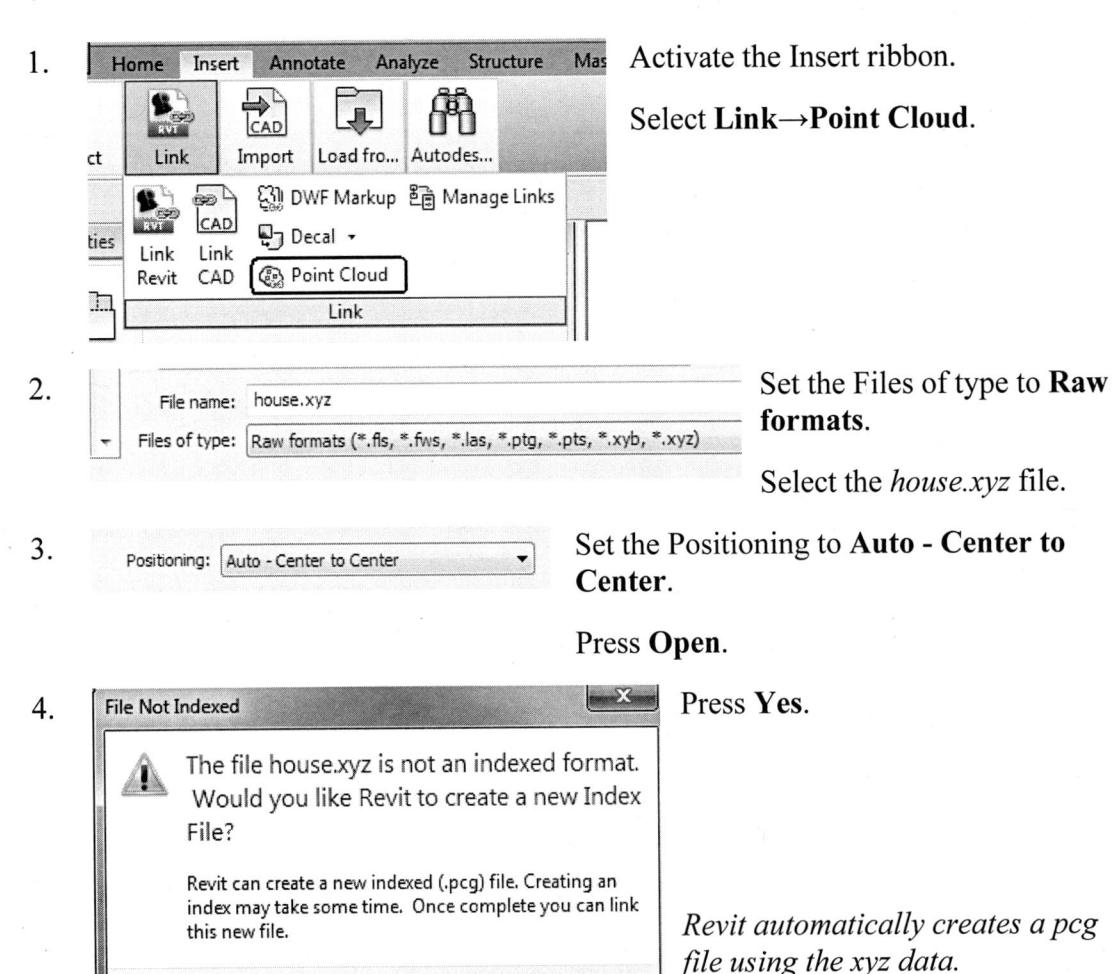

1. Activate the Insert ribbon.

   Select **Link→Point Cloud**.

2. Set the Files of type to **Raw formats**.

   Select the *house.xyz* file.

3. Set the Positioning to **Auto - Center to Center**.

   Press **Open**.

4. Press **Yes**.

   Revit automatically creates a pcg file using the xyz data.

10-18

5. Press **Close**.

6. Activate the Insert ribbon.

   Select **Link→Point Cloud**.

7. Select the *house.pcg* file.

8. Set the Positioning to **Auto - Center to Center**.

   Press **Open**.

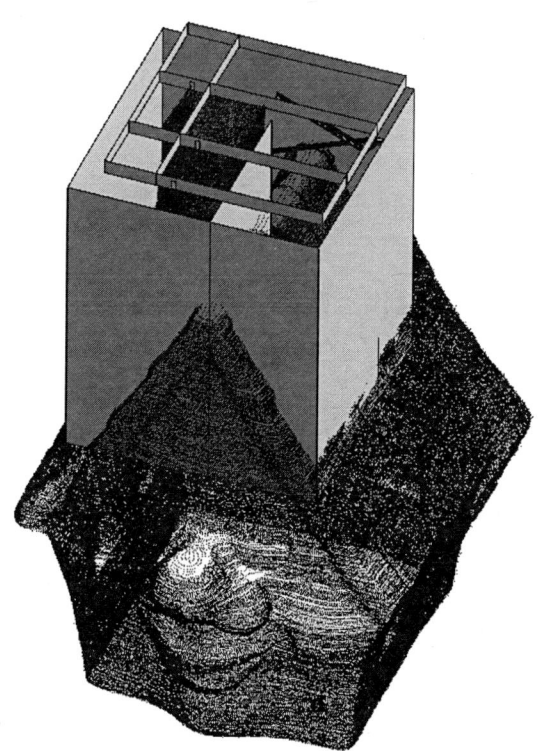

9. Switch to a 3D view to inspect the imported data.

   The data is located below the interior walls.

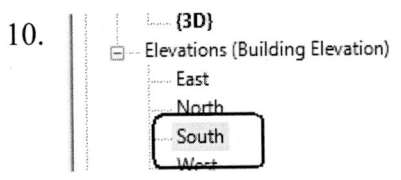

10. Activate the **South** elevation.

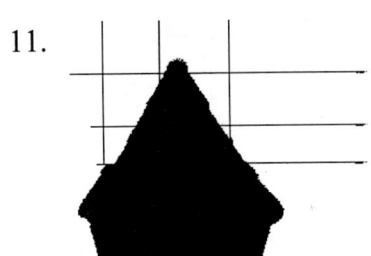

11. The scanned house is below the lowest level.

    Select the house and use the MOVE tool on the Modify panel to move the house aligned to the levels.

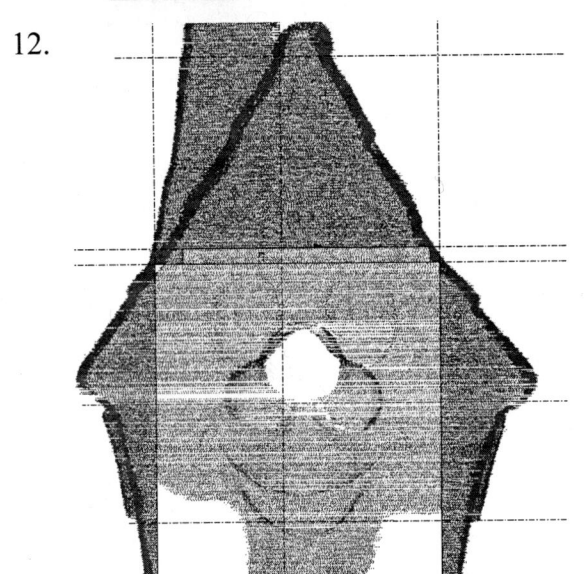

12. Position the house so that the interior walls are inside the house.

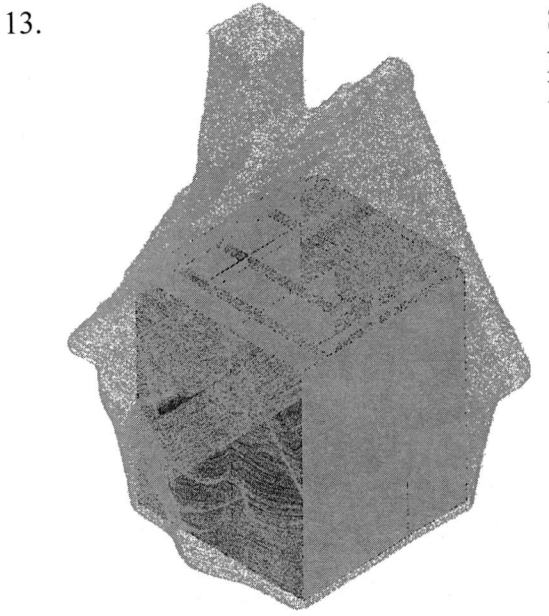

13. Switch to a 3D view and adjust the house position so that the walls are inside the house.

Collaboration

14. Activate the Insert ribbon.

    Select **Manage Links** from the Link panel.

15. Note there is now a tab for Point Clouds and the file is listed.

    Press **OK**.

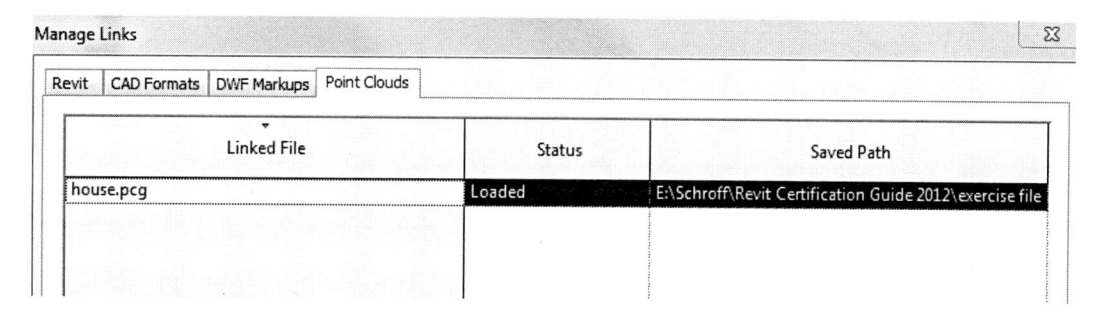

16. Close without saving.

10-21

The Unofficial Revit 2012 Certification Exam Guide

Command Exercise

Exercise 10-5 – Worksets

Drawing Name: **i_Urban_house.rvt**
Estimated Time to Completion: 90 Minutes

Scope

Use of Worksets
Use of Revisions

Solution

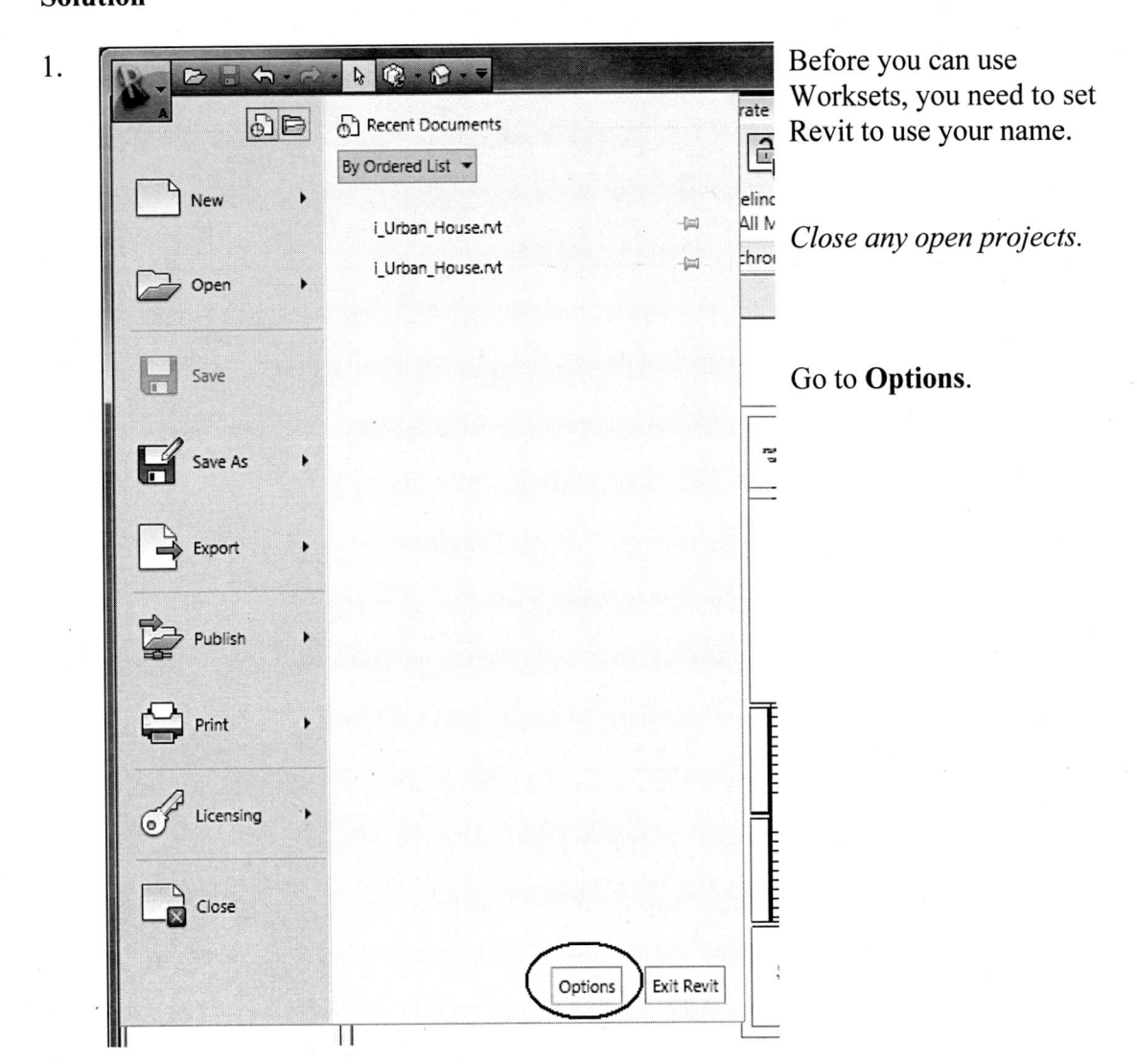

1. Before you can use Worksets, you need to set Revit to use your name.

   Close any open projects.

   Go to **Options**.

2. Select the **General** tab.
   Enter your first name in the Username text field.
   Press **OK**.

10-22

Collaboration

3. Select **Open** under Projects.

   Locate the *i_Urban_House* project.

   Press **Open**.

4. Select the **Collaborate** ribbon.

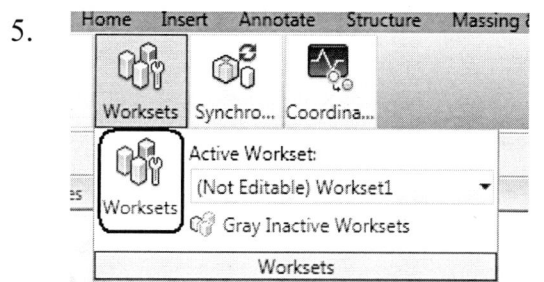

5. Select **Worksets** on the Worksets panel.

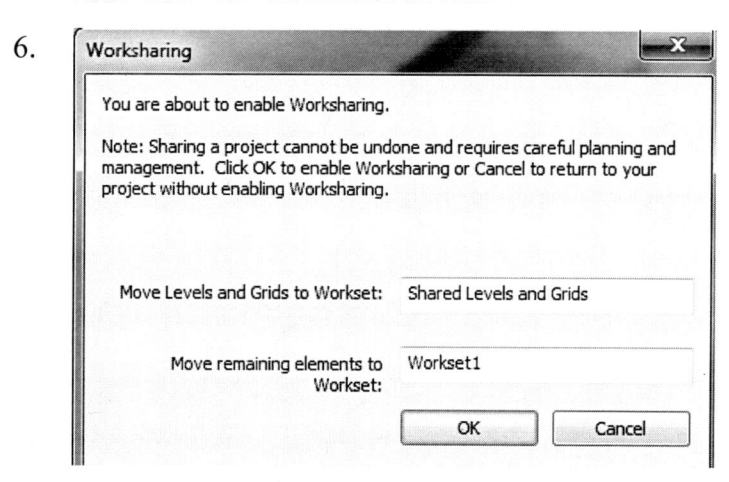

6. When you first enable Worksets, you will see this dialog.

   Press **OK**.

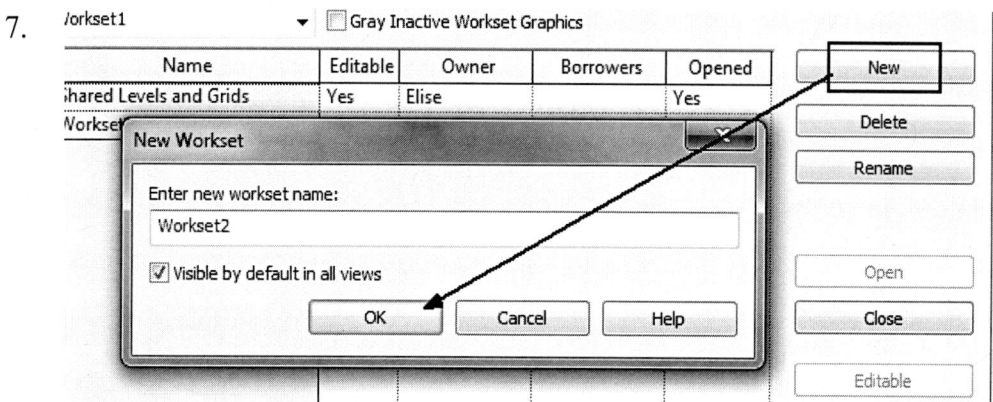

7. Create new worksets by pressing **New** and entering a name for the workset.

10-23

The Unofficial Revit 2012 Certification Exam Guide

8. | Name | Editable | Owner | Borrowers | Opened |
   |---|---|---|---|---|
   | Shared Levels and Grids | No | | | Yes |
   | Workset1 | No | | | Yes |
   | Workset10 | Yes | Elise | | Yes |
   | Workset11 | No | | | Yes |
   | Workset12 | No | | | Yes |
   | Workset2 | No | | | Yes |
   | Workset3 | No | | | Yes |

   Identify the workset assigned to you. Set Editable to **Yes**. Your name should appear as the Owner of the workset.

9. After each change, go to the Collaborate ribbon and select **Synchronize Now**.

   This ensures that your work is saved and that other team members can see your changes.

10. If you select an element which has been modified, you may receive a prompt to load the latest version of the project.

    Select **Reload Latest** from the Collaborate ribbon to ensure you are working on the latest saved version of the project.

    *You also want to **Reload Latest** after any breaks or long periods away from the project.*

11. Other team members may need to borrow elements assigned to your workset in order to make changes. You can Grant or Deny those requests.

    Every 30 minutes or so, you should check your **Editing Requests**. Editing Requests also shows any pending requests you may have.

12. Go to the View ribbon.
    Select the **Revisions** tool on the Sheet Composition panel.

10-24

13.

Sequence	Numbering	Date	Description	Issued	Issued to	Issued by	Show
37	Numeric	08.03	Add rooms and room	☐	Workset 17	Elise Moss	Cloud and Tag
38	Numeric	08.03	Add lighting fixtures t	☐	Workset 18	Elise Moss	Cloud and Tag
39	Numeric	08.03	Create Lighting Fixtur	☐	Workset 18	Elise Moss	Cloud and Tag
40	Numeric	08.03	Move Door 17 on the	☐	Workset 19	Elise Moss	Cloud and Tag
41	Numeric	08.04	Add callout for roof t	☐	Workset 19	Elise Moss	Cloud and Tag
42	Numeric	08.04	Enable Level titles on	☐	Workset 20	Elise Moss	Cloud and Tag
43	Numeric	08.04	Change roof type for	☐	Workset 20	Elise Moss	Cloud and Tag
44	Numeric	08.05	Create a section view	☐	Workset 21	Elise Moss	Cloud and Tag
45	Numeric	08.05	Create a new railing s	☐	Workset 21	Elise Moss	Cloud and Tag
46	Numeric	08.05	Create a new stair styl	☐	Workset 22	Elise Moss	Cloud and Tag
47	Numeric	08.05	Hide the ground floo	☐	Workset 22	Elise Moss	Cloud and Tag
48	Numeric	08.02	Widen Staircase next	☐	Workset 23	Elise Moss	Cloud and Tag
49	Numeric	08.03	Change second floor	☐	Workset 23	Elise Moss	Cloud and Tag
50	Numeric	08.03	Create a balcony floo	☐	Workset 24	Elise Moss	Cloud and Tag

This is the table where revisions are listed as well as the team member assigned to make the change. *I have assigned changes to a Workset number. The instructor will assign each student a workset group to make changes.*

The Sequence Number is the same as the revision number.

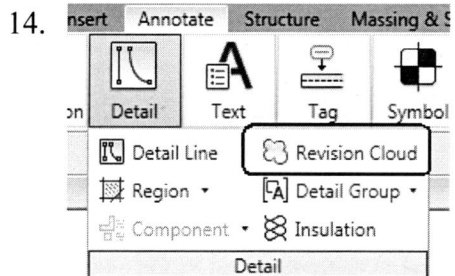

14. To place a revision cloud:
Go to the Annotate ribbon.
Select **Revision Cloud** from the Detail panel.

Revisions should be placed on the existing view.

15. Place a small cloud in the general area of the change.

16. In the Properties pane:
In the Revision field, select the Sequence Number that is used for your change.
Press **OK**.

10-25

17. Select the **Green Check** on the Mode panel to **Finish Cloud**.

18. Activate the **Annotate** ribbon.

    Select **Tag by Category** from the Tag panel.

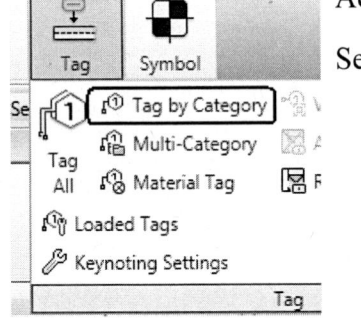

19. Pick the revision cloud.

    The first time you pick a revision cloud, you will be prompted to load the revision cloud tag. Press **Yes**.

20. Browse to the *Annotations* folder.

    Scroll down to locate the *Revision Tag* family.

    Press **Open**.

21. The tag will display the sequence number assigned to the revision cloud.

    To change the sequence number, select the rev cloud, right click, select Element Properties, and change the Revision value.

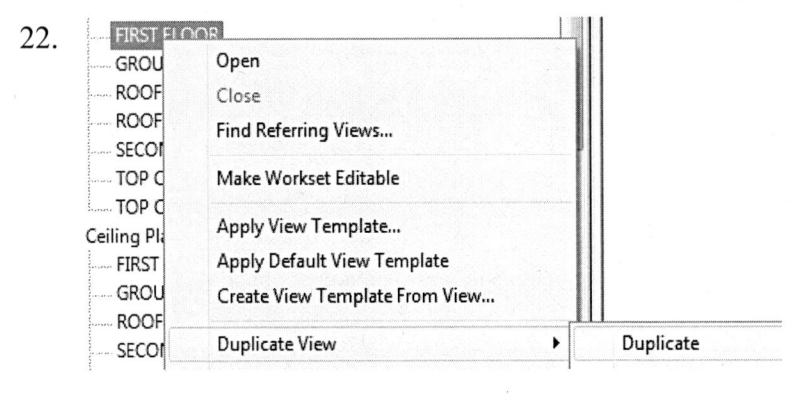

22. Highlight the view you are assigned to work on. Right click and select **Duplicate View→ Duplicate**.

23. Rename the view with the [View Name]- Existing - Workset [Number].
Press **OK**.

24. Set the Phasing for the existing view.
Set the Phase Filter to **Show Existing**.
Set the Phase to **Existing**.

25. Highlight the view you are assigned to work on.
Right click and select **Duplicate View→ Duplicate**.

26. Rename the view with the [View Name] - New Construction - Workset [Number].
Press **OK**.

27. Set the Phasing for the new construction view.
Set the Phase Filter to **Show Previous + New**.
Set the Phase to **New Construction**.

28. Create a sheet for the existing view and name the sheet.
The sheet should be named using [View] - [Phase] - [Workset Number].

29. Set Drawn By to your name.

30. Create a sheet for the new construction view and name the sheet.
The sheet should be named using [View] - [Phase] - [Workset Number].

31. Set Drawn By to your name.

32. Add revision clouds to the existing view.

33. Make the changes assigned to your workset to the new construction view.

Other Hints:

- Name any sheets you create. That way you can distinguish between your sheet and other sheets.
- Create a view that is specific to your changes or workset, so that you have an area where you can keep track of your work.
- Create one view for the existing phase and one view for the new construction phase. That way you can see what has changed. Name each view appropriately
- Use View Properties to control the phase applied to each view.
- Check Editing Requests often
- Duplicate any families you need to modify, rename, and redefine. If you modify an existing family, it may cause problems with someone else's workset.

Practice Associate Exam

1. Worksharing allows team members to:
    A. Share families from different projects
    B. Share views from different projects
    C. Work on the same parts of a project simultaneously
    D. Work on different parts of the same project

2. Set Phase Filters for a view in the:
    A. Properties pane
    B. Design Options
    C. Ribbon
    D. Project Browser

3. A rectangular column family comes with three types: 18" x 18", 18" x 24", and 24" x 24". To add a 6" x 6" type, you:
    A. Duplicate, rename and modify the instance parameters
    B. Duplicate, rename and modify the type parameters
    C. Rename and modify the type parameters
    D. Duplicate, rename the family and add a type.

4. A door is _____ a wall.
    A. hosts
    B. defines
    C. is hosted by
    D. is defined by

5. The Coordination Review tool is used when you use:
    A. Worksets
    B. Linked Files
    C. Interference Checking
    D. Phase

6. The file extension used for point cloud files when importing is:
    A. las
    B. laz
    C. xyz
    D. pcg

Answers
1) D; 2) A; 3) D; 4) C; 5) B; 6) D

About the Author

Elise Moss has worked for the past twenty years as a mechanical designer in Silicon Valley, primarily creating sheet metal designs. She has written articles for Autodesk's Toplines magazine, AUGI's PaperSpace, DigitalCAD.com and Tenlinks.com. She is President of Moss Designs, creating custom applications and designs for corporate clients.   She has taught CAD classes at DeAnza College, Silicon Valley College, San Francisco State University, Laney Community College, and Autodesk resellers. Autodesk has named her as a Faculty of Distinction for the curriculum she has developed for Autodesk products. She holds a BSME from San Jose State.

She is married with three sons. Her older son, Benjamin, is an electrical engineer. Her younger son, Daniel, is a project manager for a construction company, creating documentation in Revit. Isaiah is in high school, but says he wants to grow up to be a mechanical engineer like his mom. Her husband, Ari, has a distinguished career in software development.

Elise is a third generation engineer. Her father, Robert Moss, is a metallurgical engineer in the aerospace industry. Her grandfather, Solomon Kupperman, was a civil engineer for the City of Chicago.

She can be contacted via email at elise_moss@mossdesigns.com.

More information about the author and her work can be found on her website at www.mossdesigns.com.

Other books by Elise Moss

AutoCAD 2012 Fundamentals
AutoCAD Architecture 2012 Fundamentals